Best Places
to Stay
in the Roc

THE BEST PLACES TO STAY SERIES

Best Places to Stay in America's Cities
Second Edition/Kenneth Hale-Wehmann, Editor

Best Places to Stay in Asia
Jerome E. Klein

Best Places to Stay in California
Third Edition/Marilyn McFarlane

Best Places to Stay in the Caribbean
Third Edition/Bill Jamison and Cheryl Alters Jamison

Best Places to Stay in Florida
Third Edition/Christine Davidson

Best Places to Stay in Hawaii
Third Edition/Bill Jamison and Cheryl Alters Jamison

Best Places to Stay in the Mid-Atlantic States
Second Edition/ Dana Nadel-Foley

Best Places to Stay in the Midwest
John Monaghan

Best Places to Stay in New England
Fifth Edition/Christina Tree and Kimberly Grant

Best Places to Stay in the Pacific Northwest
Third Edition/Marilyn McFarlane

Best Places to Stay in the Rockies
Second Edition/Roger Cox

Best Places to Stay in the South
Second Edition/Carol Timblin

Best Places to Stay in the Southwest
Third Edition/Anne E. Wright

Best Places to Stay in the Rockies

SECOND EDITION

Roger Cox

Bruce Shaw, Editorial Director

HOUGHTON MIFFLIN COMPANY

BOSTON • NEW YORK

Second Edition

ISSN: 1060-7730
ISBN: 0-395-66619-8

Printed in the United States of America

Maps by Charles Bahne
Design by Robert Overholtzer
Illustration preparation by Eric Walker
This book was prepared in conjunction with
Harvard Common Press.

VB 10 9 8 7 6 5 4 3

For my family and friends in the West

Acknowledgments

Numerous people played crucial roles in helping to compile the research for this book — more than I can name. They include guests of many of these places, who talked candidly about what they liked and didn't like, owners and hosts who pointed me toward other worthy properties — even though that sometimes meant pointing me toward the competition — and knowledgeable people in the bed-and-breakfast, guest ranch, and hotel and resort industries. Their advice and perspective was invaluable.

In researching the two editions of this book, I have driven more than 22,000 miles. I could scarcely have organized my often lengthy itineraries without the help of the various state tourist boards. I want especially to thank Dave Porter of the Utah Travel Council, Victor Bjornberg of Travel Montana, Deborah Cornelius of the now dissolved Colorado Tourism Board, and Linda Sauer and Chuck Coon of the Wyoming Travel Commission for everything they did to make my travels efficient and productive. They also gave advice about new places that had opened and recommended others worth checking out.

And finally there is Kay Showker, who recommended me to Harvard Common Press; Dan Rosenberg, the Press's managing editor, who answered a myriad of questions and provided a sounding board whenever I needed one; and publisher Bruce Shaw, who gave me the opportunity to write about a part of the country I love.

Contents

Introduction

The territory covered by *Best Places to Stay in the Rocky Mountain Region* is vast. Colorado, Montana, Utah, and Wyoming cover about 434,000 square miles, or roughly one-seventh of the lower 48. They share a geologic history of volcanoes, inland seas, Ice Ages, mountainous upheavals, and dramatic erosion. Those primeval forces have produced some of the planet's most riveting scenery.

I was born in the Rocky Mountains and spent 21 of my first 22 years there, eventually graduating from the University of Colorado. Though I left after college, first for the West Coast, then the East, I've been back every year since. Part of my family still lives there, so do several of my oldest friends. My roots are in its granite peaks and sandstone monuments.

To research this book and this revised edition, I have returned to those familiar landscapes repeatedly for weeks at a time. On those excursions I have driven more than 20,000 miles as I combed Colorado, Montana, Utah, and Wyoming in search of places with character. I have personally visited every one of the nearly 250 places reviewed in the pages that follow. I have examined the rooms and public spaces, talked to the proprietors or managers, and, whenever possible, solicited opinions of guests. The decision about which to include ultimately depended on nothing other than my judgment about which places truly did rank among the best in the Rockies. No one paid to be listed in this guidebook.

This new edition adopts a different format from the last, one designed to make it easier to use. Under the old format, one chapter was devoted to each type of lodging: bed-and-breakfast homes in one place, for example, historic hotels and inns in another. That works well for vacationers seeking a particular type of accommodation, but not so well for those trying to find places to stay along a planned itinerary. And given the sometimes vast distances between towns out West, the most important consideration is usually finding any kind of lodging with character at each stop along the way rather than a particular kind of lodging.

This new format serves both types of vacationers: those looking for the best of a particular type of lodging and those looking for the best choices in towns along a planned itinerary. The book is divided into four sections, one each for Colorado, Montana, Utah, and Wyoming. At the beginning of each section is a map that shows the towns with best places. Following the map is a directory that lists the best places by types of accommodation (see Categories below). Following that are the reviews, town by town, in alphabetical order. Depending on how many best places a state has, a map may cover the entire state at once, as it does for Wyoming, or divide it into as many as four regions, as it does for Colorado. Either way, this dual system makes it easy for you to find reviews either by town or by type of lodging.

The Listings

Each entry begins with a standardized listing of crucial information. Most of that material is self-explanatory, but a few elaborations are in order.

Rates. Every effort has been made to ensure that the rates quoted were accurate at the time this book went to press, but rates inevitably change, so those cited here should be used as guidelines. In most cases I've cited what hoteliers call "rack rates," meaning the published price of a room. But many offer family or corporate discounts or reductions for those who book packages or extended stays. Ski lodges and resorts are particularly good candidates for cost-saving packages, while urban hotels often charge lower prices on weekends. So when you call for reservations, be sure to ask about discounts and packages.

Unless otherwise noted, the rates quoted are per couple per night, with single rates broken out separately when available. In most cases rates do not include taxes. Taxes and mandatory service charges are listed under the heading "Added."

Breakfast. As a kind of shorthand to describe the breakfasts included in the prices, I've used three broad categories: Continental, which consists of some form of baked goods, juice, and coffee or tea; Continental-plus, which is the same as Continental with the addition of fresh fruit, cereal, and perhaps yogurt; and Full, which means a typical American breakfast with hot entrées. Although coffee and tea are not usually mentioned in the breakfast descriptions, they are always served — even in bed-and-breakfasts in Mormon households where the hosts themselves may not drink either.

Minimum Stay. Some of the minimum stays cited under this category are fixed and immutable, like the seven-night packages at guest ranches. Others apply for reservations made months in advance but can break down as the actual date approaches. So even though the published policy is, say, a five-night minimum, it doesn't hurt to ask whether a shorter stay may be possible.

Children. This ought to be self-explanatory: children are either welcome or they're not, and if they're not, the issue is how old do they have to be and up to what age can they stay in their parents' room for free. Some states have laws, however, that ban discrimination against children of any age. In those states, lodging providers cannot come right out and say that they won't accept children, no matter how inappropriate the accommodations or atmosphere may be. Some of them hedge by saying that children are discouraged, which means that if you insist on bringing your children they legally have to let you, but they don't have to supply cribs or rollaways and may not, and they can insist that the maximum occupancy in a room is two people and require you to take a second room for your children. In short, when the book indicates that children are discouraged, it almost always means that kids won't have a very good time there and that at least some of the guests won't be pleased that you brought yours along.

Pets. There are two issues: whether you can you bring your pet, and whether the innkeepers have pets of their own. Not many establishments welcome pets, though a few provide special facilities like kennels for dogs or stables for horses. The listing spells out their policy. See the "Pets Allowed" cross-reference in the What's What listings (page 505) if you're traveling with four-legged companions. I've also noted when innkeepers have dogs or cats that roam freely throughout the inn (and sometimes if they're kept outside) for those with allergies or other aversions.

Smoking. This summarizes where you may — or may not — smoke and notes whether nonsmoking rooms are available. Unless otherwise qualified, "Prohibited" in this category means prohibited everywhere indoors but permitted outside.

Reservations. Many of the places in this book are so popular during their high season that reservations, sometimes months in advance, are essential to ensure a room. Some guest ranches have loyal clientele who book for the following year as they check out. The time to start thinking about a

July or August vacation at one of these ranches is in December. But last-minute cancellations do occur. Guest ranches and others often maintain waiting lists to fill those spaces. Others, like national park lodges, which otherwise fill up months ahead for their high season, welcome calls 24 to 48 hours ahead (but usually not more) from those hoping to find a suddenly vacant room.

The Categories

At the head of each chapter and again in an appendix, the various properties reviewed in this book have been cataloged according to type. Those lists are intended to serve travelers who know exactly what kind of lodging they prefer — whether it's a bed-and-breakfast home, a historic hotel, or a guest ranch. For this edition of the book I've used ten categories, each of which is explained below.

Ten is an admittedly arbitrary number, small enough to be manageable, yet large enough to encompass a reasonable variety of lodging. Occasionally, however, I've reviewed places that either have attributes of several categories or an identity so original that they seem to belong to none. When places are hybrids — for example, a ski lodge that also qualifies as a country inn, or a guest ranch that in winter becomes a cross-country ski center — I've listed them under any categories that apply. A knottier dilemma rises when a place doesn't quite fit any of the categories. A case in point is the Wort Hotel in Jackson, Wyoming. I've lumped it with the historic hotels because it looks and feels like one even if it isn't technically old enough to qualify. In general, whenever a hotel or inn does not obviously fit any of the prescribed categories I've picked the one it most closely resembles.

Bed-and-Breakfast Homes: Bed-and-breakfast homes are actual residences whose owners take in guests, putting them up in spare bedrooms, sharing the living room, kitchen, and other common spaces, and treating them like friends.

Bed-and-Breakfast Inns: B&B inns can be anything from a converted home to a small hotel. Their modest size ensures warmth and intimacy without any sense of intruding on someone else's life. Most — if not all — of the bedrooms have private baths. Admittedly the distinction between a home and an inn blurs when the inn is a house and the innkeeper lives there, even if he maintains his own completely separate quarters. My own litmus test is the kitchen: in a bed-and-breakfast home, the owners cook the guests' breakfast and their own meals in the same kitchen, which often becomes a gathering place. In an inn, there is usually a separate kitchen. Size, too, can help make the distinction: a Victorian mansion with a dozen rooms feels different from a Victorian house with five, even when the owners in both instances live there. Ultimately, it was my own sense of what the place felt like that determined the category to which it was assigned.

Condominiums, Apartments, and Cabins: These accommodations all amount to homes-away-from-home, with living space, complete kitchens, and complete privacy.

Country Inns: Country inns may or may not have rural locations. Their distinguishing feature is their ability to provide meals, not only to overnight guests but also to travelers passing through.

Fishing Lodges: At these classic lodges, the world revolves around fly fishing, often to the exclusion of everything else.

Guest Ranches: Guest ranches range from working cattle spreads with rustic cabins to luxurious designer retreats and virtual resorts. What they share is a passion for horseback riding and a willingness to let city slickers experience the pleasures — and sometimes the hard work — of ranch life.

Historic Hotels, Inns, and Lodges: Hotels with histories linked to the opening of the West punctuate the Rocky Mountains. The discovery of gold and silver in the Rockies created towns overnight, turned prospectors into rich men, and left a legacy of elegant Victorian hotels, many of them now restored or renovated to suggest their former elegance. Others started out as brothels, banks, or boarding houses and thus reflect the region's frontier heritage in other ways. Decades later the coming of the railroads spurred another wave of hotel construction. Many are listed on the National Register of Historic Places.

National Park Lodges: Some lodges in the national parks in the Rockies wear their history and craftsmanship like a badge. The best of them retain the feel of a bygone era, even if their amenities have improved. The floors may creak and sound may carry, but these are minor foibles, more than compensated for by having canyons, mountains, lakes, or cliff dwellings almost literally at your doorstep.

Resorts and Spas: Resorts comprise a wide range of recreational facilities, golf and tennis the most common among them, and in some cases enough shops, restaurants, and entertainment that guests may spend days there without so much as a thought to leaving. Spas often have many of the same amenities but focus on massages, body treatments, fitness workouts, stress reduction, and calorie- and health-conscious dining.

Ski Area Hotels and Lodges: Great ski lodges can be anything from a tiny inn to a luxury hotel or posh condominium. What all of them share is a location near the slopes, special attention to skiers, and ready access to the ski lifts.

Comments Please

I had a lot of help from many different quarters in compiling this second edition of *Best Places to Stay in the Rockies*. Throughout its compilation, I've made an effort not to overlook any place rich in character run by personable hosts. But the Rockies are vast. If you know of places I've missed, or agree or disagree with those I've included, I want to hear from you. There's a form you can use on the last page of this book if that makes your task easier, along with the Harvard Common Press address. Every piece of information you provide will go into making subsequent editions even more complete and authoritative. Please write.

Roger Cox

New York, New York

Colorado

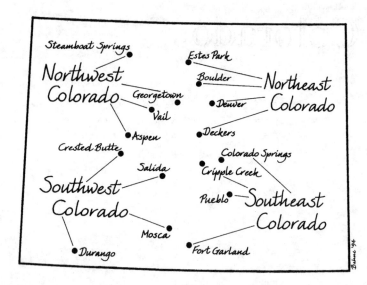

To the world at large, Colorado is a synonym for the Rocky Mountains. The majestic range sweeps north to south across the state, dividing east from west and punctuating the landscape with towering peaks. More than 50 of them soar above 14,000 feet.

For all that, Colorado's natural landscape is far more varied than its signature mountains suggest. The state begins in the east as flat, grass-covered high plains. Gradually, the last vestige of Kansas-like terrain merges with the picturesque, hilly Colorado Piedmont that parallels the Rockies themselves. Only there, halfway across the state, does Colorado begin to exhibit anything like its fabled purple mountains' majesty.

The greatest mass of the Colorado Rockies trails through the western half of the state. The Continental Divide crosses into and leaves the state at a point roughly two-thirds of the way west; it follows a drunken, meandering line as it plays connect-the-dots with many of the highest peaks. Four of the West's major rivers have their headwaters in these mountains: the Arkansas, Platte, and Rio Grande, which flow east, and the mighty Colorado, which flows west. Yet even there the terrain is varied, with high plateaus, mesas, and mountain ranges alternating with broad valleys and deep, narrow canyons.

More than 23 million acres of that rich and varied scenery is protected by the state and federal governments. That includes two national parks — Rocky Mountain and Mesa Verde — seven national monuments, 37 state parks and recreation areas, and 222 state wildlife areas. Wildlife abounds. So do opportunities for recreation. Hikers and backpackers can look forward to more than 8,000 miles of trails in the national forests, among them the 470-mile Colorado Trail, which crosses seven national forests, five major river systems, and six wilderness areas on its route from Denver to Durango. A 40-mile dedicated bike trail runs from Breckenridge over Vail Pass into Vail, while hundreds of miles of logging roads, forest service trails, and little-trafficked back roads lure mountain bikers. Fishermen have more than 8,000 miles of streams and more than 2,000 lakes and reservoirs to choose from. Skiers can carve turns through champagne-light powder at 26 areas, world-renowned Aspen and Vail among them. And this list doesn't begin to scratch the surface.

Not all of Colorado's attractions lie in the backcountry. Most of the state's 3 million inhabitants live in the major metropolitan areas along the Front Range — principally Denver, Boulder, Colorado Springs, and Pueblo — creating a demand for urban culture as well. Denver's attractions include the consistently innovative Denver Center for the Performing Arts, a fine collection of Native American arts in the Denver Art Museum, and an international showcase for western art in the Museum of Western Art. Denver and Colorado Springs both support their own symphony orchestras. Interest in the arts and culture extends beyond the major metropolises. Aspen's annual summer music festival features daily orchestral and chamber music concerts performed by talented students under the direction of master faculty. Telluride schedules a festival or two a month in the summer, including popular mountain film and bluegrass festivals.

The newest attraction is limited-stakes gambling in three historic mining towns: Cripple Creek, Central City, and Blackhawk. Almost overnight, the beep and whir of slot machines have taken over the towns' turn-of-the-century buildings. Where once miners hoped to strike it rich, hordes of quarter-toting residents and tourists now hope for the same thing. Only the methods have changed.

There are, however, certain constants in Colorado. The sun

still shines 300 days a year. Trail Ridge Road through Rocky Mountain National Park still crosses a spectacle of glaciated peaks, alpine valleys, mountain lakes, and tundra. The Anasazi cliff dwellings in Mesa Verde National Park hauntingly evoke a rich and talented culture that mysteriously disappeared. The aerial tramway to the top of Pikes Peak makes vividly clear what inspired Katherine Lee Bates to write of "the purple mountains' majesty above the fruited plain." The shops on Denver's Larimer Square may sell Laura Ashley fabrics, contemporary art, and cappuccino, but the restoration saved the turn-of-the-century architecture lining Denver's oldest street. The Red Rocks Amphitheater, in the foothills above Denver, is still the most glorious place in the Rockies to enjoy an evening concert, with the stars overhead and the lights of Denver on the plains below. Mounting a horse at a guest ranch to ride through the mountainous backcountry comes close to recalling the emotions that must have overcome the first explorers of this spectacular landscape.

There is much to see and do.

For general travel information about visiting Colorado, contact the Denver Metro Convention & Visitors Bureau, 225 West Colfax Avenue, Denver, Colorado 80202-5399 (303-892-1505 or 800-645-3446); or Colorado Ski Country USA, 1 Civic Center Plaza, 1560 Broadway, Suite 1440, Denver, Colorado 80202 (303-837-0793).

Northeast Colorado

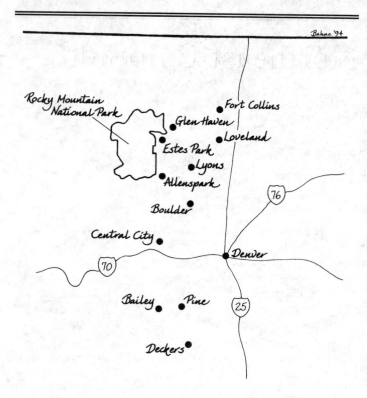

Bahne '94

Rocky Mountain
National Park

Fort Collins

Glen Haven

Loveland

Estes Park

Lyons

Allenspark

76

Boulder

Central City

Denver

70

Bailey Pine

25

Deckers

Best Bed-and-Breakfast Homes

Denver
  Victoria Oaks Inn
Estes Park
  The Anniversary Inn
Fort Collins
  Elizabeth Street Guest House

Best Bed-and-Breakfast Inns

Boulder
  Boulder Victoria
  The Briar Rose
  The Magpie Inn on Mapleton Hill
  Pearl Street Inn and Restaurant
Denver
  The Cambridge
  Castle Marne Bed & Breakfast
  Merritt House
  Queen Anne Inn
Estes Park
  RiverSong
Loveland
  The Lovelander
Lyons
  The Inn at Rock 'n River
Pine
  Meadow Creek Bed & Breakfast Inn

Best Condominiums, Apartments, and Cabins

Central City
  Winfield Scott GuestQuarters
Estes Park
  Boulder Brook

Best Country Inns

Bailey
  Glen-Isle Resort

Glen Haven
  The Inn of Glen Haven

Best Guest Ranches

Deckers
  Lost Valley Ranch

Best Historic Hotels, Inns, and Lodges

Allenspark
  Allenspark Lodge
Boulder
  Hotel Boulderado
Denver
  The Brown Palace Hotel
  The Oxford Hotel
Estes Park
  The Baldpate Inn

Colorado's northeastern quadrant encompasses attractions as unlike as the sprawling metropolis of Denver and the snow-mantled peaks of Rocky Mountain National Park. Yet to drive from one to the other takes only two hours. It is thus entirely possible to spend the day hiking above timberline and the evening watching the road company of a Broadway musical.

For many vacationers, this is where Colorado begins. Mile-high **Denver** rises from the plains on the threshold of the Rockies. Founded in 1859 after gold was discovered in Cherry Creek, it has since become the state capital and burgeoned into the most populous city within a radius of 600 miles. Almost 2 million people live in the greater metropolitan area.

For tourists, Denver is both a gateway and a destination. In 1994, a new airport, the nation's largest, opened on the plains east of the city, making access even easier. Amtrak pulls into Denver's Union Station. And Interstate 70 knifes across the city, providing a quick and direct route to the year-round recreation in the mountains to the west.

Although the impulse to take off for the backcountry and ski slopes is strong — in residents and tourists alike — Denver harbors its own considerable attractions. Businesspeople may wear cowboy boots to work, but Denver is no cowtown. A grove of reflective-glass towers in the heart of downtown epitomizes the New West. At the same time, this is also a city that has come more and more to prize its past. The impulse toward historic preservation began in the 1960s, with the restoration of Larimer Square on Denver's oldest street. Grand but derelict Victorian buildings were rehabilitated and now house shops, restaurants, art galleries, and nightclubs. More urban renewal followed with the 16th Street Mall served by a free trolley, and now there is a new LoDo (Lower Downtown) Historic District, where renovated commercial buildings have lured designers, artists, and a scattering of restaurants and boutique breweries — so many of the last, in fact, that Denver has lately been called "the Napa Valley of beer." There are two cultural anchors downtown: the Denver Art Museum, which houses one of the world's largest collections of Native American artwork; and the Denver Performing Arts Complex, which includes nine theaters, a symphony hall, and the nation's second largest performing arts center.

There are other reasons to linger. Gold launched the city, and among those to make a fortune were Johnny Brown and his wife Molly. She became famous as one of the survivors of the *Titanic* (earning her the nickname "the unsinkable Molly Brown"), and their restored mansion on Capitol Hill — one of Denver's most visited attractions — is open for tours. So is the U.S. Mint, which holds more gold bullion than any site outside Fort Knox. And another $23,000 in gold leaf covers the dome of the state capitol.

One of the capitol steps is precisely 5,280 feet above sea level. But if you stand on that step and look west on a clear day, what you see are peaks rising above 14,000 feet. The invitation to take off for the mountains is always there.

From Denver, the grandest and most accessible collection of these towering peaks lies in Rocky Mountain National Park, in Estes Park, 71 miles to the north. Its 410 square miles encompass more than 100 glacier-carved peaks above 10,000 feet, including the park's signature mountain, 14,255-foot Longs Peak. More than 350 miles of hiking trails lace its backcountry. But many of the glories of the park — including alpine lakes, glacial streams, sheer canyons, and upland meadows, can be seen from Trail Ridge Road. This serpentine highway through the park crests at 12,183 feet at "the roof of the Rockies." Much of the route is above the timberline, and because the park is a wildlife refuge, you may see bighorn sheep and other game. The 50-mile trip up and back, if you elect to do it that way, takes three to four hours, more if you stop often to photograph or to hike.

The shortest route from Denver to the park is through **Boulder,** a university town picturesquely set beneath rock formations aptly called the Flatirons, and **Lyons** (though at Lyons, lovers of devious but captivating detours should abandon Route 36 in favor of Route 7, through South St. Vrain Canyon and **Allenspark**). As you enter **Estes Park,** a well-staffed visitors' center is on the right.

For a more scenic, if indirect, route from Denver, head west (via Highway 6) through Golden to Blackhawk and **Central City,** the historic mining towns transformed into low-key Las Vegases by the introduction of limited-stakes gambling. From there, the Peak to Peak Highway shoots north on a winding but visually gripping route to Estes Park. If you have time and patience, it is by far the most rewarding byway, passing through old mining towns like Nederland and occasionally glimpsing the foothills and plains below.

ALLENSPARK

Allenspark Lodge

184 Main Street
P.O. Box 247
Allenspark, CO 80510
303-747-2552
800-206-2552

> *A landmark lodge,
> built of stone and
> ponderosa pine*

Innkeepers: Mike and Becky Osmun. **Accommodations:** 12 rooms, 7 with private bath, 3 cabins. **Rates:** Rooms $40–$80, cabins $60–$70. **Included:** Continental breakfast. **Minimum stay:** 2 nights in cabins. **Added:** 4.5% tax. **Payment:** Discover, MasterCard, Visa. **Children:** Welcome over age 14 in lodge. **Pets:** Prohibited. **Smoking:** Prohibited. **Open:** Year-round.

This 1930s lodge belongs to an era when the camaraderie guests found around the lobby fireplace meant more than private baths and luxury appointments. Set at 8,400 feet in the town of Allenspark, 17 miles south of Estes Park, it is convenient to much of the region's summer and winter recreation yet quite removed from the mainstream of traffic. In fact, except for a few cabins, a restaurant, the lodge's Wilderquest wine and beer bar, and some riding stables, there isn't much other reason to come to Allenspark.

> The rooms, like the three-story lodge, have loads of character. No two are alike except in their pine walls and ceilings, handmade antique log furnishings, and colorful quilted bedspreads.

Some of the rooms on the third floor snuggle in beneath the gabled windows. Most of the eight that share a bath have in-room sinks. Those with a private bath have either a shower or an antique tub. The sunniest and most appealing of all is Hideaway, which has a brass bed, clawfoot tub, ruffled lace curtains, and windows on three sides. All the rooms have mountain views. There are also three rustic cabins, each of which sleeps two people and has a full kitchen.

It's the public areas that make the lodge. Besides a stone fireplace, its Great Room embraces an eclectic library of books and a television. There's also a game room with Ping-Pong and billiards, and a hot tub on a screened porch. Guests can also gather in the bar, which serves beer, wine, and snacks. They meet again over a breakfast of hot or cold cereal, fruit, and pastries. The constant element in all of this is Mike and Becky Osmun, who have owned the lodge since the late 1980s and treat guests like family, with coffee and conversation available any time of the day.

BAILEY

Glen-Isle Resort

P.O. Box 128
Bailey, CO 80421
303-838-5461

A historic country inn and cabins, economically priced

Innkeepers: Gordon and Barbara Tripp. **Accommodations:** 14 rooms with shared bath, 23 cabins. **Rates:** Rooms, single $43, double $55; cabins $55–$125. **Included:** Full breakfast in rooms. **Minimum stay:** None in rooms; 2 nights in cabins. **Added:** 3% tax. **Payment:** Cash or checks. **Children:** Reduced rates under age 10. **Pets:** Allowed at $2/day. **Smoking:** Allowed. **Open:** Inn and dining rooms June into September; cabins year-round.

Around the turn of the century, the Colorado & Southern Railway began to haul vacationers to Glen-Isle, a rustic shingle and rough bark lodge with a huge turret at one corner. The 50-mile trip on the "fish train" took them up into the cooler air and pine forests at 7,800 feet. Some liked it so much they built cabins here. Relaxed and inexpensive, it was the perfect family getaway.

The public is welcome at dinner, though some who stop in assume that a complete dinner for under $10 can't be very good and move on. That's their mistake.

More than 90 years later, it still is. Set on 160 acres beside the Platte River, this National Historic Site and its kitchen-equipped cabins charms guests with its affable owners and very economical prices. Barbara Tripp's grandparents bought the lodge in 1923, and it has remained in the family's hands ever since. Barbara herself practically grew up here. Cases and cases of her dolls decorate the upstairs halls of the lodge and the log-beamed dining room, along with many Indian artifacts. Her husband, Gordon, quips about opening it as a museum.

Many of the furnishings are period pieces from the railroad era, including the oak washstands in the lodge rooms. But

Barbara replaced the original iron beds with oak and walnut antiques and added dressers with beveled mirrors. What the Tripps could not do, however, was add private baths, so the 14 rooms still share two baths at the end of the hall — too few first thing in the morning. Like the creaky floors, that's one of the foibles guests either forgive or come to cherish.

Dinner makes up for the inconvenience. Though not fancy, the nightly specials of homey entrées like chicken, baked cod, and meat loaf are delicious.

Besides the lodge, Glen-Isle has cabins with kitchens, private baths, and quarters for 2 to 20 people. The oldest cabin dates from 1902, the newest from the 1970s. Some have fireplaces, but none is so well furnished as the lodge rooms. The lodge and its restaurant are open only in the summer, but several of the cabins are available for rent year-round.

BOULDER

Boulder Victoria

1305 Pine Street
Boulder, CO 80302
303-938-1300
Fax: 303-908-1435

An 1873 cottage transformed into an elegant inn

Innkeeper: Jacki Myers. **Accommodations:** 6 rooms, 1 suite, all with private bath. **Rates:** Rooms, single $99–$125, double $114–$135; suite $154–$169. **Included:** Continental breakfast.

Minimum stay: None. **Added:** 9.3% tax. **Payment:** Major credit cards. **Children:** Welcome over age 8. **Pets:** Prohibited. **Smoking:** Prohibited. **Open:** Year-round.

This sparkling new inn makes a beguiling first impression, from its antique wrought iron fence, flower beds, and carefully painted trim to its sunny parlor, bay windows, lace curtains, and leaded glass. The Colonial Revival cottage adorns a downtown Boulder corner, just one block from the Pearl Street Mall. It has been there since 1873, but in recent decades few people noticed until it opened early in 1991 as the Boulder Victoria.

> **The staff even goes so far as to warm the robes when they turn down beds at night.**

They're noticing now. The thoughtful renovation turned the historic Dwight-Nicholson House into a cozy inn that blends Victorian architecture with country comfort and hotel amenities. A huge basket of dried flowers decorates the check-in desk in the marble entry foyer. It opens onto the sunny, brick and white parlor furnished with settees, chairs, and seats built into bay windows. Where once there was wainscoting, now there is a dark green silky fabric. Leatherbound books line an entire dining room wall. Classical music plays in the background.

The guest rooms are as cheerful as the common spaces. Whether situated in the original house or its 1962 addition, all of them have queen-size brass beds with down comforters in linen duvet covers, armoires hiding cable televisions, telephones, terrycloth robes, and private baths with pedestal sinks and brass fixtures. Though a few are very small, many open onto a porch or balcony or have decorative fireplaces and steam showers. The main-floor suite comprises two rooms, one with a white iron and brass bed, the other with an antique Murphy bed, decorative fireplace, and private entrance off a flagstone patio.

Each morning the young, amiable staff sets out a breakfast buffet of coffee cake, croissants, blueberry muffins, fresh fruit, three kinds of juice, granola, and yogurt. The inn also serves, at extra cost, espresso or cappuccino at breakfast and in the evening with desserts like fudge brownies, berries and cream, or sorbets that guests can take back to their rooms. Newspapers are also available.

Briar Rose

2151 Arapahoe Avenue
Boulder, CO 80302
303-442-3007
Fax: 303-786-8440

*A homey B&B
near the university*

Hosts: Bob and Margaret Weisenbach. **Accommodations:** 7 rooms and 2 suites, all with private bath. **Rates:** Single $65–$110, double $80–$125. **Included:** Continental-plus breakfast. **Minimum stay:** None. **Added:** 9.8% tax. **Payment:** Major credit cards. **Children:** Free under age 5. **Pets:** Prohibited (they have a dog). **Smoking:** Prohibited. **Open:** Year-round.

Shade trees and flower gardens surround this 1904 red brick cottage, whose quaint architecture would be equally at home in the English countryside as it is in a residential neighborhood a few blocks north of the University of Colorado. The delightful illusion continues inside, where stenciling decorates the parlor walls and antiques fill the rooms.

As if taking a cue from the cottage architecture, the rooms exude country warmth. All of them have been decorated with down comforters, antique furnishings, and fresh flowers. Three of the guest chambers are in the cottage itself, built on a small scale that intensifies their charm. Of those, the most often requested is the upstairs Rose Room, which has a sloping ceiling and private balcony. A carriage house across a courtyard to the east contains another four rooms, which trade the coziness of the cottage quarters for more space.

The most alluring of all the accommodations, however, are two suites in a wing off the main house. The smaller of them, really a junior suite, has a fireplace that can be seen from the bed, while the other has its fireplace in a separate sitting room.

Wherever guests bed down, they have the option of having a Continental breakfast delivered to their door or of turning up in person on the sun porch or formal dining room. Either way they

> In the afternoons, former Chicagoans Bob and Margaret Weisenbach prepare tea trays for guests and serve sherry in front of the parlor fireplace.

can look forward to hot croissants, homemade nut breads and jams, granola, yogurt, and fruit and the convivial ministrations of the Weisenbachs themselves, who live upstairs.

Hotel Boulderado

2115 13th Street
Boulder, CO 80302
303-442-4344
800-433-4344
Fax: 303-442-4378

> *A landmark hotel near Pearl Street Mall*

General manager: Sid Anderson.
Accommodations: 133 rooms, 27 suites, all with private bath.
Rates: Rooms, single $109–$129, double $121–$141; suites

$151–$180. **Minimum stay:** None. **Added:** 9.5% tax. **Payment:** Major credit cards. **Children:** Free under age 12. **Pets:** Prohibited. **Smoking:** Nonsmoking rooms available. **Open:** Year-round.

The Hotel Boulderado was born out of civic pride. By the turn of the century, Boulder had 11,000 residents and no first-class hotel, a shortcoming that many on the city council believed was inhibiting the city's growth. To remedy the situation, the council issued a stock offering of $100 a share, with the funds earmarked for just such an undertaking. On New Year's Day, 1909, admiring crowds gathered on the corner of 13th and Pearl to witness the opening of the Boulderado. Soon the elegant hotel would attract such luminaries as Theodore Roosevelt, Ethel Barrymore, Douglas Fairbanks, Sr., evangelist Billy Sunday, and Bat Masterson. More than 80 years later, the hotel remains a Boulder landmark.

> **The lobby radiates turn-of-the-century splendor, its atrium soaring past a cantilevered cherrywood staircase to a stained glass dome. The ancient safe behind the check-in desk is original, as is the Otis elevator.**

The older rooms on the upper floors tend to be small but have colorful floral wallpapers and drapes, brass and iron beds, antique and reproduction furnishings, and modern baths. The new north wing can be reached by a skywalk. Its rooms, though larger and decorated in period style, don't have the warmth and charm of the originals. All of the rooms have phones, televisions, and fresh flowers. Guests also receive complimentary passes to a nearby health club. Several rooms are wheelchair accessible. The only blight on the historic hotel is that some of the front desk staff can be brusque and aloof, as if they'd never heard of western hospitality.

Of the hotel's three restaurants, Q's on the second floor wins most acclaim for the chef David Query's contemporary American cuisine, while Winston's, a seafood house on the main level, partially redeems its uninspired fare by serving it amid the columns and leaded glass of the original 1909 dining room. Another terrific setting, this time for jazz seven nights a week, is the mezzanine lounge.

The Boulderado can't take all the credit for Boulder's growth, but the city has now grown to more than 75,000 residents and shows no signs of slowing down.

The Magpie Inn on Mapleton Hill

1001 Spruce Street
Boulder, CO 80302
303-449-6528

A grand home in a historic district

Innkeepers: Scott Coburn and Nancy Raddatz. **Accommodations:** 7 rooms, 5 with private bath. **Rates:** $72–$118; lower rates January–March. **Included:** Continental breakfast. **Minimum stay:** None. **Added:** 9.8% tax. **Payment:** Major credit cards. **Children:** Under age 13 discouraged. **Pets:** Prohibited. **Smoking:** Allowed only in parlor. **Open:** Year-round.

A grand home among grand homes, the Magpie Inn faces a tree-lined street in Boulder's Mapleton Hill Historic District. Yet the historic house is not at all the staid Victorian its architecture suggests. In converting it to an inn, owner-architect Steve Coburn opted to hire not one interior designer but nine. He assigned each of them a room to decorate and furnish as they saw fit, giving them free rein to be imaginative as long as they preserved a sense of romance with a Victorian theme. Such an approach is bound to produce surprises, like the colored squares painted on the hardwood floor of the tiny parlor, but it also ensures a consistently interesting interior. One appealing collection of antiques, custom furniture, and gorgeous fabrics follows another as you walk from room to room.

The rooms come in all shapes and sizes. Honeymooners adore the Amy Ann, seduced by its four-poster bed draped with white lace and its marble fireplace. The Cottonwood also has a four-poster bed but trades the fireplace for a separate sitting room with French doors that open out onto the front balcony and views of Boulder's landmark Flatirons. The Christopher, a corner room, combines a queen-size bed with a gas-log fireplace, wicker chair, and Victorian writing desk. There are two more small rooms on the second floor: the Rustin and the Dakota, the former with twin brass beds from the Coors Mansion and a sitting room with a balcony, the latter with stenciled walls and a full-size brass and white iron bed draped with white linen. They share a bath. Finally, the third floor contains a common area and two more guest rooms: William, which extends completely across the back of the house, and Frances, with twin beds and a detached bath.

> **Though it lies just a block above Pearl Street Mall and within walking distance of the bicycle paths and jogging trails of Boulder Creek and Central Park, this 1899 bowfront Victorian reposes in a quiet neighborhood whose character and pace owe more to the 19th century than the 20th.**

Downstairs, the quirky parlor has an assortment of games and magazines and a table laid with complimentary afternoon sherry and cookies, which guests tend to take to the spacious Great Room and its gas-log fireplace, huge sofa, and piano. Coburn and manager Nancy Raddatz often join them there. Everyone meets in the dining room for a lavish Continental breakfast of homemade granola, fresh breads and muffins, bagels, fruits, juices, and excellent coffees.

Pearl Street Inn and Restaurant

1820 Pearl Street
Boulder, CO 80302-5519
303-444-5584
800-232-5949
Fax: 303-444-6494

*An elegant little
auberge and seven-
table restaurant*

Innkeeper: Debbie Ward. **Accommodations:** 6 rooms, 1 suite, all with private bath. **Rates:** Rooms, single $68–$78, double $78–$88; suites $88–$98. **Included:** Full breakfast. **Minimum stay:** None. **Added:** 9.8% tax. **Payment:** Major credit cards. **Children:** Welcome. **Pets:** Prohibited. **Smoking:** Prohibited. **Open:** Year-round.

Extensive modifications to a 100-year-old Victorian home gave rise to the Pearl Street Inn, a small inn unusual for providing hotel amenities. Its seven exceptionally well-appointed rooms combine the old and the new, as antiques, four-poster or white iron and brass beds, fireplaces, and down comforters mix well with bleached oak floors, designer fabrics, phones, and televisions.

Art adorns the walls, fresh flowers stand in vases on the contemporary mantels, and each of the rooms has a private entrance and faces the sunny courtyard and its apple tree.

Pearl Street is no longer the only inn in downtown Boulder, but it continues to lure guests with its respect for privacy and its sumptuous Continental breakfasts. Honeymooners love the Bridal Suite, which has fireplaces in both the sitting room and the bedroom. Businessmen like the amenities. Everyone can look forward to hearty breakfasts of shirred eggs, fresh fruit, yogurt, fresh muffins, oatmeal, granola, and a hot entrée such as waffles or blueberry pancakes. Five nights a week (Tuesday–Saturday), chef Bradford Heap, a Boulder native who trained in northern Italy and southern France, draws raves for dishes like braised duck with raspberry sauce, salmon tournedos with horseradish crust, and vegetable streudel.

In summer, the courtyard invites sitting outside — it's so picturesque that it's a favorite place in Boulder for wedding receptions. In winter, the fireplaces make the rooms cozy —

crucial since the lobby is surprisingly stark and uninviting. In every season, the staff turns down the beds. One nagging question about Pearl Street remains: Has the inn become so enamored of wedding parties and business travelers that it's lost its interest in the traditional vacationer? It would be a shame if that's so, because there is so much to recommend in its cozy rooms and easy access to downtown and the University of Colorado.

CENTRAL CITY

Winfield Scott GuestQuarters

210 Hooper Street
P.O. Box 369
Central City, CO 80427-0369
303-582-3433
Fax: 303-582-3434

> *A pair of apartments in the hills behind the casinos*

Hosts: Patty and Scott Webb. **Accommodations:** 2 apartments. **Rates:** $84–$159. **Included:** Continental-plus breakfast, courtesy shuttle from Central City casinos. **Minimum stay:** None. **Added:** 7% tax. **Payment:** Discover, MasterCard, Visa. **Children:** Welcome. **Pets:** Prohibited (they have a dog). **Smoking:** Prohibited. **Open:** Year-round.

Limited-stakes gambling, introduced in 1990, transformed the economically depressed former mining town of Central City into a surreal empire ruled by slot machines and blackjack tables. Whether the town was saved or ruined remains the subject of debate, but now a steady stream of buses and cars floods its narrow streets with numbers of tourists unimaginable not so long ago, when Central City was most famous for its summer opera and drama festival. The summer festival survives, as do tours of historic houses and mines and the Central City-Blackhawk narrow-gauge railway, but most of the hotels and inns have become casinos, which means there are almost no appealing places to stay.

> **The two stylishly appointed apartments, named for local mines, are decorated with American Indian and southwestern art and artifacts. Each contains a living area, a kitchen, outdoor gas grill, a TV/VCR, phone, and a desk.**

One notable exception is Winfield Scott GuestQuarters, two blocks above the gambling emporia but still in Central City's National Historic District. Patty and Scott Webb bought this one-acre parcel — huge by Central City standards — and its 1878 homestead before the gambling fever set in. They renovated the old house for themselves and built the dormered guest quarters on the foundation of an old shed.

Each bears the name of a local mine. The Prize, on the main level, has one bedroom and a small three-quarters bath, contemporary beige-upholstered oak furnishings, down comforters, and Patty's mother's hand-pieced quilts. The Matchless, on the second story, opens onto a broad deck with views across Central City. It has cathedral ceilings, a living area with a gas-log fireplace, two bedrooms and 1¾ baths, and an array of southwestern art, pottery, sand paintings, and collectibles.

The Webbs stock the kitchen with dry cereals, orange juice, milk, bowls of fruit with honey-yogurt dressing, and everything needed for coffee, tea, or hot chocolate. Then each morning, Patty dons a Laura Ashley apron and delivers a basket of homemade rolls and muffins along with a selection of cheeses and cold cuts.

That attentiveness aside, the Winfield Scott also stands out as a terrific place for children. The wide-open grounds, completely free of traffic, hold a sandbox, croquet and badminton sets, and bird feeders. Hiking trails follow the old train beds that used to connect the mines.

The Webbs also have a free library of videotapes for use in the VCRs, and they've stocked the office with necessities like toothpaste, toothbrushes, and film since there are no convenience stores in the county. The casinos are only two blocks away, but the Winfield Scott remains wonderfully removed.

DECKERS

Lost Valley Ranch

Near Deckers, Colorado
Mailing address:
Route 2, Box 70
Sedalia, CO 80135
303-647-2311

> *A working ranch long on amenities and family programs*

Proprietors: Bob Foster and Janna and Bill Reynolds. **Accommodations:** 24 1- to 3-bedroom cabin suites. **Rates:** Summer (Memorial Day–Labor Day), $1,375/person/week; spring and fall, $75–$150/person/day, $515–$1,060/person/week. **Included:** All meals, horseback riding, gratuities, and ranch activities. **Minimum stay:** 2 nights; 7 nights from Memorial Day to Labor Day. **Added:** 4.3% tax. **Payment:** Cash, personal checks, or traveler's checks. **Children:** Reduced rates under age 20. **Pets:** Prohibited. **Smoking:** Prohibited in dining room and lounge. **Open:** February through early December.

The final nine-mile spur to this remote ranch is a dirt road that sometimes narrows to a single lane as it meanders through a forest of ponderosa pine. Though nerve-racking at times, it is the only sort of road that could credibly lead to a place called Lost Valley. The washboardlike trail ends in a clearing bisected by Goose Creek. Here you'll find a two-story log ranch house that dates from the 1880s, when this scenic parcel was first home-steaded, and its entourage of corrals, stables, and cabins, many of a more recent vintage. It looks more like a village than a ranch, an illusion height-ened by the swimming pool, hot tub, tennis courts, and a trapshooting range. Guests come here to get away, but not to do without.

Guests who come during the spring and fall can participate in the cattle drives, and they're welcome to help with chores any time of the year. That sense of being part of a real ranch, coupled with the extensive diversions, makes Lost Valley one of the most respected guest ranches in the Rockies.

Still, Lost Valley remains a working cattle ranch. Since the Foster family bought the spread in the 1960s, they have grazed Herefords on the 25,000 acres adjoining the Pikes Peak National Forest.

Families love its excellent summer children's programs. Everyone over age six can ride, and there are five hours a day of supervised activities for three- to five-year-olds. Younger children are also welcome at no charge, except for babysit-ting. Experienced wranglers take good care of adults as well. Some of the scenic, undemanding trails lead upward out of the valley to vistas of 14,000-foot Pikes Peak to the south. Others explore meadows along the creek.

For those who prefer not to ride or simply want a break there are excellent hiking trails, including one to the top of Helen's Rock for a panoramic view of the mountains and val-ley (the ranch supplies sack lunches). Guns can be signed out for the trap and skeet range. Fishing rods are available for use in the ranch's stocked ponds, and the staff will cook what you catch. However, the most significant new addition to the ranch activities menu is a fly-fishing program ($45/day surcharge) supervised by Orvis-endorsed instructors and guides.

Informality reigns, from hearty ranch meals at large tables that encourage guests to mingle, to the square dances, picnics, staff melodramas, and guest rodeo at week's end. Each room features a spacious bedroom and separate sitting room with a fireplace and a foldout sofa. All have private tiled baths, coffeemakers, refrigerators, and porches that overlook the valley. The lively staff members enthusiastically go about their business of taking care of everyone, while Bob, Janna, and Bill ensure no end of genuine western hospitality.

DENVER

The Brown Palace Hotel

321 17th Street
Denver, CO 80202
303-297-3111
800-228-2917 in Colorado
800-321-2599 in U.S.
Fax: 303-293-9204

A century-old landmark in downtown Denver

General manager: Peter H. Aeby. **Accommodations:** 205 rooms, 25 suites. **Rates:** Rooms $159–$199, suites $250–$675. **Minimum stay:** None. **Added:** 11.8% tax. **Payment:** Major credit cards. **Children:** Free under age 18. **Pets:** Prohibited. **Smoking:** 3 nonsmoking floors. **Open:** Year-round.

Fashioned from Arizona sandstone and Colorado red granite, the Brown Palace juts up among Denver's reflective glass towers and aluminum shafts like some rare, ancient tree in an ultramodern forest. Millionaire businessman Henry C. Brown had the brawny landmark built in 1892. He enlisted Colorado's leading architect, Frank E. Edbrooke, to design it, challenging him to conform its shape to a triangular plot at the edge of the downtown core. Edbrooke outdid himself, crafting a nine-story Italian Renaissance Victorian with an atrium lobby that soars past tiers of lacy balconies to a Victorian stained glass ceiling 80 feet above. In the afternoons, Denverites gather at "the Brown" for tea, striding across the Mexican onyx floor into a more gracious and elegant century.

> **The refurbishing done to prepare for the Brown's August 12, 1992, centennial has the hotel looking better than it has in years.**
> **That includes the rooms, no two of which, it seems, are alike.**

The guest rooms lean toward dark Edwardian furnishings and framed oil paintings, with occasional forays into the red velvet and burled walnut of Old West baroque, or beveled mirrors and bright art deco colors. The suites give new meaning to the word *spacious*; those in the corners are especially desirable. President Eisenhower used the suite named for him as a summer White House; he even chipped the molding in the marble fireplace while practicing his golf swing. Another suite is named for the Beatles.

Even before the centennial preparations, the Brown Palace reestablished its culinary credentials. The Palace Arms again ranks as one of Denver's foremost (and priciest) restaurants. Nineteenth-century antiques, ornate mirrors, and rich Moroccan leather banquettes provide an Old World setting for the sumptuous cuisine that weaves together traditional American and classical French cooking with southwestern and new American influences. That translates into juicy rack of Colorado lamb with herbed goat cheese crust, veal chop with black Atlantic mussels, or applewood-smoked breast of duck with black coffee and Kahlua barbecue sauce.

Some things haven't changed: the Ship's Tavern remains as

relaxed (and nautical) as ever, down to its models of frigate ships and its crow's nest. The Brown's downtown location is convenient to the state capitol (five blocks away), the comedy and jazz clubs of Larimer Square, or the Denver Center for the Performing Arts.

The Cambridge

1560 Sherman Street
Denver, CO 80203
303-831-1252
800-877-1252
Fax: 303-831-4724

> *An all-suite hotel near downtown and the capitol*

General manager: Don Rieger. **Accommodations:** 27 suites. **Rates:** $115–$209. **Included:** Continental breakfast, limo service downtown. **Minimum stay:** None. **Added:** 11.8% tax. **Payment:** Major credit cards. **Children:** Free under age 18. **Pets:** Prohibited. **Smoking:** 1 nonsmoking floor. **Open:** Year-round.

One of Denver's best-kept secrets is this jewel of a hotel on a tree-shaded street near downtown and half a block from the state capitol.

Though the hotel occupies a nondescript 1940s building, the guest suites are elegant. They come in three sizes: parlor, one-bedroom, and two-bedroom. The task of choosing a room involves more than deciding on size, however. The design motif for each of the suites ranges over a broad spectrum, from English traditional to ultramodern. The Hunt Suite features antler chairs and floor-to-ceiling bookcases; the French Country Suite conjures up the Bordeaux wine country; and the Oriental Suite seems to have been imported from Hong Kong or Singapore. The common thread is a commitment to elegance and functional comfort, whether furnishings are antique or contemporary.

> **The Cambridge has the intimacy and friendliness of a private club and pampers guests with all-suite spaciousness and grand-hotel services.**

No matter what its theme, each suite has a butler kitchen

with a coffeemaker (and complimentary supply of coffee and tea) and a refrigerator stocked with soft drinks, juices, and sparkling water. Suites also have terrycloth robes, hair dryers, phones, color televisions, and in some cases, trouser presses. Local phone calls are free; so are shoeshines. A Continental breakfast of orange juice, yogurt, and a choice of bagels, cereal, or fresh fruit is delivered to the rooms. At night, maids leave liqueurs and chocolates when they turn down the beds.

The staff could not be more attentive or friendly, willingly arranging for anything from faxes to limos and helicopters. There is someone on duty 24 hours a day. Le Profile, one of Denver's oldest Continental restaurants, is just off the lobby and provides room service. Legislators often gather in its lounge. The Cambridge enchants everyone who discovers it.

Castle Marne Bed & Breakfast

1572 Race Street
Denver, CO 80206
303-331-0621
800-92-MARNE
Fax: 303-331-0623

An imposing stone mansion reborn as an urban inn

Innkeepers: Jim and Diane Peiker, Melissa and Louis Feher- Peiker. **Accommodations:** 7 rooms, 2 suites, all with private bath. **Rates:** Rooms $85–$150, suites $160–$195. **Included:** Full breakfast. **Minimum stay:** None. **Added:** 11.8% tax. **Payment:**

Major credit cards. **Children:** Not appropriate. **Pets:** Prohibited. **Smoking:** Prohibited. **Open:** Year-round.

Castle Marne anchors a street of Victorian houses 20 blocks east of downtown, near City Park and the Denver Zoo. The silver baron Wilbur S. Raymond had the turreted and columned structure built in 1889. His architect, William Lang, is today best known for the Unsinkable Molly Brown House, but even then Lang had a reputation for ensuring that no two of his houses looked alike. And this Romanesque castle, constructed of rough-chiseled blocks of a rosy volcanic stone called rhyolite, has itself become a Denver landmark.

> A carved oak staircase winds past a six-foot circular "peacock window" of stained glass. Guests pass it every morning on their way to breakfast in the cherry-paneled dining room, where Peiker serves a feast of homemade muffins and fresh fruit, with vegetable quiche, blueberry waffles, or whatever else he feels like preparing in what he calls "Denver's smallest commercial kitchen."

Sooner or later, Jim Peiker gets around to telling the story of Castle Marne and its series of owners to every guest who will listen. He saved the mansion from a slow death as an apartment house. In order to restore it authentically, he delved into every nook and cranny of its history and ferreted out old photos that showed the original interiors and exteriors. In the end, he created not only a one-of-a-kind urban inn but a Victorian period piece.

He lavished attention on the accommodations, too. Though none of the original furnishings survived, Peiker and his family contributed their own heirlooms, combed auctions and garage sales for authentic period antiques, and, when all else failed, settled for high-quality reproductions. Each room radiates its own personality. The main floor Conservatory has a sunny bay window overlooking the garden, cabbage rose wallpaper, wicker furnishings, and a clawfoot tub. The quaint corner Balcony Room on the second floor, though small, features an antique iron and brass bed and opens onto a large deck with its own two-person jetted tub in a gazebo. The three-room Presidential Suite lures honeymooners with its king-size tester bed, decorative fireplace, solarium with jetted tub, sitting room in the tower, and private balcony with a view of downtown Denver and the Rockies beyond.

In the late afternoon Jim sets out tea, scones, and short-bread in the living room, where there's always a puzzle to work on in the turreted alcove. Downstairs is a mini guest office complete with phone, computer, and fax machine. And recently the Peikers began offering five-course candlelight dinners — exclusively for guests — that might feature Cornish game hen with wild rice one night, chicken breast with a julienne of vegetables en papillote the next.

Some member of the Peiker family is always on hand to give advice about restaurants or otherwise be of service, but Jim tells the best stories.

Merritt House

941 East 17th Avenue
Denver, CO 80218
303-861-5230
Fax: 303-832-3517

A Queen Anne Victorian turned inn and restaurant

Innkeepers: Tom and Mary Touris. **Accommodations:** 10 rooms, all with private bath. **Rates:** Single $80–$95, double $85–$110. **Included:** Full breakfast. **Minimum stay:** None. **Added:** 11.8% tax. **Payment:** Major credit cards. **Children:** Well-behaved children over age 12 welcome. **Pets:** Prohibited. **Smoking:** Prohibited. **Open:** Year-round.

Lovers of Queen Anne Victorian homes can walk the streets of Denver's Swallow Hill Historic District and see 29 examples of that architectural style, most of them built before the silver crash of 1893. Merritt House, a winsome 10-room inn at the edge of Swallow Hill, occupies the restored Queen Anne mansion Colorado Senator Elmer W. Merritt had built in 1889 from designs by architect Frank Edbrooke, who later undertook the fabled Brown Palace. While some guests choose Merritt House for its style and history, there is another compelling reason to bed down here: a menu of breakfast options.

> **Guests enjoy a pleasure rarely found at a B&B: the chance to order breakfast from a menu. Choices range from cereal and toast to berry pancakes and three-cheese omelettes.**
>
> **Denverites stopping in for breakfast on their way to work create some bustle in the dining room that recurs with the lunchtime rush. But it never extends to the guest floors above.**

The source of that amenity dates to the mid-1980s, when Mary and Tom Touris were stripping a century's accumulation of paint off the oak-paneled ceilings, walls, and door trim. They had begun thinking about opening a bed-and-breakfast five years earlier, and the more they found out about the business, the more convinced they became that it would make sense also to serve meals to the general public. Consequently, they endowed Merritt House with delightful, antique-appointed rooms and a restaurant kitchen.

All of the guest rooms have been decorated in Victorian style, with four-poster or sleigh beds, armoires, wing chairs, ornate chandeliers, Oriental carpets, and subdued floral wallpapers. But Tom also insisted on such modern amenities as remote-control televisions, phones, air conditioning, and private baths — five of them with Jacuzzi tubs.

By midafternoon the activity downstairs subsides, and guests can sit undisturbed in the glassed-in sun porch or in the adjacent living room. Mary's always around, often in a Victorian dress, to make sure guests have everything they need.

The Oxford Hotel

1600 17th Street
Denver, CO 80202
303-628-5400
800-228-5838
Fax: 303-628-5413

> *Denver's oldest grand hotel, near Larimer Square*

General manager: Jill Johnson. **Accommodations:** 73 rooms, 8 suites. **Rates:** Rooms $79–$150, suites $155–$275. **Included:** Limousine service downtown, coffee, and shoeshines. **Minimum stay:** None. **Added:** 11.8% tax. **Payment:** Major credit cards. **Children:** Welcome if well behaved. **Pets:** Prohibited. **Smoking:** Allowed. **Open:** Year-round.

The Oxford celebrated its centennial a year before the Brown Palace. Like the Brown, it was designed by renowned architect Frank C. Edbrooke, but this five-story red brick structure stands on the opposite side of downtown, one scant block from Union Station.

From the moment it opened on October 3, 1891, the Oxford was a symbol of opulence. Its classically simple facade masked lavish interiors of marble, stained glass, frescoes, elegant carpets, and sterling silver chandeliers. There was even a "vertical railway," or elevator, to whisk visitors to the upper stories for views of the mushrooming Denver metropolis, at that time the third largest city in the West.

Those views have changed dramatically over the last century, but lower downtown is again a hub of activity, following the successful rehabilitation of historic Larimer Square. And the Oxford, after closing in 1979 to undergo a four-year, $12 million restoration, is as grand and elegant as ever. Now it's listed on the National Register of Historic Places.

To furnish it, antique dealers combed England and France in search of four-poster, brass, and canopy beds and the walnut desks, brass lamps, and curved armoires that go with them. Most of what they found was Victorian, but France produced enough special pieces to decorate a dozen rooms in Art Deco style. The style fits, because most of the bathrooms, though modernized in the 1980s, still retain art deco tiles and fixtures left over from refurbishing done in the 1930s.

> **Art Deco reigns in the Cruise Room Bar, modeled after one on the *Queen Mary*, as well as amid the stained glass, rosy pillars, and little black tables of the Corner Room, a favorite spot for jazz.**

The two-story lobby reverts to turn of the century, with its marble floors, Oriental rugs, red plush sofas, wing chairs, and an ornate mahogany and marble fireplace. In the late afternoon, guests can stop by for complimentary glasses of sherry before heading off to dinner, perhaps in the adjoining McCormick's Fish House & Bar, where fresh seafood and steaks are served in an oak-paneled room with marble floors and a stained glass ceiling.

Guests can lounge in terrycloth robes, arrange for a workout or massage at the adjacent fitness club and spa, walk to nearby Larimer Square or the Denver Center for the Performing Arts, or catch the complimentary limo for a trip downtown.

Queen Anne Inn

2147 Tremont Place
Denver, CO 80205
303-296-6666
800-432-INNS
Fax: 303-296-2151

An award-winning inn carved from two Queen Anne Victorians

Innkeeper: Tom King. **Accommodations:** 10 rooms and 4 suites, all with private bath. **Rates:** Rooms $75–$125, suites $135–$165. **Included:** Full breakfast. **Minimum stay:** None. **Added:** 11.8% tax. **Payment:** Major credit cards. **Children:** Discouraged under age 15. **Pets:** Prohibited. **Smoking:** Prohibited. **Open:** Year-round.

The lovable Queen Anne Inn waltzed into Denver's bed-and-breakfast scene in 1987, promptly took over the limelight, and has basked in constant attention ever since, winning awards and loyal guests with equal ease. Its success can be traced directly to its creators, Charles and Ann Hillestad. Convinced that a great inn was more than the sum of its antiques, they set out to invest the Queen Anne with an irresistible spirit, born partly of the inn itself and partly of the personalities of the innkeepers. They sold the inn in 1992, but their successor, Tom King, a former corporate executive who'd been running his own inn in California, picked up where they left off, managing this showcase Denver hostelry with the same grace and dedication.

The beautifully restored 1879 Victorian fronts a park and fountain in a quiet historic district four blocks from downtown. Frank Edbrooke, whose plans for the Oxford and Brown Palace hotels would later make him Denver's most famous architect, designed the three-story house, shingling the sides and hoisting a turret halfway back. Though modest in appearance, the Queen Anne Inn contains 6,000 square feet of floor space, more than enough for 10 guest rooms.

> **King lives in the inn and makes a point of turning up for the 6 P.M. social hour. Like him, every member of the young, friendly nine-member staff is eager to help with anything — from restaurant recommendations to ordering a horse-drawn carriage. The Queen Anne deserves its place in the limelight.**

Each room has been decorated differently. The lace-curtained Park Room has Laura Ashley prints and antique walnut twin beds (which can be made up as a king), an armoire, and a writing desk. The Fountain Room has a canopied queen-size bed, five windows, and a black sunken tub. In Columbine, above the garden, stained glass windows soften the light that falls on a rare quarter-canopy tester bed and mirrored cherry armoire. A hand-painted mural of an aspen grove in all its golden autumn splendor covers the curved walls and peaked ceiling in the Aspen room, at the top of the turret. Since taking over, King has added more period antiques and converted the 1898 house next door — where the Hillestads used to live — into four spacious suites, each named for one of his favorite artists and outfitted with televisions, phones, and original art. The most spectacular is Remington, which contains a four-poster bed, period antiques, an outdoor shower beneath a skylight (in addition to a clawfoot tub inside), and a deck with a private hot tub.

All the rooms, whether in the main house or the one next door, have private baths designed to fit their individual decors, writing desks, and piped-in music. Many have sitting areas. Guests can make use of the abundant travel resource materials, magazines, games, and restaurant menus available in the cozy parlor (including guests' reviews of various Denver restaurants), or curl up on the dark green velvet Empire sofa with a glass of sherry. They can also help themselves to beverages in a small refrigerator on the second floor. Morning brings a generous breakfast of granola sweetened with fruit juice (a brand King has sent in from California), breads, muffins, fresh fruit, and a hot entrée, which could be quiche, streudel with fresh berries, waffles, or blintzes set out on the sideboard in the formal dining room. Breakfast in bed is also an option.

Victoria Oaks Inn

1575 Race Street
Denver, CO 80206
303-355-1818

An urban B&B for the budget-conscious

Innkeepers: Clyde Stephens and Rick Boling. **Accommodations:** 9 rooms, 1 with private bath. **Rates:** Single $45–$75, double $55–$85. **Included:** Continental breakfast. **Minimum stay:** None. **Added:** 11.8% tax. **Payment:** Major credit cards. **Children:** Welcome if well behaved (no cribs available). **Pets:** Allowed. **Smoking:** Allowed. **Open:** Year-round.

Denver's first bed-and-breakfast inn winds through three floors of an 1896 Victorian mansion on a street of historic homes 20 blocks east of downtown. Shades of its turn-of-the-century elegance survive in a dramatic hanging oak staircase, ornate brass chandeliers, leaded glass windows, and tile fireplaces. In this case, however, elegance comes wrapped in a casual atmosphere at appealing prices.

An eclectic collection of turn-of-the-century antiques gathered from Colorado, New Mexico, and Texas furnishes the rooms. Beds with dust ruffles and floral comforters stand out against walls painted vivid colors like teal blue. The molding is oak, as are the floors. The three rooms on the third floor, though small, snuggle beneath the gables.

Clyde Stephens, who took over the inn from his family in 1989, encourages guests to use the living room and the kitchen, and even to do their laundry. He serves wine in the afternoons and a Continental breakfast of pastries, croissants, bagels, and fresh fruit at a large oak dining table beneath a crystal chandelier. Since Clyde lives here, he's never far away when guests want advice about where to dine or what to see.

> **Eight rooms share two baths with clawfoot tubs, marble vanities, and original porcelain tile. The one room with a private bath, in the former parlor just inside the first-floor entrance, has a mahogany four-poster, Oriental rugs, and a fireplace. Fires burn in the fireplaces all winter long.**

ESTES PARK

For other lodging in the area, see the towns of Allenspark, Glen Haven, and Lyons.

The Anniversary Inn

1060 Mary's Lake Road
Moraine Route
Estes Park, CO 80517
303-586-6200

A 100-year-old log home near Rocky Mountain National Park

Hosts: Don and Susan Landwer. **Accommodations:** 3 rooms and 1 cottage, all with private bath. **Rates:** Rooms $85–$95, cottage $125. **Included:** Full breakfast. **Minimum stay:** 2 nights in Jacuzzi rooms and cottage. **Added:** 7% tax. **Payment:** MasterCard, Visa. **Children:** Welcome over age 14. **Pets:** Prohibited (they have a dog). **Smoking:** Prohibited. **Open:** Year-round.

Deer frequent the front yard of the Anniversary Inn, which sits back from the road in a stand of ponderosa pines, roughly a mile from the entrance to Rocky Mountain National Park. Peacefully distant from the hordes of tourists who throng downtown Estes Park in summer, the cozy little bed-and-breakfast belongs to Don and Susan Landwer, who moved here from Illinois after Don retired from AT&T. They brought along their family heirlooms.

The house dates to 1877. A floor-to-ceiling stone fireplace dominates the log-walled living room. The guest rooms, some of them small, have antique or reproduction furnishings and stenciled walls, all basically country cottage in style.

The Landwers provide a huge breakfast of fresh fruit or fruit soups, homemade breads and muffins, and a hot entrée like stuffed French toast, Belgian waffles, or cheese soufflé. It's served on tables with bases made from sewing machine treadles on a sunny porch with a woodstove to take the chill off even summer mornings in the Rockies.

> Two of the rooms have whirlpool tubs for two, while the third contains a king-size bed and large bath with a five-foot glass shower for two. The most romantic of all is a separate 400-square-foot cottage with a private bath, Jacuzzi, and fireplace.

As comfortable as the inn is, its chief asset is the Landwers. Hospitable and cordial, they go out of their way to make guests feel at home, setting out cookies and hot cider or lemonade in the afternoons, maintaining a library, and recommending things to see and do.

The Baldpate Inn

4900 South Highway 7
P.O. Box 4445
Estes Park, CO 80517
303-586-6151

> *A 75-year-old country inn, full of whimsy*

Innkeepers: Mike and Lois Smith. **Accommodations:** 12 rooms, 2 with private bath; 2 cabins. **Rates:** Rooms $65–$78, cabins $125. **Included:** Full breakfast. **Minimum stay:** 2 nights in cabins. **Added:** 4% tax. **Payment:** MasterCard, Visa. **Children:** Welcome. **Pets:** Prohibited (they have a dog). **Smoking:** Prohibited. **Open:** Memorial Day through September.

The key to the Baldpate Inn's irresistible charm does not lie exclusively in its history (which is sprinkled with famous names), in its architecture (which is unique), in its name (which has a quirky origin), or in the warmth of Mike and Lois Smith (who are unstintingly hospitable), though all of these play a part. It's a different set of keys — not figurative ones but more than 12,000 real keys, the world's largest collection — that distinguish the Baldpate.

In a curious way, all of these things tie together. The story begins in 1917, when Gordon and Charles Mace built the inn on the slopes of Two Sisters Mountain, seven miles from the newly founded town of Estes Park. They used whatever building materials they could gather locally to create a style later generations would dub Western Stick architecture. At about the same time they read a popular novel called *Seven Keys to Baldpate,* in which each of seven characters believes that he has the only key to a lodge. That was all the excuse they needed to christen their new inn the Baldpate. And in keeping with the novel's story line, they handed each guest a key as he or she checked out.

> **The Baldpate's unique collection includes keys to Mozart's wine cellar and Westminster Abbey, the Pentagon and the Royal Chapel at the Vatican, Jack Benny's dressing room and thousands of places, famous or not, all over the world.**

But when Clarence Darrow came to stay, the famous orator argued that guests ought to present the inn with a key, and allegedly he did, sowing the seeds for today's extensive collection. The Smiths acquired the keys and the inn in 1986, and since then have continued to add to the collection and to keep up the long tradition of hospitality.

The rooms, though small and unpretentious, feature pine and antique furnishings, handmade country quilts with key motifs, calico and gingham dust ruffles, and white ruffled curtains. They have the coziness of a spare room in grandmother's house, and as at grandmother's, the bath is down the hall (only two rooms have private baths; the others share five baths but have in-room sinks). The best quarters are those on the front for their glorious views across Estes Park at the mountains. There are also two cabins, one with two bedrooms off a living room, the other with three bedrooms and a living room with a fireplace.

Rough-hewn timbers and knotty pine help to engender a relaxed, casual atmosphere in the public areas, as do two massive fireplaces and broad porches with views of Dunraven Valley and 14,000-foot Longs Peak. Guests meet for cookies and juice in the lobby each evening and for "more than people can eat" breakfasts featuring Mystery Keysch and applesauce pecan breads often served on the sun porch. Some come back for lunch or an early dinner at the inn's popular soup and salad bar. When they leave, many donate a key, which is carefully tagged and hung from the rafters in the now legendary key room. There are many keys to the Baldpate Inn's irresistible warmth.

Boulder Brook

1900 Fall River Road
P.O. Box 2255
Estes Park, CO 80517
303-586-0910
800-238-0910
Fax: 303-303-586-8067

A riverfront complex of elegant vacation townhouses

Innkeepers: Jacque Traeger and Tony Sale. **Accommodations:** 16 apartments. **Rates:** $89–$175. **Minimum stay:** 2–4 nights in summer. **Added:** 7% tax. **Payment:** Major credit cards. **Children:** Welcome. **Pets:** Prohibited. **Smoking:** Nonsmoking rooms available. **Open:** Year-round.

From the highway, Boulder Brook looks like a series of elegant vacation townhouses. It consists of perhaps half a dozen structures with shingled roofs and unpainted pine clapboards nestled among the pine trees on the inside of a bend in the Fall River, roughly two miles west of Estes Park and an equal distance from the entrance to Rocky Mountain National Park.

The accommodations include 16 studio and one-bedroom apartments decorated in spiffy contemporary fashion. Each contains either a full kitchen or a wet bar and microwave, a coffeemaker and a supply of coffee, a king-size bed, a whirlpool tub, a gas-log fireplace (some with remote control), television with HBO, a phone with voice mail, and a private riverfront deck. Spa suites add a two-person spa in a glassed-in area off the deck, cathedral ceilings, and a VCR. The one-bedroom suites add a separate living area with a sofa bed and a second television in the bedroom. Some have skylights. One is totally handicapped-accessible; two others can accommodate wheelchairs. All have access to a riverfront hot tub.

> The Traegers have produced what may be the most stylish, spacious, and amenity-rich accommodations in the valley. And Boulder Brook's removal from the tourist-beleaguered streets of town ensures an ample measure of seclusion and tranquility while remaining convenient to all that Estes Park affords.

Opened in 1992, this thoughtfully designed complex is the work of the Traeger family. Jerry and Lois Traeger had been in computers and then operated a motel in Estes Park when they enlisted their son to provide the architectural plans, a daughter to do the interior design, and finally another daughter Jacque and her husband Tony Sale to manage it.

RiverSong

Off Mary's Lake Road
P.O. Box 1910
Estes Park, CO 80517
303-586-4666

> *A romantic
> couples' retreat*

Innkeepers: Gary and Sue Mansfield. **Accommodations:** 3 rooms, 6 suites, all with private bath. **Rates:** Rooms, single $85–$115, double $95–$125; suites, single $125–$170, double $135–$190. **Included:** Full breakfast. **Minimum stay:** 2 nights. **Added:** 3% tax. **Payment:** MasterCard, Visa. **Children:** Over age 12 welcome in Cowboy's Delight with prior approval. **Pets:** Prohibited. **Smoking:** Prohibited. **Open:** Year-round.

Secluded at the end of a country lane on 27 wooded acres near the entrance to Rocky Mountain National Park, RiverSong epitomizes a romantic couple's retreat. Built by an Irish earl, the luxurious timber and stone hideaway later became a summer house for a series of wealthy families who often staged raucous parties. Since Gary and Sue Mansfield converted it to an inn in 1986, the quiet has been restored.

Between the original mansion and its halo of cottages and carriage houses, the Mansfields found space for nine rooms, each named for a Rocky Mountain wildflower and decorated according to a particular theme. The smallest is Forget-Me-Not, in a corner on the main floor of the house. Though the only room without a fireplace and jetted tub, it compensates with breathtaking views of the snow-capped Continental Divide and the elegant warmth of an elaborate walnut bedroom set that used to belong to Sue's grandparents. Mountain Rose stands out for its see-through fireplace, visible from an ornate iron and brass queen-size bed and from the antique tub in the bathroom. Shooting Star features a whirlpool tub for two beneath a skylight and a corner library with a fireplace. Chiming Bells melds Victorian furnishings and a fireplace with skylights, a sunken tub, and a double redwood shower. Wood Nymph, a country cottage, holds a

> Designed as quiet, romantic cocoons, RiverSong's accommodations remain free of intrusive phones and televisions, and only one room, Cowboy's Delight, can comfortably accommodate a child.

willow four-poster bed, fireplace, reading nook, and a double whirlpool tub in a greenhouse off a private deck with views over a pond. Meadow Bright stands out for its spaciousness, massive log four-poster canopy bed, river rock fireplace, two-person jetted tub, waterfall shower, and private deck. (Both it and Wood Nymph are wheelchair accessible, from the lighted path leading to them to their roll-in showers). All have terrycloth robes, thick towels, and nightly turndown service.

Guests gather in front of a fire in the mahogany-paneled Great Room in the main house for fresh cookies and hot spiced cider. Hiking trails with panoramic views of the mountains etch the hillside. There are trout in the stream and a lattice gazebo with a stone fireplace next to a pond where guests can ice skate.

Unpretentious and welcoming, the Mansfields manage to be attentive without being intrusive. They live there too, so help in finding a restaurant in Estes Park or advice about touring Rocky Mountain National Park is never far away. Sue's special cinnamon rolls highlight a sumptuous breakfast of Irish potato pancakes, John Wayne casserole, or baked egg dishes, all served in a sunny room with one large and several small tables. Given advance notice, the Mansfields also arrange private candlelit dinners ($30 per person), for guests only.

FORT COLLINS

Elizabeth Street Guest House

202 East Elizabeth Street
Fort Collins, CO 80524
303-493-BEDS (2337)

> *A homey American*
> *foursquare near*
> *the university*

Hosts: Sheryl and John Clark.
Accommodations: 3 rooms, 1
with private bath. **Rates:** Single
$40–$55, double $55–$70. **Included:** Full breakfast. **Minimum stay:** 2 nights on special college weekends. **Added:** 9% tax. **Payment:** Cash or checks preferred; major credit cards. **Children:** Welcome over age 10. **Pets:** Prohibited. **Smoking:** Prohibited. **Open:** Year-round.

With its leaded glass windows and long front porch, this 1905 brick house graces the corner of a shady street in historic Fort Collins. That puts it a block from Colorado State University and a few blocks from the restored Old Town Square. Its front door opens onto an oak-trimmed parlor embellished with family antiques and anchored at one end by an oak staircase and a three-story fully furnished dollhouse. That old-fashioned, turn-of-the-century style makes it feel very homey.

So does Sheryl Clark. As pleasant a hostess as you could ask for, she's also the inspiration behind the decor. She refinished many of the antiques that give style to the upstairs bedrooms, picked out wallpapers and their colorful borders, and hung the lace curtains.

In the year it took her and her husband, John, to renovate the house, Sheryl developed an affection for its quirks. She loves to point out that while the decorative molding in the parlor is oak, that in the family dining room is pine, thus allowing the middle class family who built it to entertain in style while living less lavishly themselves.

> **Guests have run of the parlor and their own second-floor sitting room, which contains a desk, phone, and daybed for lounging.**

The Clarks live in the carriage house adjacent to a garden and a pond in back, but the only kitchen is the one in the main house, so that's where they have their meals.

Sheryl goes all out at breakfast. Apple-cinnamon muffins, pastries, granola and other cereals, fruit, and anything from pancakes, French toast, or Dutch babies to Scotch eggs and omelettes. Throughout the day she makes fresh fruit, coffee, and tea available. Guests can sit in the garden, borrow books and games, or get advice from the Clarks about things to see and do. It's everything a bed-and-breakfast should be.

GLEN HAVEN

The Inn of Glen Haven

7468 County Road 43
P.O. Box 219
Glen Haven, CO 80532
303-586-3897

> *A country inn
> a few miles from
> Estes Park*

Innkeepers: Tom and Sheila Sellers. **Accommodations:** 4 rooms, 2 suites, all with private bath. **Rates:** Rooms $70–$90, suites $90–$100. **Included:** Continental breakfast. **Minimum stay:** None. **Added:** 3.25% tax. **Payment:** MasterCard, Visa. **Children:** Welcome if well behaved. **Pets:** Prohibited. **Smoking:** Allowed. **Open:** Memorial Day through September; weekends in May and October through February.

Eight twisting miles of Devil's Gulch Road separate the tiny village of Glen Haven from Estes Park. Yet knowledgeable diners often make the drive, aware that the Inn of Glen Haven's intimate, antique-filled dining room consistently serves some of the best cuisine around. Once there, they order from a menu that runs from steak Escoffier and other classic French dishes to inspired variations on traditional hunting lodge fare, such as saddle of venison, Glen Haven trout, pork chops, and stuffed chicken. There's also a solid wine list with about a dozen unpretentious labels.

> **The inn has a few endearing quirks, among them a secret room and a tiny pub with a suit of armor, an antique pump organ, and seating for six very close friends.**

The excellent dining aside, this former hunting lodge and, later, bordello evolved under the direction of Tom and Sheila Sellers into a cozy bed-and-breakfast inn. Steep, narrow stairs lead to six serendipitously decorated rooms. They range from the Sherlock Holmes Room, which has a queen-size brass bed and antique dresser, to the two-room Queen Victoria Suite, done in wicker with floral wallpaper and a spindle bed with fabric canopy. The other rooms are variations on Victorian or country styles, not always fully realized but nonetheless spacious and immaculately clean. Beyond the rooms within the inn, there is a nouveau rustic cottage with a kitchen and fireplace in what used to be the stables, and a studio with a covered porch, kitchen, and fireplace in what was formerly the garage. Neither of those pretends to the style of the main inn.

The cozy parlor lobby features antique Victorian settees, a woodstove, floral window treatments, and a baby grand piano. A pianist plays through the dinner hour on most weekends, providing another excuse to linger, or to put off driving Devil's Gulch Road. Those who stay at the inn not only avoid the drive but also have the option of breakfast in bed the next morning.

LOVELAND

The Lovelander

217 West 4th Street
Loveland, CO 80537
303-669-0798
Fax: 303-669-0797

> *A romantic inn,*
> *richly decorated*
> *and well run*

Innkeepers: Marilyn and Bob Wiltgen. **Accommodations:** 11 rooms.
Rates: Single $69–$105, double $79–$115. **Included:** Full
breakfast. **Minimum stay:** None. **Added:** 6% tax. **Payment:**
Major credit cards. **Children:** Over age 10 welcome. **Pets:** Prohibited. **Smoking:** Prohibited. **Open:** Year-round.

Built in 1902 as a private residence, this rambling two-story
Victorian on the plains immediately east of the Rockies has
led numerous lives on its way through the 20th century. It
served as a boarding house for high school teachers, the office
of a country doctor, and an apartment house before Marilyn
and Bob Wiltgen transformed it into an inn as warm as it is
rich in period antiques.

Some of that warmth radiates from the Wiltgens themselves, who live in the renovated garage and are perpetually
on hand. This arrangement gives guests the run of the house
without sacrificing an ounce of personal attention. Meanwhile, the abundance of fresh and dried flower arrangements
is a constant reminder that the innkeepers really care about
their guests.

In the rooms, country blends with Victorian in vintage iron
or highback beds, colorful wallpapers with lush borders,
quilted bedspreads or comforters, and lots of pillows. There's

thick carpeting underfoot and rich fabrics drape not only the windows but sometimes the wall behind the beds as well. All have spotless private baths, three with clawfoot tubs. One room on the first floor has a private entrance and is wheelchair accessible, while those on the second floor snuggle beneath the sloping gables. Honeymooners should try to book either the oversize Columbine, which has an extra-long king-size bed, a six-foot whirlpool tub, and a wall of windows that face south; or Versailles, with regal 1860s carved walnut bed and large bathroom with skylight and clawfoot tub; or Namaqua (the original name of the settlement that became Loveland), which has an aspen log queen-size bed, two-person Jacuzzi tub, and a balcony overlooking the courtyard.

> With rooms like these, a common area isn't really necessary, but the gas-log fireplace beneath a carved oak mantel in the living room and the television, books, and plush furnishings in the parlor lure guests anyway. So does the wraparound front porch and complimentary afternoon tea or wine.

Breakfast is served at a long mahogany table in the expansive dining room. It includes fresh juice, fruit, homemade breads, muffins, and coffee cake, and a hot entrée like eggs Florentine or stuffed French toast with strawberry-tangerine sauce. The Lovelander has found its best life yet.

LYONS

The Inn at Rock 'n River

U.S. Highway 36
P.O. Box 829
Lyons, CO 80540
303-823-5011
303-443-4611 in Denver area
800-448-4611
Fax: 303-823-5011

> *A low-key,
> child-friendly
> B&B with
> fishing ponds*

Innkeepers: Marshall and Barbara McCrummen. **Accommodations:** 6 rooms, 1 2-bedroom suite, 1 cabin, all with private bath. **Rates:** Rooms $78, suite and cabins $104–$135 for up to 4 people. **Included:** Full breakfast. **Minimum stay:** 2 nights on holiday weekends. **Added:** 4.3% tax. **Payment:** Major credit cards. **Children:** Welcome. **Pets:** Prohibited. **Smoking:** Prohibited. **Open:** April–October; fishing on weekends only in April and October.

Of all the bed-and-breakfasts in the Rockies, few have as much appeal for kids as this unpretentious inn and trout farm in a scenic canyon near Estes Park. There are no Victorian antiques to worry about breaking, there are hot dogs on the lunch menu, and there is something for them to do: catch real, live rainbow trout.

Huddled among the cottonwoods and apple trees on the banks of the North Saint Vrain River, a little more than three miles northwest of Lyons, this 18-acre collection of trout ponds, waterfalls, covered bridges, manicured lawns, and flower boxes began as a homestead in 1885 and later evolved into a poultry farm and fish hatchery. Marshall and Barbara McCrummen still raise rainbow trout, smoking the succulent fillets to market commercially. Yet from late spring into fall they also welcome guests, putting them up in spacious quarters in the converted chicken house or in a 1950s cabin and treating them with unabashed hospitality.

> **The ponds teem with up to 9,000 rainbows, which means that anyone who puts a little corn on a hook is virtually guaranteed of catching a trout. Fishermen have the option of tossing a fish back, taking it home (at a cost of 48 cents per inch), or having it served for lunch or dinner at a table on the flower-laden patio or inside.**

Naturally, the very reasonably priced restaurant features trout, netting one from the ponds for those who don't catch their own. This is as fresh as trout gets. The public is welcome for lunch and dinner.

The rooms at the inn face the ponds. Immaculately kept, all have king-size beds, full kitchens, white cinder block walls stenciled with hearts and leaves, a full private bath, and enough space to accommodate a roll-away without being cramped. There's also a two-bedroom suite, a one-room cabin with a fireplace, and a two-story carriage house with a fireplace and its own glass-enclosed Jacuzzi. All the room rates include a full breakfast on the patio featuring fruit-filled pancakes, egg dishes, or maybe a breakfast burrito.

Behind the inn, hiking trails lead up the side of the scenic canyon. Traffic bound for Estes Park, 17 miles away, races past on the opposite side of the river. Parents love it as much as kids.

PINE

Meadow Creek Bed & Breakfast Inn

13438 U.S. Highway 285
Berry Hill Lane at Douglass
    Ranch
Pine, CO 80470
303-838-4167

*An escapist's dream
in the forest
west of Denver*

Innkeepers: Pat and Dennis Carnahan and Judy and Don Otis. **Accommodations:** 6 rooms and 1 cabin, all with private bath. **Rates:** Rooms $84–$120, cabin $145. **Included:** Full breakfast. **Minimum stay:** 2 nights preferred on weekends. **Added:** 4.3% tax. **Payment:** MasterCard, Visa. **Children:** Children under 12 discouraged. **Pets:** Prohibited. **Smoking:** Limited to parlor. **Open:** Year-round.

When people phone Pat Carnahan to inquire what there is to do at Meadow Creek, she frequently asks in return, "Can you handle nothing?"

Situated on 35 acres of the old Douglass Ranch, in the foothills 45 minutes west of Denver, this winsome bed-and-breakfast is an ideal place to escape, whether that means curling up on the couch in front of the native stone fireplace, hanging out on the deck, relaxing in the hot tub, or strolling through the surrounding forests and meadows. Its heart is a two-story stone house built in 1929 as a summer home by Prince Balthasar Gialma Odescalchi, a noble of the Holy Roman Empire. It stands on land that contains several old cabins and a barn. Pat and Dennis Carnahan and Pat's sister

Judy Otis and her husband Don converted it to a bed-and-breakfast in the late 1980s. The Carnahans made room for themselves in the old homesteader's cabin, leaving guests free run of the house.

> A former cake shop owner, Pat also gets rave reviews for her "extreme" breakfasts of egg dishes, fresh fruit, bacon and sausage, plus two or three pastries.

There are six guest rooms in the old house. Each has its own appeal. Grandma's Attic, a long room beneath the center eave on the second floor, has a queen-size brass bed, country quilt, windows at treetop level, and Pat's huge collection of teddy bears. The Cornerstone on the main level has its own Jacuzzi tub and a gas-log fireplace, while the Sun and Columbine rooms stand out for their large south-facing windows. For the ultimate in privacy, however, book the Room in the Meadow, a one-bedroom suite in a 1900s stone structure perched 300 yards from the main house. It contains a king-size bed, Jacuzzi tub for two, gas-log fireplace, a small refrigerator, microwave, coffeemaker, a skylighted sitting area with windows on three sides, and a private deck. Elk often graze in the meadow just beyond.

In the main house, there's a perpetual supply of coffee set out and a small refrigerator stocked with juices and sodas where guests can store any beverages and snacks of their own. The open kitchen becomes a favorite gathering place, in part because Pat puts out homemade cookies there every afternoon.

The Otises come up to help out on weekends, and from Wednesday through Saturday guests can also arrange to have homestyle dinners served at candlelit tables in the dining room. Pat describes the fare as "the sort you'd serve to entertain your friends." The table d'hôte menu may include homemade soups in winter, fresh green salad, marinated and grilled steak or perhaps chicken Cordon Bleu, steamed vegetables, homemade breads, and a choice of several desserts. Vegetarian entrées can be substituted on request, and guests may bring their own wine. All of this enhances its atmosphere of total escape.

Southeast Colorado

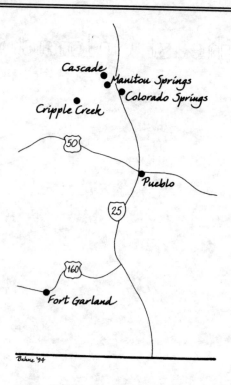

Cascade
Eastholme in the Rockies, 59
Colorado Springs
The Broadmoor, 61
The Hearthstone Inn, 63
Holden House 1902, 65
Cripple Creek
The Imperial Hotel & Casino, 66
Fort Garland
Forbes Trinchera Ranch, 68
Manitou Springs
OnALedge, 70
Red Crags, 71
Pueblo
Abriendo Inn, 73

Best Bed-and-Breakfast Homes

Cascade
Eastholme in the Rockies
Colorado Springs
Holden House 1902
Manitou Springs
OnALedge

Best Bed-and-Breakfast Inns

Colorado Springs
The Hearthstone Inn
Manitou Springs
Red Crags
Pueblo
Abriendo Inn

Best Fishing Lodges

Fort Garland
Forbes Trinchera Ranch

Best Historic Hotels, Inns, and Lodges

Cripple Creek
The Imperial Hotel & Casino

Best Resorts and Spas

Colorado Springs
The Broadmoor

Colorado's southeastern corner bears a superficial resemblance to the northeastern corner. Here, too, the western edge of the Great Plains rolls up against the Rockies, and there are large cities within easy reach of mountain peaks. But the farther south you travel in this quadrant, the more you become aware of differences in history. Though it has its great mining camps in places like Cripple Creek, it wasn't gold and silver that opened up this part of the country so much as the great trading routes and railways. And by the time you reach the southernmost tier, you cross old territorial boundaries into lands once controlled by Mexico. The two major urban centers, Colorado Springs and Pueblo, reflect those differences.

A city of broad boulevards and stylish homes, **Colorado Springs** stands in the shadow of 14,110-foot Pikes Peak. With nearly 250,000 inhabitants, it is Colorado's second largest city. Though its growth is due in part to its scenic setting, the city was founded as a summer resort and spa by General William Palmer and the Denver & Rio Grande Railroad.

Before that, the Ute Indians used to gather on the edge of what is now the city in a place called the Garden of the Gods. It remains a place to see, full of odd geologic formations and weather-beaten junipers. The city is also the home of the U.S. Air Force Academy and its striking modern chapel. The academy's visitors' center provides self-guided tour maps, and you can watch cadets march to lunch from the wall near the chapel.

But nothing draws visitors to Colorado Springs quite so powerfully as Pikes Peak. Ten miles northwest of the city along Route 24 is **Cascade** and the turnoff to the toll road that climbs 7,309 feet to the summit of Pikes Peak. If you'd rather not drive the tortuous route, you can catch the plodding cog railway (May–October) in **Manitou Springs** for the panoramic views from its 14,110-foot tip. Wait for a clear day and then choose one or the other, for this is as high as you'll get in the Rockies without climbing.

Pueblo started out as a crossroads for Indians, Spanish, and fur traders and subsequently evolved into a rail center. Now the state's third largest city, it manufactures fully half of all the goods produced in Colorado. Though often overlooked by tourists — except those who come for the Colorado State Fair in late summer — it does have an appealing downtown historic district with some 40 buildings dating to the mid-19th century, among them Rosemount House, an 1891 mansion constructed of a pink stone called rhyolite and filled with its original furnishings.

To the west of Colorado Springs and Pueblo lies a region of mountains, valleys, and high deserts that is sparsely populated. That was not always the case. The discovery of gold at **Cripple Creek** in 1891 swelled the population from a few miners to more than 25,000 in the space of less than a decade. Some of the mines still operate, but it's no longer gold fever that lures people to this remote town but limited-stakes gambling.

Among the region's other attractions are the world's highest suspension bridge over the 1,000-foot-deep Royal Gorge near Canon City; the 1858 Fort Garland, once commanded by Kit Carson and now restored as a museum; and the route of the old Santa Fe Trail from Mexico to Missouri where it cut across southeastern Colorado.

CASCADE

Eastholme in the Rockies

4445 Haggerman
P.O. Box 98
Cascade, CO 80809
719-684-9901

A landmark hotel restored as a B&B

Hosts: Joanne and Harland Jacobson. **Accommodations:** 4 rooms, 2 with private bath; 2 suites. **Rates:** Rooms $49–$59, suites $69–$74. **Included:** Full breakfast. **Minimum stay:** None. **Added:** 4% tax. **Payment:** Cash, checks, or traveler's checks. **Children:** Welcome over age 9. **Pets:** With prior approval (they have dogs). **Smoking:** Prohibited. **Open:** Year-round.

Eastholme, six miles west of Colorado Springs, is a Ute Pass landmark, the last of a group of late-19th-century hotels that once lined the route from Manitou Springs to the mining town of Cripple Creek. Authentically restored and refinished (it won Colorado's Excellence in Preservation Award in 1989), the three-story, 1885 Victorian still has many of its original furnishings, including an oak bed and matching armoire and dresser in the Eisenhower Suite, where Dwight and Mamie Eisenhower reputedly stayed (Mamie was originally from Denver). Whether that's true or not hardly matters, since Harland and Joanne Jacobson have turned the old hotel into their home and a gracious bed-and-breakfast getaway, a mere 10 miles from downtown Colorado Springs and minutes from the cog railway to the summit of 14,000-foot Pikes Peak.

> **Hummingbird feeders hang from the rafters of the wide front porch where breakfast is served, and sunlight filters through the surrounding stand of ponderosa pine.**

A pillared front porch and the balcony above it run the full width of the blue clapboard structure, providing head-on views of Pikes Peak. On warm days, it's a favorite place for Eastholme's delicious buffet breakfasts (Joanne is an award-winning cook), which, besides the usual cereals, fruits, and pastries, may include chocolate bread, turkey or ham quiche, stuffed French toast, or Cornish pasties with turkey sausage.

Inside, an inviting pink parlor has a fireplace, lace curtains, red plush sofas and chairs, rockers, a vintage Victrola, and the ruby red carpet that used to cover the floor of Colorado Springs' Old Chief Movie Theater. The guest rooms — most of them large, sunny, and tastefully furnished with antiques and handmade quilts — occupy the upper two floors. The two suites have separate sitting rooms with daybeds and private baths, though the bath for the Eisenhower Suite is detached.

Among Eastholme's unusual features is a small guest kitchen on the second floor outfitted with a microwave, refrigerator, and sink. There's also a library on the second floor and a television and VCR in the parlor.

COLORADO SPRINGS

For other lodging in the area, see the towns of Cascade and Manitou Springs.

The Broadmoor

1 Lake Circle
P.O. Box 1439
Colorado Springs, CO 80901
719-634-7711
800-634-7711
Fax: 719-577-5700

> *A multi-dimensional resort anchored by an Old World hotel*

General manager: George Fischer.
Accommodations: 483 rooms, 67 suites. **Rates:** Summer (May–October), rooms $225–$295, suites $350–$1,800; winter (November–April), rooms $145–$185, suites $235–$1,275. **Minimum stay:** None. **Added:** 8.4% tax. **Payment:** Major credit cards. **Children:** Welcome. **Pets:** Prohibited. **Smoking:** Nonsmoking rooms and suites available. **Open:** Year-round.

At the turn of the century, mining magnate Spencer Penrose set out to build a grand hotel to rival the finest in the world. He hired the architectural firm of Warren & Wetmore, which had designed New York City's Grand Central Station and the Biltmore and Ritz-Carlton hotels. From their drawing board emerged a vision of Italian Renaissance splendor in rosy-hued stucco and red tile.

A battalion of skilled artisans was imported from as far away as Italy to hand-decorate the walls, ceilings, and floors of the public rooms. Penrose and his wife traveled the world collecting paintings, sculpture, tapestries, and other fine pieces to furnish the rooms and lobbies. And finally Frederick

Law Olmsted, who laid out New York's Central Park, was charged with bringing order to the foothills landscape.

From the moment it opened in 1918, the resort acquired an international reputation for elegance and professional service. Presidents, kings, maharajahs, and generals stayed at this opulent way station at the foot of the Rockies. They were lured by the hotel's social cachet, its captivating setting, and the pure mountain air.

> The original hotel, its rosy arches and balustrades reflected in a manmade lake, has become the centerpiece of a 3,000-acre resort village with everything from extensive summer and winter recreation facilities to greenhouses and a vast convention center.

In the decades since, the Broadmoor has retained every ounce of its Old World charm. Everything looks particularly splendid now following a $15 million renovation. The rooms in the original hotel, while a trifle small by modern standards, have the Edwardian elegance only antique furnishings, original art, and hand craftsmanship can provide. Those in the Broadmoor West and South additions are newer, larger, and as tasteful as the original. Scattered throughout the resort are nine restaurants ranging from an espresso café to the English country manor decor and award-winning cuisine of Charles Court.

But man does not live by opulence alone. In 1994, the Broadmoor opened a posh new spa and fitness center as part of its new 38,000-square-foot Golf Clubhouse. It joins the already extensive panoply of recreational facilities, not the least of which are three 18-hole golf courses (the oldest designed by master golf course architect Donald Ross, the others by Robert Trent Jones and Ed Seay). The resort also has nine tennis courts (four of them covered by bubbles in winter) with plans to expand to 17, an indoor skating rink, two heated pools, riding stables, bicycling and hiking trails, and a trap and skeet range. There is even a zoo, begun by Penrose in 1926 and now home to a thousand mammals, birds, and reptiles. All that, with recreation packages and special children's programs, is gradually shifting the guest roster away from the obituary-prone loyalists, who seem to have been coming since the hotel opened, toward a younger clientele.

The Hearthstone Inn

506 North Cascade Avenue
Colorado Springs, CO 80903
719-473-4413
800-521-1885
Fax: 719-473-1322

*A rambling inn
carpentered from
two 1885 houses*

Innkeepers: Dot Williams and Ruth
Williams. **Accommodations:** 22 rooms, 3 suites, 23 with private bath. **Rates:** Rooms, single $49–$115, double $59–$125; suites, single $115–$130, double $125–$140. **Included:** Full breakfast. **Minimum stay:** None. **Added:** 8.3% tax. **Payment:** Major credit cards. **Children:** Welcome if well behaved; free under age 5. **Pets:** Prohibited. **Smoking:** Prohibited. **Open:** Year-round.

Getting lost in the maze of the Hearthstone's corridors, wandering up and down stairs and in and out of antique-embellished rooms, is one of the best ways to appreciate what former Texas psychotherapists Ruth Williams and Dot Williams (who are not related) have created. The doors to unoccupied rooms stand open to reveal brass, walnut, oak, and cherry bedsteads, marble-topped dressers, brass lighting fixtures, handmade curtains, and the occasional fireplace. Some are tiny, squeezed in beneath steeply sloping ceilings; others have bay windows and views of Pikes Peak. The Library Room has built-in bookcases and a fireplace; the Billiard Room a curved wall and large window. For elegance, nothing surpasses Fireside, a grand room in ivory, peach, and blue that features a king-size brass and blue iron bed, a fireplace, and a private latticed porch where guests can have their breakfast. So even though the same tasteful sensibility went into decorating them, the rooms are remarkable for their delightfully individual personalities. One is fully handicapped-accessible. None has a phone or television.

> Guests of the Hearthstone Inn do not receive maps when they check in.
> The inn does, however, strategically place exit signs for those who might otherwise wander the labyrinthine hallways endlessly, looking for a route back to the front desk.

The framework for this rabbit warren of an inn is two neighboring 1885 houses: one is a Queen Anne mansion built by a paper bag magnate, the other a former Victorian sanatorium. To connect them, Ruth and Dot shoehorned an old carriage house into the space between. They tied it all together visually by painting everything gray and lavender and trimming it out in lilac, peach, plum, and magenta. Dour it isn't, and neither are the Williamses and their managing staff.

By following the exit signs, guests can find their way to the dining room's long oak tables and fireplace. In the morning, it smells of coffee and freshly baked fruit breads, part of a sumptuous breakfast that might also include crustless quiche, crêpes with apples, or cheese soufflé. Coffee and tea are available all day in the parlor, whose walls have been decorated with religious needlepoint. Downtown Colorado Springs is only a few blocks away.

Holden House 1902

1102 West Pikes Peak Avenue
Colorado Springs, CO 80904
719-471-3980

> *An attentive B&B
> in a storybook
> Victorian*

Hosts: Sallie and Welling Clark.
Accommodations: 2 rooms and
3 suites, all with private bath.
Rates: Rooms $70, suites $95–$100. **Included:** Full breakfast.
Minimum stay: 2–3 nights May–October, holidays, and special events. **Added:** 8.3% tax. **Payment:** Major credit cards.
Children: Not suitable for children. **Pets:** Prohibited (they have a cat). **Smoking:** Prohibited. **Open:** Year-round.

Every evening while guests are at dinner, either Sallie or Welling Clark slips into their rooms to turn down the beds, leaving chocolates and a line or two of poetry about evening or sleep on the pillows. That kind of personal attention pervades the Holden House, a gracious, exceptionally well-run bed-and-breakfast in a residential neighborhood a mile outside Colorado Springs's historic district.

Isabel Holden, the widow of a wealthy Colorado Springs businessman, built the storybook Colonial Revival Victorian in 1902 and later added a carriage house. The Clarks, a young, savvy couple who had dreamed for years of opening a bed-and-breakfast, found the house in the mid-1980s and set about restoring it. Now the inn has a carved oak mantel, marble hearth, and authentic Van Briggle tile fireplace in the parlor, and period wallpapers throughout.

Oriental touches and classical music lend a relaxed calm to the Victorian parlor, where Mingtoy the cat presides with aristocratic nonchalance. Each of the guest rooms is a delight, from the Silverton Suite, with its queen-size four-poster and fireplace, to the Aspen Suite in the corner turret, to the Leadville Room with its white wicker. All of them have an intercom, a bottle of Calistoga water, and luggage racks. Although the rooms lack phones or televisions, the parlor has both.

> When the restoration was complete, the Clarks filled the rooms with antiques and family heirlooms, covered the brass, white iron, and four-poster beds with quilts and down pillows, and set out Sallie's great-grandmother's silver and china on the breakfast table.

Guests can have breakfast either in the formal dining room or out on the verandah, with views of Pikes Peak. Either way they enjoy homemade muffins, fresh fruit with yogurt, and a hot entrée like individual quiches or egg crêpe cups topped with sour cream and herbs. Later, when they return from sightseeing, they'll find coffee, tea, cookies, and Mingtoy waiting in the parlor.

CRIPPLE CREEK

The Imperial Hotel & Casino

123 North Third Street
P.O. Box 1003
Cripple Creek, CO 80813
719-689-7777
800-235-2922
Fax: 719-689-0416

> *A classic
> Gay Nineties hotel
> wedded to a casino*

Innkeepers: Dwayne Mays and Tom Berg. **Accommodations:** 29 rooms, 2 suites, 14 with private bath. **Rates:** Rooms $65–$85, suites $90–$100. **Minimum stay:** None. **Added:** 6%

tax. **Payment:** Major credit cards. **Children:** Welcome. **Pets:** Prohibited. **Smoking:** Prohibited. **Open:** Year-round.

At its zenith, Cripple Creek had 25,000 residents and extracted $25 million a year in gold from its 500 mines. It became a symbol of the feverish, unpredictable Wild West that could turn paupers into rich men overnight. Only a few mines still operate here in the shadow of 10,400-foot Mount Pisgah, and most of the wildness is gone, but visitors still come to Cripple Creek hoping to strike it rich. Like Central City and Blackhawk, this National Historic Mining District has introduced limited-stakes gambling. Suddenly there are slot machines and blackjack tables where once there were ice cream parlors and souvenir shops. Cripple Creek has changed — whether for better or worse depends on your perspective.

> **The one constant in Cripple Creek is the Imperial Hotel. Built after the town's great fire of 1896, it is the only one of the town's original hotels to survive. The Imperial still has a Gay Nineties decor; classic melodramas are staged in summer in its Gold Bar Theatre.**

So has the Imperial Hotel. The main level has a small Victorian parlor, a lounge with an ornate 100-year-old bar, and a dining room with stained glass windows and reasonably priced buffet dinners. A tilted staircase leads to the guest rooms, many of them larger than is typical of old hotels. Each has been individually decorated with oak dressers, colorful period wallpapers, and antique beds in white iron, brass, or oak. Yet for all the magnificence of the antique furnishings, some of these rooms look a bit ragged at the edges, and only half have full private baths, while the others share utilitarian baths with showers.

Until gambling was introduced, the Imperial closed after the fall foliage season. Its current owners, however, bowed to the inevitable and opened their own expansive two-story casino next door, with plans to operate the hotel year-round. Unlike the melodrama and the Cripple Creek–Victor narrow gauge railroad, which are summer-only fixtures, slot machines and poker tables gladly accept bets in all seasons.

FORT GARLAND

Forbes Trinchera Ranch

Fort Garland, CO 81133
719-379-3263
800-FORBES5
Fax: 719-379-3266

*A Forbes-run
fishing retreat*

General manager: Errol Ryland. **Accommodations:** 16 rooms. **Rates:** Single $250, double $400. **Included:** All meals, unlimited fishing. **Minimum stay:** 3 nights. **Added:** 5.9% tax on lodging portion. **Payment:** Cash, personal checks, or traveler's checks. **Children:** Discouraged. **Pets:** Prohibited. **Smoking:** Allowed. **Open:** Sunday to Friday, July through August.

Forbes magazine owns this 400-square-mile fishing and hunting outpost in south-central Colorado, where the sagebrush and cedar of the high desert meets pine-timbered mountains. Open only on a limited basis to a maximum of 12 fishermen at a time, the ranch encompasses 40 miles of completely private fishing streams. All of them are home to the relatively rare Rio Grande cutthroat trout, which share a few of the crystal-clear streams with rainbows and brooks. Though not particularly large — 14 inches is considered a good fish — they are abundant enough that an average fly-fisherman can look forward to catching and releasing 20 to 40 an hour.

The main lodge is a rather unprepossessing shingle-roofed structure set among the rough pine fencing and stucco outbuildings of the ranch. Inside it's another story. Crate-style chairs huddle in front of the huge stone fireplace in a spacious room whimsically outfitted with model ships and a collection of toy motorbikes. It isn't a clichéd fishing lodge, despite the meadows and trout stream right out back and the gorgeous views of the Sangre de Cristo Mountains.

The rooms, too, shy away from rustic in favor of a neo-ranch spiffiness born of western white cedar log beams, pine-paneled walls, and lodgepole pine furnishings set off by quilts, fabrics, and carpet in muted southwestern pastels. The art on the walls, some of it done by the Forbes family's friends, leans toward the offbeat. The private baths are of recent vintage.

Every room has a bowl of cookies, candy bars, fruit, and other goodies. There isn't a television in sight.

In a nod to tradition, there are some buffalo and antelope heads hanging in the dining room. But the family-style dinners of steaks, red snapper, and shrimp emerge from a kitchen headed by a chef who graduated from the Culinary Institute of America rather than the Cowboy School of Campfire Cooking.

> **Warm hospitality is the glue that binds together this otherwise unstructured environment. The ranch was designed to afford comfortable surroundings and a convivial atmosphere while providing access to an extraordinary reserve of private fishing spots.**

Guests make up the day's fishing routine, either going off on their own to cast flies in the ranch's creeks, beaver ponds, or lake or hiring one of the ranch's knowledgeable guides (at $100 a day) to accompany them. Four-wheel-drive vehicles are available for rent (at $50 a day) to get to out-of-the-way spots.

There is a caveat about the ranch: the addition of a small conference center has introduced a new orientation that encroaches on the fishing clientele. Because those conference groups are guaranteed exclusive use of the ranch, Forbes no longer takes individual bookings during any period when a conference is scheduled. Moreover, it requires a minimum of six participants in order to run the fishing program at all (the staff does, however, try to funnel prospective fishermen into the same period rather than insist upon their putting together their own groups). The quality of the fishing operation remains unchanged, but it has become more difficult for individuals to secure a reservation.

MANITOU SPRINGS

OnALedge

336 El Paso Boulevard
Manitou Springs, CO 80829
719-685-4265
800-530-8253

> A millionaire's
> 1912 guest house
> converted to a B&B

Hosts: Mel and Shirley Podell.
Accommodations: 2 rooms and 2 suites, all with private bath. **Rates:** Rooms $75–$85, suites $115–$125. **Included:** Full breakfast. **Minimum stay:** None. **Added:** 9.5% tax. **Payment:** Major credit cards. **Children:** Welcome over age 11. **Pets:** Prohibited. **Smoking:** Prohibited in rooms. **Open:** Year-round.

A Texas oil millionaire built this English Tudor–inspired home as a guest house in 1912, using red stone and rust-colored stucco. He then adorned the interiors with hardwood floors, copper light fixtures with alabaster globes, and a large copper-hooded fireplace. Still unsatisfied, he lavished another $75,000 on gardens planted on terraces sculpted from red rock.

Shirley and Mel Podell bought the secluded cottage in 1988 after selling their Manitou Springs motel. Their plan was to retire in a house big enough to allow all their children and grandchildren to visit. But, eager for company when their kids weren't around, they opened their home as a bed-and-breakfast and soon found themselves once again in the hospitality business.

The Podells opened four large rooms to guests and set aside one part of the house for themselves. Furnishings and decor vary, from the king-size canopy bed with a white comforter and white lace dust ruffle in the Rockledge Suite, to the brass bed and white wicker furnishings in the pink, mauve, and green Craftwood Room. Each of the two suites has its own hot tub, and one has a fireplace. All of the rooms have windows on either Pikes Peak or the surrounding mountains.

Every afternoon Shirley sets out coffee, tea, soft drinks, and cookies on the sideboard in the parlor, the first of many little Podell touches. She recommends restaurants and then often makes the reservation herself, though guests have a phone to use just off the parlor. Mornings begin with a huge breakfast served on the flower-decked outside patio on nice days. It might include Mel's own baked grapefruit Alaska, chicken with almonds, and raisin scones with cherries and a dribble of frosting. It's always more than most people can eat.

> **The Podells filled the former guest house with their beloved kitsch, including plaster cherubs, porcelain ducks, a carousel horse, an antique organ, two player pianos, and Mel's collection of decorative woodstoves.**

Red Crags

302 El Paso Boulevard
Manitou Springs, CO 80829
719-685-1920

> *A castlelike B&B, full of antiques and romance*

Hosts: Carrie and Kevin Maddox. **Accommodations:** 2 rooms and 5 suites. **Rates:** Rooms $75–$100, suites $125–$200. **Included:** Full breakfast. **Minimum stay:** None. **Added:** 9.5% tax. **Payment:** Major credit cards. **Children:** Welcome over age 12. **Pets:** Prohibited (they have a dog). **Smoking:** Prohibited. **Open:** Year-round.

The three-story Victorian stone mansion known as Red Crags clings to a hillside at the edge of Manitou Springs, where it commands views of Pikes Peak, the Garden of the Gods, and Manitou Valley east to Colorado Springs. The town's founder, Dr. William Bell, built the 7,000-square-foot mansion in 1870 as a sanatorium, though by the turn of the century it had counted among its guests Teddy Roosevelt and the carriage trade. A succession of owners followed. Late in 1990, former Dallas stockbrokers Carrie and Kevin Maddox completed three years of renovations and opened their castlelike home as a bed-and-breakfast.

> Teddy Roosevelt's favorite room was one with a Gothic fireplace. The Maddoxes turned it into a glorious honeymoon suite with a feather bed, claw-foot tub, and private outside deck.

Check-in formalities take place in a high-ceilinged parlor dominated by a rare Eastlake fireplace of carved cherrywood. Scattered about are antiques upholstered in red plush, an 1860 piano, and a huge marble and oak bar with a beveled mirror. The porch facing Pikes Peak has become a solarium furnished with red plush velvet couches and a wide screen television with a collection of movies. It opens at one end onto an outside deck that is a favorite place for breakfast.

One suite contains Carrie's grandmother's handmade oak bed. The smallest room — huge by other standards — has maple floors, a woodstove, a stained glass skylight, and an old-fashioned bathroom with an oak and tin tub and an oak commode. Every room showcases Carrie's gifted sense of color. Elegant Victorian wallpapers combine with the antiques to create sumptuous retreats — rooms that guests hate to leave — and all have special touches like sachets or stuffed animals.

The honeymoon suite has a private breakfast nook, but everyone else is likely to have their eggs Benedict, homemade breads, fruit punch, and butter pecan coffee on the porch or in the formal dining room. Meanwhile, the Maddoxes are at work converting their carriage house into a huge junior suite dubbed the Marionette Theatre. It, too, will have a Victorian decor and its own private Jacuzzi.

PUEBLO

Abriendo Inn

300 West Abriendo Avenue
Pueblo, CO 81004
719-544-2703
Fax: 719-542-6595

> *A brewery magnate's elegant midtown mansion, now a B&B*

Hosts: Kerrelyn McCafferty Trent and Chuck Trent. **Accommodations:** 7 rooms, all with private bath. **Rates:** Single $49–$84, double $54–$89. **Included:** Full breakfast. **Minimum stay:** None. **Added:** 11.6% tax. **Payment:** Major credit cards. **Children:** Well-behaved children over 7 welcome. **Pets:** Prohibited. **Smoking:** Prohibited. **Open:** Year-round.

This elegant foursquare mansion and its broad porch anchor an acre of parklike ground in the heart of Pueblo, two blocks from historic Union Avenue. Martin Walter, the brewery magnate, had it built in 1906 as a home for his wife and eight children.

A freelance interior designer, Kerrelyn brought her considerable skills to the task of making the enchanting rooms suggest Victorian style without verging on dark and gloomy. The Goodnight Room, in royal blue, has a Chinese Chippendale canopy bed, an Oriental rug, leaded and beveled glass windows, and a large bath. The smaller but sunny Damon Runyon, in ivory and blue, pairs a carved walnut Victorian bed with a wingback reading chair. The Orman Room, once the music parlor, has a fireplace and built-in bookcase, but the piano has been replaced by an elaborate king-size brass bed and ruby red Oriental rug. Its bedroom connects to a sitting room with three bay windows that overlook the tree-shaded grounds. In all the rooms, armoires, crocheted bedspreads, and a variety of antiques enhance the charm, while phones with data ports, desks, and televisions ensure convenience.

Listed on the National Register of Historic Places, the Abriendo features bow windows, high ceilings, inlaid wood floors, rich oak moldings and paneling, and stained glass. Even so, it took the Trents' ingenuity to turn it into Pueblo's most inviting place to stay.

Breakfast, with home-made breads, an egg and cheese casserole, fresh fruit, coffee, and tea, is served in the wainscoted dining room or outside on the sun porch. In the late afternoon, the Trents provide complimentary beverages in the living room or by the fireplace in the grand foyer. Kerrelyn and Chuck are as attentive to guests as they have been to their home.

Northwest Colorado

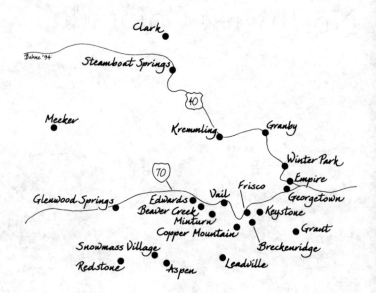

Best Bed-and-Breakfast Homes

Breckenridge
  Williams House
Georgetown
  The Hardy House
Glenwood Springs
  Kaiser House
Leadville
  Wood Haven Manor
Steamboat Springs
  Steamboat Bed & Breakfast
  Steamboat Valley Guest House
Winter Park
  Alpen Rose

Best Bed-and-Breakfast Inns

Aspen
  Hotel Lenado
  Independence Square Hotel
  Midnight Inn
  Sardy House
Breckenridge
  The Allaire Timbers Inn
Frisco
  Galena Street Mountain Inn
Leadville
  Leadville Country Inn
Minturn
  Eagle River Inn
Redstone
  Avalanche Ranch
  Cleveholm Manor
Vail
  Black Bear Inn of Vail

Best Condominiums, Apartments, and Cabins

Aspen
  Brand Building

Beaver Creek
  Park Plaza
  Trapper's Cabin
Redstone
  Avalanche Ranch

Best Country Inns

Clark
  Inn at Steamboat Lake
Keystone
  Ski Tip Lodge

Best Fishing Lodges

Kremmling
  Elktrout
Meeker
  Elk Creek Lodge

Best Guest Ranches

Clark
  Home Ranch
  Vista Verde Guest & Ski Touring Ranch
Granby
  C Lazy U Ranch
  Drowsy Water Ranch
Grant
  Tumbling River Ranch
  Kremmling
  Latigo Ranch

Best Historic Hotels, Inns, and Lodges

Aspen
  Hotel Jerome
Empire
  The Peck House
Leadville
  Delaware Hotel

Redstone
   The Redstone Inn

Best Resorts and Spas

Copper Mountain
   Copper Mountain Resort
Keystone
   Keystone Resort
Snowmass Village
   The Snowmass Lodge & Club
Edwards
   Lodge at Cordillera

Best Ski Area Hotels & Lodges

Aspen
   Alpine Lodge
   Little Nell
   The Ritz-Carlton, Aspen
Beaver Creek
   Hyatt Regency Beaver Creek
   Inn at Beaver Creek
   Poste Montane
   Trapper's Cabin
Copper Mountain
   Club Med–Copper Mountain
Snowmass Village
   The Snowmass Lodge & Club
Vail
   Christiania Lodge
   Gasthof Gramshammer
   Sonnenalp Hotel and Country Club

Whereas eastern Colorado butts up against the Front Range, the vast bulk of the Colorado Rockies — including all of the Continental Divide — marches through the state's western half. This has tended to discourage the growth of large towns — Grand Junction with a population of 30,000 is as large as they get — while promoting an endless variety of recreation, summer and winter. The northwestern region is particularly rich in ski areas, having more than two-thirds of the state's entire total. That includes Aspen and Snowmass, Vail and Beaver Creek, Steamboat Springs, Winter Park, and the quartet in Summit County: Arapahoe Basin, Breckenridge, Copper Mountain, and Keystone. Colorado owes its reputation for world-class skiing to the resorts in the northwest quadrant. Once the snows melt, however, the region becomes if anything even more beautiful and accessible for a far greater variety of distractions. Back roads and high mountain passes reopen. Rivers run with trout. Wildflowers bloom. Several routes officially designated as scenic byways lace the high country, including one from Yampa to Meeker along the Flat Tops Wilderness and Route 133 south from Carbondale through **Redstone** and beyond. Highway 82 over Independence Pass, on the other hand, carries no such official recognition, but it is every Coloradan's favorite back route into Aspen. The scenic but often hair-raising alpine highway begins by skirting Mt. Elbert — at 14,433 feet the tallest peak in Colorado — and then winds upward toward 12,095 feet and the Continental Divide. There's a turnout at the top, which is well above the timberline, and a path leading to an overlook along the peaks of the Divide. At that point the road descends as it ascended; looking barely wide enough for two cars, it is riddled with blind, hairpin curves.

It's a relief to arrive in **Aspen,** the fabled ski town that is even more appealing in summer and fall. Recreation and trendy shops abound in this former mining town, which has a smart pedestrian mall, excellent restaurants, and a fine summer music festival. Hikers who don't mind crowds can take a bus to Maroon Bells (it's so popular, cars have been banned from the trailhead); those who prefer a quieter route head for the Snowmass–Maroon Bells Wilderness Area instead.

Aspen stands out for its elegant restoration and chic clientele, but it is only one of many late 19th-century mining towns dotting the mountains in this region. In **Georgetown,** for example, more than 200 structures in various states of repair survive from the last century, while **Leadville** recalls the gold and silver era with attractions like the Matchless Mine, the 1879 Tabor Opera House, and the lavishly furnished 1878 Healy House.

Not all the ski towns are old, of course. **Vail** dates to the early 1960s and was modeled on a European village — evidently one that sells furs and designer fashions — while **Keystone** is not a town at all but a lodge-and-condominium development at the base of the slopes.

The nature of this northwestern quadrant is an ability to satisfy a variety of inclinations. There are hot springs pools in **Glenwood Springs** and **Steamboat Springs,** guest ranches of every stamp from working cattle spreads to luxury havens, superb paved bicycle trails from **Breckenridge** over the Continental Divide to Vail, Gold Medal trout fishing in half a dozen rivers, and whitewater rafting on the Colorado, and uncounted miles of hiking and mountain biking trails.

In the far west, the Rockies give way to the arid landscapes of the great deserts. Near Grand Junction, Colorado National Monument shows the power of wind and erosion to sculpt sandstone into awesome shapes. Within its boundaries, towering monoliths stand like sentinels in deep canyons framed by sheer cliffs. The landscapes are particularly dramatic when seen from above off Rim Rock Drive, a 22-mile road along the canyon edges. The bleak gray landscape in the extreme northwest corner holds part of Dinosaur National Monument, where 140-million-year-old dinosaur fossils have been unearthed.

ASPEN

For other lodging in the area, see Snowmass Village.

Alpine Lodge

1240 East Cooper
Aspen, CO 81611
303-925-7351
Fax: 303-925-5796

> *A funky old
> ski lodge, at
> attractive prices*

Innkeepers: Jim and Christina Martin. **Accommodations:** 7 rooms, 4 with private bath; 4 cabins. **Rates:** Rooms, summer (mid-May–Thanksgiving) $45–$60, winter $55–$95; cabins, summer $65–$70, winter $98–$130. **Included:** Continental-plus breakfast in summer. **Minimum stay:** 7 nights over Christmas and February–March. **Added:** 7.7% tax. **Payment:** Discover, MasterCard, Visa. **Children:** Welcome. **Pets:** With prior approval in cabins (they have a cat and a dog). **Smoking:** Prohibited. **Open:** Year-round.

In glitzy Aspen, any room priced below $200 a night is considered a relative bargain during the winter ski season. And while it's possible to pay less, those who do often get just what they pay for: a place to sleep and very little else. One notable exception, though, is the funky Alpine Lodge, an Aspen institution almost as old as the ski area itself.

Rough-hewn beams, textured stucco walls, and shelves of beer steins suggest Bavaria, and so does the green ceramic tile woodstove in the sitting room. That provides an appropriate atmosphere for the entertainment: once a week the previous owner stops by to play the zither and sing German songs.

> **The Alpine Lodge's tenure as a ski lodge dates back 40 years; the two-story, stucco and timber house itself has been around since before the turn of the century.**

Jim and Christina Martin bought the lodge in 1989. They replaced the old patchwork quilts with down comforters, spruced up the carpets and fabrics, and modernized the baths, but they haven't interfered with the casual atmosphere, attractive prices, or the lodge's longstanding commitment to treating guests like family. Guests still bed down in clean, cozy rooms decorated with antiques and knotty pine wainscoting or in a cabin with a fully equipped kitchen, a tiny bedroom, and a private bath.

By midsummer, the lodge is often completely booked for the winter. That has less to do with its cozy rooms than its reasonable prices and its convivial ambience. At a $300-a-night hotel you may never meet a soul; guests at the Alpine Lodge pay hundreds of dollars less, are greeted by name, and meet everybody. The Martins encourage it, in part by scheduling margarita Mondays (most people arrive on Saturday), with free drinks and a Mexican dinner to bring everyone together for what amounts to a party. Many become friends and plan to come back the next year at the same time.

Although rates do not include meals, the lodge does offer breakfasts ($5) and dinners ($14) and posts the weekly menu. In summer, rates include a Continental-plus breakfast. Both are served family style. There's also an outdoor hot tub.

The Alpine Lodge's minor drawback is its location; at the edge of town, it's beyond easy walking distance to the slopes. It is, however, right on the free shuttle bus line that serves all four ski areas. It's Aspen's best bargain; just be sure to make your reservations early.

Brand Building

205 South Galena Street
Aspen, CO 81611
303-920-1800
Fax: 303-920-3602

> *A half dozen sybaritic apartments in the heart of Aspen*

General manager: Bill Stolz. **Accommodations:** 6 condominiums. **Rates:** Summer (June–September) $260–$660, winter (late November–March) $315–$1,200, off-season $200–$400; higher over Christmas holidays. **Included:** Health club privileges, admittance to Caribou Club. **Minimum stay:** 14 nights over Christmas holidays. **Added:** 8.2% tax. **Payment:** Major credit cards. **Children:** Welcome. **Pets:** With prior approval. **Smoking:** Allowed. **Open:** Year-round.

Built in 1891 from rough-hewn blocks of native sandstone, this Victorian fortress in the center of Aspen originally housed a mining company and a bank, whose safe once held the largest silver nugget ever found. Decades later, the Brand provided studio space for Roy Lichtenstein, Andy Warhol, and Christo. Ice cream and tie-dyed clothing were sold in the shops on the street level. But it still hadn't begun accepting overnight guests, except those who may have spent the night on a couch in an artist's studio.

The transformation of the Brand from fortress to lodge occurred in the mid-1980s, when street-peddler-turned-Aspen-entrepreneur Harley Baldwin converted the second floor into six apartments that would later be featured in *Architectural*

Digest. Individually designed and furnished, the suites have one or two bedrooms, fireplaces, huge marble baths, and full kitchens. Each is named for a famous Aspen mine: Cascade's antique Scandinavian furnishings, twig stands, and blue and white chintz suggest an elegant country cottage; the Park Regent features southwestern accents and Mexican earthenware; and the Silver Echo soars through three levels to a balconied master bedroom.

> The Brand isn't priced for the faint of pocketbook, but then neither is Aspen; and with only half a dozen rooms, this is the most exclusive address in town.

Guests arrive to find fresh flowers, bowls of fruit, and champagne. Each living room has a complete stereo system. Original art accents the walls. Concierge service is available. So is an optional Continental breakfast from one of Aspen's foremost bakeries.

The back stairs access a small workout room with a Jacuzzi, sauna, and a personal trainer on call. Guests may also use the posh Grand Champions Fitness Club and dine at the otherwise private Caribou Club.

Hotel Jerome

330 East Main Street
Aspen, CO 81611
303-920-1000
800-331-7213
Fax: 303-925-2784

> *A grand mining-era hotel has had a $5 million makeover*

General manager: Anthony M. DiLucia. **Accommodations:** 44 rooms and 49 suites. **Rates:**

(higher over Christmas holidays) Rooms, summer (April–mid-December) $199–$239, winter $229–$439; suites, summer $299–$439, winter $329–$439. **Included:** Airport transfers and ski area shuttle. **Minimum stay:** 6 days over Christmas holidays. **Added:** 7.7% tax. **Payment:** Major credit cards. **Children:** Free under age 3. **Pets:** Prohibited. **Smoking:** Prohibited in rooms. **Open:** Year-round.

Built during Aspen's mining heyday, this three-story Victorian charmer can still pamper body and spirit with the best of them. It was the grandest hotel in town when it opened in 1889, boasting not only electricity and steam heat but also a rare elevator. Each of its original rooms contained a fireplace capped by a mirror made of diamond dust.

Jerome B. Wheeler, the financial backer behind the landmark, made a fortune investing in Aspen's mines after giving up his position as president of Macy's. Like many at the time, he believed that the booming town needed a hotel that would reflect its prosperity. He donated the land, hired the architects, and ultimately poured the equivalent of $1.6 million into its construction and furnishings. It opened with great fanfare and hyperbolic praise on Thanksgiving Day 1889.

> One aspect of the hotel survives unchanged: the legendary and immensely popular Jerome Bar. Despite competition from upstarts nearer the slopes, this western artifact remains one of the best places in town for après-ski.

The current owners put $4.5 million into restoring the timeworn National Historic Landmark to its original Eastlake-Gothic elegance. They reduced the number of rooms in the original hotel from 90 to 27, making up the difference by building a new wing containing 67 rooms and suites, all of them spacious and opulent. Each contains an antique brass or cast-iron bed and an authentic Eastlake armoire with a beveled glass mirror. Bold floral wallpapers copied from 19th-century patterns set off the moiré drapes and lace sheers. The large bathrooms have whirlpool tubs, but enough Carrara marble surrounds them and the double sinks to continue the turn-of-the-century feel. The rooms also feature terrycloth robes, cable televisions, VCRs, telephones, hair dryers, humidifiers, and mini-bars. Some of the suites harbor even more exquisite pieces, like carved antique beds and armoires, glass lamps, and decorative fireplaces.

Diffused light from a skylight three floors above illuminates the lobby parlor, falling on the carved oak mantel of an impressive fireplace and the silver-dust mirror above it. A baby grand piano stands to one side, out of the way of clusters of vintage furniture.

During the summer, the patio at the well-known Jerome Bar, which has a small pool, attracts a crowd with its live bands. The adjacent Century restaurant, under chef Jeffrey Troiola, has lately attracted cuisinary attention for contemporary American creations like grilled Colorado trout on orzo, seared lamb loin with vegetable couscous, and low-fat, low-cholesterol orrechetti pasta with grilled vegetables.

Beyond that, the Jerome offers room service, valet parking, ski storage, a concierge, and turndown service. The newest additions to the Jerome's panoply of amenities are a ski-tuning room and a state-of-the-art fitness center. Its only shortcoming is the staff, who can be anything from attentive to indifferent, snooty to western friendly.

Hotel Lenado

200 South Aspen Street
Aspen, CO 81611
303-925-6246
800-321-3457
Fax: 303-925-3840

> *An award-winning inn that celebrates the beauty of wood*

General manager: Jayne Poss. **Accommodations:** 19 rooms. **Rates:** Winter (Thanksgiving to mid-April) $129–$299 (higher over Christmas holidays), rest of year $95–$215. **Included:** Full breakfast. **Minimum stay:** 3–4 nights on some summer weekends; 4 nights over weekends February–March; 7 or more over Christmas holidays. **Added:** 8.2% tax and $1.50/person/day gratuity for breakfast. **Payment:** Major credit cards. **Children:** Free under age 3. **Pets:** Prohibited. **Smoking:** Prohibited in breakfast room. **Open:** Year-round.

Leñado means "wooded" in Spanish, and the Hotel Lenado lives up to its name, with furnishings crafted from apple, birch, cherry, pine, fir, willow, hickory, and ironwood. Bent-willow chairs and sofas with overstuffed cushions cluster near the contemporary fireplace that soars through the three-story atrium lobby. Fir has been used on the walls and hemlock for the floors. Every room has either a carved applewood or four-poster twig bed. The hotel's magnificent obsession even carries out to the sundeck and its wood-encased hot tub.

Situated next to a park in the heart of Aspen, a block from Main Street and six blocks from the ski lifts on Aspen Mountain, this delightful inn opened in 1984.

> **Not only was this the first new hotel to open in Aspen in a decade, it also took the unusual step of rating its own rooms with one to five stars according to their size and amenities.**

According to the hotel's own rating system, one-star rooms, though warmly appointed, have twin beds and a minimum of extras. Three-star accommodations combine larger space with a vaulted ceiling and a balcony. Four- and five-star rooms boast wet bars, balconies or decks, whirlpool tubs, and in some cases woodstoves, vaulted ceilings, and corner locations. Every room, whether one star or five, has down comforters, terrycloth robes, a phone, and a nine-inch television.

For a small hotel, the Lenado has an exceptional array of amenities. Apart from the hot tub and sun deck — which have views of the trees or the ski slopes, depending on the time of year — there is a library with books, newspapers, restaurant menus, and games; a screening room with a VCR and big-screen TV; and heated ski-boot lockers. Breakfast is a generous feast of homemade granola, oatmeal, fresh muffins, eggs, bacon, and daily specials like Belgian waffles, eggs Lenado with home fries, or blueberry pancakes. There are complimentary hors d'oeuvres in Markhams Bar (which doubles as the breakfast room) every afternoon, and the first-rate staff strives to get to know all the guests and make them want to come back.

Independence Square Hotel

404 South Galena Street
Aspen, CO 81611
303-920-2313
Fax: 303-925-1233

*A century-old
brothel redone
as a spiffy inn*

General manager: Julie Adams. **Accommodations:** 28 rooms. **Rates:** Summer (mid-April–late November) $80–$185, winter $95–$300. **Included:** Continental breakfast, privileges at Aspen Club, airport transfers. **Minimum stay:** 3–5 nights in winter (7 over Christmas). **Added:** 7.9% tax. **Payment:** Major credit cards. **Children:** Welcome. **Pets:** Prohibited. **Smoking:** Allowed. **Open:** Year-round.

The Independence Building was constructed in 1889 and almost immediately became a brothel, one of 25 at that time in a mining town that had blossomed into a city of 12,000.

These are bright, functional spaces (when the Murphy bed folds up, a table drops down) with tiled baths (some with shower only) and extra amenities like phones, televisions, and terrycloth robes.

Decades later, after snow-covered slopes had replaced silver and gold as the town's chief attraction, the three-story brick structure became employee housing. Then in 1985 it joined Aspen's lodging renaissance (see the Hotel Lenado above) with its conversion to an inn.

Designers steered clear of traditional dark Victorian style in favor of what the brochure describes as French country. That has a nice sound to it even if it does leave guests wondering just which region of provincial France provided the inspiration for rooms with Murphy beds, wet bars, and lots of built-in cabinetry covered, like the ceiling, with fir wainscoting. Maybe the brochure is alluding to the pillow-covered banquette windows or duvet covers.

These rooms can sometimes be noisy, the staff at times indifferent, but the hotel's location couldn't be better: on the mall and a short 2½ blocks from the Silver Queen Gondola and the ski slopes of Aspen Mountain. A second-floor sitting area open to a skylight two floors above has a gas-log fireplace, purple couches, and quilts hanging on its walls. Higher up, the hotel's rooftop Jacuzzi enjoys a 360-degree view of town and the surrounding mountains. Guests also enjoy privileges at the Aspen Club, an exclusive fitness and tennis club in the aspens along the Roaring Fork River east of town. And every morning there is a complimentary breakfast laid out in the library with trays to make it easy to carry it back to the rooms.

The Little Nell

675 East Durant Street
Aspen, CO 81611
303-920-4600
800-525-6200
Fax: 303-920-6345

A sybaritic ski hotel and fabulous restaurant

General manager: Eric Calderon.
Accommodations: 79 rooms, 13 suites. **Rates:** Rooms, winter (mid-December–early April) $375–$485 (higher over Christmas holidays), summer (late May–late September) $225–$315, spring/fall, $175–$240; suites, winter $650–$2,300, summer $450–$1,400, spring/fall $325–$1,100. **Minimum stay:** 3–4 nights on weekends; 7 nights over Christmas holidays. **Added:** 8.2% tax. **Payment:** Major credit cards. **Children:** Welcome. **Pets:** Prohibited. **Smoking:** Prohibited in restaurant; nonsmoking rooms available. **Open:** Year-round.

Here is the answer to a skier's prayers, the ultimate ski-in lodge. A valet parks cars in front; in back, a ski concierge collects equipment as guests come off the slopes, then returns the skis tuned and waxed and the boots and gloves warmed the next morning as they head back out to ski. In between, guests can curl up in extra large rooms extravagantly decked out in country French comforts.

This $34 million boutique hotel set a new standard of ski-in/ski-out luxury and superlative service when it opened in December 1989. Situated at the base of Aspen Mountain, it is 30 paces from the Silver Queen Gondola and not much farther from Aspen's pedestrian-oriented shopping district.

No two rooms have the same layout. Even lowly standard quarters with a town view feature a gas-log fireplace, down sofas and ottomans, wool carpeting, and an oversize bed with a down comforter. The remote-control TV comes with a VCR; the spacious marble bathroom with two vanities, a steam shower, and alabaster tissue holders and wastebaskets. He has his closet, she has hers. More deluxe digs have better views, even more space, and balconies overlooking the slopes. Most opulent of all are the suites, which encompass more square footage than some homes.

Not the homes of the people who rent them, though. The Little Nell appeals unabashedly to the carriage trade, and the meek of pocketbook need not apply. Still, it doesn't scrimp on amenities. The courtyard behind the hotel frames a small heated swimming pool with filtered rather than chlorinated water and a flagstone deck whose radiant heat ensures that winter swimmers or those bound for the Jacuzzi never have to tread across snow or ice. Designed to afford views of the mountain, it nonetheless shelters bathers in semi-seclusion, out of sight of prying eyes (a strategically placed planter at Shlomo's Deli prevents the crowd there from peering into the coutryard). And a doorway off the patio leads to sauna and steam rooms and a small exercise room just inside.

The lobby is less a lobby than a living room furnished with plump down-filled couches and chairs in front of a two-sided flagstone fireplace. Modern western art and historic photos of Aspen decorate the walls, and there are views across the pool and the ski slopes and gondola. This living room gives onto a cozy bar with live jazz in one direction and a restaurant featuring the innovative "American alpine" cuisine — charred tuna steak with wasabi potatoes, grilled veal T-bone with compote of cannellini beans — of executive chef George Mahaffey in the other.

For lighter fare, the hotel has Shlomo's, a deli with decks on the ski slopes. It provides the best in people-watching to go with sandwiches, burgers, or bagels and cream cheese. All in all, the Little Nell is one of the great inns in ski country.

Midnight Inn

0786 Midnight Mine Road
P.O. Box 3053
Aspen, CO 81612
303-925-2349
Fax: 303-920-9722

A secluded inn, quirky and comfortable, set in the aspens

Hosts: Fritz and Melina Greve. **Accommodations:** 6 rooms, 4 with private bath. **Rates:** Summer $90–$156, winter $130–$270. **Included:** Full breakfast. **Minimum stay:** None. **Added:** 6.5% tax. **Payment:** Major credit cards. **Children:** Welcome. **Pets:** Prohibited (they have a dog and a cat). **Smoking:** Prohibited. **Open:** Year-round.

The Midnight Inn is a secluded three-story timber house set on an aspen-covered hillside 3½ miles from town on the road to Ashcroft. Inside, the main room is an expansive open kitchen with a blue ceramic tile floor and a raised dining area.

Beyond it, a few more steps lead to a small living room with a woodburning fireplace, TV/VCR, player piano, and an old phone booth, reputedly from the Jerome Hotel. From there, an irregular staircase provides the first clue to the Midnight Inn's engaging but quirky character. It is not, as it first seems, a simple boxy house but a renovated barn connected in peculiar fashion to a log cabin farther up the hillside.

> In summer, columbines, roses, and other flowers bloom in terraced beds, luring hummingbirds. Umbrella tables dot a brick deck, and a hammock stretches between two trees. In winter, steam rises from a glassed-in hot tub with views of Castle Creek Canyon and the slopes of Aspen Highlands.

Fritz and Melina Greve, the thirtysomething couple who own the inn, had nothing to do with its construction. The odd design resulted from the collision between the independent spirit of the inn's former owner, Steve Coolidge, and county zoning laws. Coolidge had been living in the cabin when he decided to convert the barn to guest quarters. He promptly ran afoul of county officials, who insisted that he couldn't have two residential buildings on his property. In response, he gerrymandered an enclosed wooden tunnel to connect the two. And thus the Midnight Inn was born.

Interior design was not, however, Coolidge's forte. It took the Greves' efforts to transform the rooms into sleeping quarters as endearing as the inn itself. They outfitted the six rooms with antique iron or brass beds, some armoires, new linens and floor coverings, down comforters, and cutwork shower curtains. Fritz set many of the sinks in old treadle sewing machines (in some, the treadle opens and closes the drain). He turned an old chicken egg hatcher into a table for the living room.

Each room is unique. The Midnight Room has a woodburning stove, a queen and separate daybed, an armoire with an oval beveled mirror, and its own deck overlooking a pond and creek. The Berry Room stands out for its many windows, skylight, and private bath in a turreted alcove. Even the small Lilac and Spruce Rooms, which share a bath, are cozy chambers with queen beds tucked under the eaves and skylight.

The Greves live in the log cabin, leaving guests full run of the inn. He's a former ski racer, she's a hair stylist, and both love having guests. They come down each morning to fix huge breakfasts of oatmeal, pancakes, whole-wheat poppy-seed French toast, eggs Benedict — "Anything," says Fritz, "depending on how brave we get. We always overfeed them."

In summer, the inn can be a base for hiking, mountain biking, fishing; in winter, Fritz himself plows the road, assuring easy access to the inn, which is convenient to all the ski areas.

The Ritz-Carlton, Aspen

315 East Dean Street
Aspen, CO 81611
303-920-3300
800-241-3333
Fax: 303-920-7353

> *A late-vintage hotel, close to the ski slopes*

General manager: Joseph Violi. **Accommodations:** 231 rooms and 26 suites. **Rates:** Rooms, winter (Thanksgiving–mid-April) $350–$500, rest of year $145–$400; suites, winter $700–$2,800, rest of year $475–$2,000. **Included:** Use of fitness center. **Minimum stay:** 10 days over Christmas holidays. **Added:** 8.2% tax. **Payment:** Major credit cards. **Children:** Welcome. **Pets:** Prohibited. **Smoking:** Non-smoking rooms available. **Open:** Year-round.

The eagerly awaited and long-delayed Ritz-Carlton, Aspen finally opened late in 1992 on a prime parcel of real estate a block and a half west of the Silver Queen gondola and within walking distance of all of Aspen's shops, restaurants, and entertainment. A multigabled structure made of 800,000 Colorado red bricks, the five-story hotel borrows aspects of the town's historic mining-era architecture while investing them with a suggestion of modern style and elegance. It manages at once to blend in and stand out.

> The lobby lounge, which has views of Aspen Mountain, is a homey place for après-ski or afternoon tea, and there's nightly entertainment each evening in the bar.

Its 257 rooms make it almost three times the size of any other hotel in town, yet it feels more intimate. Doormen in cowboy hats and dusters — the avant garde of an infallibly polite, attentive staff — greet guests at the porte cochere, ushering them into a wood-paneled lobby with a wall of windows on the hotel's two-tiered interior courtyard, a comfortable-looking lounge with a green marble bar and a baby grand piano, and a two-sided fireplace of lichen-covered rock. The rooms inhabit the upper floors, where they have views of the courtyard and ski slopes or the town.

Tastefully if conservatively appointed in shades of peach, green, or mauve, the rooms cleave to the traditional elegance of wood furnishings, floral-print draperies, and crown moldings, while the bath is a symphony of gray-grained white marble. Amenities abound, from the obligatory remote-control television with sports channels and first-run movies to three dual-line phones (one in the bath), personal safes, plush terrycloth robes, hair dryers, and humidifiers. At the same time, basic quarters at this Ritz seem small by luxury hotel standards, and once the drapes are closed there is nothing in these elegant appointments to remotely suggest Colorado or the Rockies, not even the botanical and wildlife prints used to accent the walls.

That is, perhaps, a quibble in a hotel that also has a heated outdoor swimming pool and whirlpool, a state-of-the-art fitness center, and massage and beauty treatments. In winter, ski and boot storage is as close as the full-service Aspen Sports shop opposite the entrance, and so are lift-ticket sales.

Whether you stay at the Ritz-Carlton or not, one irresistible reason to stop by is Executive Chef Xavier Salomon's delectable cuisine. Trained in Europe and now influenced by America, Salomon has devised menus that inventively blend both traditions. Selections vary but could include an appetizer of seared, black-peppered ahi with jicama and ginger, a potato and arugula risotto, or such entrées as oven-roasted salmon in horseradish crust and honey-thyme Colorado rack of lamb.

Sardy House

128 East Main Street
Aspen, CO 81611
303-920-2525
800-321-3457
Fax: 303-920-4478

*An enchanting inn,
at once antique
and opulent*

General manager: Jayne Poss. **Accommodations:** 15 rooms, 5 suites. **Rates:** Rooms, winter (Thanksgiving–mid-April), $175–$330 (higher over Christmas holidays), rest of year $175–$250; suites, winter $230–$550, rest of year $275–$430. **Included:** Full breakfast. **Minimum stay:** 3–4 nights on some summer weekends, 4 nights over weekends February–March, 7 or more nights over Christmas holidays. **Added:** 8.2% tax and $2/person/day gratuity for breakfast. **Payment:** Major credit cards. **Children:** Free under age 3. **Pets:** Prohibited. **Smoking:** Prohibited in breakfast room. **Open:** Year-round except mid-April–mid-June and mid-October–mid-November.

In 1910, anyone with $1,000 could have picked up this exquisite red brick Victorian and still have $200 left over for furniture. In 1985, the same partners who'd successfully opened the Hotel Lenado needed $3 million to transform the turreted 1892 Queen Anne mansion and its carriage house into Aspen's most luxurious bed-and-breakfast inn in Aspen. It was worth every cent.

> The rooms are delights, each different enough to inspire loyalty (the staff keeps track of guests' preferences). The rooms' most talked-about feature is the cherrywood bed copied from an old French design. The beds are covered with down comforters and topped with scads of pillows.

Part restoration, part recreation, the enchanting inn blends the turn-of-the-century opulence of its original golden oak staircase and sliding parlor doors with such 20th-century amenities as a heated swimming pool, Jacuzzi, and sauna (all discreetly tucked away at the side of the inn behind a stand of spruce trees). Classical music plays in the cozy, lace-curtained front parlor, whose velvet settees face Aspen Mountain. Beyond it, tables set with ivory linen await those who opt to come down to one of the inn's superb breakfasts rather than have it sent to their room.

Whether in the main house or the carriage house — an enclosed gallery bridge connects them — the distinctive style continues in custom-woven carpets with the Sardy House signature rose. Many rooms feature arched windows and high vaulted ceilings paneled in beaded fir. They have white tile baths with whirlpool or antique clawfoot tubs, terrycloth robes, and heated towel bars. Armoires conceal televisions.

Of the suites, the most famous is the Manfred Smith, for its sunken living room and vaulted ceiling (suites also have stereos and VCRs), though others love Atkinson for its balcony and views of Aspen Mountain parlor, and O. J. Wheeler for its two bedrooms. All of them are wonderful.

In the evenings, the Sardy House dining room opens as a candlelit restaurant featuring American cuisine, which translates into roast rack of Colorado lamb, various types of wild game including pheasant, venison, and caribou, and perhaps fresh broiled salmon with citrus vinaigrette. Next to the dining room is Jack's Bar, a plush, intimate space for cocktails.

Sardy House's one minor inconvenience is that it's not within walking distance of the ski slopes. But it is on the route of the free shuttle that serves all four of Aspen's ski areas. And even if it weren't, that would be a small price to pay for so much luxury.

BEAVER CREEK

Hyatt Regency Beaver Creek

Beaver Creek Resort
136 East Thomas Place
P.O. Box 1595
Avon, CO 81620
303-949-1234
800-233-1234
Fax: 303-949-4164

> *A chateau hotel where the slopes meet the village*

General manager: Steve Dewire. **Accommodations:** 286 rooms, 9 suites. **Rates:** (higher over Christmas holidays, lower in shoulder periods) Rooms, summer (late May–early September) $185–$295, winter (mid-December–March) $290–$550; suites, summer $385–$970, winter $525–$2,220. **Minimum stay:** 4 nights over winter holidays. **Added:** 9.2%. **Payment:**

Major credit cards. **Children:** Free under age 18. **Pets:** Prohibited. **Smoking:** Prohibited in some public areas; nonsmoking rooms available. **Open:** Year-round except 3 weeks in fall.

Before the winter of 1989, even those who loved Beaver Creek, Vail's soignée little sister eight miles down the canyon, had the nagging suspicion that something was missing. The resort had a perfect little village, manicured slopes, and celebrity snowbirds — former President Gerald Ford has a house there, and former Vice President Dan Quayle comes every Christmas — so why this vague malaise, this sense that it was still somehow incomplete?

> **Modeled on the great European hotels and castles at some of Europe's famous mountain resorts, the ski-in/ski-out Hyatt rambles along the base of the mountain where the apron of the slopes meets the pedestrian village.**

It wasn't until the new Hyatt Regency Beaver Creek opened that December that the void was filled and everyone understood what had been missing. The ritzy 296-room Rocky Mountain chateau instantly became the gregarious hub of the village, the social focal point it had never had, the place to meet. Beyond snagging a prime location, it has succeeded in creating exactly the right sophisticated yet relaxed atmosphere. People love meeting here.

It doesn't look anything like a cookie-cutter chain hotel. The custom-designed interiors make extensive use of native stone and woods, and everything from the carpets and furniture to the murals and artwork was produced by local craftsmen and artists. It is at once distinctive and full of character, and yet cozy and familiar.

The same attention to detail extends to the rooms. The smallest have 400 square feet and reflect rustic comfort in their hand-stenciled wall coverings, raised country beds, and distressed pine armoires. Many of the deluxe rooms add a fireplace. Rich colors — forest green, fireweed red, and cornflower blue — have been used throughout.

There's no shortage of amenities, from the coffeemakers and heated towel bars in the rooms to an indoor-outdoor pool, six slope-side Jacuzzis, a ski valet (to store skis and boots overnight), and excellent Camp Hyatt summer and winter children's and teens' programs. There is even a place in the lobby to buy lift tickets, and the very popular Lobby Bar features piano music and a fireplace. Excellent cuisine is as close as a gourmet deli and the popular Patina Ristorante Italiano, whose Italy-meets-the-Rockies menu ranges from stuffed lobster ravioli, pheasant mousse tortellini, and build-your-own pizzas to grilled elk with wildberry compote and pan-seared breast of duck. All in all, it is a spectacularly well thought-out ski hotel.

The Inn at Beaver Creek

10 Elk Track
P.O. Box 36
Beaver Creek, CO 81620
303-845-7800
800-859-8242
Fax: 303-949-2308

An engaging little inn beside the ski slopes

General manager: Kathy Ferguson Allen. **Accommodations:** 37 rooms, 8 suites. **Rates:** Rooms, winter (late November–mid-April) $150–$290 (higher over Christmas holidays), summer (mid-June–late September) $130–$150, spring/fall $85–$110; suites, winter $225–$475, rest of year $150–$190. **Included:** Continental breakfast, shuttle to Vail. **Minimum stay:** 4–7 nights in winter. **Added:** 9.2% tax. **Payment:** Major credit cards. **Children:** Free under age 12. **Pets:** Prohibited. **Smoking:** Nonsmoking rooms available. **Open:** Year-round.

Patterned after small European hotels, the Inn at Beaver Creek is set alongside Beaver Creek's Chair 12, just a hundred yards beyond the village core. Built for smart comfort and conviviality, the guest rooms are attractively decorated in American traditional furnishings and floral comforters in a color scheme of beige with claret or green. Though generally small, the rooms feature such thoughtful amenities as a coffeemaker, a microwave, a small refrigerator, and an assortment of dishes.

The small size of the rooms is offset by two expansive parlors (one with a grand piano) on either side of a gray stone fireplace. An après-ski bar is a quiet place for guests and their friends to settle into the elegant rolled-arm sofas and relax.

The inn also has an outdoor heated pool and Jacuzzi and indoor heated parking.

The back door, which opens automatically as guests approach, affords almost direct access to Chair 12, and thus both downhill slopes and Beaver Creek's Nordic ski center. Reentering by the same door at the end of the day puts guests just steps from their ski lockers.

> **The hotel's convenience shows most at the beginning and end of the ski day.**

Beaver Creek's restaurants and shops are just close enough to be easily reached and just far enough away to ensure complete quiet. It's a grand little lodge.

Park Plaza

46 Avondale Lane
P.O. Box 358
Beaver Creek, CO 81620
303-845-7700
800-528-7275
Fax: 845-9342

> *A stylish condominium hotel in the village*

General manager: Tamara Cartmill. **Accommodations:** 36 condominiums. **Rates:** Winter (late November–mid-April) $400–$895, summer (mid-June–late September) $210–$285, spring/fall $175–$255. **Included:** Continental breakfast in winter. **Minimum stay:** 7 nights in winter. **Added:** 9.2% tax. **Payment:** Major credit cards. **Children:** Welcome. **Pets:** Prohibited. **Smoking:** Allowed. **Open:** Year-round.

Dubbed the Cadillac of ski-in/ski-out lodgings when it opened in 1985, the 36-unit Park Plaza remains one of the most stylishly appointed condominium hotels in the Rockies. One side borders the pedestrian plaza in the heart of Beaver Creek, directly across from the Centennial Express chair lift. Original artwork graces the walls of a lobby appointed with granite floor tiles, antique oak furnishings, and brass chandeliers. A lounge on one side holds a marble fireplace and sideboard, where coffee and tea are set out all day.

> **Beyond the lounge is an indoor swimming pool in buff and blue tile, and a Jacuzzi. There are also ski lockers with boot dryers.**

The rooms subscribe to the same tasteful elegance. The quality shows in marble fireplaces, fabric wallcoverings, wool carpets, and the extensive woodwork of the oversize living room. VCRs complement the televisions. Kitchens come fully equipped, down to microwaves and coffeemakers. There's even a washer/dryer.

Most of the units have two bedrooms, the master with a king-size bed and whirlpool tub and either a second master bedroom or a smaller room with twin beds and its own bath. The couch folds out to provide yet another bed. The three-bedroom units have even larger living rooms, with a two-story vaulted ceiling and two master bedrooms, one of them upstairs. Each unit, regardless of its size, has a deck with views of the village or the mountains.

During ski season, a Continental breakfast is set out on the coffee bar in the lobby. And like a hotel, the Park Plaza offers bell service, 24-hour staffing, and a heated underground parking garage.

Poste Montane

76 Avondale Lane
Beaver Creek, CO 81620
303-845-7500
Fax: 303-845-5012
Mailing address:
P.O. Box 36
Avon, CO 81620

> *A French country
> auberge close to
> the ski slopes*

General manager: Tish Land. **Accommodations:** 7 rooms, 17 suites. **Rates:** Rooms, winter (late November–mid-April) $195–$295 (higher over Christmas holidays), summer (mid-June–late September) $105, fall/spring $70-$85; suites, winter $225–$495, summer $115–$170, fall/spring $95–$150. **Included:** Continental-plus breakfast. **Minimum stay:** 4 nights; 7 nights in winter. **Added:** 9.2% tax. **Payment:** Major credit cards. **Children:** Free under age 13. **Pets:** Prohibited. **Smoking:** Prohibited in lobby. **Open:** Year-round except for 1 week in spring and fall.

Beaver Creek's oldest and smallest inn exudes Old World charm. Its doors open into a rich world of custom mahogany woodwork. A beveled glass mirror caps the marble fireplace in the intimate lobby parlor, where guests come for Continental breakfast and the comfort of green velvet sofas and wing chairs.

> **These elegant digs are enhanced by period furnishings and rich carpets. In the bath, a marble counter tops a mahogany vanity.**

That theme carries over to the accommodations. Most of the rooms and suites occupy the top floor and have fireplaces, king-size beds, and refrigerators. Framed pressed wildflowers add a touch of the Rocky Mountains. The decor is similar in the one- and two-bedroom suites, which add a separate sitting room with a foldout couch and in many cases a separate bath.

Its location in the center of the village falls just short of ideal because guests must walk across the plaza to reach the lifts. It makes up for it, at least partially, by having a whirlpool, sauna, and steam room, and an elegant seafood and pasta restaurant, Legends, on the premises.

Trapper's Cabin

Beaver Creek Resort
P.O. Box 915
Beaver Creek, CO 81620
303-845-7900
Fax: 303-845-7809

> *An isolated
> cabin, with chef
> and hot tub*

Cabinkeeper: R. G. Jacobs. **Accommodations:** 1 cabin. **Rates:** Summer (late June–early October) $1,800 (up to 4 people), winter (Thanksgiving–mid-April) $2,200; $200/night less on multinight stays in any season. **Included:** All meals, chef, cabinkeeper, liquor; lift tickets in winter. **Minimum stay:** 2 nights preferred. **Added:** 9.2% tax. **Payment:** Major credit cards. **Children:** Free under age 6; reduced rates under age 12. **Pets:** Prohibited. **Smoking:** Allowed. **Open:** Thanksgiving–mid-April, late June–mid-October.

Half hidden by stands of aspen and spruce on a panoramic 9,500-foot ridge above the resort village of Beaver Creek, Trapper's Cabin is accessible in summer by Jeep or horseback and in winter by skis or snowmobile. This cabin achieves a seemingly impossible standard: the freedom of an isolated wilderness sanctuary combined with all of civilization's creature comforts.

To ensure exclusivity, the cabin rents to one family or

group of friends at a time. Everyone gathers at the Inn at Beaver Creek in the village to meet their guide/cabinkeeper. In winter, he escorts them to the top of Beaver Creek's Chair 12 for an easy five-minute ski run down to the secret hideaway (luggage arrives later, via snowmobile). After a quick cabin orientation, guests gather in front of the fireplace for assorted wild-meat hors d'oeuvres, cheeses, and champagne, followed by a sumptuous feast of rack of lamb, grilled salmon, elk steaks, or pheasant breasts, served with fine wines at a hickory table beneath an elk antler chandelier. At that point, the chef and cabinkeeper clean up and depart, leaving guests in complete privacy with a roaring fire, a bubbling hot tub, an upright piano, a kitchen full of snacks, fresh fruit, and beverages, and an emergency phone.

> The two-story, rustically elegant lodgepole pine cabin features hedonistic amenities no mountain man ever dreamed of, including a front porch hot spa with vistas of the majestic Gore Range, a fully stocked kitchen and bar, and a cabinkeeper and personal chef.

The two-person staff returns the next morning to fix breakfast before the group takes off to ski Beaver Creek's slopes (lift tickets are included in the package). Rather than have guests return to the cabin for lunch, Trapper's arranges a gourmet repast at Beano's, an exclusive, members-only, mid-mountain restaurant on the ski slopes.

In summer, the routine is much the same, except the cabin functions as a personal guest ranch with its own stable of horses. Riders can often get near the herds of native deer and elk. Those not riding can spend the day hiking or mountain biking (the cabin has four bikes).

Trapper's has three bedrooms upstairs, furnished with wicker or lodgepole pine beds, braided rugs, pine armoires, terrycloth robes, and large bathrooms with deluxe toiletries. The billiard room downstairs has another wicker double bed, a pine trundle, and a fourth bath. Those determined to rough it need not apply.

BRECKENRIDGE

The Allaire Timbers Inn

9511 Highway 9/Main Street
P.O. Box 4653
Breckenridge, CO 80424
303-453-7530
800-624-4904

*A modern
log-and-stone inn
in a Victorian
mining town*

Innkeepers: Jack and Kathy Gumph. **Accommodations:** 8 rooms, 2 suites, all with private bath. **Rates:** Rooms $115–$175, suites $150–$225. **Included:** Full breakfast in winter, Continental-plus in summer. **Minimum stay:** 2 nights on weekends and in suites; 3–7 nights in ski season. **Added:** 7.5% tax. **Payment:** Major credit cards. **Children:** Over 12 welcome. **Pets:** Prohibited. **Smoking:** Prohibited. **Open:** Year-round.

The cozy, two-story Allaire Timbers Inn perches on a tree-studded rise at the southern end of town, convenient to Breckenridge's National Historic District but removed, literally and architecturally, from the self-conscious Victorian quaintness of downtown. Though constructed in 1991, the log-and-stone inn looks and feels like a classic mountain lodge.

Each of the eight cozy rooms — one of them fully handicap accessible — bears the name of the Colorado mountain pass that inspired its decor. So though all have log-veneer walls, pine armoires, comforters, tiny private baths (with showers but not tubs), and outside decks, each is distinctive. The one named for Tomichi Pass, for example, has been done up in a southwestern motif, while Rabbit Ears sports — what else? — rabbits. Each bears a wall plate with hand-lettered information about the pass it's named for. Those on the second floor, while no larger, feel more spacious and airy thanks to their cathedral ceilings. None, however, has a television or phone.

> A huge river rock fireplace anchors the Great Room, which soars two stories to a vaulted pine ceiling, while outside, a deck with a hot tub commands views of town and the majestic Ten Mile Range.

There are also two junior suites. Located on corners, they have in-room spas adjacent to river rock fireplaces and large private decks. Their decors differ, however. The Victorian-inspired Breckenridge Suite on the first floor combines turn-of-the-century antiques with a king-size four-poster bed, whereas the second-floor Summit Suite has the rustic charm of log furnishings, including a king-size log canopy bed.

Innkeepers Jack and Kathy Gumph live at the inn. Their presence, coupled with the friendliness of the staff, creates a warm atmosphere. The Gumphs are often around during breakfast — which consists of a buffet of homemade granola, fresh breads, fruit, and yogurt in summer supplemented in winter by a sit-down feast of French toast, quiche, or pancakes. They also tend to be there to greet guests in the late afternoon, setting out complimentary appetizers and beverages.

Besides the hot tub, the inn has ski lockers, boot warmers, and bike and golf club storage. There's also a TV/VCR and sound system on the mezzanine above the Great Room. And the town trolley stops 100 yards away, providing free transportation to the Breckenridge ski slopes.

Williams House

303 North Main Street
P.O. Box 2454
Breckenridge, CO 80424
303-453-2975
800-795-2975

> *A two-story*
> *Victorian dollhouse*

Hosts: Diane Jaynes and Fred Kinat. **Accommodations:** 4 rooms, 1 cottage, all with private bath. **Rates:** Rooms $89–$140, cottage $150–$225. **Included:** Full breakfast in winter, Continental-plus in summer. **Minimum stay:** 4 nights in ski season; 2 nights rest of year. **Added:** 9.9% tax. **Payment:** American Express. **Children:** Not suitable for children. **Pets:** Prohibited (they have a dog). **Smoking:** Prohibited. **Open:** Year-round.

Painted pale yellow and trimmed in forest green, Williams House stands behind a wrought-iron fence and postage-stamp yard on Main Street in Breckenridge's historic district. The house, which dates to around 1885, typifies the homes built during the mining-era heyday. Since 1989, however, the charming little cottage has been both a home to Diane Jaynes, Fred Kinat, and their children and a charming little bed-and-breakfast. Inside, high ceilings tower above oak floors covered with Oriental carpets, and lace curtains set off the painted woodwork. A quiet sitting area in front has a gas-log fireplace framed by a gorgeous cherry surround, an antique rolltop desk, a library, and a guest phone. A second parlor in back has a hidden TV/VCR and sound system. There's a deck and hot tub out back with views of the mountains and a storage room for skis containing boot and glove dryers.

The accommodations consist of four guest rooms in the

main house and a cottage next door. The rooms have been simply but tastefully done in period fashion with antique beds, dressers, and bureaus. Quilted comforters cover the beds, lace curtains the windows. Each room has its own bath, modern except for a clawfoot tub. The two-room Willoughby Cottage is even older than the house, dating to 1880. Its Victorian bedroom set is oak, to match the mantel over the bedroom fireplace, and its bath has a two-person shower.

> **The cottage has a cozy Victorian parlor, furnished with antiques but with such unexpected amenities as a TV/VCR, stereo, wet bar, refrigerator, and microwave. From the bedroom, a wide door (the cottage is wheelchair accessible) leads to an enclosed deck with a two-person Jacuzzi.**

As wonderful as these accommodations are, it's Diane, a nurse, and Fred, a teacher, whom guests remember most. Engaging and enthusiastic, the former Houstonites relish being around others who, like them, adore an outdoor-oriented lifestyle. To spend time with guests, they provide refreshments every afternoon and fresh-baked bread and muffins every morning to go with the hearty fare of breakfast burritos, fritattas, or quiche in winter and fresh fruit and yogurt in summer.

The trolley to the ski area stops less than a block away, and the inn is convenient to a superb network of biking trails that have made Breckenridge a haven for mountain bikers. At any season, Williams House is just steps away from the shops, restaurants, and entertainment in Breckenridge's historic district.

CLARK

The Home Ranch

54880 Country Road 129
P.O. Box 822
Clark, CO 80428
303-879-1780
800-223-7094
Fax: 303-879-1795

A picturesque guest ranch offering boots-and-jeans luxury

Proprietor: Ken and Cile Jones.
Accommodations: 6 rooms, 8 cabins, all with private bath.
Rates: Rooms $350–$415/day, $2,450–$2,905/week, cabins $400–$475/day, $2,800–$3,325/week. **Included:** All meals, horseback riding and guided hikes in summer, cross-country skiing and sleigh rides in winter, other ranch activities, weekly laundry, airport transfers. **Minimum stay:** 3 nights; 7 nights in summer and over Christmas holidays. **Added:** 4% tax, 15% service charge. **Payment:** Major credit cards. **Children:** Over age 4. **Pets:** Prohibited. **Smoking:** Prohibited in dining room and discouraged in guest rooms. **Open:** June to mid-October; mid-December to March.

Ken Jones likes to call his Home Ranch "an antidote to modern living." Guests are more likely to think of it as the Tiffany's of guest ranches, because of its quality and its dedication to pampering service. Set in a mountain clearing at the edge of Routt National Forest, 20 miles north of Steamboat Springs, the picturesque ranch basks in peaceful seclusion, all views and pine-scented air. Its 35 to 40 guests share the 750-acre oasis of luxury only with the very attentive staff.

The heart of any dude ranch is its riding program, and that is true of Home Ranch as well. However, since it is also a member of the prestigious Relais & Châteaux association, a preride breakfast consists of nothing so pedestrian as bacon and eggs but rather orange-cumin chicken, duck sausage, or buttermilk-cornmeal pancakes with blueberries.

Yet the ranch is more than horseback tours of the scenic backcountry. There are also hiking guides who lead outings on trails within the ranch and beyond; up to Hahn's Peak, for example, or into the adjacent Mt. Zirkel Wilderness. Fly-rodders, too, have guides available for the two miles of private beats along the Elk River, with additional access to streams in the neighboring property. There's also a swimming pool, sauna, and Jacuzzi, and a library and sundeck for those who would rather just relax. During the summer, the ranch adds a fully supervised children's program for kids age three and older, with riding for those over six, and picnics, hikes, gold panning, pool parties, and more for the others.

> Each Home Ranch guest is provided with his or her own horse and an opportunity to learn about saddling and currying. By the end of the week, and after many trail rides, goodbyes at the stables sometimes take longer than those at the lodge.

Three nights a week children eat with their counselors, leaving their parents to savor grilled breast of duck with raspberry-orange demi-glace or rack of Colorado lamb with tomato-mint chutney in the company of other casually dressed adults at candlelit tables set with linen, silver, and crystal. Later, adults and kids alike gather around the hand-painted 1912 Steinway in the lounge for cowboy songs, tall tales, and singalongs instigated by Jones and some of his musician friends.

The east wing of the lodge holds six comfortably large and elegantly rustic guest rooms with handsome wooden beds and full modern baths. Two have sleeping lofts for children.

The glory of the ranch, though, is its cabins, sequestered in a grove of aspens a hundred yards from the lodge. Similar in style to the lodge rooms but larger, the cabins feature fireplaces and very private outdoor Jacuzzis. The newest, and largest, has three bedrooms, three baths, and a living room with a fireplace. All of the accommodations, however, have added little touches like coffeemakers, hand-loomed bedspreads, down comforters, cotton sheets, Indian rugs, and a cookie jar kept perpetually full of homemade chocolate chip cookies.

In winter the emphasis shifts from horseback riding to cross-country skiing on 40 kilometers of laid track. Guests can also partake of sleigh rides and venture into Steamboat Springs for downhill skiing or shopping.

Life on the range doesn't get any better than this.

The Inn at Steamboat Lake

Highway 129
P.O. Box 867
Clark, CO 80428
303-879-3906
800-934-STAY
Fax: 303-879-3906

> *A modern log lodge near lakes, streams, and wilderness*

Manager: Jennifer Harris. **Accommodations:** 8 rooms, all with private bath. **Rates:** $75. **Included:** Full breakfast. **Minimum stay:** None. **Added:** 4.5% tax. **Payment:** Major credit cards. **Children:** Free under age 10. **Pets:** Prohibited. **Smoking:** Allowed. **Open:** Year-round.

This modern, two-story log lodge squats at the base of Hahn's Peak, 25 miles north of Steamboat Springs. The inn is ideal for taking advantage of the region's abundant outdoor recreation, though there always seem to be a few guests who've come for no other reason than to escape.

Built in 1989 and modeled on the homey comfort of the grand old national park lodges, the eight-room inn is well appointed in American country style. The rooms, each of moderate size with a private bath, are filled with custom-made pine furnishings, puffy quilts, and coordinated draperies and wallpapers. Even the artwork matches the decor. One is fully wheelchair accessible.

> **Covered decks wrap around two sides, one of them containing a hot tub where guests come to recover from days spent fishing the nearby streams, windsurfing or canoeing on the lake, or hiking or cross-country skiing in the nearby Mt. Zirkel Wilderness.**

The decor is much the same in the cozy restaurant on the main level. The changing menu features the likes of linguini in clam sauce with artichokes, smothered burritos, and chicken-fried steak. By the time dinner's over, half the diners know each other. Those staying in the inn probably met earlier, either in the bar, the hot tub, or in front of the woodstove that warms the second-floor guest lounge, where there's a satellite TV, sound system, refrigerator, and microwave for guests to use. They will certainly meet again at breakfast for the French toast, eggs, or pancakes along with fruit, cereal, and Danish pastries included in the price of a night's stay. If the inn falters at all, it's in the fact that some of the staff treat their work as a job and lack the warmth and charm of the log lodge itself.

Vista Verde Guest & Ski Touring Ranch

Seedhouse Road
Clark, Colorado
Mailing address: Box 465
Steamboat Springs, CO 80477
303-879-3858
800-526-7433
Fax: 303-879-1413

A family-oriented guest ranch and ski touring center

Proprietors: John and Suzanne Munn. **Accommodations:** 9 cabins, all with private bath. **Rates:** Summer (late May–September) $1,295–$1,395/person/week; winter (mid-December–mid-March) $135/person/day. **Included:** All meals, horseback riding in summer and cross-country skiing in winter, other ranch activities, and airport transfers. **Minimum stay:** 7 nights in summer, 2–5 nights in winter. **Added:** 4% tax. **Payment:** Cash or checks. **Children:** Reduced rates under age 12. **Pets:** Prohibited. **Smoking:** Prohibited. **Open:** Late May–September, mid-December–mid-March.

Vista Verde's spruce lodge and its attendant cabins stand against a grove of aspens and pines behind a hay meadow, seven miles from the nearest paved road and 25 miles north of

Steamboat Springs. Bordered by the Elk River, and surrounded by the Routt National Forest and Mt. Zirkel Wilderness, the 540-acre ranch and its pristine valley have changed little since homesteaders settled here in the 1920s.
Guests often see elk, deer,
coyotes, or beavers; eagles
and sandhill cranes soar
overhead.

The Munns are former
guests who bought the
ranch in 1991, trading In-
diana plains for Colorado
peaks. Under the previous
owners, Vista Verde had
become one of the most
talked about ranches in
Colorado, so they kept
many members of the
staff and changed little.
They buried the eyesore
of a power line that ran
across the hay meadow,
dug a lake, and built a

> **Included in every week-long package is a float trip down the Colorado River, guided backpacking trips into the Mt. Zirkel Wilderness, mountain bike tours, rock climbing, fishing, gold-panning expeditions, hay rides, and a night at the Steamboat rodeo. The ranch also arranges, at extra cost, hot air balloon trips, fly-fishing instruction, and two-day wilderness pack trips.**

spacious lodge. They also added an enclosed hot tub to go with the one outdoors and beefed up their supply of mountain bikes, fishing gear, and cross-country ski equipment. Finally, they introduced even more flexibility into what had long been the ranch's fairly unstructured routine.

Its scenery aside, much of Vista Verde's charm lies in its enthusiasm for all things western. The heart of the program is an extensive horseback riding program with instruction both in the ring and on the trail. Riding groups are kept small to ensure personal attention. As a small working ranch, Vista Verde entices guests with both scenic rides and a chance to help ride herd on its 200 head of cattle. Meanwhile, its love of families shows in a separate riding program for children over six, while little kids get to help care for two tiny ponies as part of their own program.

Accommodations consist of nine cabins, ranging in size from one to three bedrooms. All have a separate living area, woodburning stove, a scattering of antiques, wall-to-wall carpet, tasteful wallpapers, full baths, down comforters on lodgepole pine beds, coffeemakers, and refrigerators.

Guests follow their individual enthusiasms by day, but they meet in the antique-filled lodge at night for delicious, plentiful meals prepared by a graduate of New York's Culinary Institute of America. The staff soon knows all 25 guests — the most the ranch accepts — by name, and the long tables in the dining room and nightly gatherings mean that every guest soon knows every other. In winter, the focus shifts to cross-country skiing on the ranch or beyond into the national forest. Though the seasons change, the camaraderie remains the same.

COPPER MOUNTAIN

Club Med–Copper Mountain

50 Beeler Place
Copper Mountain, CO 80443
303-968-2161
Fax: 303-968-2166
Reservations:
Club Med Sales, Inc.
P.O. Box 29805
Phoenix, Arizona 85038
800-CLUB-MED

> *A ski haven*
> *for singles*
> *and families*

Head of customer service: Sonia Laviera. **Accommodations:** 236 rooms. **Rates:** $940–$1,340/week; higher over Christmas holidays. **Included:** All meals, lift tickets, ski instruction, entertainment, taxes, and gratuities. **Minimum stay:** 7 nights. **Added:** Nothing. **Payment:** Major credit cards. **Children:** Welcome over age 2; reduced rates under 12. **Pets:** Prohibited. **Smoking:** Allowed. **Open:** Early December–early April.

Club Med's only snowy venue in North America is this haven for singles and families at the base of the ski slopes on Copper Mountain, 75 miles west of Denver. The modern, seven-story lodge stands at the western edge of the village, adjacent to the ski lifts and just a short stroll from shops and restaurants. Its all-inclusive price bundles excellent skiing and optional large-group instruction with bountiful food, nightly entertainment, and superb children's programs.

For adults who want the free ski lessons, the Club Med week at Copper begins with a ski-off to sort everyone into groups according to their ability. Lessons start immediately and go on for two hours twice every day throughout the week. The classes tend to be very large — a dozen is typical — and are taught by instructors whose only credentials may be their own love of skiing. Still, most people improve, thanks to the hours of supervision and the occasional videotaping session that lets them view their progress. From time to time the

> The children's programs run from 9 A.M. to 9 P.M., so parents remain at leisure to ski and dine guilt-free. The kids have so much fun, and the counselors are so good, that the end of the vacation can seem to them like the end of the world.

Schnapps Patrol skis by, bearing peppermint Schnapps. And there's a Jacuzzi waiting at the end of the day.

While adults hone their downhill technique or learn to snowboard on Copper's 1,360 acres of alpine slopes (or on its cross-country trails, though the Club doesn't provide instruction or equipment there), kids are indulging their own notions of a perfect vacation in either the Petit Club (age 3), Mini Club (ages 4–7), or Kids Club (ages 8–11) with sledding, face painting, and other diversions for the very young and ski lessons for those older. They even have their own special kids' food.

As good as it is for families, the club also welcomes singles. Large, convivial tables ensure that those who come alone never have to dine alone. What's more, they can avoid having to pay two-person hotel prices by asking the Club to assign a roommate. The rooms at this Club Med are little more than places to sleep. Though some have mountain views, all are small and outfitted with twin beds and private baths. Recluses need not apply.

The Club has two restaurants: one with a bountiful hot and cold buffet and seating at large tables; the other more intimate, with tables for two or more. As entertainment, the Copper Mountain Club Med features a piano bar, skits (starring the staff, kids, and anyone else who wants to participate), talent shows, and dancing. It's a very well-run program that lures people from all over the world.

Copper Mountain Resort

P.O. Box 3001
Copper Mountain, CO 80443
303-968-2882
800-458-8386
Fax: 303-968-6227

*A four-season
resort with skiing,
golf, tennis, and
fishing*

General manager: Bill DeForrest.
Accommodations: 424 condos
(studios–4 bedrooms). **Rates:** Summer (Memorial Day–Labor
Day) $135–$350, winter (mid-December–early April) $155–
$645. **Included:** Use of athletic club. **Minimum stay:** 7 nights
over Christmas holidays; 4 nights in March. **Added:** 5.5% tax
plus 2.3% resort surcharge. **Payment:** Major credit cards.
Children: Free under age 12. **Pets:** Prohibited. **Smoking:** Nonsmoking units available. **Open:** Year-round.

This year-round resort village huddles at the base of 12,441-
foot Copper Peak in an alpine valley 75 miles west of Denver
via I-70. Copper's assets as a ski area begin in its well-
designed layout. Its 1,360 skiable acres on two fused mountains range from untamed bowls and steep glades for experts
to gentle, immaculately groomed slopes for rank beginners,
with plenty of intermediate terrain in between. In general, the
slopes become more challenging as skiers move from west to
east, effectively providing each ability level with its own
domain. Families love it. Cross-country skiers can look forward to 25 kilometers of set track and skating lanes. Copper
even has the only winter Club Med in America (see above).

Come summer, Copper sheds its mantle of snow but continues to run a free chairlift to a mountaintop restaurant and
nature center. Golfers have the 6,129-yard Pete and Perry Dye
course, which at 9,700 feet above sea level is the highest
championship course in the nation (it typically opens in late
June). The $3 million Athletic Club holds a restaurant, an in-
door heated lap pool with views of the ski mountain, a complete weight room, an aerobics center, racquetball courts, and
eight tennis courts, two inside and six out. Copper also lies
on the 40-mile paved bicycle trail running from Breckenridge
over the mountains to Vail. Its stables offer guided trail rides
into the surrounding Arapaho National Forest.

There are three condo villages at Copper, each built at the
base of a different ski lift and thus within walking distance of
the slopes. Most of the restaurants and what little nightlife

exists, however, are concentrated in the central Village Square. Condos have as many as two bedrooms as well as fireplaces, full kitchens, and decks with views of the mountain. For gracious European ambience, a family favorite is Telemark Lodge in the West Village. It has a lobby anchored by a fireplace, a large Jacuzzi, and its own bar. The most luxurious choices are the Legends and the Woods, which have deluxe amenities and as many as four bedrooms. Among Copper's handful of restaurants, Rackets, in the athletic club, attracts the biggest crowds for its savory southwestern cuisine and great salad bar.

> **Copper features not only a highly regarded ski mountain with a 2,601-foot vertical drop but also an 18-hole golf course, a splendid tennis and athletic club, and fly-fishing in Ten Mile Creek, which runs right through the property.**

EDWARDS

The Lodge at Cordillera

Cordillera Way
P.O. Box 1110
Edwards, CO 81632
303-926-2200
800-877-3529
Fax: 303-926-2486

> *An elegant country inn and spa with resort amenities*

General manager: Keith Halford. **Accommodations:** 20 rooms, 8 suites. **Rates:** Rooms, summer (June–September) $180–$235, winter (mid-December–March) $175–$315, spring/fall $130–$205; suites, summer $265–$310, winter $250–$345, spring/fall $185–$295. **Included:** Continental-plus breakfast, shuttle to ski slopes. **Minimum stay:** 2 nights on weekends. **Added:** 4.2% tax. **Payment:** Major credit cards. **Children:** Free under age 16. **Pets:** Prohibited. **Smoking:** Prohibited. **Open:** Year-round.

Built of stone and stucco and capped by a green slate roof and peaked gables, the Lodge at Cordillera perches in splendid isolation atop a ridge high in the Rocky Mountains, 25 minutes west of Vail. It looks more like an elegant European manor than an exclusive inn, right down to the tapestries hung on the hand-troweled plaster walls and the wormy silver maple of its coffered ceiling. Nonetheless, its balconied rooms and broad terraces command incomparable views of rolling ranchlands and majestic peaks that belong unmistakably to Colorado.

> **The Lodge at Cordillera pampers guests with a full range of spa services, from facials to total body fitness classes, each conducted by a cheerful and altogether healthy-looking cast of locals.**

The sophisticated lodge is the centerpiece of a 3,200-acre resort residential development and has only 28 rooms. While most are average in size, every one has that stunning view, most from private balconies that look out on New York Mountain and the rest of the Sawatch Range. Carved reproductions of antique Catalan armoires and wrought-iron desks with vine motifs stand out boldly against the white plaster walls, which are unadorned except for the wormy maple moldings, bold draperies, and an occasional capricious reminder of the West, like elk antlers in a willow wreath. About half have fireplaces; five have lofts. All come with down comforters in duvet covers, terrycloth robes, bottled spring water, bowls of fresh fruit, and spacious marble and tile baths complete with bidets.

The staff will supervise a workout in the well-equipped health club, which has a full range of exercise equipment, or provide towels for the indoor and outdoor swimming pools.

Guests determined to take the first steps toward a healthier lifestyle will also find ultra-fresh spa cuisine available in the dining room.

Those not obsessed with counting calories can splurge on some of the region's most elegant, unusual — and expensive — cuisine in the lodge's Restaurant Picasso, which *Esquire* ranked the best deluxe dining room in Vail Valley.

Cordillera has a beautifully laid out 18-hole Hale Irwin golf course, tennis (on two courts), croquet, hiking, and mountain biking in summer, and its own system of cross-country ski trails in winter (as well as a free shuttle to the slopes in Beaver Creek and Vail).

EMPIRE

The Peck House

83 Sunny Avenue
P.O. Box 428
Empire, CO 80438
303-569-9870
Fax: 303-569-2743

A cozy inn with roots in the 1860s mining era

Innkeepers: Gary and Sally St. Clair. **Accommodations:** 10 rooms, 9 with private bath; 1 suite. **Rates:** Rooms $45–$80, suite $95. **Included:** Continental breakfast. **Minimum stay:** None. **Added:** 8.9% tax. **Payment:** Major credit cards. **Children:** Welcome. **Pets:** Prohibited. **Smoking:** Allowed. **Open:** Year-round.

Colorado's oldest continuously operating inn dates from 1860, when Chicago merchant James Peck, lured west to prospect for gold, built a home for his family. The location he chose, at the eastern foot of the steep stage and wagon road over Berthoud Pass, made his house a logical place for travelers to stop before attempting the ascent. To better entertain them he expanded the original four-room house by adding a second story, a verandah, and the luxury of running water. He and his wife then filled the rooms with the handsome oak, maple, and walnut furniture they'd brought with them by stage from Chicago.

> **Some of the original furnishings survive, among them the gorgeous bird's-eye maple bedroom set in the Garden Room and the etched glass gaslight shades, which hung in the state capitol until it converted to electricity.**

Antiques decorate not only the cozy parlor and the rooms but also the halls, where oak tables and vanities topped with dried flower arrangements decorate the carpeted but still creaky halls. Over the years many famous people have stayed here, among them General Sherman, P. T. Barnum, and Ulysses S. Grant.

For all its history, Peck House is not a museum of Victoriana. Only a few rooms still have dark Victorian wallpapers. Most have a country decor with brass beds, floral comforters, cheerful wallpapers, and just enough antiques to give them character. More than half have clawfoot tubs. Peck House also has such un-Victorian amenities as a hot tub and ski lockers.

Travelers still get a warm reception and excellent meals. A fireplace anchors the dining room, whose walls have a changing display of contemporary artwork and colored lithographs depicting the mining era. Among the choices on the menu are trout amandine, chicken maison, medallions of venison, and raspberry duck. There's a bar off to one side.

FRISCO

Galena Street Mountain Inn

First Avenue & Galena Street
P.O. Box 417
Frisco, CO 80443
303-668-3224
800-248-9138

> *A friendly inn
> with easy access
> to four ski areas*

Innkeeper: Brenda McDonnell. **Accommodations:** 14 rooms, 1 suite, all with private bath. **Rates:** Summer (Easter–Thanksgiving), single $70–$95, double $75–$100; winter, single $85–$155, double $90–$160. **Included:** Full breakfast in winter, Continental-plus in summer. **Minimum stay:** 2 nights on weekends. **Added:** 7.5% tax. **Payment:** Major credit cards. **Children:** Over 12 except in suite. **Pets:** Prohibited. **Smoking:** Prohibited. **Open:** Year-round.

This two-story neo-Victorian opened in early 1992 on a corner a block off Main Street in downtown Frisco. Blue-green weathered shingles cap a tan stucco structure set off by porches, blue and white trim, and decorative latticework. Behind the lattice is a patio courtyard covered with decking.

Inside, a tiny lobby gives onto a parlor with a cathedral ceiling, gas-log fireplace, comfortable chairs and sofas, and a library of books. A hallway on one side leads to a glassed-in hot tub (with an adjacent sauna) and sunny breakfast room, both of which have windows on the courtyard. Most of the sleeping quarters, meanwhile, occupy the two floors of the west wing.

Down comforters and pillows in pastels and florals cover beds — most of them queen-size. Some rooms have window seats, others open onto porches. Two are fully handicap accessible, with access to the floor via ramps in the patio. All have wall-to-wall carpet, open shelving, televisions, phones, and private baths (half with shower only). A few have two double beds and somewhat more room. Largest of all is the Tower Room, a high-ceilinged junior suite with a four-poster bed and views of Mount Royal. During the peak months of February and March, the inn also rents a family suite (Room 200), which has a sitting area with an alcove containing a single bed and a separate bedroom. This is the only room where small children are allowed, but it has the disadvantage of lying above the common area and can thus be noisy.

In summer, breakfast generally consists of fruit, yogurt, cereal, Martha's high-altitude muffins, and home-baked items such as custard-filled cornbread or pear-cranberry crisp. In winter, that fare is supplemented with eggs and meats or gingerbread waffles. Year-round the inn sets out afternoon snacks of cookies, brownies, hot chocolate, and cider. Coffee and tea and other snacks are available all day from a self-service refreshment bar.

> These are not the usual bland, just-a-place-to-sleep rooms typical of so much of ski country. Their most distinguishing feature is the Mission-style furniture, which was custom-crafted for the inn.

General manager Brenda McDonnell has lived in Summit County for more than a decade, making her an invaluable source of information about what to see and do. She also sets a tone of warm, personable service that the rest of the staff adopts. The free shuttle to the skiing at Copper Mountain and Breckenridge leaves from across the street (the inn provides ski lockers), and Frisco's restaurants and shops are just a block away.

GEORGETOWN

The Hardy House

605 Brownell Street
P.O. Box 156
Georgetown, CO 80444
303-569-3388

> *An irresistible Victorian dollhouse*

Host: Mike and Carla Wagner.
Accommodations: 2 rooms, 2 suites, all with private bath.
Rates: Rooms $73, suites $77. **Included:** Full breakfast. **Minimum stay:** None. **Added:** 8.9% tax. **Payment:** Cash, personal checks, traveler's checks. **Children:** Discouraged. **Pets:** Prohibited. **Smoking:** Prohibited. **Open:** Year-round.

Painted a vivid red and trimmed in white, this two-story Victorian house is one of 200 19th-century structures still standing in historic Georgetown. None, however, can match Hardy House's irresistible charm — not even the famous Hotel de Paris, which is now a museum. So it only makes sense when visiting this once-booming mining town to stay in the house the Georgetown Historical Society praised for its sensitive restoration.

The public rooms have been done in cheerful colors, including the tiny dining room, which has red and coral striped wallpaper, a brass chandelier, and a few antiques. The sleeping quarters have also been decorated with unfettered exuberance. They have stenciled walls, a few antiques, down comforters, and tasteful textured carpets. Most of the baths have clawfoot tubs. The suites add extra amenities like gas-log fireplaces and televisions with VCRs.

Only one of the rooms, called Ruby, is tiny, its queen-size bed tucked beneath a second-floor dormer window and its bath down the hall. Otherwise, the rooms are comfortably spacious. Two open onto second-floor decks: Loui-Ans, a two-bedroom suite with a private entrance, and the Peak Room. The only room on the main floor is the Victoria Suite, just off the dining room. It has a very large bedroom with a king-size bed and a small sitting area.

> Like the narrow-gauge railway that still chugs up the canyon, this 1877 house seems to have been built to a smaller scale. Even so, the cozy bay-windowed parlor has room for a pot-belly stove, a couch and chair upholstered in rose-covered fabric, a grand-father clock, and a jar of cookies.

Mike and Carla Wagner bought the Hardy House late in 1993 and changed little of what they found except to introduce their own antiques — they had been living in a Queen Anne Victorian in Cincinnati — and to add a hot tub to the back yard. "Carla loves to cook and we both love to entertain," Mike says of their decision to give up their Midwest careers — he'd worked in research and development for Proctor and Gamble, she'd been an orthopedic technician — to realize a dream to move to Colorado.

Under them, breakfast remains an elegant, candlelit affair. They set the dining room table with crystal, rose-patterned Victorian china, and gold flatware. Carla makes baked goods to serve with fresh fruit, eggs, French toast, Belgian waffles, or blueberry pancakes. Afterwards, historic Georgetown is right outside the front door.

GLENWOOD SPRINGS

The Kaiser House

932 Cooper Avenue
P.O. Box 1952
Glenwood Springs, CO 81602
303-945-8827
Fax: 303-945-8826

*A colorful
Victorian home
near a fabled
hot springs*

Hosts: Glen and Ingrid Eash. **Accommodations:** 7 rooms, all with private bath, 1 suite. **Rates:** Rooms $60–$112, suite $120. **Included:** Full breakfast. **Minimum stay:** 2 nights on holidays and summer weekends. **Added:** 7.75% tax. **Payment:** Discover, MasterCard, Visa. **Children:** Welcome over age 8. **Pets:** Prohibited (they have dogs). **Smoking:** Prohibited. **Open:** Year-round.

All gables and turrets, this colorful Victorian stands on the corner of a wide residential street a few blocks from Glenwood's fabled Hot Springs Pool and Vapor Caves. Hints of its turn-of-the-century grace survive in the oak mantel above its marble-hearth fireplace and in the oak flooring, pocket doors, and bay windows. But in converting the 1902 home to a bed-and-breakfast, the Eashes banished dark Victorian interiors in favor of a much more cheerful country house decor, while keeping a scattering of antiques.

By exiling themselves to the house next door, they found space for eight tidy rooms, all with private baths, carpeted floors, lace curtains, comforters, and ceiling fans. Most appealing of all is the second-floor tower room, which stands out for its large size, views to the east and south, and antique white wicker furniture accented with red hearts. Families gravitate toward the third-floor attic suite, a single huge room beneath the eaves decorated in delft blue and rose and furnished with a queen and a single bed, dresser, wet bar, and refrigerator. It's also the only room that has (or needs) air conditioning. The largest and most amenity-rich of all is the Studio Suite above the garage, an oversize room with a kitchenette and balcony.

> The living room with its fireplace belongs to guests and so does the parlor, where they can curl up on the French Provincial settee to read or watch television or videos. There's also a hot tub on the private patio.

Depending on the season, breakfast is served either in the dining room beneath an etched glass chandelier or outside. Never less than hearty, it typically consists of homemade pastries and muffins, cereals, and something substantial like egg casserole, waffles, or pancakes.

Longtime Glenwood residents, the Eashes have an intimate knowledge of nearby diversions, from skiing at Sunlight and Aspen (the latter is 40 miles away) to the hiking, four-wheeling, whitewater rafting, and other summer activities in the surrounding canyons and mountains.

GRANBY

C Lazy U Ranch

3640 Colorado Highway 125
P.O. Box 378
Granby, CO 80446
303-887-3344
Fax: 303-887-3917

An elegantly rustic ranch with excellent children's programs

General manager: John Fisher.
Accommodations: 42 rooms. **Rates:** Summer $1,250–$1,725/person/week, winter $90–$165/person/night. **Included:** All meals; horseback riding and instruction, ranch activities in summer; cross-country skiing, equipment, and instruction in winter. **Minimum stay:** 2 nights; 7 nights in summer. **Added:** 4.2% tax. **Payment:** Cash, personal checks, traveler's checks. **Children:** Welcome. **Pets:** Prohibited. **Smoking:** Allowed. **Open:** Late May–mid-October and mid-December–March.

The C Lazy U trails along Bald Mountain in its own alpine valley two hours west of Denver. The family-owned operation lets city slickers experience as much time in the saddle as they can handle without having to give up the good life of heated swimming pools, hot tubs, and tennis courts.

The heart of the 3,000-acre spread is the log lodge where adults gather for cocktails in a room with a hand-hewn log ceiling, a stone fireplace, and leather sofas. Its windows frame a landscape of Peaceful Valley, Willow Creek, and the Continental Divide. A door on one side opens into a dining room with polished log walls, another fireplace, western chairs at tables for 10, and still more valley views. In winter, the lodge becomes a staging area for cross-country skiing on 22 kilometers of groomed track and acres of backcountry powder (equipment, lessons, and guide services are all part of the package) and for sledding, sleigh rides, and ice skating. There's also a free shuttle to the downhill slopes of Winter Park/Mary Jane. In summer, it remains the morning and evening gathering place, but the focus of activity shifts to the stables.

> This classic among upscale dude ranches puts guests up in tastefully appointed one- to three-bedroom cottages, feeds them on beef tenderloin en croûte and jalapeño-stuffed trout, and entertains their children from breakfast until after dinner.

The outstanding riding program affords adults as much or as little instruction as they desire and a choice of rides geared to their abilities, slow and scenic for some, exhilarating bursts of cantering or galloping for others. Meanwhile, the ranch's experienced counselors sort the kids into groups according to age (3–5, 6–12, and teens) and entertain them with appropriate activities: pony rides for the little ones, trail rides and extensive riding instruction for older kids. Either way, they're kept busy almost continuously from 9 A.M. to 9 P.M. (kids eat separately from adults). The highlight of the week for adults and older kids is an all-day ride to Gold Run, through a tunnel of aspens to a scenic overlook with views of Grand Lake and Rocky Mountain National Park.

Afterward, guests return to rooms whose only rustic quality is their log walls or wood paneling. Even the most basic have quilted bedspreads, wall-to-wall carpet, modern, fully stocked baths, coffeemakers, in-room safes, and enough space for a desk and two comfortable chairs. Towels are replenished twice a day; at turndown, a staff member leaves mints. Most rooms have fireplaces. The more deluxe units add Jacuzzi baths and a separate shower, a refrigerator with soft drinks and beer, and walk-in closets.

A wonderful staff, as patient as they are friendly, oversees the operation. Beyond riding, there's fishing in streams or stocked ponds, trap and skeet shooting, racquetball, tennis, and a masseuse. The C Lazy U is a family classic in boots and a cowboy hat.

Drowsy Water Ranch

U.S. Highway 40
P.O. Box 147
Granby, CO 80446
303-725-3456
800-845-2292

*A family-run
guest ranch that
loves families*

Proprietors: Ken and Randy Sue Fosha. **Accommodations:** 8 rooms, 9 cottages, all with private bath. **Rates:** Rooms $975/person/week. **Included:** All meals, horseback riding, ranch activities. **Minimum stay:** 3 nights; 7 nights from mid-June–August. **Added:** 4% tax. **Payment:** Cash, personal checks, or traveler's checks. **Children:** Reduced rates under age 5; family rates available. **Pets:** Discouraged. **Smoking:** Prohibited in dining room, discouraged in cabins. **Open:** Early June–mid-September.

On Thursdays, after guests have become acquainted with their horses and with riding, Drowsy Water Ranch schedules a backcountry ride to the top of Stag Mountain. Just short of the summit the riders spread out, forming a long line in a meadow full of wildflowers. At a signal from the wranglers they mount a cavalry charge, whooping and hollering as they gallop to the top, arriving exhilarated by the ride and awestruck by panoramic views of the Continental Divide.

Drowsy Water Ranch is not the grandest or the largest or the best-known dude ranch in the Rockies, but Ken and Randy Sue Fosha, who have owned and operated the 600-acre spread since the mid-1970s, know and love people. They understand that whatever else brings guests to a dude ranch, everyone secretly wants just once to let loose and ride at full speed (or at least as fast as he or she dares) across a spectacular mountain landscape, as they imagine the camera drawing back and the music swelling to a crescendo.

The core of the ranch is a cluster of red-roofed log buildings built in the 1920s beside Drowsy Water Creek, which trickles along the bottom of a draw seven miles west of Granby. Sagebrush lines the hills on either side, giving way to aspens, ponderosa pines, and spruce trees higher up in Arapaho National Forest. Guests can stay in the remodeled lodge, which features polished pine beams and floors, log furniture, and brass beds, or in any of nine renovated log-and-chink cabins, each with one to three rooms, a fireplace, and modern bath.

Parents and kids meet for all-you-can-eat dinners served family style in the dining room. Afterward, unless there's a hayride, they head for the Teepee, actually a round log structure, for the night's entertainment, which could be Ken calling a square dance, a staff show, or carnival games.

> **The Foshas and their crew of warm-hearted wranglers set out to teach the fundamentals of riding, beginning with pointers in the ring and continuing with coaching and suggestions on the trail. Kids as young as six can ride, and by the second day even they have learned to lope.**

Throughout the week the ranch runs fully supervised children's programs, one for kids ages three to five, another for those six to twelve. In addition, there is a small heated pool and a hot tub, stocked fishing ponds, a horseshoe pit, the option (at extra cost) of whitewater rafting or overnight pack trips, fishing and boating on nearby lakes and rivers, and even two easy-to-reach golf courses. But the most memorable few moments of your stay will probably be that exhilarating cavalry charge, up a hill into a flower-strewn meadow in the very heart of the Rockies.

GRANT

Tumbling River Ranch

P.O. Box 30
Grant, CO 80448
303-838-5981
800-654-8770

> *A well-run guest ranch that's a well-kept secret*

Proprietors: Jim and Mary Dale Gordon. **Accommodations:** 12 rooms, 13 cabins, all with private bath. **Rates:** Summer (early June–August) $1,100–$1,400/person/week, fall $150/person/day, $900/person/week. **Included:** All meals, horseback riding, and most activities. **Minimum stay:** 2 nights; 7 nights June–August. **Added:** 3.2% tax. **Payment:** Cash, personal checks, or traveler's checks. **Children:** Reduced rates under age 12. **Pets:** Prohibited. **Smoking:** Prohibited in dining room, discouraged in cabins. **Open:** June–September.

For half a century this secluded ranch has been introducing its guests to the joys of horseback riding in the Rocky Mountain high country. Beginning at 9,200 feet, it hopscotches for 14 miles along Geneva Creek, alternating its acreage with land in the Pike National Forest, before finally ending at a high camp, 12,000 feet above sea level near the creek's headwaters. By then, Denver seems far more than 50 miles away.

> **Colorado has a handful of famous guest ranches that seem to garner most of the publicity. Tumbling River is not among them, which makes this outstanding spread one of the best-kept secrets in the Rockies.**

Life at the ranch centers around a 1920s lodge, the staging area for most activities and a favorite place for late afternoon cocktails (BYOB) and scanning the Mt. Evans Wilderness for herds of bighorn sheep. There is also a second lodge, a quarter mile away, built in southwestern style by the daughter of Adolph Coors (a waterfall just up the canyon inspired the original Coors Beer logo). Both lodges have their own dining rooms and a handful of guest rooms with fireplaces and private baths, though those in the Coors lodge are larger. There are also 13 cabins, each with a fireplace and furnished (as are the rooms) with Jim's handmade lodgepole pine beds, refinished antiques, and complimentary fruit baskets.

The ranch has 80 horses for its 50 to 60 guests, enough to schedule several daily rides. In addition, there are Jeep tours to a ghost town and whitewater rafting trips (both at additional cost), and an excellent children's program that divides kids into three groups by age and organizes appropriate activities. Except for two nights a week, when adults dine by candlelight, kids and parents eat together. Meals are western staples like a steak fry or barbecued ribs and chicken. Everything is a cut above the usual ranch fare, long on salads and homemade breads and pastries, and as beautifully presented as it is tastily prepared.

Mary Dale in particular puts her heart and soul into the ranch, and it shows in everything from the cleanliness of the rooms to the well-trained and enthusiastic staff of college students. This is, after all, the Gordons' home. And while it may not be as famous as some of the other Colorado ranches, it is as warm and hospitable as anyone could want.

KEYSTONE

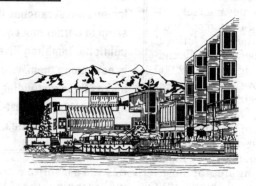

Keystone Resort

Highway 6
P.O. Box 38
Keystone, CO 80435
Information: 303-468-2316
Keystone Lodge: 303-468-4246
800-222-0188
Fax: 303-468-4215

> *A year-round destination resort long on activities*

Executive vice president of lodging: Brian Smith. **Accommodations:** 152 rooms, 850 condos (studios–4 bedrooms). **Rates:** summer (May–mid-October), rooms $170–$220, condos $115–$600; winter (mid-October–April), rooms $165–$220, condos $120–$800 (higher over Christmas holidays). **Minimum stay:** 5 nights in Chateau D'Mont year-round; 3–7 nights in condos in winter. **Added:** 5.5% tax, 4.7% Keystone surcharge. **Payment:** Major credit cards. **Children:** Free under age 18 in summer, under 12 in winter. **Pets:** Prohibited. **Smoking:** 1 nonsmoking floor in lodge. **Open:** Year-round.

Keystone perches at 9,300 feet in a narrow, scenic valley about 90 minutes west of Denver. A subsidiary of Ralston Purina, it began as a modest ski area only to grow into a year-round destination resort — a self-contained village, really — with its own lengthy roster of summer and winter activities to complement the abundant recreation in the mountains that embrace it.

> **Keystone once had a reputation as a ski area for wimps, but has since beefed up its unintimidating terrain with more challenging runs and, most recently, 700 acres of glades, trails, and back-country skiing on a third mountain, the Outback. Lights allow skiing under the stars until 10 P.M.**

The core of the village is the Keystone Lodge, which faces a lakefront plaza lined with restaurants, shops, and the most central of several clusters of condominiums. Each of Keystone's 152 oversize rooms has a view of the mountains, a balcony or patio, quasi-country decor, and lots of little extras like remote-control cable TVs and terrycloth robes. But it's the convenience of having so much so close at hand — except the ski lifts, which are three quarters of a mile away — that seduces guests to stay here rather than at one of the more elaborately appointed studio to four-bedroom condominiums (the newest and most luxurious of them, Chateau D'Mont, is a snowball's throw from the chair lift at North Peak).

In either case, it's what happens outdoors that sets Keystone apart. In winter, in addition to downhill skiing, Keystone operates a cross-country center with both groomed and backcountry trails and maintains the lake in the village as an ice skating rink.

Summer means even more choices, among them tennis on 12 hard courts (two indoors), golf on an 18-hole, 7,090-yard Robert Trent Jones, Jr., course, water sports on Keystone Lake and nearby Lake Dillon, plus guided fly fishing, horseback riding, hiking, four-wheeling, llama trekking, gondola rides, bicycling on a magnificent network of paved trails throughout the valley, a summer music festival, and much, much more. During both summer and winter, Keystone operates an exceptional children's program, making it one of the most popular family resorts in the Rockies. The lodge added a small fitness center with exercise equipment, an indoor/outdoor swimming pool, Jacuzzis, sauna, steam, and tanning beds. And finally, the resort has two stellar restaurants, one in Ski Tip Lodge (see below) and another in a rustic 1930s log house called the Ranch, where somewhat casually attired diners sit down to scrumptious, six-course feasts of sophisticated fare like lamb with baby artichokes, strudel of forest mushrooms, duet of Rocky Mountain rainbow trout, and a chef's special of seasonal game.

Ski Tip Lodge

Montezuma Road
P.O. Box 38
Keystone, CO 80435
303-468-4202
800-222-0188

> *A stagecoach stop
> that evolved into a
> superb country inn*

Innkeeper: Erin Clark. **Accommodations:** 10 rooms, 8 with private bath, and 2 suites in lodge; 8 rooms with private bath in annex. **Rates:** Rooms, summer (June–September) $63–$113, winter (late November–mid-April) $62–$140, spring/fall $44–$92; suites, summer $126–$144, winter $123–$170, spring/fall $105–$123. **Included:** Continental-plus breakfast in summer; full breakfast rest of year. **Minimum stay:** None in summer; 4 nights over winter weekends; 7 nights during Christmas holidays. **Added:** 5.5% tax and 4.7% Keystone surcharge. **Payment:** Major credit cards. **Children:** Welcome. **Pets:** Prohibited. **Smoking:** In bar only. **Open:** Year-round.

Ski Tip Lodge is not as ancient as the Rockies, though it is older than virtually everything else that now surrounds it, including the state of Colorado. Built as a stagecoach stop in 1860, the quaint log two-story, with its massive stone fireplaces and hand-hewn beams, resonates warmth and hospitality. Plans for the nearby Arapaho Basin Ski Area were hatched in the living room in the 1940s, and soon Ski Tip became Colorado's first skier's guest ranch. Continual upgrading since 1985 has transformed it into an exquisite country inn, well known for its congenial atmosphere, welcoming staff, and superb cuisine.

> **Though part of Keystone Resort (see above), Ski Tip nestles in wooded seclusion a mile east of the condominium village. Window boxes a-riot with petunias in summer give it the look of a Swiss hostel, but the interiors are richly American.**

The cozy living room — all low ceilings and rustic beams and pillars — gets its style from a fireplace, framed quilts, and terra cotta tile floors with oriental rugs. New age music wafts through the rooms. Outside, the bent willow chairs on the patio off the popular Rathskeller Bar overlook a beaver pond, tennis courts, and a llama corral. In winter, the landscape turns white and the focus shifts to the cross-country ski center just a few gliding steps from the lodge.

The homey rooms at Ski Tip have been decorated in elegant country fashion with Victorian antiques and brass, four-poster, or bleached pine-log beds covered with comforters or patchwork quilts. Hand stenciling accents the white walls. All the rooms have thick carpets; all but two have private tiled baths with modern fixtures. Few have views, however, and none has a television or phone. There is also an annex 20 yards from the inn, overlooking the beaver pond. Though its rooms are larger, its decor is 1960s motel style, completely lacking the character of the old lodge.

In summer, rates include a breakfast of homemade granola, yogurt, fresh fruit, croissants, muffins, and vanilla bean coffee. In winter, breakfast expands to a full buffet, and the daily package also includes scrumptious four-course dinners. The restaurant is open to the public year-round. Its menu changes daily but always features regional cuisine like Rocky Mountain trout with three-pepper chutney, sesame-smoked breast of duck over bowtie pasta, whole roasted sirloin with tomato-tarragon hollandaise, or paella. The fixed price menu costs $35, not including wine, taxes, or tips. Since this is one of the great restaurants in the valley, reservations are essential.

KREMMLING

Elktrout

1853 County Road 33
P.O. Box 614
Kremmling, CO 80549
303-724-3343
800-722-3343
Fax: 303-724-9063

> *A fishing retreat
> dedicated to
> little else*

General manager: Marty Cecil. **Accommodations:** 8 rooms, all with private bath, 2 cabins. **Rates:** $1,050–$1,125/person/3 days. **Included:** All meals, fishing guides. **Minimum stay:** None. **Added:** 5.8% tax on lodging portion. **Payment:** Master-Card, Visa. **Children:** Discouraged unless avid about fishing. **Pets:** Discouraged. **Smoking:** Allowed. **Open:** Mid-May–mid-October.

Once a private fishing retreat, Elktrout retains an air of exclusivity. The modern log lodge and an executive cabin hold a maximum of 20 guests, each of whom has guided access to 15 miles of private beats along the Colorado and Blue Rivers and spring-fed Troublesome Creek, as well as to 15 ranch ponds. All of the fishing is catch-and-release, mainly for rainbow and brown trout, and most of it is just minutes away. The rivers often yield fighting two-pounders, while the ponds, several of them spring-fed, regularly produce fish weighing four pounds or more. Anyone whose catch is 21 inches or longer becomes a member of the lodge's exclusive "21 club."

Elktrout has no horses, tennis courts, hot tubs, swimming pools, playgrounds, or other nonfishing diversions, though the staff can arrange activities if guests request them. It does have an amiable staff of professional guides, one assigned to every two fishermen, capable of advising anyone from beginners to experienced fly rodders. Its devotion to fishing runs so deep that dinner is served early, at 5:30 P.M. when the wind picks up, to provide the opportunity to stalk large trout during the productive hours after 6:30 P.M.

Meals — fried chicken, rack of lamb, Mexican dishes, and the like — are served in a turn-of-the-century tent outfitted with crystal chandeliers, kerosene lamps, and a woodstove. The lodge has a convivial lounge with a fireplace, self-service bar stocked with beverages and mixers (bring your own liquor), coffee and tea, cookies and snacks. Upstairs, there is a fly-tying table and a VCR with a selection of fishing videos. Patios outside invite sunning, relaxing, and enjoying the views of the snow-capped peaks of the Gore and Byers ranges.

> **The first Colorado lodge to garner an Orvis endorsement, this fly-fishing sanctuary perches at 7,300 feet in a meadow-covered bluff overlooking a stretch of the Colorado River, 2½ hours west of Denver.**

The lodge rooms vary in size but share a rustic decor of twin beds, full baths (some with steam showers), rough pine paneling set off by paisley wallpaper, and a few tanned hides for decoration. Those on the second floor have vaulted ceilings. The executive cabin features two bedrooms, vaulted ceilings, a fireplace, kitchen, and screened porch. A second, small cabin has one room and a loft. The complex also contains a fully equipped tackle shop. At certain times during the summer, the lodge runs special three-day fly-fishing schools in addition to its regular three- and six-day packages.

Latigo Ranch

P.O. Box 237
Kremmling, CO 80459
303-724-9008
800-227-9655
Fax: 303-724-9009

> *A high-mountain guest ranch set in scenic grandeur*

General managers: Kathie and James Yost and Lisa and Randy George. **Accommodations:** 10 cabins. **Rates:** Summer $955–$1,325/person/week, winter

$110/person/day. **Included:** All meals; taxes and gratuities; horseback riding, ranch activities, and overnight pack trip in summer; cross-country skiing and instruction in winter. **Minimum stay:** 6 days in summer. **Added:** Nothing. **Payment:** Major credit cards. **Children:** Under 3 free; reduced rates under 14. **Pets:** Prohibited. **Smoking:** Prohibited in dining room, nonsmoking cabins available. **Open:** Memorial Day–early October and December–March.

The 1926 lodge, cabins, and various outbuildings of Latigo Ranch huddle in a clearing at the edge of a heavy spruce and pine forest 17 miles from Kremmling, seven miles from the highway. The Arapaho National Forest wraps around three sides, adding to its seclusion, but it is the breathtaking panorama across a valley to the east at the Indian Peaks and Continental Divide that seduces everyone who visits.

> Perched on the side of a mountain 9,000 feet above sea level, Latigo Ranch has what another Colorado rancher described as "a knock-your-hat-in-the-creek view."

That alpine setting and access to 35,000 acres of spectacular mountain terrain invest Latigo with uncommon grandeur. The surrounding terrain varies from near-level open meadows to steep escarpments. Sagebrush-tufted hills roll up against stands of quaking aspen and thick forests of spruce and pine, and mountain streams, interrupted here and there by beaver ponds, etch delicate lines in the landscape. Deer and elk abound.

This is country that begs to be explored on horseback, and twice each day rides leave Latigo's corrals for the surrounding high country. "We try to offer horse instruction, not just nose-to-tail riding," notes Kathie Yost, one of the owners. "And since we can handle a maximum of 35 people, we can do that." For the most part, the instruction takes place on the trail, with riders divided into groups of four or five according to their ability. There's also a weekly sunset ride — with views of the rock formation that inspired the name of Rabbit Ears Pass — and a midweek overnight pack trip (included in the price).

Kathie and James Yost and their friends Lisa and Randy George bought the ranch in 1987 after giving up professional careers — Randy had been a university professor, the Yosts had conducted anthropological studies while living with an Indian tribe in Ecuador — and apprenticing at the C Lazy U Ranch in nearby Granby (see above). Latigo has a history of dude-ranch hospitality dating to the 1920s, and it has blossomed under the Yosts and Georges, earning a reputation not only for spectacular rides but also for its family orientation and superb children's programs.

Kids are divided by age into two groups. Those ages six to thirteen have their own riding program supplemented by an overnight pack trip, nature hikes, swimming (Latigo has an outdoor pool), fishing, hayrides, and square dancing. Those three to five spend the day feeding ranch pets, going for nature walks to learn about plants, animals, and rocks, hearing stories about Indians, and being led around on a pony. One old western cabin, dubbed the Sheriff's Office, functions as a meeting place and arts and crafts center. None of this is mandatory, allowing families to do as much together as they want.

Accommodations consist of one- and three-bedroom cabins, each with a sitting room, fireplace or woodburning stove, modern tile bath, and extra amenities like coffeemakers and small refrigerators. The decor in the older cabins runs to 1970s earth tones, but all are comfortable and immaculate, as cozy in summer as they are in winter, when the emphasis shifts to cross-country skiing on 30 kilometers of groomed track.

During either season, guests gather for meals of updated, health-conscious western fare in the original 1926 lodge, which has a low ceiling of rough pine, pine log tables, and country fabrics. But the heart of the ranch is in many ways its recreation hall, a two-story wood-frame building containing a mossrock fireplace, indoor whirlpool, dance floor, library, and game room. The nightly entertainment ranges from country dancing to a video of the Yosts' experiences with that Ecuadoran tribe. The rec hall also has an outside deck on the second floor that makes the most of that "knock-your-hat-in-the-creek view."

LEADVILLE

Delaware Hotel

700 Harrison Avenue
Leadville, CO 80461
719-486-1418
800-748-2004
Fax: 719-486-2214

A mining-era mercantile building turned engaging hotel

Proprietors: Susan and Scott Brackett. **Accommodations:** 32 rooms, 4 suites. **Rates:** Rooms $55–$80, suites $80–$100. **Included:** Full breakfast. **Minimum stay:** None. **Added:** 8.9% tax. **Payment:** Major credit cards. **Children:** Free under age 2. **Pets:** Prohibited. **Smoking:** Prohibited in dining room. **Open:** Year-round.

It was not gold or silver fever that lured the Calloway brothers to Leadville but the prospect of catering to those who had caught it. To that end they built the Delaware Block Store in 1886, giving it retail space on the ground level and 50 rooms on the top two floors suitable for bedrooms or offices. It took four years for their enterprise to fail, at which point they leased the retail space to a dry goods store, which remained until the late 1970s. Not until 1986 and the building's centennial did it finally become the hotel the Calloways envisioned.

The best rooms have views to the west or south across the Arkansas Valley at the Continental Divide. The rooms on the third floor are a little larger than those on the second, while the most spacious of all are the two-room suites in the corners, which can sleep four with ease.

When Susan and Scott Brackett bought the Delaware early in 1992, they completed its evolution from dry goods store to hotel by banishing the retail shops on the main level and opening up space for an elegant Victorian lobby, which features nightly entertainment on weekends, and a restaurant with entrées such as chateaubriand for two, trout amandine, and pasta primavera. Guests now get a full breakfast along with their room. Those who stay here rave about the convivial atmosphere and pleasant staff, who dispense cheerful advice about what to see and do besides visiting the Matchless Mine and Tabor Opera House. There is also a library and Jacuzzi, the latter in a windowless room off the lobby. Yet for all these improvements, prices remain very reasonable, making the Delaware an excellent value.

> **Now on the National Historic Register, the Delaware has 36 high-ceilinged rooms outfitted with antique dressers and brass, iron, or four-poster beds. Lace curtains drape the windows, and new carpet runs wall to wall. All have cable televisions and private baths. Presumably, the creaky floors are original.**

The Leadville Country Inn

127 East Eighth Street
P.O. Box 1989
Leadville, CO 80461
719-486-2354
800-748-2354
Fax: 719-486-3886

> *A theatrical inn
> even the owners call
> "overplayed Victorian"*

Innkeepers: Sid and Judy Clemmer. **Accommodations:** 10 rooms, all with private bath. **Rates:** Single $52–$102, double $67–$117. **Included:** Full breakfast. **Minimum stay:** 2 nights over holiday periods. **Added:** 7% tax. **Payment:** Major credit cards. **Children:** Well-behaved children over age 5. **Pets:** Prohibited. **Smoking:** Prohibited. **Open:** Year-round.

Built in 1893 by a mining executive, this Queen Anne mansion had become rather run down by the time Sid and Judy Clemmer bought it in 1988. The personable West Texans restored the mansion and its carriage house as a bed-and-breakfast inn, filling its rooms with English antiques or, failing that, whatever else they could find that seemed appropriate, and adding a gazebo-topped hot tub to the yard alongside.

Molly's room, on the first floor of the carriage house, is typical of the owners' "overplayed Victorian" style. Its private entrance opens onto a large room filled with ribbons and roses and dominated by an antique walnut bedroom set with a queen-size four-poster. Old linens and lace dresses drape a camelback trunk at one end, while the large bath has stained glass windows, a clawfoot tub, and two china lavatories set in an antique walnut sideboard. Though not all are quite that busy, each has its own personality and a decor that runs from elegant Victorian to country cabin.

As the rooms have evolved, the inn has come to be more and more a retreat for couples. One contributing reason may be that the tiny parlor doesn't invite guests to mingle, though there are cookies, coffee, and tea out all day. Still, guests do meet, in the hot tub or at breakfast, a family-style affair of caramel pecan cinnamon rolls, fruit smoothies, breads,

> **Strait-laced historians might shudder at the liberties they've taken, but the Clemmers never set out to create a museum; the inn leans more toward the theatrical.**

and an egg dish, waffles, or casserole. Lately the inn has also begun using the tea room to serve lunch to the general public, dishing out such entrées as puff pastry topped with vegetarian cream sauce or seafood Newburg along with soup, salad, hot breads, and homemade, hand-cranked ice cream.

Wood Haven Manor

809 Spruce
P.O. Box 1291
Leadville, CO 80461
719-486-0109
800-748-2570

> *A B&B created from two turn-of-the-century houses*

Innkeeper: Jolene Wood. **Accommodations:** 6 rooms, 2 suites, 5 with private bath. **Rates:** $47–$87. **Included:** Full breakfast. **Minimum stay:** 2 nights over holidays. **Added:** 8.9% tax. **Pay-**

ment: Major credit cards. **Children:** Welcome over age 3. **Pets:** Prohibited. **Smoking:** Prohibited. **Open:** Year-round.

Wood Haven Manor consists of two turn-of-the-century houses set side by side on Bankers Row, a block and a half from Leadville's historic main street. Jolene Wood restored them in 1989 and decorated with antiques.

> **Guests meet for breakfast in the dining room, where Jolene serves homemade pastries and breads, smoothies, and perhaps French toast stuffed with apricot preserves and cream cheese. Jolene dispenses friendly advice about what to see and do in the area — she's lived in Leadville for more than a decade — along with hot coffee and tea.**

The door to 809 Spruce opens onto an elegant living room containing the original oak and Italian marble fireplace and a television and VCR. The dining room beyond — where guests staying at both houses gather for breakfast — holds two spectacular antique sideboards. Upstairs are two country Victorian rooms with queen-size beds and private baths, but the room that best reflects Wood's style is a two-room suite. In its living area, pale lavender walls capped by a wallpaper border set off draperies in paisley and lace. An antique armoire stands across from a foldout sofa. Pocket doors separate that room from the sleeping quarters containing a highback headboard and a big whirlpool tub.

Next door, at 807 Spruce, Wood has installed French provincial furnishings in the oak-floored living room and hidden the TV/VCR in an antique armoire. An oak fireplace stands out against the emerald green wallpaper in the dining room, while an oak staircase leads to the rooms on the floors above. This house, too, has a suite. Located on the second floor, it contains a four-poster canopy bed, antique dressers, two armoires with beveled glass mirrors, a sitting room with a foldout sofa, and a three-quarter bath. There are four more rooms, two on the second floor with private baths and two rather less fulsomely decorated quarters on the third with shared bath. They have been variously appointed with iron or aspen beds, quilts, and scattered antiques.

MEEKER

Elk Creek Lodge

1111 County Road 54
P.O. Box 130
Meeker, CO 81641
303-878-5454 in summer
303-878-5232 in winter
Fax: 303-878-5311

> *A fly-rodder's sanctuary renowned for varied fishing*

General manager: Chris Lockwood. **Accommodations:** 11 suites, all with private bath. **Rates:** $2,750 for 6 nights. **Included:** All meals, fishing guides and instruction, fishing equipment, one fly-out to Utah, non-angling activities, airport transfers. **Minimum stay:** 6 nights. **Added:** 6.8% tax on lodging portion. **Payment:** Personal checks preferred. **Children:** Over age 14 and enthusiastic about fly-fishing. **Pets:** Prohibited. **Smoking:** Prohibited in main lodge. **Open:** Late June through mid-October.

As part of the 20,000-acre family-owned Wheeler Ranch in northwestern Colorado, Elk Creek Lodge has access to five miles of private fishing on Elk Creek, another 11 miles of privately owned water on the White River, and three more miles on Marvine Creek. That and its Orvis-endorsed fly-fishing school and fully equipped tackle shop would be all it needed to rank among the West's foremost fly-fishing getaways, but there's more. The Wheeler family also owns Trapper's Lake Lodge on Trapper's Lake in the nearby Flat Tops Scenic Wilderness, thus Elk Creek's guests can arrange trail rides and fishing expeditions both to Trapper's and the alpine lakes in the surrounding wilderness, casting for a pure strain of wild cutthroat trout.

The heart of Elk Creek is a modern two-story log lodge in a meadow surrounded by hayfields and sagebrush. It contains a bar with a woodstove, several comfortable sitting areas, and a dining room known for its grilled steaks, Maine lobster, stuffed veal, and fresh fish. The highlight is the Wednesday night traditional Greek barbecue hosted by the guides.

The suites occupy two new log cabins and two log-faced two-story structures. They have long decks, furnished with director's chairs oriented up the valley toward the high mesa of the Flat Tops. Half have sleeping lofts above a living area furnished with crate-style furniture. The others have separate, if tiny, bedrooms. They are basically just places to sleep.

> **Packages include a one-day fly-out to Utah's incomparable Green River, a tailwater fishery with an incredible 10,000 trout per mile. No other Colorado lodge can match Elk Creek's variety of fishing options.**

Elk Creek's reputation revolves around its exclusive and varied fishing. Its knowledgeable, friendly, and highly regarded staff instruct those who want to learn the art of fly-fishing and guide those who want to practice their skills. The waters hold brook, brown, rainbow, and wild cutthroat trout. Easy, rewarding wade fishing is as close as Elk Creek itself, 50 yards from the lodge's front door. Meanwhile, nonfishermen can horseback ride, hike, and mountain bike on the ranch or in the wilderness beyond.

MINTURN

Eagle River Inn

145 North Main Street
P.O. Box 100
Minturn, CO 81654
303-827-5761
800-344-1750
Fax: 303-827-4020

> *A Colorado inn
> with New Mexico's
> adobe architecture*

Proprietor: Richard Galloway. **Innkeeper:** Jane Leavitt. **Accommodations:** 12 rooms, all with private bath. **Rates:** Winter (mid-November–late April) $109–$190, summer (late May–October) $89. **Included:** Full breakfast. **Minimum stay:** 5 nights over Christmas holidays. **Added:** 8% tax. **Payment:** Major credit cards. **Children:** Over age 12 preferred. **Pets:** Prohibited. **Smoking:** Prohibited in common areas. **Open:** Year-round except November 1–15 and late April–late May.

The Eagle River Inn's warm pueblo architecture contrasts dramatically with the weathered wood storefronts lining Minturn's one street. Camped beneath the willows alongside the Eagle River, two miles south of I-70 and roughly midway between Vail and Beaver Creek, the hotel dates, as does much of the town, from the 1890s railroad era. The inn's metamorphosis occurred in 1986, when Richard Galloway bucked the trend toward lace-ruffled Victorians and conjured up the adobe elegance of Santa Fe.

The southwestern motif carries into the cozy guest rooms. Here custom-made furnishings, king-size beds with hand-crafted headboards, and quilts with pastel prints suggest New Mexico, as do the colorful tiles in the private baths. The rooms also have fresh flowers, thick towels, and remote-control TVs, but no phones.

> **A porticoed entrance opens into a cheerful white stucco lobby with a beehive fireplace in one corner and traditional vigas and latillas in the ceiling. Indian baskets, rugs, and fabrics and original southwestern art decorate the walls and floors.**

It isn't, however, an entirely straight take on Santa Fe style. The handles of the front door are brass sculptures of coyotes, and capricious hand-painted drawings of cactus, pottery, and the night sky adorn the hallways and stairwells.

The friendly, accommodating staff helps make everything go smoothly. On winter afternoons, they serve hot soup, light hors d'oeuvres, and beer and wine to returning skiers. In summer, they rent mountain bikes and outline the region's recreational options, beyond the riverfront deck with hot tub. And year-round they dish out a sumptuous breakfast of homemade granola, baked goods, Belgian waffles, peach pancakes, or frittatas. All of that helps make the Eagle River Inn and Minturn an engaging alternative to trendier Vail.

REDSTONE

Avalanche Ranch

12863 Highway 133
Redstone, CO 81623
303-963-2846

> *A B&B for adults,
> cabins and an
> animal farm for kids*

Proprietors: Jim and Sharon Mollica. **Accommodations:** 4 rooms, 2 with private bath; 12 cabins. **Rates:** Rooms $85–$95, cabins $75–$118. **Included:** Continental breakfast in rooms. **Minimum stay:** 2 nights over summer weekends and holidays. **Added:** 6.5% tax. **Payment:** Discover, MasterCard, Visa. **Children:** Free under age 9 in cabins. **Pets:** Allowed with prior approval. **Smoking:** Prohibited. **Open:** Year-round.

Lost in the beauty of the Crystal River and its red rock canyon, you can easily pass right by the sign marking the drive to Avalanche Ranch. The 45-acre spread huddles beneath the pine trees at the base of 12,953-foot Mt. Sopris. Though just off the highway and a mere four miles north of the art galleries and souvenir shops in the historic town of Redstone, it gives the wonderful illusion that civilization is much farther away.

Jim and Sharon Mollica bought the ranch in 1988, after almost three decades of living in Aspen, where he had a real estate appraisal firm and she led a campaign against smoking. Both felt it was time to get away, and the ranch, originally a silver miner's homestead, seemed to offer a way out. They turned the 1913 red farmhouse into a bed-and-breakfast inn, the red barn into an antiques shop, refurbished the old log cabins, and added children's play areas and an animal farm.

The accommodations in the main house have early country antiques, folk art, claw-foot tubs, and homey touches like braided rugs and extra lace-trimmed pillows. Each occupies a corner location on the second floor. The dining room on the main level runs the full depth of the house and has picture windows that frame arresting views of the valley and Mt. Sopris. It has old pine tables decorated with dried flowers and a fireplace with a carved wood mantel. Off to one side is a small parlor with a couple of old rockers, a couch, and a library. It couldn't be cozier.

> **Kids can pet and feed llamas, horses, donkeys, and goats. There are also chickens and ducks, pigs, and a cat and dog. The last, named Abby, gets mail from kids who've visited.**

Guests in the house come down to a breakfast of homemade cranberry scones, peach muffins, lots of fresh fruit, granola, yogurt, and more. There's always coffee out in the parlor.

The log cabins stand in two rows on a hillside behind the barn where all have views of Mt. Sopris. They range in size from studios to two bedrooms. More rustic than the rooms in the house, they sport pine-paneled walls, pine floors, pine tables and chairs, and country fabrics. All come with fully equipped kitchens, private baths, outdoor barbecues, and picnic tables. Some have clawfoot tubs and wood-burning stoves, among them numbers 8 and 11, which, lying at the far end of the rows, also have more privacy. Cabin guests can have breakfast in the inn, though it's not included in the cost.

Cleveholm Manor

0058 Redstone Boulevard
Redstone, CO 81623
303-963-3463
800-643-4837

A romantic castle of opulent suites and regal furnishings

Innkeeper: Cyd Lange. **Accommodations:** 13 rooms, 5 with private bath; 3 suites. **Rates:** Rooms $95–$125, suites $155–$180. **Included:** Continental-plus breakfast. **Minimum stay:** None. **Added:** 6.5% tax. **Payment:** Major credit cards. **Children:** Welcome. **Pets:** Allowed. **Smoking:** Limited to game room. **Open:** Year-round.

Most vacationers take the drive to Redstone after hearing rumors of its gorgeous setting beneath red cliffs alongside the Crystal River. They arrive to find its one street lined with art galleries and antiques shops and, a little south of town, something unexpected: a fantastic castle capped by turrets and guarded by a sandstone gatehouse.

John Cleveland Osgood, a coal and steel magnate, built the 42-room, 27,000-square-foot mansion just as the gilded 19th century drew to a close. Traveling to Europe with his second wife, he collected a king's ransom in regal furnishings: Stickley chairs, carved cherrywood sideboards, mahogany tables, inlaid Moorish thrones, and Carrara marble for the fireplaces. Anything less would have been out of place among the gold-embossed leather ceilings, French silks and damasks, oriental carpets, and Tiffany lamps that decorated the grandiose rooms. When it was finished, he dubbed it Cleveholm Manor, though everyone else called it Redstone Castle. John D. Rockefeller and J. P. Morgan visited, and so did Teddy Roosevelt and the king of Belgium.

Nearly a century later, the manor was transformed into a bed-and-breakfast inn nearly as opulent as it was when Osgood built it. Seventy percent of the original furnishings survive, making the interiors even more fantastic than the architecture.

> Guests have the run of the palace, free to roam the brocade and velvet Great Hall, the library with its Tiffany lamps and gold-tooled ceiling, and the game room (the only place where smoking is allowed) with its stone walls, pool table, and television.

Palatial appointments survive in the rooms on the upper floors. Guests dream gilded dreams in original canopy, sleigh, or brass beds. Three of these rooms are splendid tower or turret suites with marble fireplaces, big sitting rooms or sun porches, and views of the Crystal River or the red mountain cliffs.

The additional rooms are sequestered in the former servants' wing. What's missing from that part of the inn, aside from private baths, is the drop-dead opulence of the mansion proper, something not even four-poster beds and eiderdown comforters can make up for.

Continental-plus breakfast is served in the dining room. Guests and the public alike can reserve a place for Friday and Saturday night candlelit dinners prepared by a chef from Aspen.

The Redstone Inn

82 Redstone Boulevard
Redstone, CO 81623
303-963-2526
800-748-2524

> *A historic inn
> in a scenic,
> art-filled town*

General manager: Deborah Strom.
Accommodations: 31 rooms, 27
with private bath; 4 suites. **Rates:** Summer (June-September)
and winter weekends, rooms $40–$110, suites $99–$150; midweek in winter, rooms $32–$78, suites $85–$105. **Minimum
stay:** 2 nights over holidays. **Added:** 6.5% tax. **Payment:**
Major credit cards. **Children:** Welcome. **Pets:** Prohibited.
Smoking: Nonsmoking rooms available. **Open:** Year-round.

John Osgood, the coal baron responsible for Redstone's fantasy castle (see Cleveholm Manor above), built the Redstone
Inn in 1902 as quarters for unmarried miners. As in his own
mansion, he used locally quarried stone, but in this case he
opted for a more down-to-earth, half-timbered Tudor style.
His mines later closed, but the structure survived, becoming
a hotel in 1925 and a showcase for the late 19th-century arts
and crafts movement.

The antique furnishings include unusual hand-crafted
wrought-iron wall sconces and chandeliers and early 20th-
century photographic works of L. C. McClure. The original
Seth Thomas clock in its tower has kept time for the village
since 1902.

Since they were built for bachelor miners, the rooms in the
inn have been decorated in a more masculine style than is
typical of bed-and-breakfasts. A color scheme in burgundy

and emerald predominates, and there's the suggestion of a hunting lodge in the pheasant-motif wallpaper that extends across the top of the wainscoting in the hallways. Freshly re-done, the rooms showcase better than ever the splendid antiques that provide so much of the inn's character.

> **Now on the National Register of Historic Places, the 35-room inn contains more than 60 pieces of Gustav Stickley hand-pegged antique furniture, among them the beds and dressers in many of the guest rooms.**

The best accommodations in the original wing have mountain views. A second wing was added in 1950, however. Its rooms are generally larger, and some have desirable outdoor sitting areas. What they lack are the Stickley furnishings. All the rooms have phones and televisions, so the issue comes down to a choice between great antiques and space.

There are plenty of other pieces to admire in the library, reception area, and parlor, though these areas can become congested with sightseers. The Redstone Inn's main dining room serves classics like rack of lamb, veal piccata, trout with piñon nuts and cilantro butter, and lemon chicken at tables decorated with linen and fresh flowers, while its informal Patio Grill dishes out burgers, salads, and inexpensive pastas.

The Patio Grill overlooks a small swimming pool, the nucleus of a small recreation complex containing a hot tub, tennis court, and modest fitness center overlooking East Creek. There's also a petting zoo and a concessionaire who rents mountain bikes in summer, cross-country ski equipment in winter. Meanwhile, Redstone itself is a haven for artisans, sculptors, and antique dealers, whose wares are on display in historic houses just steps from the inn.

SNOWMASS VILLAGE

The Snowmass Lodge & Club

Snowmass Club Circle
P.O. Drawer G-2
Snowmass Village, CO 81615
303-923-5600
800-525-6200
Fax: 303-923-6944

> *An intimate lodge with a panoply of resort facilities*

General manager: Karen A. Short. **Accommodations:** 76 rooms, 63 condos. **Rates:** Rooms, summer (late June–mid-September) $150–$225, winter (mid-December–late March) $255–$350 (higher over Christmas holidays), spring/fall $105–$155; condos, summer $150–$250, winter $295–$670, spring/fall $125–$190. **Included:** Airport transfers; 2 lift tickets per bedroom in ski season. **Minimum stay:** 3 nights in summer and winter; 7 nights over Christmas holidays. **Added:** 11.5% tax. **Payment:** Major credit cards. **Children:** Free under age 12. **Pets:** Prohibited. **Smoking:** Nonsmoking rooms available. **Open:** Year-round.

In Brush Creek Valley, 12 miles west of the town of Aspen, the elegant Snowmass Lodge & Club is that rare intimate hotel to anchor a full-service golf, tennis, and ski resort. The cozy lodge and its cluster of condominiums bask in semi-isolation a short mile from the ski slopes at Snowmass and within easy access of the breathtaking Rocky Mountain scenery of the 172,000-acre Snowmass–Maroon Bells Wilderness Area.

> **The lodge is a short drive from Aspen's trendy shops, art galleries, restaurants, and Summer Music Festival, yet completely removed from its congestion and traffic.**

The lodge has the feel of an intimate, elegant inn. The lobby has floors of 300-year-old pine, a huge rock fireplace, and several sitting alcoves with views of the valley, among them one with a piano bar. Elk antlers and local art decorate the walls. And an unfailingly friendly staff adds to the homey, comfortable feeling of the place.

The unusually spacious standard rooms feel more like junior suites than basic quarters. Furnished with pine reproduction antiques, they have a contemporary country look. Huge windows look out on either the mountains or the valley. With their foldout couches, these rooms can easily accommodate a family of four. Two rooms are wheelchair accessible. The condos, which range from one to three bedrooms, come equipped with full kitchens, fireplaces, living and dining areas, and patios or balconies with views of the peaks.

Dining at the lodge's main restaurant has shuttled between family style and elegant, sometimes with a featured chef. It has currently settled on what may be called Colorado bistro fare — think sage-roasted chicken — prepared by a team of chefs. Given the restaurant's volatile history, however (even the name has changed), inquiries may be merited before making reservations.

Never in doubt are the club's extraordinary recreational amenities. Its year-round facilities include a state-of-the-art fitness center, recently expanded and refurbished, two heated outdoor swimming pools, and two indoor tennis courts. In summer, guests have an 18-hole golf course designed by Arnold Palmer and Ed Seay, 11 outdoor tennis courts, and access to mountain bikes. In winter, shuttles deliver skiers to the downhill slopes of any of the region's four areas. Cross-country skiers have 30 kilometers of groomed track right outside the lodge door, and that system links up with another 60 kilometers of track on one of the largest free trail networks in the country, spanning three valleys from Aspen to Snowmass. And finally, at any time of year the lodge encourages families by offering kids-stay-free programs, children's menus and activities, and a nursery.

STEAMBOAT SPRINGS

Steamboat Bed & Breakfast

442 Pine Street
P.O. Box 772058
Steamboat Springs, CO 80477
303-879-5724

A neo-Victorian B&B on the ski shuttle line

Host: Gordon Hattersley. **Accommodations:** 7 rooms, all with private bath. **Rates:** Summer (May–Thanksgiving) $70, winter $125. **Included:** Full breakfast. **Minimum stay:** 5 days over Christmas holidays. **Added:** 9.5% tax. **Payment:** Discover, MasterCard, Visa. **Children:** Discouraged under age 10. **Pets:** Prohibited (he has a dog and cat). **Smoking:** Prohibited. **Open:** Year-round except mid-April–early May and mid-October–early November.

Until it was struck by lightning, what is now the Steamboat Bed & Breakfast had been a turn-of-the-century Congregational church. The damage was so extensive that even the parishioners elected to start over on another site. But from the burned-out shell a Steamboat Springs builder and entrepreneur created a 2½-story neo-Victorian charmer, with dormers, bay windows, gingerbread trim, and stained glass windows on either side of the oak front door. Late in 1992, he sold it fully furnished to Gordon Hattersley, a twenty-something Cornell Hotel School graduate who'd wanted his own business.

> The pale yellow clapboard house sits atop a hill in a residential neighborhood only two blocks from Steamboat Springs's main drag and a free shuttle bus to the ski slopes.

The house has seven largish rooms, some of them tucked under sloping ceilings and all of them irregular in shape. They showcase an eclectic collection of antiques and reproductions, including some white iron and some carved wood beds. All of them have lace curtains, wallpapers with tiny flowers, chenille bedspreads, and modern baths. The largest is the Sunset Room on the third floor. Honeymooners like it for its highback oak bed, views through half-round windows, and gabled charm.

Terraced gardens cascade down the front lawn, below a deck. A hammock stretches between two trees, and there is an outdoor hot tub. The entrance foyer has a woodstove and so doubles as a small sitting room, though there's a larger parlor on one side with white wainscoting and couches upholstered in tapestry prints, and a music room on the other with an upright piano and television. An oak staircase leads to the rooms on the upper floors. Beyond the larger parlor lies the breakfast room, which has spindleback chairs and an oriental rug. There Hattersley dishes out hearty skiers' fare of homemade breads, his own granola, fresh fruit, and possibly blueberry pancakes or Belgian waffles with bacon or eggs Benedict or Florentine.

Along with breakfast, Hattersley dispenses advice about what to see and do in Steamboat, from visiting the hot springs to fishing, hiking, rodeos, and downhill and cross-country skiing. He's a very gracious host.

Steamboat Valley Guest House

1245 Crawford Avenue
P.O. Box 773815
Steamboat Springs, CO 80477
303-870-9017
800-530-3866

> *A charming
> hilltop B&B with
> views of the slopes*

Hosts: George and Alice Lund.
Accommodations: 4 rooms, all with private bath. **Rates:** Rooms $65–$110, suite $85–$140. **Included:** Full breakfast. **Minimum stay:** None. **Added:** 9.5% tax. **Payment:** Major credit cards. **Children:** With prior approval. **Pets:** Prohibited. **Smoking:** Prohibited. **Open:** Year-round.

A two-story western log home with a cantilevered roof, Steamboat Valley Guest House stands on a hill at the western end of town surrounded by an acre of grounds. It used to be an administration building until George and Alice Lund — he's a former Lutheran minister, she a former school teacher — converted it in early 1993 into a bed & breakfast in the Swedish tradition. It's distinguished by the charm of its four rooms and its hilltop vistas of the ski slopes and ski jump. One place to take in that view is the two-story living room, which has log walls, a brick fireplace, a baby grand piano, a library, and a wall of windows.

The house shows no traces of its administrative past. The Lunds, who previously operated B&Bs elsewhere in Colorado, have filled it with family treasures and antiques and transformed offices into unusual bedrooms full of charm. Two of these rooms — the Margaret Gear and Anna Bernice — are on the second floor with balconies overlooking what the Lunds have dubbed the Great Room. Anna Bernice, the smaller of the two, has a mountain flower decor, a queen-size white antique bed, oak floors, an emerald green comforter, and a three-quarter bath. Margaret Gear (named for Alice's mother) adopts a romantic Victorian motif, with a queen-size antique brass bed, lace curtains, family memorabilia such as her mother's wedding slippers and parasol, and lots of ruffles and pastel florals. French doors open onto its balcony, which is large enough to hold a tiny table and two ice-cream parlor chairs.

> The bureaucrats who worked here must have had trouble keeping their minds on their work. Now the expansive deck, furnished with umbrella tables in summer, and the hot tub in the backyard are both pleasant places to enjoy the view.

Downstairs, the smallish room called George Lawrence has been decorated in an early American whaling motif. It has a queen-size brass bed, an old chest, starboard lanterns, large windows that frame views of town and the ski hill, and a full bath across the hall. Largest of all is the Telemark Honeymoon Suite, an oversize sunny room colorfully decorated in a type of painted Scandinavian furniture called rosemål. Yellow predominates, from the wicker furniture to the hand-painted headboard on the king-size bed and the fleurs-de-lis in the wallpaper to the yellow primroses in the ceramic tiles of the gas-log fireplace.

Breakfast sometimes shows a similar Scandinavian inspiration in its Swedish pancakes with strawberries and sour cream, but could just as easily be a green chile cheese soufflé with salsa or poppyseed French toast. The main dish always comes with homemade granola, fresh-baked breads, and fruit: the Lunds, who love to ski and hike, understand the need for hearty morning fuel. After more than two decades in Colorado, they're also valuable sources of information about what to do.

The guest house is modestly removed from the heart of downtown, which can be viewed as either an asset or a drawback, and the shuttle to the ski area stops on the road below, a walk of perhaps 150 yards, downhill in the morning, uphill coming back. But those are quibbles with what is otherwise Steamboat's most charming new B&B.

VAIL

For other lodging in the area, see also Beaver Creek, Edwards, and Minturn.

Black Bear Inn of Vail

2405 Elliott Road
Vail, CO 81657
303-476-1304
Fax: 303-476-0433

> *A spacious, modern log lodge, four miles from the slopes*

Innkeepers: Jessie and David Edeen. **Accommodations:** 12 rooms, all with private bath. **Rates:** Summer (May to before Thanksgiving) $90, winter $100–$185. **Included:** Full breakfast. **Minimum stay:** 2–6 days in winter. **Added:** 4% tax. **Payment:** MasterCard, Visa. **Children:** Welcome. **Pets:** Prohibited. **Smoking:** Prohibited. **Open:** Year-round except mid-April to Memorial Day.

The Black Bear Inn is a great barn of a lodge built alongside Gore Creek, four miles from the alpine village of Vail. David Edeen, who used to work for the restaurant division of Vail Associates (owners of the ski resort), and his wife, Jessie, built it in 1990 to house themselves and their two sons, with a few thousand square feet left over for guest rooms and a cavernous, many-windowed great room.

Crafted from honey-colored Engelmann spruce, the inn radiates homey warmth, from the antique woodstove and comfortable couches in the main room to the decks overlooking the creek. The Edeens lure guests outside late every afternoon, setting out beer, wine, hot cider, and hors d'oeuvres. But where once the conversation may have been about stalking prey, now it focuses on the glories of skiing Vail's back bowls.

> Unlike Vail, which strives to be a European village, the Black Bear belongs to the great American tradition of the hunting lodge, without the animal trophies.

After a hard day on the slopes, guests could probably sleep soundly, as hunters did, in a tiny room whose bath is down the hall, but they don't have to. Now the accommodations are generous, with David's own hand-crafted queen-size log beds, down comforters, modern pine furnishings, a sofa sleeper, thick wall-to-wall carpeting, phones, and modern tile baths. The accommodations on the second floor have cathedral ceilings; those on the first floor have bay windows. There's a storage area for boots and skis downstairs.

The price of a night's lodging is about half what it is in Vail Village, and it includes a generous breakfast of granola, fruit, juice, homemade muffins and breads, and hot entrées like ham and cheese croissants, French toast, or pancakes.

Though slightly outside the city center, Black Bear lies on the Vail bus route, so getting to and from town and the slopes doesn't require driving. It's a distinctive new addition to Vail's lodging options.

Christiania Lodge

356 East Hanson Ranch Road
Vail, CO 81657
303-476-5641
800-530-3999
Fax: 303-476-0470

A family-run ski lodge, 150 yards from the lifts

General managers: Paul and Sally Johnston. **Accommodations:** 16 rooms, 5 suites, 1 studio. **Rates:** Rooms, summer (mid-June–mid-September) $90–$135, winter (mid November–mid-April) $195–$325, rest of year $75–$100; suites and studio, summer $125–$175, winter $250–$400, rest of year $100–$150. **Included:** Continental-plus breakfast. **Minimum stay:** 7 nights, February–March and over Christmas holidays. **Added:** 8% tax. **Payment:** Major credit cards. **Children:** Welcome. **Pets:** Prohibited. **Smoking:** Discouraged. **Open:** Year-round.

As one of the original lodges in Vail and one of the few that are family run, Christiania has always had an endearing charm and a roster of hearty perennial guests who come back winter after winter. Yet for all its assets, its age had begun to show until it underwent a thorough refurbishing late in 1992 that has this charming little Bavarian lodge looking better than ever.

The tiny lobby, which has a flagstone floor set off by an oriental rug and fireplace, is not so much a place to gather as a place to check in and make contact with the Johnstons or members of their amiable staff. The place to congregate is Sarah's Lounge (named for Sally Johnston, whom everyone calls Sarah), where guests gather for buffet breakfast beneath a pine ceiling (or outside on the patio in summer) or for après-ski or evening entertainment around the bar and fireplace.

The rooms, all newly painted and carpeted, have traditional Bavarian carved pine furnishings, including an armoire with a television, and pine ceilings, rough plaster walls, and a color scheme in dusky green and rose. Down comforters cover the beds. Private baths have marble vanities.

> **Christiania's location, slightly removed from the heart of town but only 150 yards from the Vista Bahn lift, strikes many as ideal, and though it lacks a hot tub — the quintessential ski lodge amenity — it makes up for it with an outdoor pool kept at 103 degrees.**

The most deluxe rooms have mountain views and balconies, others overlook the village, still others look out onto the garden (making up for that restricted perspective by having a Jacuzzi tub). All of the suites look toward the majestic Gore Range and have large outside decks, a few antique Bavarian furnishings, a separate living room with a gas-log fireplace, and two full baths. There's also one studio apartment with a fireplace and kitchen.

Among the Christiania's other amenities are a ski room with individual boot dryers, a dry sauna, and that outdoor pool. This tiny lodge is once again one of Vail's great little inns.

Gasthof Gramshammer

231 East Gore Creek Drive
Vail, CO 81657
303-476-5626
Fax: 303-476-8816

> *A small,
> European-style hotel,
> close to the lifts*

Proprietors: Pepi and Sheika Gramshammer. **Manager:** Kelly DeGuire. **Accommodations:** 28 rooms. **Rates:** Summer (April to mid-December) $85–$375, winter $195–$555. **Included:** Continental-plus breakfast in winter; Continental in summer. **Minimum stay:** 7 nights in winter. **Added:** 8% tax. **Payment:** Major credit cards. **Children:** Welcome. **Pets:** Prohibited. **Smoking:** Discouraged. **Open:** Year-round except 2 weeks in April.

One of Vail's oldest and best small hotels, the Gasthof Gramshammer dominates a corner in the heart of Vail Village, one very short block from the Vista Bahn chair lift. The cozy little 4-story inn looks like a refugee from the Austrian Alps — all white stucco, timber, and cut-out balconies. Austrian Olympic skier Pepi Gramshammer and his wife, Sheika, opened their very European hotel in 1964, only two years after the first lifts started carrying skiers to Vail's fabled slopes. It has since become a landmark.

The inn's endearing charm begins in the cozy lobby, which is anchored by a bulging fireplace coated in rough white plaster. Small brass and crystal chandeliers hang overhead from sculpted wood beams. An archway beyond the lobby leads into Pepi's Bar and Restaurant, a place as bustling as the lobby is quiet.

Upstairs, the handsome rooms in blue and beige feature hand-carved custom-made furnishings, down comforters, and original art. An armoire conceals a remote-control television. Thick wool carpet is underfoot. Almost all have balconies with views of the mountain and town.

Though the Gramshammers leave the management of the hotel to staff, they cling to Old World traditions of innkeeping and make a point of trying to meet every guest. In winter, when everyone spends at least a week, they usually succeed. Many of their guests are European, drawn by that ambience.

If the Gasthof had only that one restaurant and bar, it could pass for a country inn, but there is a second restaurant featuring wild game and veal, and Sheika's Nightclub in the basement, where dancing goes on until all hours. There's also Pepi Sports, a shop specializing in high-fashion skiwear and equipment. Those who can't warm up to the Gramshammer point to that commercialism and to the one-week minimum bookings in winter as the cause. Still, this is one of Vail Village's few small inns, and it's right in the heart of town, just steps from the lifts and everything else Vail has to offer.

Sonnenalp Hotel and Country Club

20 Vail Road
Vail, CO 81657
303-476-5656
800-654-8312
Fax: 303-476-1639

A necklace of Bavarian hotels, one all suites and opulence

General managers: Rosana and Johannes Fässler. **Accommodations:** 92 rooms and 94 suites. **Rates:** Rooms, winter (mid-November–mid-April) $245–$300, summer (mid-April–mid-November) $100–$145; suites, winter $345–$1,100, summer $160–$600. **Included:** Full breakfast. **Minimum stay:** 3–7 nights in winter. **Added:** 8% tax. **Payment:** Major credit cards. **Children:** Free under 6 in winter, under 13 in summer. **Pets:** Prohibited. **Smoking:** Allowed. **Open:** Year-round.

The endearing Sonnenalp is not one lodge but a trio — Austria Haus, Swiss Haus, and Bavaria Haus — strung along Gore Creek as it rushes through the heart of Vail. Together they encompass 186 rooms and suites. Guests at any of them bed down no more than a few short blocks from the Vista Bahn Express and closer still to a myriad of upscale restaurants, shops, and galleries.

One inn stands out: the landmark Bavaria Haus. During 1992 and 1993, this largest of the three Sonnenalp inns was completely leveled and then rebuilt. What rose from the rubble is an 88-suite gem that far and away outshines everything else in Vail.

Hand-troweled plaster walls and Bavarian pine furnishings invest the suites — which range in size from junior to two-bedroom — with homey warmth. Nonetheless, the secret to their seductiveness lies in a profusion of amenities, including oversize marble baths with two-person Jacuzzi tubs and heated floors, walk-in closets, down comforters, gas-log fireplaces, VCRs, and French balconies. Six of these rooms are handicap accessible. The original woodburning fireplace in the lobby survives (it was the only thing left standing after the demolition)

> **Owned by a German family that has operated resorts in Bavaria for three generations, these three inns exude Old World charm and warmth from their affable, international staff to their hand-carved Bavarian furnishings.**

and opens now to a sitting area on one side and a quiet book-lined library on the other. With the reconstruction came new facilities, among them a state-of-the-art fitness center and a heated outdoor pool, both overlooking Gore Creek. Bavaria Haus also has an inexpensive and locally popular restaurant called Bully Ranch that provides an alternative to the more formal Ludwig's.

Meanwhile, Austria Haus and Swiss Haus have been refurbished in recent years. Their cheerful rooms feature hand-painted doors, Bavarian pine armoires and two-poster beds, down comforters, and terrycloth robes. Those in Austria Haus, the oldest and most like a European inn of the trio, tend to be somewhat smaller but are closest to the lifts and have balconies that look south across the creek to Vail Mountain. Swiss Haus stands out for the massage therapy offered in its small fitness spa.

Each of the three properties has at least one restaurant and includes a huge buffet breakfast of meats, fruits, cheeses, Bavarian muesli, freshly baked breads and pastries, Belgian waffles, and hot entrées in its rates. Each has at least one penthouse suite with a fireplace and fully equipped kitchen.

When winter ends, the Sonnenalp shifts gears and provides guests with access to the Singletree Country Club, 17 miles to the west, with its award-winning golf course, golf school, four tennis courts, and relaxed restaurant and bar. Sonnenalp is a wonderful haven year-round.

WINTER PARK

Alpen Rose

244 Forest Trail
P.O. Box 769
Winter Park, CO 80482
303-726-5039
800-531-1373

*A B&B with
Austrian style
and engaging hosts*

Hosts: Robin and Rupert Sommeraur in winter; Jim and Ray Carey in summer. **Accommodations:** 4 rooms, 1 suite, all with private bath. **Rates:** Summer $65–$75, winter $85–$95. **Included:** Full breakfast. **Minimum stay:** None. **Added:** 9% tax. **Payment:** Major credit cards. **Children:** Accepted; no roll-aways or cribs available. **Pets:** Prohibited. **Smoking:** Prohibited. **Open:** Mid-November–mid-September.

Of the half dozen or so bed-and-breakfasts in Winter Park, the one with the most character is the Alpen Rose. The house itself mirrors the Austrian background of its owners and their love of the mountains in the decorative wood trim in the eaves and the painting of the Alps adjacent to the entrance. So do the rooms, each of which bears the name — often in German — of an alpine wildflower and harbors treasures that Robin and Rupert Sommerauer brought over from their Austria and Germany.

The Sommeraurs opened Alpen Haus in the winter of 1989 to take in skiers attracted to the downhill slopes of the Winter Park/Mary Jane ski area (the free shuttle bus stops outside). The rustic two-story green house they lived in with their two children afforded ample space for four charming guest rooms on the main level (they live on the second floor) plus a large, functional, if rather less charming suite downstairs, appropriately named the Keller (or "cellar"). They expanded the back deck to make room for a hot tub with a southern exposure and commanding vistas of James and Perry peaks, as spectacular at sunrise as in the alpenglow of evening. The common room with its woodburning stove provided a place to gather for snacks and hot beverages at the end of the day.

> **The Sommerauers enjoy the company of active people. Robin is a licensed mountain climber and was one of an expedition of women to make an assault on the Himalayan peak of Dhaulagiri. Both are licensed ski instructors; in summer they operate an alpine hut in Germany.**

The Sommerauers' warmth finds another expression in the decor of the rooms. The one called Alpen Rose has a pine armoire, turned spindle bed, views of the Continental Divide, and a whirlpool bath for two. Enzian stands out for its four-poster pine bed, handmade by friends of the Sommerauers' in Germany. Only the downstairs suite, rented mostly during periods of peak demand in winter, seems spartan by comparison. It has low seven-foot ceilings, a sitting area heated by a wood-burning stove, and two quilt-topped twin beds.

Breakfast picks up the European theme again with Robin's own homemade granola, Austrian pancakes (served with blueberries or apples and maple syrup) or stuffed croissants, homemade coffeecake, and fresh fruit.

Southwest Colorado

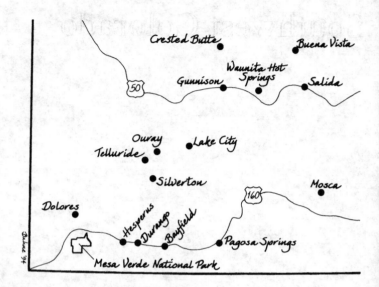

Best Bed-and-Breakfast Homes

Durango
  Logwood–The Verheyden Inn
Gunnison
  The Mary Lawrence Inn
Ouray
  The Manor
Pagosa Springs
  Echo Manor Inn

Best Bed-and-Breakfast Inns

Buena Vista
  The Adobe Inn
  Trout City Inn
Crested Butte
  The Claim Jumper
  Crested Butte Club
Dolores
  Lost Canyon Lake Lodge
Hesperus
  Blue Lake Ranch
Lake City
  Old Carson Inn
Ouray
  The Damn Yankee Bed & Breakfast Inn
  Wiesbaden Hot Springs Spa and Lodgings
Salida
  The Poor Farm Country Inn
Telluride
  Pennington's Mountain Village Inn
  The San Sophia

Best Country Inns

Mosca
  Great Sand Dunes Country Inn

Best Guest Ranches

Bayfield
 Wilderness Trails Ranch
Durango
 Colorado Trails Ranch
Telluride
 Skyline Guest Ranch & Ski Lodge
 Waunita Hot Springs
 Waunita Hot Springs Ranch

Best Historic Hotels, Inns, and Lodges

Crested Butte
 Elk Mountain Lodge
Durango
 General Palmer Hotel
 Strater Hotel
Ouray
 St. Elmo Hotel
Silverton
 Grand Imperial Victorian Hotel

Best National Park Lodges

Mesa Verde National Park
 Far View Lodge

Best Resorts and Spas

Durango
 Tall Timber
 Tamarron
Telluride
 The Peaks at Telluride

Best Ski Area Hotels & Lodges

Crested Butte
 Irwin Lodge

Mountainous grandeur is almost as commonplace in Colorado as blue skies, yet even in that context the southwestern region stands out for the majesty of its landscapes. Whole ranges soar above 14,000 feet, the Collegiate Peaks of Harvard, Yale, Columbia, and Princeton near **Buena Vista** among them. But the drama does not always depend on elevation alone. The San Juan Mountains, though not generally among the tallest in the state, make an uncommon impact because of their chiseled features. Around Ouray and Telluride, two former mining towns set in box canyons, they rise directly at the edge of town, gaining in grandeur by their very closeness. At the eastern edge of this region, near **Mosca,** the Sangre de Cristo Mountains tower above the vast San Luis Valley and what appears to be a mirage: a desertscape of 700-foot-high sand dunes mysteriously piled at the base of snow-capped peaks. Mystery of another sort surrounds the disappearance of the Anasazi Indians, whose palatial cliff dwellings cling to the sandstone canyons of Mesa Verde National Park.

Several of the roads through these mountains bear an official designation as scenic byways. One follows the Black Canyon on the Gunnison River before looping up over Kebler Pass into the historic mining town and ski area at **Crested Butte** and then back to **Gunnison.** Another, the San Juan Skyway, loops through the historic mining towns of Telluride, Ouray, Silverton, and Durango on a 236-mile circle that encompasses the towering peaks and evergreen forests of the San Juans as well as Mesa Verde and the high desert.

Mesa Verde National Park preserves the remnants of a civilization of Anasazi Indians who mysteriously disappeared more than 700 years ago. Though lacking in metal of any kind, they constructed elaborate stone cities in the sheltered recesses of canyon walls. By visiting the park you can walk through some of their architectural masterpieces, including the 200-room Cliff Palace, the largest cliff dwelling in North America, and Balcony House, where ladders and tunnels connect room after room of fine stonework.

The gateway to all of this is the town of **Durango.** Founded in 1880 by the Denver & Rio Grande Railroad, whose initials inspired the name, the once rowdy town now has a university and more than 12,000 people. ("It's growing too fast," complained one local resident. "I mean, they just had to build a fourth grocery store.") It is best known to vacationers as the starting point for the Durango & Silverton Narrow Gauge Railroad. Its coal-fired steam engines carry passengers on a scenic 90-mile route to the old mining camp of Silverton high in the San Juans.

The train goes no farther, but a section of the San Juan Skyway called the "Million Dollar Highway" climbs over Red Mountain Pass and then clings precariously to the mountainsides as it descends past abandoned mines into **Ouray.** Named for a Ute Indian chief, this historic mining town nestles in a high valley narrowly hemmed in on three sides by the 12,000- to 13,000-foot peaks of the San Juans. There you can relax in its hot springs pool, hike up to Box Canyon Falls, or stroll among the galleries and shops of Main Street, which has preserved much of its 19th-century architecture.

The shortest distance from Ouray to Telluride is a four-wheel-drive jeep road, one of several rugged byways that make jeeping popular in this corner of the state. By highway it's 50 miles, all of them scenic. Like Ouray, **Telluride** hunkers down in a hanging valley boxed in by skyscraping red and gray granite peaks (the name derives either from a corruption of "to hell you ride" or, more probably, from tellurium, the semimetallic ore that was mined there). Butch Cassidy and the Sundance Kid are said to have robbed their first bank there. That was before it became the chicest and most dramatic of the southwestern ski areas. In summer there is a festival almost every weekend, variously showcasing jazz, bluegrass, and films. Ralph Lauren has a ranch nearby, as does Sylvester Stallone.

Beyond the peaks and mining towns and cliff dwellings, southwestern Colorado has one other notable attraction. Beyond Mesa Verde a 21-mile detour leads to the Four Corners, the crossroads where Colorado, Utah, Arizona, and New Mexico meet.

BAYFIELD

Wilderness Trails Ranch

23486 County Road 501
Bayfield, CO 81122
303-247-0722
800-527-2624
Fax: 303-247-1006
Winter: 776 County Road 300
Durango, CO 81301

A Morgan horse ranch, family-run and family-oriented

Proprietors: Gene and Jan Roberts. **Accommodations:** 10 cabins, all with private bath. **Rates:** $2,600/couple/week; reduced before mid-June and in September. **Included:** All meals, horseback riding, water skiing, other ranch activities, and gratuities. **Minimum stay:** 7 nights. **Added:** 5% tax. **Payment:** Major credit cards. **Children:** Welcome under age 3; reduced rates under 18. **Pets:** Prohibited. **Smoking:** Prohibited. **Open:** Late May–early October.

Wilderness Trails Ranch butts up against the Los Pinos River in the scenic Pine River Valley, 7,600 feet above sea level and 35 miles northeast of Durango. Ute Indians used to hunt in this backcountry during the summers, and the Weminuche Wilderness Area to the north has changed little since they were here. Like the Ute, Gene and Jan Roberts spend their summers in the valley, not hunting but tending to the Morgan horses they breed and train and taking guests on long rides into the surrounding wilderness.

The Robertses bought the scenic guest ranch and its hand-hewn log lodge and cabins in 1970. During their tenure they added a 72-foot pool, a hot tub, and a few cabins. They made room for 70 guests, but soon found that was too many to allow them to get to know everyone. Something important had been lost in the expansion, they discovered, so they cut back and now limit the number to 50.

Gene and Jan's heartfelt concern for quality makes Wilderness Trails outstanding. They get help from their children and from an enthusiastic crew made up mostly of college students. Their excellent children's program for ages 3–5, 6–11, and 12 and over began because of their kids and continues to evolve.

In addition to the popular riding program, the ranch offers four-wheel-drive tours, raft trips when possible, and water skiing on nearby Lake Vallecito. For those who'd rather hike, there are superb trails into the wilderness.

The cabins range in size from two to five bedrooms. Some have fireplaces and coffeemakers; all feature spiffy country appointments. Although nestled in the woods, none of the accommodations is far from the dining room or the Watering Hole, whose lounge with leather sofas and a stone fireplace is a fun place to meet (BYOB). In a break from guest ranch tradition, the kitchen serves generous breakfasts cooked to order, and dinners of Cajun catfish, chicken Durango, and grilled salmon, often accompanied by a salad bar, in addition to staples like barbecued ribs and grilled steaks. There's a game room with billiards and a television, and nightly entertainment ranging from square dances and campfire singalongs to a staff show or a magician. The real magic, though, is in the setting.

> **The ranch-bred Morgan horses are even-tempered, and the riding instruction is excellent. Half-day and full-day rides climax at lookouts like Vista Grande, with views of the valley floor 2,000 feet below and the 14,000-foot peaks in the Weminuche Wilderness to the north.**

BUENA VISTA

The Adobe Inn

303 North Highway 24
P.O. Box 1560
Buena Vista, CO 81211
719-395-6340

> *A family-run inn,
> inspired by the
> Southwest*

Innkeepers: Michael, Paul, and Marjorie Knox. **Accommodations:** 3 rooms, 2 suites, all with private bath. **Rates:** Rooms $55–$79, suites $65–$79. **Included:** Full breakfast; $10/couple less without. **Minimum stay:** None. **Added:** 8.9% tax. **Payment:** MasterCard to hold reservations; cash or check preferred. **Children:** Welcome. **Pets:** Prohibited. **Smoking:** Prohibited. **Open:** Year-round.

Visitors to Buena Vista discover a few things very quickly. First, locals pronounce it *byew-nuh* vista. Second, the best Mexican food for miles around can be found at the Casa del Sol Restaurant. And finally, the one place along the motel strip with soul-soothing character is the quaint, southwestern-style Adobe Inn. The Knox family opened the inn in 1982, converting a former art gallery into an intimate bed-and-breakfast with southwestern style.

The style of the inn reflects the Knoxes' extensive travels in Mexico and their love of the Southwest, which carries over into the individually decorated rooms. One has Mexican tile, pigskin chairs and tables, and hand-tooled fixtures. Another combines a classic beehive fireplace with Aztec prints, a hand-carved headboard, and a loft suitable for kids. The larger of the suites has wicker furnishings, stained glass windows, potbelly stove, and original southwestern art. All the rooms have televisions and use of a two-person Jacuzzi.

Guests often meet in the livingroom-like solarium in the sunny late afternoons and convene again in the morning for substantial breakfasts of Mexican-style dishes like eggs with wild green chili served with sausage, croissants, fruit, juice, and Mexican hot chocolate.

The Knoxes' son Michael now handles the day-to-day operations. He knows the area and its attractions intimately and has a stock of maps and local information. And the Casa del Sol, that restaurant with the best Mexican food for miles around, is right next door, another Knox family enterprise.

> **The heart of the inn is a solarium anchored by a kiva-style fireplace of white stucco. Like a classic southwestern living room, it has terra cotta tile floors and Native American and Hispanic crafts. It also has comfortable couches, a library, and a baby grand piano.**

Trout City Inn

Highway 24/285 at McGee Gulch
  Road
P.O. Box 431
Buena Vista, CO 81211
Inn (June–October): 719-395-8433
Reservations (year-round):
  719-495-0348

> *A singular inn:
> part B&B, part
> railroad museum*

Innkeepers: Juel and Irene Kjeldsen. **Accommodations:** 2 rooms, 2 railroad cars, all with private bath. **Rates:** $38/couple. **Included:** Full breakfast. **Minimum stay:** None. **Added:** 5% tax. **Payment:** MasterCard, Visa. **Children:** Age 10 or older except in caboose. **Pets:** Prohibited. **Smoking:** Prohibited. **Open:** Mid-June to mid-September.

Passionate about trains almost to the point of obsession, Juel and Irene Kjeldsen built Trout City to recreate the atmosphere of a station stop on the 19th-century South Park narrow-gauge line. They chose the historic site of McGees Station, near the top of Trout Creek Pass, seven miles east of Buena Vista. There, on the hillside above the beaver dams in Trout Creek, they erected a cluster of ersatz western buildings, chief among them a clapboard depot. Eventually, the Kjeldsen's hope to make their complex the centerpiece of a living history museum of the rail era.

> The Kjeldsens have made staying here fun, especially for kids. Guests can try to pump the handcar replica along Trout City's quarter mile of siding or pan for gold. At night, Juel runs vintage Toonerville Trolley cartoons in a screening room inside a half-size reproduction of a steamboat (inexplicably run aground on Trout City's only street, but never mind).

The idea for Trout City seems to have been filtered through Disney World's Frontierland, but there's nothing bogus about the Kjeldsens' infectious enthusiasm or their eagerness to please. Juel, who often dresses in a bowler hat and leather vest, is never more animated than when discussing local history or train lore. For him, everything from the authentic telegraph key in the depot to his replica of a Mason Bogie locomotive (like those once used on the South Park railroad) seems to conjure up images of a bygone era. He knows a great deal about the area, including hiking and biking trails (there are some excellent mountain biking trails on the reopened Midland and South Park Railway beds) and the gamut of restaurants.

Even the accommodations are distinctive. Two small rooms in the depot have a Victorian flare and brass or four-poster beds covered with Irene's handmade quilts. On the rails in front of the depot stand modern versions of old railroad stock, one a parlor car with a bedroom and sitting room done in red plush and oriental rugs, the other a caboose with a decorative potbelly stove and two rooms with bunk beds. All four have private baths with showers. What they don't have are televisions or phones.

The rail cars have no place to plug a television in anyway, since they continue to operate on solar power. Committed environmentalists, the Kjeldsens reluctantly abandoned their efforts to run the whole inn on solar power, however, after guests complained of the lack of heat on cool nights and of having no outlets for shavers or hair dryers. Now the rooms also have conventional power (and the rail cars have automatic heat).

Breakfast is a lavish buffet set out in the depot waiting room. On any given morning it's likely to have everything from eggs and sausage to Amish friendship bread, delicate pastries, fruit, and buttermilk biscuits with homemade jams.

CRESTED BUTTE

For other lodging in the area, see the town of Gunnison.

The Claim Jumper

704 Whiterock
Crested Butte, CO 81224
303-349-6471

A witty inn, full of popular Americana

Innkeepers: Jerry and Robbie Bigelow. **Accommodations:** 6 rooms, all with private bath. **Rates:** $69–$109. **Included:** Full breakfast. **Minimum stay:** 2 nights preferred on weekends. **Added:** 9.9% tax. **Payment:** MasterCard, Visa. **Children:** Over 11. **Pets:** Allowed with prior approval. **Smoking:** Prohibited. **Open:** Year-round.

Great bed-and-breakfasts inevitably express the style and personality of their owners, but few succeed as thoroughly as the Claim Jumper. Its six guest rooms and various common areas exhibit Jerry Bigelow's mammoth collection of sports memorabilia and artifacts of popular American culture, its sumptuous breakfasts showcase Robbie's restaurant and catering background, and the whole house vibrates with their witty sense of humor. It is unrivaled for its sheer sense of fun.

> **"Jerry used to put 'Not For Sale' signs on everything in our antiques store because he couldn't bear to part with it," says Robbie Bigelow. The Claim Jumper provided a venue for displaying that amazing collection.**

The house itself was built in 1960 by the Verplanck family. They used 100-year-old timbers, visible in places like the second-floor common area and dining room. The Bigelows bought it in 1989, abandoning their antique shop and catering business for the ski slopes of Crested Butte. Among the possessions they brought with them was a virtual Smithsonian of popular 20th-century Americana, from old Coke machines to signed photographs of members of baseball's 500-homerun club.

Each of the six rooms has a different assortment of artifacts tied to a particular theme. In Soda Creek, guests curl up in a queen-size brass bed amid a flurry of Coke memorabilia, including signs, bottles, an old-fashioned Coke machine, and the door of a Coke delivery truck with a Mel Gibson cutout peering through the window. A tape in the room plays old Coke ads. Ethyl's Room runs riot in gas station and car artifacts, including a Shell gas pump, stop light, license plates, and old oil cans. A car door serves as a towel rack. The top-floor Sportsfan Attic, the largest room of all, houses a hoard of sports memorabilia encased in glass around a queen-size brass bed. Among its decorations are scores of signed photos of sports stars, Wayne Gretzky's hockey stick, Bruce Jenner's Olympic jacket, a 1917 Princeton blanket, and countless hats, pennants, and jerseys. This room also has a kind of loft called the Press Box with a twin bed and memorabilia from the

1940s and '50s. Of the other rooms, Prospector's Gulch and Rough and Ready have mining and cowboy themes respectively, while Commodore Corrigan's Cabin adopts a nautical motif. The rooms lack phones (though the Bigelows make cordless phones available), but all have VCRs to take advantage of the inn's library of 100 videotapes.

The fun continues in the second-floor common area and dining room, where an old Crested Butte gondola carries life-size mannequins of George Bush, Richard Nixon, and Mikhail Gorbachev. A biplane flies from the rafters.

It's here that guests meet at a long table for huge breakfasts of buckwheat pancakes with Bavarian cream, Robbie's own elk sausage, or Santa Fe pastry stuffed with eggs and feta cheese and served with homemade salsa. Every afternoon, Robbie puts out more goodies, like salsa and chips or artichoke heart pâté. Guests can also arrange for intimate six-course candlelit dinners.

The Claim Jumper also has a game room with bumper pool and a puzzle table, a living area with a Sensurround TV/VCR, and an indoor hot tub (with glow-in-the-dark stars) and steam shower. The free shuttle to Crested Butte's ski slopes leaves from across the park, about a 50-yard walk; the inn sells discounted lift tickets. And anyone who wants to get married while they're there can enlist the Bigelows' wedding services. They specialize in unusual locations — on the ski slopes, atop a peak, wherever. The Claim Jumper is a rare find.

Crested Butte Club

512 Second Street
P.O. Drawer 309
Crested Butte, CO 81224
303-349-6655
800-492-6655
Fax: 303-349-7580

19th-century elegance meets 20th-century fitness

General manager: Joe Rous. **Accommodations:** 6 rooms, 1 suite, all with private bath. **Rates:** Rooms, summer and winter $125–$135, spring and fall $60–$70; suites, summer and winter $165, spring and fall $85. **Included:** Continental-plus breakfast. **Minimum stay:** 2–3 nights on summer weekends; 4–7 nights in winter. **Added:** 9.9% tax. **Payment:** Major credit cards. **Children:** With prior approval. **Pets:** Prohibited. **Smoking:** Prohibited. **Open:** Year-round.

Part Victorian hotel, part health club, the Crested Butte Club merges 19th-century elegance with a 20th-century preoccupation with fitness. Anywhere else, that may have been an unexpected combination, but not here.

The National Historic Landmark that houses the Crested Butte Club began in 1886 as the Croatian Social Club. Although it was moved from its original location to a spot just off Crested Butte's main drag, the false-front timber structure still contains the original Victorian back bar. Its dark wood and beveled glass became a point of departure for the extensive interior renovations carried out in 1989.

> The club in many ways reflects the restored mining town it inhabits, for although Crested Butte was born in the gold and silver rushes of the 1880s, it has since become noted chiefly as a haven for skiers, mountain bikers, and hikers.

The layout and decor of each of the seven rooms differs, except in their turn-of-the-century elegance and spaciousness. All of them have antique or reproduction furnishings, sitting areas dominated by marble fireplaces with mahogany or walnut surrounds, lace or floral curtains, wall-to-wall carpeting, and such amenities as phones and remote-control cable televisions. All have decoratively tiled private baths, pedestal sinks, and clawfoot or ancient copper tubs. The more deluxe rooms open onto a deck where many couples like to have their breakfast or even watch the sunrise, and the expansive one-room suite radiates Edwardian warmth from its brass chandelier to its four-poster bed. The rooms couldn't be more romantic.

The original bar remains in service, though it is framed now by a refined room with a fireplace, coffered ceiling, and dark wood paneling. In the mornings, guests find cereal, yogurt, pastries, juice, and fruit laid out for them to eat there or take back to their rooms. Guests also have free access to an adjacent health club and its aerobics classes, cardiovascular equipment, Universal weight machines, indoor lap pool, hot tubs, and steam rooms. Those who prefer to ski can catch a free shuttle to the mountain right outside the front door.

Elk Mountain Lodge

129 Gothic Road
Crested Butte, CO 81224
303-349-7533
800-374-6521
Fax: 303-349-5114

> *A former mining hotel rumored to have a ghost*

Innkeepers: John and Patty Vermillion. **Accommodations:** 16 rooms, all with private bath. **Rates:** Summer $69–$79, winter $98–$108. **Included:** Full breakfast. **Minimum stay:** 3 nights Christmas and spring break. **Added:** 9.9% tax. **Payment:** Major credit cards. **Children:** Free under 12. **Pets:** Prohibited (they have a dog). **Smoking:** Prohibited. **Open:** Year-round.

Built in 1919 as a hotel for single miners, the three-story Elk Mountain Lodge underwent a thorough remodeling in 1992 after Dallasites John and Patty Vermillion bought it. The three-story clapboard and stucco structure retains its early 20th-century look, with a gabled roof and red and black trim, but the extensive renovation transformed the interiors.

Ceiling fans twirl above a seating area anchored by a gas-log fireplace and baby grand piano. There's a television and stereo there and a Queen Anne–style table and chairs set in the adjacent dining room, where a leaded and beveled glass beer cooler from the original hotel now functions as a sideboard. The sun porch in front holds an intimate lobby bar, while to the back there is a small library and Patty's boutique of hand-painted western wear. The hallway beyond leads to an indoor hot tub and ski storage lockers.

The rooms upstairs differ in layout and style depending on location. Those on the third floor snuggle beneath dormer windows. Though on the small side, they are redeemed by having balconies (in all but one case), a generally country decor with eyelet lace pillows and bedspreads, handmade quilts, and paintings by local artists. Rooms on the second floor, though somewhat larger, are less appealingly decorated in contemporary Edwardian fashion. Room 11 is said to have a resident ghost.

> There is a Queen Anne-meets-Dallas elegance to the parlor and dining room, where the Vermillions remodeled in Victorian style and then installed the furnishings from their Texas home.

Breakfast consists of homemade granola, fresh fruit, fresh breads or rolls, and a selection of hot dishes, which could be French toast, apple crisp, cheese grits, biscuits and gravy, or an occasional soufflé. In winter, the Vermillions also set out high tea on Sunday afternoons. The free shuttle to the ski slopes stops a few blocks away.

Irwin Lodge

P.O. Box 457
Crested Butte, CO 81224
303-349-5308
800-2-IRWIN-2
Fax: 303-349-5309

> *A haven for powderhounds*

General manager: Lynne and Richard Curtis. **Accommodations:** 23 rooms, 1 suite. **Rates:** Summer, rooms $80–$95, suite $150; winter (2-day/3-night package), rooms $580/person, suite $1,430/couple. **Included:** Full breakfast and tax in summer; all meals, unlimited guided Sno-Cat or cross-country skiing, Sno-Cat tours, transportation from Crested Butte, tax in winter. **Minimum stay:** None in summer; 3 nights in winter. **Added:** Nothing. **Payment:** MasterCard, Visa. **Children:** Nonskiers discouraged in winter; reduced rates under age 10. **Pets:** Prohibited. **Smoking:** Prohibited in dining room, allowed in guest rooms. **Open:** June 15–October 15, Thanksgiving–April 15.

None of the roads leading to Irwin Lodge is open in the winter, which is only one of the things guests like about it. The great hulk of a three-story structure squats on a plateau above the frozen surface of Irwin Lake, 12 miles from Crested Butte at an elevation of 10,700 feet. To reach it, guests board Sno-Cats for the serpentine trip along snow-covered forest trails. They are lured to this snowy mountain aerie by the promise of run after run of perfect powder skiing on 2,500 acres accessible to no one but them and their guides.

Next to the bar is a restaurant where guests gather for nightly repasts of halibut with raspberry cream sauce, Cornish game hens marinated in lime and tequila, prime rib, or a low-fat, high-carbohydrate fuel in the

> **A certifiable eccentric built the immense cedar lodge in 1976. The 120-foot lobby stretches almost the entire length of the building and soars 30 feet to the peak of the roof. The Alferd Packer Bar (Packer was a notorious Colorado cannibal) anchors one end, a medallion of reindeer skins the other.**

form of manicotti with artichoke heart marinara or toasted ravioli with three sauces. Meals are part of the winter package.

Except for one huge suite with some Victorian furnishings and a living room that runs the entire width of the building, the large, functional rooms are all alike, with queen or double beds, new convertible sofas, and private baths with showers. The reason everyone comes has nothing to do with chenille spreads or new quilts and everything to do with the Sno-Cats that haul guests to the top of the slopes for long runs through untracked powder and then pick them up at the bottom for a ride back to the top. The average skier makes six to eight such trips a day, collapsing happy and exhausted in one of the lodge's two 20-person Jacuzzis when it's over. Those who'd rather not downhill have 12 kilometers of groomed trails or can hop aboard snowmobiles for sightseeing excursions through a winter wonderland spiked with 13,000-foot peaks.

There is also a summer side to the lodge. Then it can be reached — slowly — by car, and the focus shifts from skiing to horseback riding, hiking, mountain biking, and fishing. It makes an appealing backcountry retreat then, too, but it's as a ski lodge that the Irwin shines as a truly unique place.

DOLORES

Lost Canyon Lake Lodge

County Road 35.3
P.O. Box 1289
Dolores, CO 81323
303-882-4913
800-992-1098

*A secluded,
contemporary
log inn on a lake*

Innkeepers: Beth Newman and Ken Nickson. **Accommodations:** 5 rooms, all with private bath. **Rates:** $70–$90. **Included:** Full breakfast. **Minimum stay:** None. **Added:** 1.9% tax. **Payment:** Major credit cards. **Children:** Free under 6. **Pets:** With prior approval (they have kennel, cats, and dogs). **Smoking:** Prohibited. **Open:** Year-round.

This two-story log home huddles beneath the ponderosa pines in the hills overlooking Lost Canyon Lake Reservoir, roughly midway between Dolores and Mancos. Set on 40 acres, it has both seclusion and comfort to recommend it. A broad deck runs along the back. It has been furnished with umbrella tables for those who want breakfast outdoors or a place to enjoy the sunsets. Below the deck, a lawn slopes away toward an outdoor hot tub and the lake shore. Flowers in window boxes and half-barrel planters provide splashes of color. The entrance to Mesa Verde National Park is 20 miles away, but the house seems close to nothing but the forest and sky.

Beth Newman was an intensive care nurse and Ken Nickson was an emergency care physician in California when they bought this house and opened it as a bed-and-breakfast in 1992. Ken still spends part of each month working on the coast, but Beth has taken up Colorado residence full time, living in the house they built next to the lodge. She has a knack for making guests feel at home and a nurse's attentiveness to their needs.

Because she and Ken live next door, guests have free run of the very

> Two rooms have lofts with a queen-size bed accessible by a steep ladder to supplement the queen-size bed below. Two others look out on vistas of the lake.

comfortable inn. A broad living room, paneled in pine and anchored by a mossrock fireplace, runs the entire width. A wall of windows faces the deck and lake beyond. Furnished in contemporary ranch fashion, the room is spacious enough to hold two pairs of couches. A Remington sculpture stands on one of the tables, and Beth and Ken have installed a telescope and television for guests to use. There are even pets: they have lots of cats and dogs, though none is allowed in the house.

The rooms occupy the first and second floors. Like the rest of the house, they tend to be very spacious. Though individually decorated with lodgepole pine, white wicker, or four-poster beds, they all have country warmth. Each has a modern bath with added amenities like heat lamps and a selection of toiletries. There are even laundry facilities.

Beth serves huge breakfasts of ham and cheese strata, sour cream coffeecake, hot breads, and granola at a big table at one side of the living room. "I get attached to my guests if they're here more than a few days," she says, "and then I really don't want them to leave."

DURANGO

For other lodging in the area, see Dolores, Hesperus, and Mesa Verde National Park.

Colorado Trails Ranch

12161 County Road 240
Durango, CO 81301-6306
303-247-5055
800-323-3833
Fax: 303-385-7372

A ranch for families and serious riders

Proprietors: Dick and Ginny Elder. **Accommodations:** 27 cabins. **Rates:** Single $1,175–$1,500/week, double $1,975–$2500/week. **Included:** All meals, horseback riding and instruction, ranch activities. **Minimum stay:** 7 nights in summer, 3 nights after Labor Day. **Added:** 18% to cover taxes and gratuities. **Payment:** Major credit cards. **Children:** Discouraged under age 5. **Pets:** Prohibited. **Smoking:** Prohibited in public areas. **Open:** Late May to early October.

The heart of this 500-acre ranch is a recreated western village complete with a trading post, opera house, and blacksmith shop. This vision of the Old West owes more to Hollywood than to history, and thus variously strikes guests as either extremely hokey or unabashedly fun. Those same guests are much less likely to disagree about the horseback riding program, however. Both Dick and Ginny Elder, who have operated Colorado Trails for more than three decades, are certified riding instructors with a passion for horses and for teaching guests the skills they need to handle them. Their ambitions thus go far beyond merely using horses to visit the scenery.

Poised at the edge of the San Juan National Forest, 13 miles northeast of Durango, the ranch seems more remote than it actually is. Although the Durango-Silverton narrow-gauge railway and the Benetton and Ralph Lauren Polo factory outlets are an easy 25-minute drive away, from the porch of the lodge there is nothing to see but pine-forested hills, corral, and sky.

That proximity to town coupled with an ambitious children's program make it a haven for families. Not only are kids taught to ride, they're also taken whitewater rafting, water skiing, and on overnight campouts. The nightly entertainment is geared to families as well, with square dancing, a steak fry and campfire singalong, and occasional performances by the staff in Shaefer's Opera House, part of the ranch's western village. In addition, there is a weekly trip into Durango to see a melodrama.

> **Of all the dude ranches in the Rockies, this one comes closest to being an equestrian school, right down to the option of English or western riding, dressage, and jumping.**

Though kids may eat with their parents, most prefer the company of their counselors and new friends. That leaves the adults free to enjoy the ranch fare — barbecued chicken or ribs, roast beef, spaghetti, or lasagna — at tables for six in the raftered dining room. The guest rooms are similarly unpretentious. Paneled in pine and decorated in 1960s earth tones, the rooms range from small to spacious in everything from a classic western cabin to an A-frame or X-shaped pod.

There is also a swimming pool, a heated spa, two tennis courts, a trapshooting range, and a volleyball court at the ranch, and the option of a variety of water sports at nearby Vallecito Lake, where the ranch keeps a boat. But riding is the point. Divided by ability into groups of no more than six, guests start their instruction in the ring. Once they know the basics, wranglers take them out on the trail. But rides are not follow-the-leader outings but opportunities to practice skills under the watchful eye of an instructor. "Rather than take people on rides," says Dick Elder, "we teach the sport of equitation. The rider is in complete control." Open meadows allow riders to learn to canter. Horsemanship comes first, and the reward is often breathtaking vistas.

General Palmer Hotel

567 Main Avenue
Durango, CO 81301
303-247-4747
800-523-3358
Fax: 303-259-0536

A turn-of-the-century hotel beside the railway depot

General manager: Sandra Medearis. **Accommodations:** 37 rooms, 2 suites. **Rates:** Rooms, summer (May–October) and Christmas $98–$165, winter $65–$105; suites, summer and Christmas $185–$195, winter $130–$145. **Included:** Continental breakfast. **Minimum stay:** None. **Added:** 9% tax. **Payment:** Major credit cards. **Children:** Free under age 12. **Pets:** Prohibited. **Smoking:** Prohibited except in lobby. **Open:** Year-round.

The Denver & Rio Grande Railroad started the town of Durango to serve the gold and silver mines in nearby Silverton, Ouray, and Telluride. Much of the downtown today belongs to a National Historic District, including the architecturally unprepossessing General Palmer.

Though guests of the inn still awaken to the whistle of the narrow gauge, the hotel has changed markedly since the turn of the century. It now encompasses both its original building and the old Palace Hotel, which lies across a parking lot and even closer to the depot. Their bland exteriors mask Victorian hearts, the result of a thorough redecoration undertaken in the mid-1980s.

Together, the two hotels comprise a modest 39 rooms. No two guest quarters are alike except in having modern baths. Some feature brass beds or pewter-colored iron beds, others oak or walnut, and still others four-posters or canopies of cameo lace. The turn-of-the-century motif continues in lace curtains, plush burgundy and beige carpets, brass fixtures, and dark wood moldings. Mauve, peach, and burgundy tones enrich the wallpaper, rugs, and upholstery. And all of the rooms have accents like standing mirrors and dried flower arrangements and such amenities as terrycloth robes, cable televisions, and phones.

> **Built in 1898, the three-story brick hotel stands on a corner in a prime location just a short block from the depot of the Durango & Silverton Narrow-Gauge Railroad depot.**

The rooms in the General Palmer tend to be a little smaller than those in the Palace, but guests are just an elevator ride away from the wicker-furnished solarium where Continental breakfast is served, and from the quiet, intimate lobby and library, which has a woodburning stove and red plush chairs. Cranberry glass lamps further enhance the rich, turn-of-the-century atmosphere.

Logwood–The Verheyden Inn

35060 Highway 550 North
Durango, CO 81301
303-259-4396
800-369-4082

> *A secluded river-front log home*

Hosts: Debby and Greg Verheyden.
Accommodations: 6 rooms, all with private bath. **Rates:**

$65–$90. **Included:** Full breakfast. **Minimum stay:** None. **Added:** 6.9% tax. **Payment:** MasterCard, Visa. **Children:** 8 and over. **Pets:** Prohibited (they have a cat). **Smoking:** Prohibited. **Open:** Year-round.

This western red cedar log home stands amid the cottonwoods, ponderosa pine, and Gambel oaks on the banks of the Animas River, 12 miles north of Durango. Designed as a bed-and-breakfast by Debby and Greg Verheyden's predecessors, it makes the most of its seclusion.

> A fabulous deck looks east across the river, and rooms with picture windows have the same view. Guests often see deer, elk, badgers, and birds.

Inside, an expansive L-shaped common area encompasses a two-story vaulted living room with a river rock fireplace, a dining area with a long pine table, and a library. If guests tend to linger there and in the kitchen it's because the Verheydens have a rare capacity to make everyone feel that the house is theirs. Coffee and tea are available in the kitchen all day long, and guests are invited to use the refrigerator. The Verheydens' warm, open personalities make Logwood an unusually homey bed-and-breakfast.

Guest rooms occupy the upper and lower levels. Though smallish, they are redeemed by those picture windows and views and by their engaging western decor. All have log beds, comforters or hand-pieced quilts, timber ceilings, and modern private baths. Those on the second floor have cantilevered ceilings and thus feel more spacious than the downstairs rooms, though the latter tend to be cooler and are large enough to accommodate a roll-away or cot. The most appealing of all is Mesa Verde, a sunny corner room on the second floor.

Breakfast varies seasonally. In summer, Debby and Greg serve casseroles with fresh fruit, yogurt, biscuits, scones and waffles, pancakes, or French toast. In winter, the fare becomes even heartier, with casseroles of ham and eggs or baked fruit and oatmeal. In any season, guests rave.

Debby is a registered nurse, Greg a chemical engineer formerly with Dupont. They bought Logwood in 1991, moving from Texas with their teenage sons, Michael and Alan. They'd been attracted to the abundance of outdoor recreation the region offers. They dispense advice about what to see and do over breakfast and again in the late afternoons or evenings when they reconvene guests to sample their award-winning desserts, among them one called "Berries on a Cloud." They also provide bike and ski storage and encourage fly-fishing on the river (their son Alan has developed a passion for fly-tying since moving from Texas). Hospitality runs deep here.

Strater Hotel

699 Main Avenue
P.O. Drawer E
Durango, CO 81302
303-247-4431
800-247-4431
Fax: 303-259-2208

A grand old hotel, rich in Victorian furnishings

Vice president/Co-owner: Rod Barker. **Accommodations:** 91 rooms, 2 suites. **Rates:** (Higher during Christmas holidays) Rooms, summer (mid-May–October) $105–$135, winter $68–$125; suites, summer $145, winter $135. **Minimum stay:** None. **Added:** 9% tax. **Payment:** Major credit cards. **Children:** Welcome. **Pets:** Prohibited. **Smoking:** Nonsmoking rooms available. **Open:** Year-round.

When it opened in 1887, the Strater was one of the grandest hotels west of the Mississippi. The five-story red brick structure featured hand-carved white stone sills and cornices and posh interiors rich with Victorian furnishings. Louis L'Amour worked on his best-selling western novels in rooms 222 and 223, and over the centuries the southwestern Colorado landmark has entertained Kit Carson, Tom Thumb, Will Rogers, and Presidents Eisenhower, Truman, Kennedy, and Ford.

> The hotel successfully mixes turn-of-the-century grandeur with Wild West flamboyance, from the red velvet drapes and period light fixtures in the lobby to the costumed bartenders and waitresses in the gilded Diamond Belle Saloon. Its theater is renowned for authentic Victorian melodramas.

Presidents have tended to prefer the suites (one of which has seven windows, eight wallpapers, and an antique half-tester bed), but even the average guest can look forward to a dose of 19th-century opulence. The Strater has one of the world's largest collections of American Victorian walnut furnishings, so every room features an ornate hand-carved bed, a swooning couch or love seat, marble-topped tables, and plush drapes. The Barker family, who bought the hotel in 1926, not only collected most of these pieces — repairing them when necessary in their own shop — but also lavished meticulous attention on providing a proper context for displaying them by decorating the rooms with richly patterned wallpapers typical of the 19th century. When possible they left the old-fashioned hexagonal and decorative tile in the bathrooms intact. Only the phones, remote-control televisions, air conditioning, and a hot tub break the spell.

Henry's is a well-regarded restaurant specializing in prime rib. If the service in the hotel can be hit or miss and the lobby swarms with gawkers and tourists on their way to the restaurant or melodrama, the Strater nonetheless remains a grand reminder of Colorado's mining era.

Tall Timber

San Juan National Forest
Silverton Star Route Box 90
Durango, CO 81301
303-259-4813

> *An uncommonly
> civilized hideaway,
> accessible only by
> rail or helicopter*

Proprietors: Dennis and Judy Beggrow. **Accommodations:** 10 rooms. **Rates:** $1,000–$1,200/person/3 nights or $1,400–$1,700/person/6 nights . **Included:** All meals, most activities, helicopter or train transfers. **Minimum stay:** 3 nights. **Added:** 6% tax. **Payment:** Cash, personal checks, or traveler's checks. **Children:** Discounts under age 12. **Pets:** Prohibited. **Smoking:** Allowed. **Open:** Mid-May to late October, before Christmas to after January 1.

Tall Timber exists in that rarefied domain beyond roads in a place evocatively named "the canyon of the river of lost souls." There are, thus, only two ways of reaching this 180-acre sanctuary deep within the nearly two-million-acre San Juan National Forest: by helicopter or narrow-gauge train out of Durango. Either way, as new arrivals disembark at the tiny depot they can expect to be personally welcomed by several members of the amiable staff. That often includes Denny and Judy Beggrow, who started building this retreat with their own hands in 1970.

The Beggrows wanted to recreate the experience of traveling in the 1920s and 1930s, when people spent extended periods at their destination, often after taking a long journey. Those lengthy stays made it easy to get to know both the staff and the other guests. And though hardly anyone vacations for months at a time any longer, at Tall Timber the Beggrows and their amiable retinue strive to make even new arrivals feel like old friends.

They've made settling in uncommonly easy. Guests bed down in duplex suites scattered beneath a canopy of aspen and fir trees. Furnished in contemporary fashion, these two-level hideaways have separate living rooms dominated by two-story stone fireplaces that soar to the top of the cathedral ceilings. The loft above holds a king- or queen-size bed, a spacious marble bath, and terrycloth robes that guests are encouraged to keep. There are neither phones nor televisions but there are such unexpected touches as wet bars, refrigerators, and coffeemakers (and an unlimited supply of coffee and tea). Every evening, guests find logs and kindling laid out in the fireplace ready to light and something special left behind

> This emphasis on making life easy and sumptuous for guests extends to the daily routine. Except for fixed mealtimes, the Beggrows have banished structure. Thus Tall Timber manages to be a haven both for the incurably active and the congenitally indolent.

along with the turndown service: fruit and cheese one night, cookies and milk another, liqueurs on a third.

Those who crave exercise can hike into the wilderness (or helicopter up and walk back), fish, golf on the 9-hole Executive course, play tennis, swim against an artificial current in the solar-heated pool, exercise in the workout room, or, for a fee, ride horses. Guests can also read, choosing books from the resort's 5,000-volume library, languish in a riverside Jacuzzi, or do nothing at all. Missing from the formula are any kind of organized children's programs or a children's supervisor; like adults, they're on their own.

Everyone comes together for cocktails in the 16,000-square-foot clubhouse before sitting down at window tables draped with linen for a table d'hôte dinner that is elaborate one night, simple and homespun the next, but always punctuated by superb breads and as many of its own vegetables as Tall Timber can grow.

Tamarron

40292 Highway 550 North
P.O. Drawer 3131
Durango, CO 81302-3131
303-259-2000
800-678-1000
Fax: 303-259-0745

> *A golf resort in a cliff-flanked setting*

General manager: Bob Nelson. **Accommodations:** 103 rooms, 280 condos. **Rates:** (Higher over Christmas holidays) Summer (May–October), rooms $129–$169, condos $225–$354 (not available rest of the year); winter (November–April), rooms $95–$110. **Included:** Full breakfast, service charges, use of health club. **Minimum stay:** None. **Added:** 6.9% tax. **Payment:** Major credit cards. **Children:** Free under age 18. **Pets:** Prohibited. **Smoking:** Allowed; nonsmoking rooms and condos available. **Open:** Year-round.

A golf course rated one of the toughest resort courses in Colorado and the golf schools that complement it make Tamarron, 18 miles north of Durango in the nearly two-million-acre San Juan National Forest, an obligatory stop on any duffer's tour of Rocky Mountain fairways. A wall of gray and buff volcanic peaks looms to the west, punching skyward above a carpet of evergreens, aspens, and Gambel oaks. Perched atop the cliff amid all that greenery is the rambling, 103-room lodge.

> **Designed by Arthur Hill, the golf course is a 6,885-yard scenic wonder that wraps around a cliff in a breathtaking 20-mile-long valley.**

Tamarron's fame may revolve around its golf, but the 750-acre property is in fact a full-service resort. A steep set of stairs down the cliff face ends at a small tennis complex with three courts, two platform courts, a pro shop, and an enthusiastic full-time summer pro. A path leads away to a series of nature trails, a stocked fishing pond for kids, and the stables. The lodge itself shelters an indoor/outdoor heated swimming pool, whirlpool, a modest fitness center, and aerobics and massage rooms. In winter, Tamarron grooms eight kilometers of cross-country track and runs shuttles to Purgatory for those who prefer downhill. Summer and winter, the lodge is the staging area for supervised children's programs.

The lodge rooms, while far from elegant, have trendy pastel color schemes, two-poster beds (one king or two doubles), original southwestern art, a remote-control cable television, and enough extra space to accommodate a foldout sofa and a tiny kitchen complete with pots, pans, dishes, a toaster, a percolator, and a small refrigerator filled with overpriced beverages and snacks. Every room has views of the colorful cliffs lining both sides of the valley. There's even a free washer and dryer down the hall.

Besides the lodge, Tamarron has three clusters of condominiums along the cliffs and golf fairways. They range in size from townhouse studios barely larger than the rooms to deluxe, 2,200-square-foot, three-bedroom hideaways.

The restaurants, while fine, are in no danger of winning culinary awards — not even the Continental fare in Remington's, which features barbecued salmon, steaks, pork chops, and burritos. The good news is that for those nights when guests don't feel like a full meal, Tamarron also has the Caboose Café, which serves pizza, sandwiches, and ice cream. Kids love it.

In spring and fall, the atmosphere sometimes changes for the worse as badge-toting conventioneers outnumber vacationers. On the other hand, while in meetings they aren't competing for golf tee times. Besides, they usually leave before the weekend.

GUNNISON

For other lodging in the area, see the towns of Crested Butte and Waunita Hot Springs.

The Mary Lawrence Inn

601 North Taylor
Gunnison, CO 81230
303-641-3343

A convivial home near skiing and a university

Host: Jan Goin. **Accommodations:** 3 rooms and 2 suites, all with private bath. **Rates:** Rooms $69, suites $85–$135. **Included:** Full breakfast. **Minimum stay:** 2 days over some holidays and special college weekends. **Added:**

8.9% tax. **Payment:** MasterCard, Visa. **Children:** Welcome. **Pets:** Prohibited (she has a dog). **Smoking:** Prohibited. **Open:** Year-round.

Painted a tasteful jade green and trimmed out in white, mauve, and pale blue, this century-old Victorian home stands on a corner in a quiet residential neighborhood just a few blocks from Western State College. Nathan Weinberger, a saloon keeper, had it built in 1885 as his private residence, but the couple who turned it into a bed-and-breakfast chose to name it instead for Mary Lawrence, a woman who operated it as a rooming house for years while pursuing her own career as a teacher, then superintendent of schools and college administrator. Giving it her name seemed to keep alive its link to hospitality.

> On warm afternoons, guests gather in the Adirondack chairs on the deck for iced tea, and kids frolic in the fenced backyard, which has a large playhouse. At any time of day, the coffee station on the second floor has cookies and coffee, tea, and hot chocolate. Hospitality reigns.

For Jan Goin, a 20-year resident of Colorado, the inn was a ticket to a small town and a chance to pursue a career that allowed her to merge her background in property management and business with her love of people and cooking.

Each of the rooms has been individually decorated. A double wedding ring quilt graces a queen-size brass bed in the two-room Nathan Weinberger Suite. The Cow Camp Suite also has two rooms, one an oversized chamber with a decorative fireplace, an Indian-inspired quilt atop a queen-size bed, strong earth colors, and rustic furnishings, the other an ideal children's room with twin beds and lots of toys. Mullin Patch has white wicker and chintz, stenciled walls, a hand-appliqued quilt atop a brass bed, and a bath across the hall with a clawfoot tub. Galloping Goose, a smallish room with a large bath, leans to a simple country decor of blue sponged and stenciled walls, plants, and an assortment of homemade stuffed animals and dolls. All four of these line the second-floor hallway accessible only by a set of very steep stairs. The fifth room, Kathryn Firebaugh's, occupies the first floor.

Named for one of the inn's original owners, this large chamber stands out for its Mission oak antiques and Amish quilt.

Although there is no parlor, a walk-through kitchen connects to a sunny bay-windowed breakfast area where Goin serves a scrumptious breakfast that may feature eggs Taos, a hot berry compote, sausage clafouti, or grilled grapefruit. Off to one side is a sun room with shelves of books and racks of maps where guests can gather to read or chat, and there's also a porch in front and that deck and yard in back.

HESPERUS

Blue Lake Ranch

16919 Highway 140
Hesperus, CO 81326
303-385-4537
Fax: 303-385-4088

A delightful inn and cottages, surrounded by gardens

Innkeepers: David and Shirley Alford. **Accommodations:** 4 rooms, 1 suite, and 3 cabins, all with private bath. **Rates:** Rooms $85–$150, suite $165, cabins $165–$225 (lower rates November–March). **Included:** Continental-plus breakfast. **Minimum stay:** 2 nights. **Added:** 6.9% tax. **Payment:** Cash, personal checks, or traveler's checks. **Children:** At innkeepers' discretion. **Pets:** Prohibited. **Smoking:** Prohibited. **Open:** Year-round.

David Alford bought the 100-acre Blue Lake Ranch in the mid-1970s, when it had little more to recommend it than a woebegone homesteader's shack, a trout-filled lake, and views of the Rocky Mountains. It still has the lake and the views, but the early-1900s homestead has evolved, with no obvious plan, into an exquisite bed-and-breakfast inn, supplemented by two cottages and a two-story log cabin. Colorful, fragrant gardens bloom all around them. Alford and his physician wife, Shirley, banished themselves to a converted barn, so guests have the run of the antique- and flower-filled house without any sense that they're intruding on their hosts' lives.

Not that David would make anyone feel that way in any

case. Animated and gracious, he is one of those people seemingly born to hospitality. Guests relax the moment they enter the cozy living room, with its woodstove and oil painting of David's grandmother as a young girl. Off to one side is a solarium, chock full of flowers and plants, where the Alfords serve a traditional European breakfast of cheese, fruits, meat, and pastry, highlighted by their own peach-raspberry preserves and lavender jelly.

> **One cottage, three-quarters of a mile from the main house, basks in complete seclusion amid a stand of cottonwoods alongside a river. It has separate living and sleeping quarters and a full kitchen.**

Every room reflects David's buoyant personality. No two are alike, though all have family heirlooms — among them his grandfather's hand-carved mahogany canopy bed — and colorfully tiled baths, down comforters, hidden televisions, and walls decorated with hand-painted flowers. Two open directly onto the gardens. There's also a very private suite with a living room, full kitchen, a bedroom with a pine bed, and a private bath tiled in teal blue. The suite occupies one end of a European-style barn, a few steps from the house, and opens into another garden, one full of delphiniums and surrounded by a white picket fence.

The smaller of the cottages stands just a hundred yards away beyond an edible-flower garden. Inside, a single large room with an alcove kitchen holds a woodstove and a roomy bed covered with a pink and white quilt and set beneath a beamed ceiling hung with dried flowers. The two-story log cabin, which looks onto the lake, has a floor-to-ceiling stone fireplace, log and willow furniture, a loft bedroom (with its own fireplace) accessible by a spiral staircase, a second bedroom with its own entrance, and a full kitchen.

All of these lodgings have views of the La Plata Mountains and herds of grazing sheep. Mesa Verde National Park is a 45-minute drive in one direction, Durango 15 minutes in the other. At night, the only sign of civilization visible in any direction is a single, dim light at a distant mine.

LAKE CITY

Old Carson Inn

P.O. Box 144
Lake City, CO 81235
303-944-2511
800-294-0608

*A modern log inn
among ghost towns
and mountains*

Hosts: Don and Judy Berry. **Accommodations:** 7 rooms, all with
private bath. **Rates:** $60–$95. **Included:** Full breakfast. **Minimum stay:** None. **Added:** 8.9% tax. **Payment:** Discover, MasterCard, Visa. **Children:** Welcome (roll-aways available). **Pets:** Prohibited. **Smoking:** Prohibited. **Open:** Year-round.

The plant-filled sun room at the Old Carson Inn seems to have its windows pressed up against the Continental Divide. This off-the-beaten-path valley in the Rockies encompasses five peaks higher than 14,000 feet, and two of them rise virtually on the inn's doorstep. Yet for all their towering majesty, it looks as if you could stroll out the front door and shortly arrive at the top of the world.

That's because the inn itself perches high in the mountains. Set in a grove of aspens 9,200 feet above sea level, the 5,000-square-foot log and pine home is a contemporary take on an old lodge. Don and Judy Berry, who've lived in Lake City for more than a decade, built the house in 1990 as a bed-and-breakfast, with seven spacious rooms and several common areas for guests and quarters for themselves as well. They then named it for a mining camp ghost town on the mountain slopes above.

Using family heirlooms and furniture their son built, they decorated the inn in essentially country fashion, giving each of the rooms the name of a local mine. The accommodations range from the cozy Bachelor Mine, with an extra-long double bed and three-quarter bath, to the expansive Bonanza King Mine, whose king-size bed and sitting area bask in stunning views of the forest and the mountains through massive windows. Most occupy the second and third floors, accessible by a massive log staircase. The exception is the Maid of Carson, whose private entrance off the front patio opens into a mountain room of spruce logs and aspen paneling.

Though all the rooms have log and wood trim and private baths, no two are alike. In some, Judy sponge-painted the walls, in others she applied wallpaper. There are headboards of log, wicker, and, in one case, a mirror. Throughout the house the Berrys have scattered an assortment of collectibles and American Indian artifacts, some of them capricious, like a bench from the ghost town of Carson and a sharpening stone now converted to a planter.

> In summer, guests typically head off to hike, mountain bike, or explore the scenic four-wheel-drive backcountry byways into Silverton, Ouray, and the ghost town of Capital City. In winter, there are 120 miles of groomed snowmobile trails and a wilderness of backcountry skiing. In any season, they come back to a refrigerator stocked with wine and an enclosed hot tub.

The front door opens onto a common area with a wood-burning stove. That connects to the sun room on one side and the dining room on the other. Breakfast takes place at a long deal table (one of the pieces their son crafted) and consists of egg and meat dishes, pancakes, homemade breads or biscuits, muffins, and fruit.

Part of the lure of this area is that the small town of Lake City has not suffered the glitz and commercialism typical of other Colorado towns. It also has Lake San Cristobal, the second largest natural lake in the state. The Old Carson Inn provides the most appealing lodging in this remote and scenic valley.

MESA VERDE NATIONAL PARK

For other lodging in the area, see the towns of Dolores, Durango, and Hesperus.

Far View Lodge

Mesa Verde National Park, CO
    81330
303-529-4421
Reservations: ARA Mesa Verde
P.O. Box 277
Mancos, CO 81328
303-529-4421
Fax: 303-529-4411

> *A blufftop motel among ancient Indian cliff dwellings*

General manager: Brad Barker. **Accommodations:** 150 rooms. **Rates:** $72–$86. **Included:** Coffee. **Minimum stay:** None. **Added:** 4.9% tax. **Payment:** Major credit cards. **Children:** Under 13 free. **Pets:** Allowed. **Smoking:** Nonsmoking rooms available. **Open:** Mid-April through mid-October.

The 150 rooms of Far View Lodge occupy a score of buildings in the heart of Mesa Verde National Park. Strictly speaking, it is not a lodge but rather a complex of 20 motel blocks scattered across an 8,000-foot bluff. Its mid-park location puts guests within an easy drive (about six miles) of the most spectacular of the Anasazi Indian cliff dwellings at Cliff Palace and Balcony House and within walking distance of the Visitors Center.

> **What makes the lodge itself appealing is that each of the rooms opens out onto a private balcony with see-forever vistas across the canyons and mesas of southwestern Colorado.**

That location and see-forever views compensate for what is otherwise a somewhat small room laid out in fairly standard motel fashion, though without the usual phone and television. What the rooms lack in amenities they partially make up for in unaccustomed style. Decorated to reflect the region, all have quilted comforters in southwestern prints in pastel colors, modern oak and brass furnishings, and an Indian sand painting. The best have views to the south across a high plateau etched by deep canyons. The first to go are those right on the edge of the mesa. Particularly popular are numbers 101–120, whose generally southern exposure faces just enough west to catch the sunset, and numbers 121–140, oriented to take in sunrise and the jagged peaks of the San Juan Mountains.

All of the rooms (a few of which are wheelchair accessible) are a short walk from the main lodge and its sunset patio. Inside there's a gift shop, lounge, and an informal, dinner-only restaurant that specializes in western and southwestern fare such as carne asada, barbecued quail, trout, and Indian barbecued rabbit. The hotel stages multimedia shows each evening about the history of the area's ancient inhabitants, all of whom mysteriously disappeared centuries ago, and about the region's modern peoples as well.

MOSCA

Great Sand Dunes Country Inn

Zapata Ranch
5303 Highway 150
Mosca, CO 81146
719-378-2356
800-284-9213
Fax: 719-378-2428

*A resort
and country inn
among bison
and sand dunes*

Innkeeper: Olivier Chang. **Accommodations:** 14 rooms, 1 suite, all with private bath. **Rates:**

Rooms $130–$180, suites $170–$250. **Included:** Continental-plus breakfast, shuttle from Alamosa airport. **Minimum stay:** None. **Added:** 7.1% tax. **Payment:** Major credit cards. **Children:** Free under 8. **Pets:** Prohibited. **Smoking:** Prohibited. **Open:** May through October.

By a stroke of geological fate, the tallest sand dunes in the western hemisphere appear high in the Colorado Rockies, along the base of the Sangre de Cristo Mountains. Trapped by 14,000-foot peaks, they are constantly shifting, reaching heights as great as 700 feet as they create a 55-square-mile miniature Sahara in the otherwise agriculturally rich San Luis Valley. This strange, timeless place is full of legends about web-footed horses and disappearing wagon trains. Bison still roam the surrounding sagebrush country.

> **This legendary spread dates from the 1880s. The same stand of cottonwoods that once shaded a Pony Express stop now canopies one of the West's most distinctive country inns.**

The bison, at least, can be logically explained: the neighboring Zapata Ranch, which dates to the 1880s, runs over 2,500 head of buffalo — the third largest herd in America — on its 100,000 acres. Several of the log buildings that were part of the original ranch now form the core of a mini-resort. There are 15 homey rooms, 10 of them in log-and-chink cabins, the rest — including one that is wheelchair accessible — in Stuart House, the rather charmless home of the former owner. All have been furnished with pine beds made by the ranch's caretaker, armoires, Indian print or handmade quilted comforters, and modern baths with terra cotta tile floors and pedestal sinks. None has a phone or television (though there is a TV in the Stuart House living room), and newspapers have been banned to enhance the sense of seclusion.

Yet the ranch is far from primitive. Within steps of the rooms guests will find a 6,800-yard golf course, a heated outdoor swimming pool and Jacuzzi, a small health club with exercise equipment and a Universal weight machine, mountain bike rentals, and an on-call masseuse. Plans also call for adding one tennis court. Hiking trails lace the surrounding mountains, leading to such dazzling sights as Zapata Falls. There are even tours of the bison ranch.

A breakfast of fruit, yogurt, granola, cold cuts, and pastry comes with the room, but the inn also has a 40-seat restaurant whose specialty is, of course, bison steaks, though it also serves shrimp tarragon, brandied veal, and pasta and vegetable platters.

There are views of the dunes from anywhere on the ranch, and the entrance to Great Sand Dunes National Monument is seven miles to the north. Let the rangers know if you see any wild, web-footed horses.

OURAY

The Damn Yankee Bed & Breakfast Inn

100 Sixth Avenue
P.O. Box 709
Ouray, CO 81427
303-325-4219
800-845-7512

A warm, thoughtfully designed inn near a famous hot springs

Host: Mike Manley. **Accommodations:** 8 rooms, 2 suites, all with private bath. **Rates:** Rooms, summer (June–August), $88–$115, winter $58–$98; suite, summer $125–$145, winter $98–$125. **Included:** Full breakfast. **Minimum stay:** 3 days over holidays. **Added:** 7.25% tax plus $1.25/room/day. **Payment:** Major credit cards. **Children:** Welcome over age 12. **Pets:** Prohibited. **Smoking:** Prohibited. **Open:** Year-round.

In a town of historic buildings that date to the turn of the century, the Damn Yankee is a mere infant. Built in the 1980s and dramatically expanded in the 1990s, this winsome bed-and-breakfast inn perches near the river, two blocks from the galleries, restaurants, and shops of Ouray's main street and an easy drive from its famous hot-springs pool. What it lacks in historic character it more than makes up for in thoughtful design and elegant appointments.

Mike Manley furnished each of the eight oversize rooms with reproduction antiques and covered the queen-size beds with down comforters and pillows. Rooms on the second floor have vaulted ceilings. A hot tub is set beneath a gazebo at the river end of the house.

The first floor has a breakfast room with a long oak table and a cozy parlor with a woodstove and grand piano. But the most popular gathering place is the third-floor tower, a sunny aerie with windows on the San Juan Mountains. Apart from comfortable couches, it has a soft drink dispenser and a refrigerator with ice.

> **The inn's most unusual feature is that every room has a private entrance from the decks that wrap around the first and second stories — the better to view the soaring granite peaks of "the Switzerland of America."**

Mike Manley moved to Ouray from Missouri, where he was a civil engineer, because he loved the mountains. Gracious and casual, he makes a wonderful host, setting out plates of hors d'oeuvres in the tower every afternoon and serving either a light breakfast of granola, yogurt, and breads or a huge repast highlighted by hot entrées such as eggs Benedict in pastry cups or stuffed French toast. He also invested his B&B with special touches, from the brass fixtures, thick towels, and deluxe toiletries in the bathrooms to the remote-control cable televisions in every room. Guests rave.

The Manor

317 Second Street
P.O. Box 745
Ouray, CO 81427
303-325-4574

> *A Victorian B&B run by an outdoorsy young couple*

Hosts: Diane and Joel Kramer. **Accommodations:** 7 rooms, all with private bath. **Rates:** Summer (May–October) $75–$90, winter $60–$80. **Included:** Full breakfast. **Minimum stay:** 3

nights over July 4. **Added:** 7% tax plus $1.25/room/night. **Payment:** MasterCard, Visa. **Children:** No children under 10. **Pets:** Prohibited. **Smoking:** Prohibited. **Open:** Year-round.

Dressed in Birkenstock sandals, Diane and Joel Kramer bustle about the parlor and dining room of their seven-room bed-and-breakfast, eagerly greeting new arrivals or guests returning after a day of recreation. To encourage this gathering they've set out sodas, herbal teas, juices, fresh-baked cookies or muffins, Diane's own biscottis, scones, and popcorn to go with the bowl of fruit that is a household fixture. They had been in

> **Avid hikers and mountain bikers themselves, the Kramers have more than the usual interest in how their guests have spent the day.**

other people-oriented professions — working at Canyon Ranch in Arizona and the Peaks at Telluride — before buying this established bed-and-breakfast in 1993.

The three-story Georgian-Victorian stands on a quiet residential street just a block from Ouray's main drag. Although Diane and Joel did not themselves convert this 1890 house into a bed-and-breakfast, since taking it over they have done much to invest it with their personality. Some of the antiques came with the house; others, like the carved oak chairs in the dining room, they brought with them from Telluride. Joel's black-and-white and color photos adorn the walls, and there's a growing collection of books and maps about what to see and do in the craggy San Juan Mountains.

Sunlight filters through stained glass windows into the small front parlor. It falls on a fireplace and on tastefully chosen wallpapers and period furnishings, some of them antiques, others reproductions. The Kramers' quarters are off to one side, the guest rooms on the second and third floors above. Individually decorated with wall-to-wall carpet, down comforters, feather beds (in winter), and miscellaneous antiques, each has mountain views, an immaculate bath, and a queen-size white wicker, oak, or brass bed. Those on the second floor tend to be somewhat small — though numbers 2 and 3 in the front of the house have the best views — while those in the third floor attic tend to be somewhat larger but have low, sometimes sloping ceilings. What none of them has is a phone, television, or small children, on the assumption that guests come to get away.

The hot tub on the back deck gets plenty of use, basking in

vistas of the San Juan mountains, and the Kramers hand out free passes to the hot springs, which are within walking distance. The Kramers have also provided indoor storage for various kinds of recreational equipment, whether it's mountain bikes in summer or skis in winter. Also in winter, Diane, who's a licensed massage therapist, is available for Swedish or shiatsu massages.

The buffet breakfast, meanwhile, reflects the Kramers' active lifestyle and former spa training by emphasizing high-carbohydrate dishes like whole wheat buttermilk waffles, French toast with fresh peaches or apples, or spinach-mushroom whole wheat soufflé, supplemented by their own homemade breads and muffins (both like to bake), crêpes, and perhaps an egg dish heavy on apples, oatmeal, and cinnamon.

St. Elmo Hotel

426 Main Street
P.O. Box 667
Ouray, CO 81427
303-325-4951
Fax: 303-325-0348

A diminutive mining-era lodge tricked out in Victorian finery

Innkeepers: Dan and Sandy Lingenfelter. **Accommodations:** 7 rooms, 2 suites, all with private bath. **Rates:** Summer (June–early October) and Christmas, rooms $79–$84, suites $86–$94; rest of year, rooms $58–$69, suites $65–$89. **Included:** Full breakfast. **Minimum stay:** 2 nights over holidays. **Added:** 7% tax plus $1.25/room/night. **Payment:** Major credit cards. **Children:** Welcome. **Pets:** Prohibited. **Smoking:** Prohibited. **Open:** Year-round.

The little St. Elmo started out as a hotel for miners who had more hope than money. The two-story hotel opened on Main Street in 1898 while Ouray was still a booming mining camp, but unlike the Strater in Durango or the Jerome in Aspen it never aspired to be anything other than workingmen's lodgings until Dan and Sandy Lingenfelter bought it in 1983 and turned it into an intimate Victorian inn.

> **The St. Elmo's location puts it just steps from Ouray's galleries and shops, while exceptional Italian specialties and seafood are as close as the Bon Ton restaurant in the hotel's basement.**

Oak doors with ovals of etched beveled glass open into a lobby with red flocked wallpaper, French Empire chairs and sofas, Oriental carpet, crystal chandelier, and lots of plants. Farther back there's a second, more subdued parlor with a piano, television, and reading area, and finally a breakfast room, where sunlight floods through a bay window. Here a buffet of homemade breads and muffins, French toast, Belgian waffles, cereal, and juice is served.

The Lingenfelters invested each of the rooms with its own take on Victorian style. Antiques mix with reproductions in spacious havens decorated with bold Victorian wallpapers, brass beds, marble-topped end tables, and lace curtains. All have private baths, some with showers only, but none has a phone or television. There is also a pair of two-room suites, each on a corner. The Cascade Suite consists of two bedrooms, one with a king-size bed and antique armoires, the other with a double; they share a bath with a shower only. Honeymooners and romantics opt instead for the Alpenglow, which has a separate sitting room to complement sleeping quarters that feature a half-tester bed topped by a lace and eyelet coverlet and a floral quilt with lace ruffles. It has a full bath.

After a day of hiking to Bear Creek Falls or the Box Canyon, touring old mines, or exploring the majestic San Juan Mountains, guests can look forward to using the hot tub and sauna.

Wiesbaden Hot Springs Spa and Lodgings

625 Fifth Street
P.O. Box 349
Ouray, CO 81427
303-325-4347
Fax: 303-325-4845

*A B&B inn
on the site of
sacred hot springs*

Proprietor: Linda Wright-Minter.
Accommodations: 16 rooms, 4 apartments and cottages.
Rates: Rooms $80–$95, apartments and cottages $115–$135 (lower rates midweek in winter). **Included:** Access to hot springs spa. **Minimum stay:** None. **Added:** 7% tax plus $1.25/room/night. **Payment:** MasterCard, Visa. **Children:** Under age 5 not allowed in spa. **Pets:** Prohibited. **Smoking:** Prohibited. **Open:** Year-round.

The Ute Indians believed that all hot springs had curative powers, yet revered one above all others. Lifted high in a box canyon in southwestern Colorado, that particular spring's source was inside a cave in the glacier-chiseled San Juan Mountains. Convinced of its miraculous powers, the Ute Chief Ouray went so far as to build an adobe dwelling near the cave entrance in order to be close to the sacred waters.

Linda Wright-Minter knew nothing of the spring's history when she toured southwestern Colorado in the late 1970s. After years of running a child care center in Germany, she moved to New Mexico intent on starting her own preschool. Taking a break first, she arrived in Ouray, the once-booming mining town that took its name from the Indian chief. While there, a chance visit to the hot springs, which had come to be called Wiesbaden Spa, changed everything. She couldn't stop thinking about the improvements she'd make if she owned it. Within months she did.

Under her direction, it has become an intimate, European-style spa. The pure, continuously flowing waters remain the principal tourist draw. Guests come, as the Ute Indians did, to bask in the soothing warmth. To enhance their stay, Wright-Minter offers other services, among them massages, facials, reflexology, a flotation tank, and a private outdoor soaking pool beneath a sycamore tree.

Warm and chatty herself, Linda chooses staff who are

equally personable. Her taste and sensibility show throughout. The lobby has become a skylighted solarium, like a greenhouse with its abundant plants. An old woodstove is in one corner, and an antique sideboard contains herbal teas and decaffeinated coffee.

She also transformed the small motel rooms using an eclectic decor of contemporary and country furnishings punctuated by antiques — many of them treasures she collected in Europe.

> **Free of chlorine and other additives, the hot springs feed the 104-degree outdoor swimming pool and the 110-degree soaking pool in the natural vapor cave.**

Some have decorative stenciling along the tops of the walls. All have modern baths and televisions. One large room has a wall that is actually the side of the mountain. The accommodations also include a cottage that stands on the site of Chief Ouray's adobe dwelling, another across the street holds more antiques, and a variety of townhouses and flats, some with complete kitchens. But it's the waters and Linda that make the spa what it is. "There's a lot of spiritual stuff here," says Wright-Minter. "I think it's a very healing place; it's not just me saying that. People tell me that all the time." To this day, the Indians continue to use the springs for ceremonial purposes.

PAGOSA SPRINGS

Echo Manor Inn

3366 Highway 84
Pagosa Springs, CO 81147
303-264-5646
Fax: 303-264-4617

A labyrinthine inn, all gables and turrets

Hosts: Ginny and Sandy Northcutt.
Accommodations: 8 rooms, 6 with private bath; 2 suites. **Rates:** Rooms $45 single, $54–$64 double; suites $69–$125. **Included:** Full breakfast. **Minimum stay:** None. **Added:** 8.1% tax. **Payment:** Discover, MasterCard, Visa. **Children:** Welcome if well behaved. **Pets:** Prohibited (they have a dog and outside cat). **Smoking:** Prohibited. **Open:** Year-round.

Big families require big houses, though whether the man who built this residence in a mixture of Queen Anne and Dutch Victorian styles really needed 35 rooms for his five children is debatable. He seems to have succumbed regularly to an urge to add on, until he eventually created an elaborate cottage of gabled dormers and turrets.

Ginny and Sandy Northcutt bought it in 1986 and turned it into an inn, naming it for the lake across the road. Stairways and hallways take off in every direction. Guests joke about needing a map to find their rooms.

Though individually decorated, most of the sleeping quarters have a few antiques and handmade quilts. One hides away beneath the sloping roof of the turret at the top of a steep, circular staircase. Curiously, its best view is from the bathroom window, which looks toward the majestic mountainscape from Wolf Creek Pass to the San Juan Range. Honeymooners adore the viewful Royal Suite (actually one large room), which has a sitting area with an electric fireplace and loveseat and a king-size brass bed tucked into an alcove whose bay window frames the inn's best views of the San Juans. Families have a choice of

> This "cottage" contains, among other things, three family rooms, two kitchens, and a 1,600-square-foot suite larger than many houses.

a two-bedroom suite under the gables reached via a narrow spiral staircase or that 1,600-square-foot suite downstairs, which has a very western living room (equipped with a king-size bed and pull-out sofa), fireplace, full kitchen, and private entrance.

The Northcutts have also earned a reputation for unstinting hospitality and legendary breakfasts of such fare as strawberry, cherry, or blueberry crêpes, potato bake, quiche, scrambled eggs, fresh rolls, and carrot, banana, or blueberry muffins served on a sunny glassed-in porch just off the kitchen, with views of the San Juans and Continental Divide. Guests have the run of the vast house, with several living rooms (one for adults only), a game room with television and many of Sandy Northcutt's hunting trophies (among them a 2,000-pound moose), a sun deck, and 6½ acres of property containing a hot tub, barbecue grill, and swings. The town of Pagosa Springs and its hot mineral springs are 3½ miles away. There is fishing and water skiing in the lake across the road, and snow skiing at Wolf Creek Pass, 30 minutes away.

SALIDA

The Poor Farm Country Inn

8495 Country Road 160
Salida, CO 81201
719-539-3818

> *A budget-priced inn overlooking a river*

Hosts: Herb and Dottie Hostetler. **Accommodations:** 7 rooms, 3 with private bath; 1 coed dorm with 1 bath. **Rates:** Rooms $45–$55, dorm $22. **Included:** Full breakfast. **Minimum stay:** None. **Added:** 7% tax. **Payment:** MasterCard, Visa. **Children:** Free under age 5. **Pets:** Prohibited (they have dogs). **Smoking:** Prohibited. **Open:** Year-round.

Though it is now a warm-hearted bed-and-breakfast, the Poor Farm Country Inn once did, as its name suggests, house the county's poor. The century-old brick dwelling stands among the open fields lining the Arkansas River, in a quiet country setting two miles from downtown Salida. Though listed on the National Register of Historic Places, the rather boxy dwelling stands out for quite another reason: Herb and Dottie Hostetler's exceptional ability to make guests feel at home.

Behind the etched glass in the front door lies a high-ceilinged parlor with a television and upright piano and a wall of library shelves complete with an attached rolling ladder. Country wallpapers in subdued colors help set off the wood moldings. Cheerful rugs accent hardwood floors. Scattered throughout are the Hostetlers' antiques, which they brought with them from California, where he used to restore old houses. They did much of the work on this house themselves.

Children are welcome. They love to slide down the old-fashioned fire escape, fish in the stocked pond, and play in their own playground. For adults, there's good fishing in the Arkansas River just out the back door, coffee and tea available all day, and complimentary wine or beverages in the library in the afternoons. Everyone begins the day with a huge country breakfast served family-style.

But it's Herb and Dottie that everyone remembers. They've turned the Poor Farm into an amiable country retreat.

> **Most of the bedrooms have mountain views. There are a few antiques, but for the most part the Hostetlers shied away from period decor and glamour in favor of simple comfort.**

SILVERTON

Grand Imperial Victorian Hotel

1219 Greene Street
P.O. Box 57
Silverton, CO 81433
303-387-5527

> *An 1882 hotel in a once-thriving mining camp*

General manager: George Foster II.
Accommodations: 38 rooms and 2 suites, all with private bath. **Rates:** Summer (March–mid-Oc-

tober), rooms $60–$125, suites $150; 50% less rest of year. **Minimum stay:** None. **Added:** 7% tax. **Payment:** Discover, MasterCard, Visa. **Children:** Welcome. **Pets:** Prohibited. **Smoking:** Nonsmoking rooms available. **Open:** Year-round.

The mountain town of Silverton, 9,300 feet above sea level, has only 800 or so year-round residents. The last mine closed in 1991, so now most of its residents live and die by the tourist trade. Throughout the summer, they arrive from Durango, borne by the narrow-gauge railway that puffs up through the San Juan Forest several times each day. Another contingent arrives by car, white-knuckled after negotiating the cliff-hanging Million Dollar Highway out of Ouray. Both groups converge on Main Street, lined with 19th-century buildings and anchored at both ends by 12,000-foot peaks.

> In its heyday a century ago, Silverton was a thriving mining camp, and the Grand Imperial Victorian Hotel was regarded as one of the finest examples of Victorian architecture on Colorado's Western Slope.

The three-story, mansard-roofed Grand Imperial Victorian Hotel stands on a corner on Main Street, two blocks from the narrow-gauge railway depot. Painted gray and trimmed in red and blue, it does not have the look of a hotel, and in fact it originally housed shops on its street level and professional offices on the second, leaving only the third level divided into separate rooms for travelers.

There are still shops on the street level to either side of the lobby and adjacent Hub Saloon and Gold King Dining Room. But now both upper stories have quarters for guests. What once were offices, however, have now become the hotel's most appealing rooms. Most there have been redone either in Victorian style with bold floral wallpapers or in lighter colors more typical of country style. All have antique brass or canopy beds and refurbished bathrooms. Those on the corners are large enough to be called junior suites.

There are some oddities in the hotel, too. The third-floor rooms look like something out of the 1950s — the date of their last major overhaul — and both floors have some tiny interior rooms with windows, though one does have twin four-poster beds. Floors creak.

The narrow lobby on the street level has a crystal chandelier, high pressed-tin ceilings, antique leather couches, and a life-size portrait of Lillian Russell. A door from there leads directly into the saloon, notable for its original ornate cherrywood back bar, and the restaurant, whose fare runs to steaks, chicken, and shrimp. Those, too, have been part of the general refurbishing still going on at the hotel. There are also plans for a train museum in the basement. Best of all, George Foster brings a new level of hospitality and warmth to the hotel's management.

TELLURIDE

The Peaks at Telluride

136 Country Club Drive
Telluride, CO 81435
303-728-6800
800-789-2220
Fax: 303-728-6567

*A ski-in, golf-in
resort hotel
and spa*

General manager: Richard M. Houston. **Accommodations:** 149 rooms, 28 suites. **Rates:** Rooms, winter (late November–early April) $200–$435, summer (early April–late November) $120–$275; suites, winter 375–$1,750, summer $265–$750. **Included:** Use of fitness center, airport transfers. **Minimum stay:** 4 nights over winter holidays. **Added:** 12% tax. **Payment:** Major credit cards. **Children:** Free under age 2. **Pets:** Small, with prior approval. **Smoking:** Nonsmoking rooms available. **Open:** Year-round.

There are really two Tellurides: the original mining town that dates to the last century and the Mountain Village that dates to last week (okay, parts of it have been around since the late 1980s). Though physically two miles apart, both butt up against the ski slopes, which plunge off the mountain into town on one side and into the Mountain Village on the other. The broad main thoroughfare through town is lined with Victorian-era or Victorian-inspired buildings, many of them now housing restaurants, shops, and real estate offices. The Mountain Village has been fertile ground for palatial homes and condominiums, some in the woods, others on the slopes and around a golf course.

The Peaks at Telluride inhabits the Mountain Village. Its Great Room frames views of 14,246-foot Mt. Wilson, and so does the sundeck at the Legends of Telluride restaurant (which specializes in "Ranchlands" cuisine of game, local lamb, seafood, and pasta). Even the indoor pool and weight room in its four-story spa have mountain views.

> **The Peaks at Telluride snagged an upper Mountain Village location that allows its guests to ski out the back door in winter and golf out the back door in summer.**

Pampering treatments, state-of-the-art exercise equipment, aerobics classes, an indoor lap pool, and a host of other facilities and services have consistently garnered the spa rave reviews since it opened in 1992. The same cannot be said of the hotel, though through no fault of the current owners. Carefree Resorts purchased it in the fall of 1993, and has only just started to attempt to bring the hotel up to the standards of others it owns, most notably the Boulders in Arizona.

Their task is complicated by what they have to work with. The rooms tend to be of average to smallish size for a hotel of this caliber, though they are partly redeemed by balconies (on two-thirds of the rooms), custom oak woodwork, TVs with VCRs, and baths with separate showers and tubs. New soft goods have already given them vitality they lacked. Moreover, this new management stresses services, like a ski valet to tune skis and heat boots overnight and a KidSpa to entertain 6- to 11-year-olds while their parents go off to ski.

The hotel does have other assets, including five tennis courts, squash and racquetball courts, and a climbing wall. The Great Room draws a crowd in front of its fireplace for a winter après-ski of light hors d'oeuvres and entertainment. And lift tickets can be purchased right on site. But for now, the Peaks must be regarded as a work in progress.

Pennington's Mountain Village Inn

Telluride Mountain Village
100 Pennington Court
P.O. Box 2428
Telluride, CO 81435
303-728-5337
800-543-1437
Fax: 303-728-5338

> *A seductive inn
> enhanced by
> awesome
> mountain vistas*

Innkeepers: Judith and Michael Maclean. **Accommodations:** 9 rooms, 3 suites. **Rates:** (Higher over Christmas holidays) Rooms, winter (late November–early April) $125–$150, summer (early June–mid-September) $175–$200, spring/fall $140; suites, winter $175–$250, summer $200–$225, spring/fall $165. **Included:** Full breakfast. **Minimum stay:** 2 nights over summer and winter weekends, 3–4 nights during summer festivals, 3–7 nights over Christmas holidays. **Added:** 12% tax. **Payment:** Major credit cards. **Children:** Welcome. **Pets:** Prohibited. **Smoking:** Prohibited except in one room. **Open:** Year-round except first 2 weeks in May and first 2 weeks in November.

Even if Pennington's were not a seductive French country bed-and-breakfast, all elegance and upscale amenities, its to-die-for views of the majestic San Juan Mountains could probably keep all its rooms filled.

Though decorated and furnished differently, the sumptuous rooms share a love of warm colors and stylish window treatments. Some have brass and iron beds, others canopy, sleigh, or pine four-posters. All have large private baths with deluxe toiletries. Tucked into every room is a sitting area, telephone, remote-control color television, and a private refrigerator stocked with complimentary soft drinks, juice, and snacks (though the television really ought to be hidden from sight in an armoire as it is in the suites — both the TV and the exposed refrigerator obtrude on the room's French country ambience). Most prized are the balconies, which command unobstructed views of the mountains.

Poised on a ridge alongside a golf course, 4½ miles from the historic town of Telluride and a mile below the ski lifts, this stone and stucco inn opened in 1989 with justified fanfare. It quickly took a place among Colorado's most distinctive inns.

Guests who can't bring themselves to leave their sleeping quarters in the morning can have breakfast delivered. Others gather in the sunny, high-ceilinged Victorian dining room downstairs. Both have a choice of daily specials — perhaps blueberry pancakes, or egg blossoms — served with meats, fruit, and juice. The Macleans, who manage the inn, are often on hand to see to guests' other needs.

Its generally accommodating service aside, the elegant inn lavishes guests with creature comforts. A two-sided fireplace warms a library lounge with books and games and the adjacent living room, both of which look out on the golf course and mountains. Hors d'oeuvres and beverages set out in the late afternoon bring guests together, as does a 12-person indoor Jacuzzi, huge steam room, and a game room with a pool table. There are lockers for ski or golf equipment and even laundry facilities.

If Pennington's has a drawback, it's the neither-here-nor-there location. Nothing is within convenient walking distance. Skiers face a short commute to the mountain (though a free shuttle stops half a block away), while Telluride's shops and restaurants are a 10-minute drive. But for many people, that's a small price to pay for those breathtaking views.

The San Sophia

330 West Pacific Avenue
P.O. Box 1825
Telluride, CO 81435
303-728-3001
800-537-4781
Fax: 303-728-6226

> *A neo-Victorian inn,*
> *smack in town,*
> *steps from the lifts*

Innkeepers: Gary and Dianne Eschman. **Accommodations:** 16 rooms. **Rates:** Summer (early May–late October) $85–$120, winter (late November–early April) $125–$180, higher over Christmas holidays and during some summer festivals. **Included:** Full breakfast. **Minimum stay:** During the Christmas holidays and some summer festivals. **Added:** 10% tax. **Payment:** Major credit cards. **Children:** Over age 10. **Pets:** Prohibited. **Smoking:** Prohibited. **Open:** Year-round.

Historic Telluride's most talked about inn, the San Sophia has been dazzling guests with its luxurious rooms and what-else-can-we-do-for-you hospitality since it opened in 1990.

Gary and Dianne Eschman, who designed the inn, carved out irregularly shaped rooms and furnished them with queen-size brass beds, handmade quilts, two-person tubs, pedestal sinks, pine armoires with remote-control televisions (and in some cases VCRs), phones, terrycloth robes, thirsty towels, and an array of toiletries. They designed the breakfast room with a two-story wall of windows so it's flooded with light. They installed a hot tub beneath a gazebo on the deck to take advantage of commanding views of the San Juan Mountains and Telluride's fabled ski slopes. They made room for a library with a gas-log fireplace and a complimentary video library of their favorite movies. They hung Gary's arresting black-and-white photos around the inn. They even thought of covered parking, boot warmers, and storage lockers for ski equipment. And they included a huge breakfast served at tables topped with apricot linens and fresh flowers.

> Set in the middle of the former mining town's National Historic District, the gabled and turreted neo-Victorian pays homage to the architecture around it, right down to its stained glass and bay windows.

The inn's convenient location, a block from the Oak Street ski lift and an easy walk to the town's shops and restaurants, is another asset. So is the amiable staff. All that attention to detail has made the San Sophia the finest place to stay in town.

Skyline Guest Ranch and Ski Lodge

7214 Highway 145
P.O. Box 67
Telluride, CO 81435
303-728-3757
Fax: 303-728-6728

> *A guest ranch near the top of the world*

Proprietors: Dave and Sherry Farny.
Accommodations: 10 rooms, 6 cottages, all with private bath.
Rates: Rooms, summer (June–October) $960/person/week, winter (mid-December–March), single $75, double $125; cabins, summer $960/person/week, winter $200/couple. **Included:** All meals, horseback riding, and most ranch activities in summer, full breakfast and shuttle to Telluride ski slopes in winter. **Minimum stay:** 7 nights in summer. **Added:** 6%

tax. **Payment:** Major credit cards. **Children:** Free under age 2. **Pets:** Prohibited. **Smoking:** Prohibited. **Open:** Mid-June through early October and mid-December through March.

Cradled in the awesome grandeur of the snow-capped San Juan Mountains, the 160-acre collection of funky weathered buildings, sparkling lakes, and meadows splashed with wildflowers basks in mystical beauty. The heady, rarefied air at 9,600 feet no doubt contributes to the sensation. But those who go back time and again agree, the ranch's most irresistible elements are Dave and Sherry Farny. Lovers of the outdoors themselves, they never seem happier than when introducing others to the joys of riding, hiking, and exploring in Colorado's magnificent high country.

> At any season, the Farnys' strong sense of community binds the ranch together. It's because of them as much as the spectacular alpine setting that one guest described Skyline as "a spiritual retreat masquerading as a ranch."

Originally, the Farnys bought a former logging camp as a base for their Telluride Mountaineering School. They later purchased another 320 acres higher in the mountains where they could go on overnight pack trips. Those two parcels and the surrounding Uncompahgre National Forest allow them many options for activities. Among the elements that distinguish Skyline from other ranches is the serendipitous quality to the weekly summer schedule. More often than not, the Farnys decide on each day's activities at dinner the night before, learning guests' preferences and making up plans as they go along. They choose staff who, like themselves, thrive on being accommodating.

There is always a lot of time on horseback in the mix, and the Farnys are committed to teaching riding. They encourage guests to learn every aspect of horse care, too, including saddling, feeding, and currying the animals. Beyond that, a typical summer week affords opportunities for hiking, four-wheeling, climbing to the top of a 14,000-foot peak, trout fishing, or an excursion to the Indian cliff dwellings in Mesa Verde National Park. All of these are part of the ranch package, as is use of the hot tub and sauna.

Everyone gathers in the lodge for breakfast and tasty ranch-style dinners (lunch is usually eaten somewhere out on the trail) and around the potbelly stove in the living room after helping to clear the table — guests aren't here to be waited on but to participate. Entertainment could be chamber music or a square dance. Some people drive into Telluride, eight miles away, to catch a movie or any of its many summer festivals. The rooms they come back to are clean and cozy.

In winter, Dave and Sherry turn the ranch over to their daughter, Cindy. The emphasis shifts to cross-country skiing in the surrounding back country and to superb cuisine — some say better than anything available in Telluride — with the restaurant open to the public as well.

WAUNITA HOT SPRINGS

Waunita Hot Springs Ranch

8007 County Road 887
P.O. Box 1
Gunnison, CO 81230
303-641-1266

*A guest ranch
with hot springs*

Proprietors: Rod and Junelle Pringle. **Accommodations:** 22 rooms. **Rates:** Rooms, single $900/week, double $1,680/week. **Included:** All meals and most activities. **Minimum stay:** 7 nights in summer, 3 nights after Labor Day. **Added:** 3.75% tax. **Payment:** Cash, personal checks, or traveler's checks. **Children:** Reduced rates under age 16. **Pets:** Prohibited. **Smoking:** Prohibited, as is alcohol. **Open:** Early June to late September.

As the name suggests, Waunita Hot Springs Ranch, 26 miles east of Gunnison, is an unusual hybrid: a traditional guest ranch supplemented by its own private artesian hot springs. Its history dates back hundreds of years to the era when American Indians hunted deer, elk, and buffalo in the area near what is now Gunnison, Colorado. Between hunts, they often relaxed in the springs, which are said to be the hottest in Colorado, to cure ailments and relieve aching muscles.

> **The Pringles also run an excellent riding program. Every trip begins with instruction, whether it's a one-hour ride into the surrounding ranchlands or an all-day excursion above the timberline to a 12,000-foot aerie with sweeping views of the spectacular West Elk, Collegiate, and San Juan ranges.**

The hot springs' transformation from public pools to commercial spa occurred in 1890, when a Chicago doctor became convinced of the springs' therapeutic potential and built permanent structures to house guests and patients. Among them were cabins, a three-story guest house, a bathhouse, swimming pool, and a complete hospital. Its heyday as a health retreat lasted until the doctor's death in 1928.

The spa changed hands many times over the years and was badly neglected until 1962, when Rod and Junelle Pringle resurrected Waunita as a guest ranch. Miraculously, a few of the original buildings survived, among them one cabin from 1890, the guest house built in 1915, and the 1921 clubhouse. The Pringles converted the latter two into lodges, upgrading the baths with modern fixtures but preserving the old ranch decor. Earth tones, heavy oak furnishings, and paneling, some of it depicting western wildlife, predominate.

The simplicity of the rooms fits with the tone of the ranch. Warm and unpretentious, the Pringles and their staff make guests feel like family, right down to inviting them into the kitchen. They encourage families to stay by having some adjoining rooms, with bunk beds on one side and a queen-size bed on the other. Alcohol is banned. Evenings begin with hearty family-style meals, followed almost every night by some kind of activity, whether it's a hayride, square dance, movie, or the Pringle family and ranch staff's music show.

Though there is no organized children's program, children as young as five can learn basic horsemanship, and the program is designed so that even rank beginners can handle some of the longer trail rides offered late in the week. At the end of the day, guests return to enjoy the hot springs, which now feed a 90-foot swimming pool, in much the same way as the Indians did, relaxing after a day of riding in the high country.

Montana

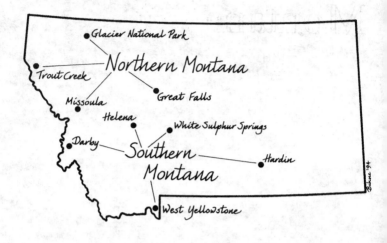

Meriwether Lewis and William Clark logged roughly 8,000 miles on their journey to explore America's newly acquired Louisiana Purchase and search for a route to the Pacific Ocean. More than a quarter of those miles were in Montana, as they followed the course of the Missouri River through the northern tier and the Yellowstone through the southern. The two centuries since have wrought unalterable changes, of course, yet in places Montana seems as exciting and new as the territory Lewis and Clark traversed. It remains a fascinating place to explore.

To anyone who has not visited Montana, the nickname "the Big Sky State" may seem like breathless boosterism. Once there, however, visitors discover something unexpected in the landscapes. Maybe it's a trick of light in the clear air, the rare beauty of its fertile valleys, or the way glacier-sculpted mountains form majestic palisades, but whatever it is creates a sense of extraordinary expansiveness, as if the sky over Montana were in fact somehow bigger. And in a way, that is true: only three states (Alaska, California, and Texas) cover more area. Yet fewer than 800,000 people live in Montana's 147,000 square miles; only Alaska and Wyoming are more sparsely populated.

The name itself, from the Spanish word for "mountain-ous," evokes partially misleading images of a state hump-backed with peaks. Nevertheless, the eastern three-fifths of the state owe their topography to the Great Plains rather than the Rockies. Nearly one-fifth of the state's residents live in just two cities on those plains: Billings, with 68,000 residents, and Great Falls, with 57,000. Elsewhere, millions of cattle and sheep graze over the gently rolling landscape, filling in the spaces between the generally small and widely scattered towns. It is western Montana whose topography inspired the state's name. There, mountain ranges alternate with valleys to create green corridors lined with jagged peaks. The scenery is most dramatic in Glacier National Park along the Canadian border. Rugged and unspoiled, its one million glacier-chiseled acres have changed little since Meriwether Lewis first saw them in 1806. Nor has the backcountry of the Bob Marshall Wilderness just to its south.

In many ways, Montana remains close to its frontier roots. Without sounding ridiculous, people can say, "God made man with two legs — one for each side of a horse." Cowboy boots continue to be more fashionable than shoes. The state's guest ranches rank with the best on the planet, ranging from genuine working spreads where guests can help work cattle to resort ranches with tennis courts and racing sloops and posh, sybaritic havens known as much for their creature comforts as the quality of their mounts.

Ranchers helped to make Montana what it is. So did miners, lured to the gold fields in Bannack and Alder Gulch, an atmosphere now recreated in Virginia City and Nevada City. The state capital of Helena also began as a gold mining camp known as Last Chance, then evolved into the state capital. Elsewhere, towns sprang up along the rail lines. All of those left legacies of historic buildings in the form of hotels, log lodges and cabins, and turn-of-the-century houses and mansions, many of which accommodate overnight visitors.

What they come for varies. Recreation abounds, of course. All told, Montana has 17 million acres of national forest, three million acres of wilderness, seven national wildlife refuges, and 313 state parks, recreation areas, and fishing accesses, and two national parks: Glacier and a portion of Yellowstone. Large game animals abound, among them moose, elk, deer, grizzly and black bears, bighorn sheep, and mountain goats. Herds of skittish pronghorns run free on prairie. And a flock of 500 trumpeter swans, once almost extinct, live around Yellowstone, Hebgen, and Red Rocks lakes.

The state's fly-fishing is legendary, especially on such Blue Ribbon waters as the Gallatin, Madison, and Yellowstone Rivers. Montana also has the largest natural freshwater lake west of the Mississippi, plenty of golf courses, and several notable winter ski areas — Big Mountain, Big Sky, and Bridger Bowl among them. Every June, the battle between General Custer and the Northern Plains Indians is reenacted at Little Bighorn Battlefield National Monument. And there is summer theater in Bigfork, outdoor music festivals in Big Sky, and rodeos everywhere.

For an exceptionally useful free guide to Montana's varied attractions, contact Travel Montana, 1424 9th Avenue, Helena, MT 59620 (406-444-2654 or 800-847-4868).

Northern Montana

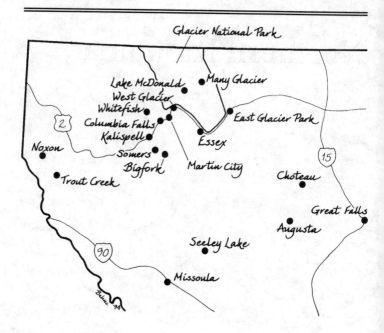

Best Bed-and-Breakfast Homes

Bigfork
O'Duach'Ain Country Inn
Columbia Falls
Plum Creek House Bed & Breakfast
Turn in the River Inn
Great Falls
The Sarah Bed-and-Breakfast Inn
Sovekammer Bed and Breakfast
Seeley Lake
Emily A. Bed & Breakfast
Somers
Osprey Inn Bed & Breakfast

Best Bed-and-Breakfast Inns

Columbia Falls
Bad Rock Country Bed & Breakfast
Missoula
Goldsmith's Bed & Breakfast
Noxon
Bighorn Lodge
West Glacier
Mountain Timbers Lodge
Whitefish
Duck Inn
The Garden Wall

Best Condominiums, Apartments, and Cabins

Martin City
Abbott Valley Accommodations

Best Guest Ranches

Augusta
Klick's K Bar L Ranch "Beyond All Roads"
Bigfork
Averill's Flathead Lake Lodge & Dude Ranch

Choteau
  Pine Butte Guest Ranch
Trout Creek
  Blue Spruce Lodge & Guest Ranch

Best Historic Hotels, Inns, and Lodges

Essex
  Izaak Walton Inn
Kalispell
  Historic Kalispell Hotel

Best National Park Lodges

  Glacier National Park
  Glacier Park Lodge
  Lake McDonald Lodge
  Many Glacier Hotel

Best Resorts and Spas

Whitefish
  Grouse Mountain Lodge

Best Ski Area Hotels & Lodges

Whitefish
  Kandahar Lodge

Apart from the Fort Union Trading Post National Historic Site in Sidney on the border with North Dakota, all of the major attractions in Montana's northern tier lie west of center, where the plains end and the mountains begin. In practical terms, that means virtually everything of interest in northern Montana lies within a 2½-hour drive of **Glacier National Park.** That's as it should be, for if you see nothing else, you ought to visit Glacier.

Established in 1910, the park merged in 1932 with Canada's Waterton Lakes National Park to form the Waterton-Glacier International Peace Park. Together they cover 1,600 square miles on both sides of the Continental Divide. About

50 small glaciers remain, the largest of them Grinnell, which covers 300 acres and is up to 400 feet deep in places. However, it's less the glaciers themselves that lure two million people each year than the wonderland of craggy peaks and ridges, deep valleys, and sparkling lakes they sculpted during several Ice Ages. It is a primitive, rugged place that shelters some 60 species of mammals — grizzly bears and wolves among them — and 200 species of birds.

More than 700 miles of trails lace the interior, but there is only a single highway, leaving much of the backcountry accessible only to those willing to take off on foot. Nevertheless, that one highway, the two-lane Going-to-the-Sun Road, ranks among the most glorious routes in the country. Fifty miles long, it links the east and west sides of the park on a cliff-hanging zigzag route best suited to mountain goats, many of which can be seen along the way. It crosses the Continental Divide at Logan Pass, whose 6,680-foot elevation affords 100-mile views in every direction of the surrounding peaks, glaciers, and lakes.

Below the park is the fabled Bob Marshall Wilderness, the nation's second largest and best known tract of primitive backcountry. Two other wildernesses border the "Bob," and together they make up a 1.5-million-acre complex devoid of roads but open to fishermen, hikers, campers, and horseback riders along 1,800 miles of trails.

There is more to Montana than wilderness, however. To the west of Glacier and the Bob stretches the Flathead Valley, a broad, green plain framed by the Mission and Swan mountain ranges to the east and the Flathead range to the west. It contains Flathead Lake, the largest freshwater lake in the western U.S. and renowned for its salmon fishing. The valley itself abounds in recreation, including eight golf courses. In winter, Big Mountain at the head of the Flathead Valley near **Whitefish** lures skiers with its 4,000 skiable acres — more even than Vail — consistent snow, and short lift lines.

Scattered elsewhere across this tier are two important cities: **Helena,** the state capital, whose Montana Historical Society Museum has a fine collection of Charles M. Russell's art, a historical library, and a gallery of Montana photography; and **Great Falls,** the largest of the northern cities, whose C.M. Russell Museum Complex holds the most complete collection of Russell's works and memorabilia as well as his original log cabin studio and home.

AUGUSTA

Klick's K Bar L Ranch
"Beyond All Roads"

Augusta, MT 59410
Summer/fall: 406-467-2771
Winter/spring: 406-562-3589

*A guest and
fishing ranch
inaccessible
by road*

Proprietors: Dick and Nancy Klick. **Accommodations:** 14 cabins with shared baths. **Rates:** $690/person for 6 days. **Included:** All meals, activities, and taxes. **Minimum stay:** 6 days. **Added:** Nothing. **Payment:** Cash, personal checks, or traveler's checks. **Children:** Over age 5 preferred. **Pets:** Prohibited. **Smoking:** Allowed. **Open:** Early June to early September.

As its nickname suggests, Klick's K Bar L Ranch literally lies "beyond all roads." The 40-acre spread trails along the upper end of Gibson Reservoir, roughly 25 miles west of Augusta on the very doorstep of the Bob Marshall Wilderness Area. There are only two routes in: by boat up the reservoir or by pack mule or on foot over a scenic seven-mile mountain trail.

That far-flung location seems to promise an escape from the rigors of 20th-century living, but physical remoteness is only the first of the ranch's assets. From the time it was founded, it has been a family operation. Dick Klick's parents built the log ranchhouse in 1927 on the banks of the Sun River's trout-filled North Fork. The main house is a classic western lodge, now with electric power supplied by the ranch's own hydroelectric generators. Guests gather before a soot-blackened stone fireplace in a living room fitted out with pine furnishings, Indian blankets, animal hides, hunting trophies, and library.

Paths from the main house lead to the edge of the woods and 14 rustic cabins, ranging in size from one to three rooms. All have porches, wood floors, Navajo rugs, woodstoves, Hudson Bay blankets, tin washbasins, and a tap just outside that supplies filtered drinking water. They share several clean, strategically placed bathhouses containing toilets and hot showers.

Dick Klick himself is a master guide who was born in nearby Great Falls, grew up on the ranch, and says he doesn't know anything else. He and his wife Nancy belong to that tough breed of westerner: self-reliant, a little slow to warm up to strangers, but absolutely committed to tradition and to old-fashioned standards of excellence. Wranglers wear cowboy hats, not baseball caps. Those staff members who aren't family are people the Klicks know and trust.

> **Riding enthusiasts can mount superb, professionally trained horses. Anglers have a professional fly fishing guide at their disposal and can, if they're adept, catch and release as many as 70 trout a day.**

With a million and a half acres of some of the Rocky Mountains' most rugged and imposing backcountry wilderness at its back door, the K Bar L has miles of riding trails. Several of the most popular climb steeply before reaching buttes and open meadows, with panoramic views of the lake and mountains. Other rides approach salt licks where elk congregate. The ranch also operates overnight pack trips that make it possible to spend days at a time deep within the wilderness. Children may ride, but there is no organized program for them.

Dinners at the ranch are typically hearty western fare: steaks, fried chicken, spaghetti, or ham, served with homemade breads and pies. Beer and soda are available, but guests must bring their own wine and liquor. After dinner, some guests head for the ranch's hot springs pool to soak under the stars, others gather at friends' cabins for drinks and conversation. Occasionally, there are volleyball and softball games. Fishermen often head back out for a few more casts. Mainly, though, people relax and enjoy this remote outpost of tranquility, far from the rigors of civilization.

BIGFORK

Averill's Flathead Lake Lodge and Dude Ranch

Flathead Lake Lodge Road
P.O. Box 248
Bigfork, MT 59911-0248
406-837-4391
Fax: 406-837-6977

> *The guest ranch*
> *as resort,*
> *with superb*
> *family programs*

Proprietor: Doug Averill. **Accommodations:** 20 rooms and 17 cabins, all with private bath. **Rates:** $1,343/person/week. **Included:** All meals and activities. **Minimum stay:** 7 nights. **Added:** 4% tax on lodging portion. **Payment:** MasterCard, Visa. **Children:** Reduced rates under age 20. **Pets:** Prohibited. **Smoking:** Allowed. **Open:** Mid-June–early September.

In 1945, everyone thought Don Averill was crazy to buy 2,000 timbered acres along Flathead Lake with the notion of opening a dude ranch. Half a century later, with his son Doug at the helm, Averill's Flathead Lake Lodge has become one of the country's most successful operations, with a reputation for energetic staff and topnotch children's programs. Every Sunday in summer a new batch of 120 guests — about a quarter of them kids — arrives, new cowboy hats and boots in hand, lured by the horseback riding and a feast of other recreation.

The road into the ranch edges along the corrals through fir and cedar forest before coming to the massive log lodge. Rustic and welcoming, with a huge stone fireplace and the obligatory moose heads, this gathering place sets the tone of informality that extends to fancy home-style meals. "Guests don't dress up for dinner," says Doug Averill, "they clean up," before chowing down on baron of beef, Cornish game hen, or perhaps ribs.

The lodge anchors a line of cabins, the oldest of them with moss-covered roofs but all ideal as family accommodations. They have two or three bedrooms, a sitting room, log furniture, country fabrics, and pine paneling. The rooms, most in a second log lodge, feature cozy western decor with quilts.

Cabins and lodges constitute standard western fare, as do the morning and afternoon trail rides and the weekly steak fry. But Averill's is far from a simple dude ranch. That vast

> **Averill's has evolved far beyond the off-the-shelf dude ranch into a virtual resort.**

lake at its doorstep has inspired an array of water sports, among them sailing, canoeing, and water skiing. The ranch also acquire the *Questa*, a 51-foot racing sloop, which it uses for sailing lessons and cruises. A heated swimming pool and tennis courts supplement hiking trails. During the week the ranch offers special activities (at added cost), such as fly-fishing, whitewater rafting, and tours to Glacier National Park, an hour north.

To free parents to enjoy all of this, Averill's runs a highly structured and diversified children's program, which effectively entertains kids age 6 and up from morning until night (with babysitters available for those younger). Kids can learn to ride (the ranch even has small saddles) and care for horses, camp out in a tepee, fish, swim, sail, or do arts and crafts, all under the staff's watchful eye. They even eat dinner early and go off for an evening ride so parents can dine in peace. Just don't expect them to be happy to leave, and don't wait until after February to make reservations.

O'Duach'Ain Country Inn

675 Ferndale Drive
Bigfork, MT 59911
406-837-6851
800-837-7460
Fax: 406-837-4390

> *A homey B&B near art galleries and summer theater*

Innkeepers: Tom and Margot Doohan. **Accommodations:** 5 rooms, 2 with private bath. **Rates:** Single $70–$90, double $80–$100. **Included:** Full breakfast. **Minimum stay:** None. **Added:** 4% tax. **Payment:** Major credit cards. **Children:** Welcome. **Pets:** Prohibited. **Smoking:** Prohibited. **Open:** Year-round.

O'Duach'Ain is the Gaelic version of Doohan and means "of the black hound." There are no black hounds at this three-level log home on five acres of woods a few miles south of the arty town of Bigfork. There is, however, a bulldog named Winston who placed first in the Kalispell auditions for David Letterman's "Stupid Pet Tricks" by demonstrating his penchant for playing with a 16-pound bowling ball. Though Winston was never called on to make a national appearance, he performs hopefully for every guest who comes to stay at this warm country house, upstaging the other dogs, cats, peacocks, horses, birds, tropical fish, and even the rare 34-inch-tall Sicilian donkey that completes the Doohans' menagerie.

> **Homey rather than luxurious, most rooms have brass or four-poster beds, comforters, decanters of brandy, and eccentric touches — a jumble of things Japanese in one, 1940s and 1950s memorabilia in another.**

Margot and Tom Doohan have the innate warmth and accommodating personalities of born innkeepers. They opened their lodgelike home to guests in 1985, using its three small downstairs bedrooms, which share one bath, as guest rooms. Later, they added on, creating two more rooms with private baths and outside decks in what had been a hayloft above the detached garage out back.

The main attraction of the house may be its two-story vaulted living room, with log walls, timber roof, antiques, western saddles, Indian blankets, and southwestern art. But guests (including former President George Bush's son Neil, when he stayed here) tend to gather in the kitchen with the Doohans or in the hot tub outside on the deck.

Breakfasts are hearty; Margot prepares stuffed Irish toast, Irish soda bread, "Dutch babies," or eggs and bacon and other American favorites. There are hiking trails in the woods that are good for cross-country skiing in winter. Nearby Bigfork has art galleries, a couple of good restaurants, and summer theater.

CHOTEAU

Pine Butte Guest Ranch

HC 58, Box 34C
Choteau, MT 59422
406-466-2158

> *A dude ranch for the
> environmentally aware*

General managers: Lee and Genny Barhaugh. **Accommodations:** 10 cabins. **Rates:** June–August $950/week, otherwise $110/day, $750/week. **Included:** All meals, most activities; airport transfers on week-long stays. **Minimum stay:** 2 nights; 7 nights early June–mid-September. **Added:** 4% tax to lodging portion only. **Payment:** Cash, personal checks, or traveler's checks. **Children:** Reduced rates for children under 12; recommended for those over age 8 interested in nature. **Pets:** Prohibited. **Smoking:** Prohibited in lodge. **Open:** May through early October.

Set in the rolling prairie just east of Montana's vast Bob Marshall Wilderness, Pine Butte Guest Ranch could pass for a typical dude ranch, which it was for almost half a century. But in 1979 The Nature Conservancy — a private, nonprofit organization dedicated to saving plants, animals, and their habitats from extinction — bought both the ranch and 18,000 acres of wetlands nearby now designated as the Pine Butte Swamp Preserve. Since then, the ranch has sought to lure not so much would-be cowboys as people interested in learning about nature and the environment.

During the core of the summer, from early June to mid-September, the main activities are optional: twice-a-day horseback rides and a daily hike or tour led by a resident naturalist. The rides — most of them nose-to-tail sorties lasting roughly two hours — typically light out for the high country in the hope of getting close to wildlife. The scenery can be breathtaking; the meadows are full of purple lupine, yellow hornbells, and monkey flowers. But city slickers hoping to gallop across the prairie will be disappointed: the horses provide a means of transportation, not a chance to master equestrian skills.

In the spring and fall, the emphasis shifts to natural history tours and workshops on everything from mammal tracking to photography and paleontology. Passionate in their concern for habitat, the guides occasionally interject appeals for contributions to the Nature Conservancy cause.

Guests stay in timber and stone cabins scattered across an open, grassy slope above the aspens and cottonwoods that line the South Fork of the Teton River. The oldest date from the 1930s, the youngest from the 1980s, but all have native stone fireplaces, porches, private baths, and handmade hardwood or pine furniture (two of them readily accommodate families, though the ranch does not offer organized children's programs or babysitting). None is far from the heated pool or the main lodge, which has a dining room (the fare is lighter and healthier than traditional ranch cuisine), sitting room, laundry room, and an adjacent cabin with displays of fossils and photographs and a gift shop with books, maps, and souvenirs.

Emphasis is on nature hikes. Some treks head up to a crystal blue alpine lake in search of shaggy mountain goats; others visit the preserve looking for signs of grizzly bears. Birds abound, making it a paradise for bird watchers. Another guided hike visits the excavation site of Egg Mountain, one of the world's richest fossil beds, famous for its dinosaur eggs.

COLUMBIA FALLS

Bad Rock Country Bed & Breakfast

480 Bad Rock Drive
Columbia Falls, MT 59912
406-892-2829
800-422-3666
Fax: 406-892-2930

*A 1970s home in
a pastoral setting*

Innkeepers: Sue and Jonathan Alper. **Accommodations:** 7 rooms, all with private bath. **Rates:** $90–$125; lower rates spring and fall. **Included:** Full breakfast. **Minimum stay:** None. **Added:** 4% tax. **Payment:** Major credit cards. **Children:** Over age 9. **Pets:** Prohibited (but free boarding of horses). **Smoking:** Prohibited. **Open:** Year-round.

A ranch-style home built in the late 1970s, Bad Rock Country Bed & Breakfast reposes on 30 acres of alfalfa fields and pasture 15 miles west of the entrance to Glacier National Park. Its circular drive swings past a restored red and green 1918 John Deere grain wagon parked in the front yard. A barnlike garage stands to one side, not far from two cabins constructed of square-hewn logs.

This pastoral vision was in fact built by a bank executive. Sue and John Alper bought it in 1992. For Sue, it marked a return to her Montana roots; for them both, it was a chance to realize a dream of introducing visitors to Montana country living. To do so, they filled their new home with period furnishings, mainly from the 1850s to 1920s, many of them her family's heirlooms, and converted the garage into quarters for themselves. What emerged was a bed-and-breakfast long on understated elegance and attentive hospitality.

The house itself has three guest rooms, all of them decorated in contemporary western style and outfitted with brass beds, a mixture of antiques and reproduction furnishings, and private bath. The master bedroom stands out for its four-poster brass bed, private balcony, and bath with steam shower (but no tub). The cabins have locally made lodgepole pine beds, sitting areas with convertible sofas, and private decks. All of the rooms have the added amenities of thermal loft comforters, robes, beach towels, and thongs — those last few to make it easy to use the outdoor hot tub in the back yard, with views across the pasture to the slopes of Big Mountain.

> **The Alpers added the two cabins in 1994, replicating the Old West style of a Montana settler's dwelling. The cabins have two oversize rooms, both equipped with fireplaces.**

Hot tubs are normally communal affairs, but at Bad Rock the Alpers have guests sign up for half-hour private soaking sessions. So guests gather instead in the front room, which has a fireplace, a library of books about Montana, and views east to Columbia Mountain, or in the downstairs family room, where the Alpers have installed a television, a microwave for popcorn, and a refrigerator stocked with juices, seltzers, and ice.

The best of hosts, the Alpers greet guests every afternoon with hors d'oeuvres and every morning with huge breakfasts often featuring Sundance eggs (a Mexican egg dish) or a phyllo sausage bake, Montana potato pie, and huckleberry muffins.

Plum Creek House Bed & Breakfast

985 Vans Avenue
Columbia Falls, MT 59912
Reservations:
406-892-1816
800-682-1429
Fax: 406-892-1876

A former timber baron's home overlooking the Flathead River

Innkeepers: Caroline and Bob Stevens. **Accommodations:** 5 rooms, all with private bath. **Rates:** June–September, $80–$95, otherwise $65–$75. **Included:** Full breakfast. **Minimum stay:** None. **Added:** 4% tax. **Payment:** Major credit cards. **Children:** Welcome; roll-aways available. **Pets:** Kennel available. **Smoking:** Prohibited. **Open:** Year-round.

This 5,000-square-foot country manor trails along a bluff above the Flathead River in a residential neighborhood a mile from Columbia Falls and 15 miles from the Camus Entrance to Glacier National Park. It was built in 1957 by D.C. Dunham, the founder of the Plum Creek Timber Company, who hand-picked every piece of interior wood. Yet it is neither the house's ultra-solid construction nor the charm of its plum-colored board-and-batten architecture that seduces guests, but its unobstructed views across a wild and scenic stretch of the river to 7,200-foot Columbia Mountain.

Caroline and Bob Stevens, who had run their own bed-and-breakfast in Oregon before retiring to Montana, bought the house in 1990 and spent two years renovating the interiors. Her eye for color and style has given it an elegance and charm to match the views out the windows. Dunham's original dining room set survives, but otherwise the furnishings — a mixture of contemporary and antique — are the Stevenses'.

Of the five guest rooms, the former master bedroom stands

out for its views of the river, mountains, and park. It has a two-poster bed covered with a floral-print quilted comforter, wallpaper in rich pinks, Caroline's collection of dolls, and a large bath with separate tub and shower. The two rooms at the front of the house lack that view (although one does have an oblique perspective on the river) but feature queen-size beds, TVs and VCRs (the Stevenses have a collection of 300 videotapes for guests to use), phones,

> **To make the most of the river and mountain panorama, decks extend all along the back of the house, ending at a heated pool and Jacuzzi.**

coffeemakers, thick terrycloth robes, a scattering of antiques, and private baths.

There are two additional rooms on the pine-paneled lower level, which opens out onto yet another scenic deck. Both of these bedrooms have river views, though the larger features a fireplace, private patio, fold-out couch, and enough room for a roll-away, making it the best choice for a family. There's also a kitchen exclusively for guests' use, complete with dishes, pots and pans, a stove, microwave, refrigerator, and dishwasher. This entire level can be rented as a kitchen suite to accommodate two couples or a family.

A huge breakfast, served either in the dining room or on the sun porch — both of which have views of the river — may consist of a French bread and cheese casserole with ham, bacon, or sausage, Grand Marnier French toast, or scrambled eggs, ham and biscuits. Guests are welcome to use the barbecues on the outside decks, and there's Montana Coffee Traders coffee whenever they want it. But beyond that, the Stevenses have an innate sense for catering to guest needs and a love of conversation.

Turn in the River Inn

51 Penney Lane
Columbia Falls, MT 59912
Reservations: P.O. Box 1356
Whitefish, MT 59937
406-257-0724
800-892-2474

*A contemporary
farmhouse
as appealing
as its owners*

Innkeepers: Judy and Don Spivey.
Accommodations: 4 rooms, all with private bath. **Rates:** $85–$110. **Included:** Full breakfast, airport or train pickup. **Minimum stay:** None. **Added:** 4% tax. **Payment:** MasterCard, Visa. **Children:** Welcome. **Pets:** With prior approval (they have a dog). **Smoking:** Prohibited. **Open:** Year-round

The open kitchen at the two-story Turn in the River Inn was designed so that Judy and Don Spivey, whose house this is, could remain in contact with their guests. They succeeded beyond their hopes: "It seems to be the place everyone likes to gather," says Judy.

Built as a bed-and-breakfast, the house has other wonderful public spaces: a great room with a massive river rock fireplace, a music room with a baby grand piano, a TV/VCR lounge with a collection of John Wayne movies and nature videos. Yet guests seem to spend mornings and late afternoons in the kitchen when they're around, probably because that's where they're most likely to encounter Judy and Don.

The Spiveys' personal exuberance shows in the house itself, which their architect son designed as a contemporary farmhouse. The two-story home perches on 35 acres overlooking the Whitefish River, half an hour from Glacier National Park and 20 minutes from the ski slopes at Big Mountain. Inside, sunlight streaming through the windows gives added warmth to interiors abounding in wood, larch and fir mostly, and to the craftsmanship of local carpenters and masons who built the cabinets, stair rails, and fireplace. Walls display the memorabilia of their lives — Judy's sister's colorful handmade quilts, for example, or found objects like an old Coke sign or quirky sculptures made from junk.

That same warmth extends to the rooms. The largest is the wheelchair-accessible Alaska Room on the main floor. It has larch built-ins, a bent-willow headboard, and wicker furnishings. The two upstairs rooms, though smaller, have windows on two sides and pine and maple beds, and comforters in Judy's colorful duvet covers. Phones and cable televisions can be installed on request. And children too old to share a room with their parents can sometimes be accommodated in Judy's workroom downstairs.

> The Spiveys bring a rare enthusiasm to their role as innkeepers. Native Californians who retired to Montana after living all over the western U.S. and in Germany, they seem to thrive on having people in the house, dishing out hors d'oeuvres and beverages every afternoon as an opportunity to find out what their guests have been up to all day.

Besides the guest quarters in the house, there is a fourth, even larger room above the garage. It has two queen-size beds, a large bath, and kitchenette. Guests can have breakfast there or in the house, and have full access to the inn's facilities.

Wherever guests stay, they can look forward to finding a tray of coffee or tea outside the room early in the morning before breakfast, and at night a turned-down bed with fresh sheets and locally made truffles or huckleberry cordials. In summer, there are fresh flowers from the gardens outside.

Breakfast could be quiche, blintzes, an omelet with artichokes, or a show-stopping Belgian waffle with fresh fruit and cream. Whatever the Spiveys decide to make, it comes with their own fresh-baked breads and as much advice as guests need to plan their day.

That doesn't necessarily mean leaving Turn in the River. Nature trails wind down to a calm stretch of the river — safe for swimming — and a beach where the Spiveys keep a canoe for guests to use. They also have a bike or two around to loan out and a workroom for minor bike or ski repairs.

Late afternoon finds guests in the outdoor hot tub or settling into the bent-willow chairs on the long deck out back, watching as whitetail deer emerge from the forest to forage in the hay fields. Sooner or later, however, they wander back into the kitchen to see what the Spiveys are up to.

ESSEX

Izaak Walton Inn

Highway 2
P.O. Box 653
Essex, MT 59916
406-888-5700
Fax: 406-888-5200

> *An inn and four cabooses from the great railway era*

General managers: Larry and Linda Vielleux. **Accommodations:** 31 rooms, 11 with private bath; 4 cabooses. **Rates:** Rooms, $72–$92, cabooses, $425 for 3 nights. **Included:** Cross-country skiing. **Minimum stay:** 2 nights on weekends in inn (November 15–April 15), 3 nights in cabooses year-round. **Added:** 4% tax. **Payment:** MasterCard, Visa. **Children:** Free under age 2. **Pets:** Prohibited. **Smoking:** Prohibited in dining room and cabooses. **Open:** Year-round.

The Great Northern Railway built the Izaak Walton Inn in 1939, chiefly to house its train crews. The three-story timber and stucco hotel faces the railroad yards in Essex, where helper engines stand ready to assist freight trains over the Continental Divide at nearby Marias Pass. At the time the inn was built, however, Essex was of strategic importance to the railroad. The tiny town — little more than a clutch of houses and the hotel — lay at a proposed southern entrance to Glacier National Park, midway between the current east and west entrances. Great Northern thus expected to house not only its personnel but tourists as

> **Train buffs will want the red Great Northern Caboose. Its original interior is largely unchanged, except for the addition of four single beds, two of them in the cupola.**

well, and so erected a far larger hotel than it really needed. Plans for the southern entrance evaporated with the coming of World War II, but the hotel is now on the National Register of Historic Places.

The rooms, though hardly elegant, are very large, with ample space for both a double and a single bed. All have knotty cedar paneling, high ceilings, white curtains trimmed in lace, quilts in pastel pinks and greens, and carpeted floors. Some have private baths with modern fixtures; the rest share a bath on each floor.

The newest accommodations are the cabooses, set on the hillside across the tracks from the hotel. Built in the late 1960s or early 1970s, these cars have been converted into pine-paneled apartments complete with modern kitchenettes, microwaves, and coffeemakers. Newlyweds and romantics opt for the wooden Chicago, Burlington & Quincy caboose, which dates to 1885 and has been decorated as a honeymoon suite with an iron bed, antique dresser, and lace curtains. The remaining two have had more of the original train paraphernalia removed to make way for a double bed and more dining and living space. All four have private baths.

Wherever guests stay, they are likely to cross paths in the small lobby, especially on nights chilly enough to merit a fire in the fireplace. Railroad memorabilia lines its walls and display cases. Downstairs, there is a usually quiet bar with an old Wurlitzer jukebox (seven plays for 50 cents and selections like "Mood Indigo," "Sentimental Journey," and "Stardust") and a recreation room with Ping-Pong and billiards tables, while an annex across the parking lot holds a sauna and laundromat.

In winter, the inn has 30 kilometers of cross-country ski trails and runs guided ski tours of the park. In summer, the local attractions include hiking trails and a variety of excursions into Glacier, with pickup and dropoff at the inn. Either way it's easy to reach on Amtrak, whose Empire Builder stops there daily. But some railroad buffs may be content to sit on the porch swings waiting for any kind of train to pass by.

GLACIER NATIONAL PARK

For other lodging near Glacier National Park, see the towns of Columbia Falls, Essex, Kalispell, Martin City, West Glacier, and Whitefish.

Glacier Park Lodge

Glacier National Park
East Glacier, MT 59434-0147
Off-season:
Glacier Park, Inc.
Dial Tower
Phoenix, AZ 85077-0928
406-226-5551 summer
602-207-6000 winter
800-332-9351 in Montana

> *A rambling old park lodge with resort amenities*

General manager of Glacier Park, Inc.: Dale Scott. **Accommodations:** 147 rooms, 8 suites. **Rates:** Rooms, single $94–$124, double $100–$130; suites, $140–$180. **Minimum stay:** None. **Added:** 4% tax. **Payment:** Discover, MasterCard, Visa. **Children:** Free under age 12. **Pets:** Prohibited. **Smoking:** Allowed. **Open:** Early June to mid-September.

The oldest of the Glacier National Park lodges, this rambling structure is the only one to lie outside the park boundaries. It was built by the Great Northern Railway in 1913 to be close to the train depot, with a broad apron of lawn and a circular drive in front to welcome arriving passengers, and a porch at the back with sweeping views of the park and its 8,000-foot peaks, two miles west.

In the lobby, massive Douglas-fir trunks soar 40 feet beyond rafters hung with cast-iron chandeliers A huge stone fireplace anchors one end. The most easily accessible of the lodges, it is continually abuzz with gawkers and guests who come to see the lobby or buy souvenirs.

The lobby would be a tough act to follow under any circumstances, but the rooms are a distinct disappointment after the grandeur of this public space. Small, with battered oak furniture and outdated earth tones, they don't remotely live up to one's hopes. Rooms in the newer annex show only slight improvement, having more space and balconies.

> **Massive Douglas fir trunks, 40 feet tall and two feet thick, support the sky-lighted roof of Glacier Park Lodge's four-story lobby.**

As compensation, however, guests get a heated swimming pool and access to the lodge's 9-hole golf course. There's a dining room that serves steak, trout, chicken, and pasta, and other places to eat in and around East Glacier. Lake McDonald and Many Glacier (see below) have far better locations, but that doesn't prevent Glacier Park Lodge from booking out months in advance for July and August. Reserve early.

Lake McDonald Lodge

Glacier National Park
West Glacier, MT
Summer:
East Glacier, MT 59434-0147
Off-season:
Glacier Park, Inc.
Dial Tower
Phoenix, AZ 85077-0928
406-226-5551 summer
602-207-6000 winter
800-332-9351 in Montana

> *The smallest and most appealing of Glacier National Park's lodges*

General manager of Glacier Park, Inc.: Dale Scott. **Accommodations:** 32 lodge rooms, 35 cottage rooms, 33 motel rooms. **Rates:** Rooms, single $64–$94, double $70–$100; cottages, single $54, double $60. **Minimum stay:** None. **Added:** 4% tax. **Payment:** Discover, MasterCard, Visa. **Children:** Free under age 12. **Pets:** Prohibited. **Smoking:** Allowed. **Open:** Early June to late September.

Built from logs and timber, this rustic hunting lodge on the shores of Lake McDonald crouches among a stand of giant cedars 10 miles inside Glacier National Park. It holds a mere 32 rooms (the rest are scattered through log cottages and a motel), making it the most intimate and captivating of the park's historic lodges.

Huge unpeeled cedar logs tower three stories above the lobby floor, supporting a roof of smaller log beams. Dozens of hunting trophies — moose, bighorn sheep, elk, deer, eagles, and mountain goats — peer down from their perches. Couches with Indian print upholstery face a massive stone fireplace whose hearth and sides have been etched with pictographs that, legend says, were the work of the great western artist Charles Russell, who had a cabin nearby.

> The best rooms face the lake and its sunsets, including a few on the third floor that have French doors onto their own balconies. Some rooms on the first floor are wheelchair accessible.

Now a National Historic Site, the Lake McDonald Lodge was built in 1913–1914 as a tourist hotel by a furrier who later sold it and several of the surrounding cabins to the park company. The rooms were last refurbished in 1988. Their new but bland contemporary pine furnishings and pastel floral fabrics don't fit with the overall style of the lodge, but there's something to be said for their cheerfulness. Each room has a tiny modern bath with a shower but no tub, electric heat, and a phone.

Apart from the main lodge, there are large and small rooms in a line of log cottages that follow the shoreline. The most desirable of them are the rooms in front with views of the water. The last group of accommodations occupies a two-story motel whose rooms, while decorated with colorful but inappropriate Aztec print bedspreads, have surprising appeal thanks to their knotty pine walls and space enough for two double beds.

Back in the lodge, there is a cedar-timbered dining room where college-age waiters serve passable to good pasta, steaks, pan-fried trout, and baked chicken with hit or miss efficiency. Rangers give talks several nights a week in the auditorium next door, and music and drama students recruited for the summer perform nightly in the lobby. Boats leave from the dock behind the lodge for cruises of the lake, and motorboats, rowboats, and canoes are available for rent. Besides the hotel, the Lake McDonald complex contains a post office, general store, coffee shop, and gas station. It is also home to a fleet of 1930s White Company buses with canvas sun roofs, which are still used to ferry guests between lodges and on guided tours of the park.

Many Glacier Hotel

Glacier National Park
Many Glacier Lake, MT
Summer:
East Glacier, MT 59434-0147
Off-season:
Glacier Park, Inc.
Dial Tower
Phoenix, AZ 85077-0928
406-226-5551 summer
602-207-6000 winter
800-332-9351 in Montana

A rambling lakeside lodge with glacier views

General manager of Glacier Park Inc.: Dale Scott. **Accommodations:** 208 rooms, 2 suites. **Rates:** Rooms, single $79–$134, double $85–$140; suites, $150. **Minimum stay:** None. **Added:** 4% tax. **Payment:** MasterCard, Visa, Discover. **Children:** Free under age 12. **Pets:** Prohibited. **Smoking:** Allowed. **Open:** Early June to mid-September.

Many Glacier's viewful setting on the shores of Swiftcurrent Lake and its endearing Swiss alpine architecture make it one of the favorite places to stay in the park. The National Historic Landmark rambles in two directions from the off-center circular fireplace in its tree trunk–pillared lobby. When its 200 rooms are full, which is most of July and August, it can be crowded, but the hotel makes up for it with its vistas of Grinnell Glacier across the lake and by its strategic proximity to several of the favored hiking trails.

Like many old lodges, Many Glacier has thin walls and

creaky floors. The hallway floors slope toward the lake. The generally wide hallways zig and zag and change character as you pass from one section to the next, as if it had been stuck together in pieces — and indeed it was: the main lodge was built in 1914 and its annex added three years later.

> There is something endearing about the old-lodge atmosphere. It's rather like a beloved but doddering uncle: people love Many Glacier because of its quirks and foibles, not despite them.

In keeping with the Swiss theme, the room doors bear the same cross as the Swiss flag, and the banners of the Swiss cantons fly in the dining room. However, the Glacier Company ignored all of that when they set about refurbishing some of the rooms. They adopted a variation on the characterless decor used in the Lake McDonald Lodge, which is no more appropriate here than it is there.

There are three categories of rooms: Alpine, Aspen, and Evergreen. The Alpine rooms stand out for their lake views from high floors (though note that there are no elevators). Aspen rooms also overlook the lake, though from a lower vantage point. Evergreens are the smallest of the lot and at best have only partial views of the mountains across a parking lot.

As at Lake McDonald, music and drama students provide free entertainment in the lobby during the evenings. Many Glacier also has a restaurant that serves reasonably priced — and quite good — chicken, steak, and pasta. But its greatest asset is that mid-park location. Narrated tours of Swiftcurrent and Josephine Lakes leave from its docks, where boats, rowboats, and canoes are available for rent. Naturalists give guided walks to Grinnell Lake twice a day, and, weather permitting, horseback rides depart daily from the corral next to the upper parking lot.

GREAT FALLS

The Sarah Bed-and-Breakfast Inn

626 4th Avenue North
Great Falls, MT 59401
406-452-5906

*A Victorian B&B
near the
Russell Museum*

Innkeepers: Lynne and Paul Stubbs. **Accommodations:** 5 rooms, 2 with private bath, 1 suite. **Rates:** Rooms, $55–$65; suite, $100–$125. **Included:** Full breakfast. **Minimum stay:** None. **Added:** 4% tax. **Payment:** Cash, checks, or traveler's checks. **Children:** Welcome. **Pets:** Prohibited. **Smoking:** Prohibited, as is drinking. **Open:** Year-round.

A winsome Victorian in gray clapboard and lilac trim, the Sarah stands on a quiet street a few blocks from the heart of downtown and not far from the C. M. Russell Museum complex. It dates to 1903 and is one of the stops on a walking tour of historic downtown. Its rebirth as a bed-and-breakfast, however, dates to 1989, when Lynne and Paul Stubbs, who have a renovation business, undertook to restore and modernize this three-story house as a place for them to live and guests to enjoy.

The original maple floors, quarter-sawn oak woodwork, and oak wainscoting survive, as do the pocket doors and leaded glass windows. The parlor features a bow window and a mix of contemporary and antique furnishings, including a pastel floral couch and loveseat and a television. Local art adorns the walls there and in the second-floor sitting area, which has a decorative fireplace and track lighting. "I'm not totally old," says Lynne of the decor. "In fact, I'm modern."

Rather than Victorian charm, the rooms have a contemporary country flare. Four of them open onto that second-floor sitting area. They have antique beds and dressers, comforters, lace curtains, and rather spare walls. Three of them share a bath containing a modern pedestal sink and a shower/tub. The fourth sports a highback oak bed and antique oak dresser, pink curtains, and a private bath.

> The Sarah feels less like a turn-of-the-century home than a fresh, clean, modern one, for all its Victorian architecture. That can be either an asset or a drawback, depending on your perspective.

The third floor is taken up largely by an air-conditioned three-room suite containing a sitting area with a stereo, two bedrooms — one with a double bed in white wood, the other with a double bed and single brass bed — and a full bath with a clawfoot tub and hand-held shower. There's also a third, supplementary small bedroom on this floor containing a single twin bed and children's toys.

Breakfast at the Sarah takes place either in the wainscoted dining room or in nooks in the parlor and living room. Either way it consists of Treasure State coffee cake (a local recipe), fresh fruit, some kind of egg dish or, perhaps, cornmeal or rye pancakes, and meat.

Sovekammer Bed and Breakfast

1109 3rd Avenue North
Great Falls, MT 59401
406-453-6620

> *A B&B with Danish accents and abelskiver*

Innkeepers: Irene and Dean Nielsen. **Accommodations:** 4 rooms, all with private bath. **Rates:** $55–$65. **Included:** Full breakfast. **Minimum stay:** None. **Added:** 4% tax. **Payment:** Cash, personal checks, or traveler's checks. **Children:** Welcome. **Pets:** Prohibited. **Smoking:** Prohibited. **Open:** Year-round.

Of the half dozen or so bed-and-breakfasts in Great Falls, none exudes as much warm and charm as the Sovekammer. Located on a quiet residential street, a few blocks from the Charles M. Russell Museum, this clapboard two-story building has four bedrooms (*sovekammer* means "sleep chamber" in Danish), each tricked out in bold paints, exuberant wallpapers, and antique furnishings. Capricious touches like collections of old hats or ladies' purses reflect Irene Nielsen's sunny disposition.

A case in point is the Evergreen Room on the main floor. Done up in reds and greens, this sleep chamber has a queen-size bed, plaid loveseat, and a private purple bath awash in purple ladies' hats and purses. It's also the only room with its own television.

> The apparent joy Irene took in decorating finds another expression in her huge Danish breakfasts. These tend to feature *abelskiver,* a sort of pancake made from recipes from Dean's grandmother's cookbook. Irene serves them with cranberry-orange compote, raspberries or apples, caramel rolls, and potatoes, dishing out as much of all this as guests can hold.

Upstairs, honeymooners seem to prefer the Master Bedroom, which has black floral wallpaper accented in reds and pinks, a queen-size bed, and a private bath with a shower. Guest Quarters, meanwhile, runs to cheery blues and rose florals. It has a full-size iron bed and a private bath whose clawfoot tub stands in the bedroom itself. Finally, there is Brandee's Chamber, with both a double sleigh bed and twin bed, burgundy and teal wallpaper, and a detached bath with a clawfoot tub. Guests on this floor share a sitting room with a television.

One aspect of this otherwise delightful B&B may make guests who don't share the Nielsens' religious beliefs uneasy: a gallery of paintings of Jesus covers the walls of the stairs leading to the guest rooms on the second floor, and the landing there displays plaques explaining the Biblical meaning of various given names. The Nielsens point this out in their brochure, noting, "You'll especially enjoy the collection of old & new pictures of Christ displayed throughout the Bed & Breakfast."

KALISPELL

Historic Kalispell Hotel

100 Main Street
P.O. Box 986
Kalispell, MT 59901
406-751-8100
800-858-7422
Fax: 406-752-8012

> *A logging-era hotel in the gateway to the Flathead Valley*

General manager: Valerie Vassil. **Accommodations:** 40 rooms. **Rates:** Rooms, single $43–$94, double $50–$102. **Included:** Continental breakfast, parking. **Minimum stay:** None. **Added:** 4% tax. **Payment:** Major credit cards. **Children:** Free under age 12. **Pets:** Prohibited. **Smoking:** Nonsmoking rooms available. **Open:** Year-round.

When the Historic Kalispell Hotel went up in 1909, across the street from the Opera House in the heart of downtown, it was only the second building in town to top two stories. Grand for its time, with a lobby that swept back from Main Street, it seemed to symbolize the logging town's growing sophistication. But like so many old hotels, a changing economy forced it into hard times, and the once grand dame was reduced to taking in weekly and monthly tenants.

> **From the lobby, archways and halls lead variously to a bar, two restaurants, and a casino, the latter containing poker tables and slot machines.**

Its fortunes changed early in 1991 when, following a complete renovation, it reopened with some of its old dignity restored. The entrance off Main Street now opens onto a turn-of-the-century lobby. Sunlight streams through the tall windows onto comfortable Victorian rolled-arm sofas and chairs. Toward the back, the exposed brick walls of a small parlor serve as a gallery for the work of local landscape artists.

The smallish rooms on the two floors above project traditional elegance in their reproductions of walnut antiques, pale blue wallpapers capped by a border, and lavender paisley bedspreads and drapes. Baths have marble countertops and showers. There is more local artwork above the beds, and all the rooms come equipped with phones, remote control cable televisions, and air conditioning. For something more deluxe, book one of the corner rooms, several of which have Jacuzzi tubs. The staff is excellent, too, but does not include bellmen, so be prepared to cart your luggage upstairs without benefit of an elevator.

That caveat aside, checking in here means having all of downtown Kalispell just out the door.

MARTIN CITY

Abbott Valley Accommodations

P.O. Box 98
Martin City, MT 59926
406-387-5774

*Log cabins
near Glacier
National Park*

General managers: Marion and Brian Foley. **Accommodations:** 1 apartment, 4 cabins. **Rates:** $90–$150/day, $499–$799/week. **Minimum stay:** None. **Added:**

4% tax. **Payment:** Major credit cards. **Children:** Welcome. **Pets:** With prior approval. **Smoking:** Prohibited. **Open:** Year-round.

In the 1950s, Marion Foley's lumberjack father, Red, purchased a turn-of-the-century homestead and adjacent timberlands in the Abbott Valley, 10 miles south of Glacier National Park. Then as now, two creeks, the North and South Abbott, trailed through the meadows and forests of the secluded 300-acre ranch. It was an exciting era, as loggers cut timber for the Hungry Horse Reservoir and sawmills turned it into lumber.

> The most appealing lodgings are two ancient log cabins secluded in a meadow alongside South Abbott Creek. The cabins have rustic, heavily weathered exteriors, but they've been thoroughly remodeled inside, with modern kitchens and contemporary furnishings.

The valley is quieter now, but it remains the habitat of beaver, geese, ducks, loons, and great blue herons. Deer, elk, and moose frequent it as well. That peaceful seclusion adds to the appeal of a handful of individual lodgings — all with fully equipped kitchens and washer-dryers — that reflect the valley's history.

An original trapper's cabin, dubbed Baptiste, is capable of sleeping six. A deck adjoins the master bedroom, providing views of the north meadow and log haybarn. Firefighter is somewhat older, a hand-built log house with an open main floor and a two-bedroom loft upstairs. It has a wood-burning stove, a porch with a sofa, and a large picture window framing the south meadow. It, too, sleeps six. Groups or families needing still more space can rent the adjacent log bunkhouse — once used for tanning hides and now fitted out with four single pine beds (but no kitchen of its own).

On the opposite side of the meadow, next to the Foley home, is the Apikuni Rose, a studio apartment for four with a protected deck overlooking the meadow across a gurgling creek. In the woods a mile or so away stand two gray clapboard houses with knotty pine interiors. While functional, these lack the pioneer charm of the cabins and the wonderful open feeling of the meadow setting. The small two-bedroom home called Quintonken is, however, wheelchair accessible. It was built by Red Foley and contains a wood-burning stove and room to sleep six. Its large backyard contains a swing set and picnic table. The other, called, F.K. & L. (after a sawmill that operated nearby in the 1950s), is a two-bedroom, one-bath home with views from the living room of sunsets in the Canyon and North Fork areas.

Nature and mountain bike trails begin on the ranch and continue into the surrounding national forest; in winter, cross-country skiers have four miles of groomed track and access to the neighboring backcountry.

MISSOULA

Goldsmith's Bed & Breakfast

809 East Front Street
Missoula, MT 59802
406-721-6732

A riverfront inn near the university

Proprietors: Jeana and Richard Goldsmith. **Accommodations:** 6 rooms, 1 suite, all with private bath. **Rates:** Rooms, single $55–$65, double $65–$75; suite, $85–$95. **Included:** Full breakfast. **Minimum stay:** None. **Added:** 4% tax. **Payment:** Major credit cards. **Children:** Free under age 10. **Pets:** Prohibited. **Smoking:** Prohibited. **Open:** Year-round.

Built in 1911, this two-story red brick house was originally the residence of the University of Montana's second president. But in 1989, Jeana and Richard Goldsmith had it physically moved — in two pieces — from the campus to its current location on the opposite bank of the Clark Fork River, a few blocks from downtown Missoula. Reassembling it next to their family's ice cream parlor, they then restored the interiors and opened it as a bed-and-breakfast inn. Part country, part Victorian, the seven guest rooms share a predilection for cheerful wallpapers, stenciled designs, spacious tiled baths, ceiling fans, telephones, and Victorian, sleigh, or brass and iron beds. Views of the river make numbers 3 and 4 in front by far the most appealing, though the third-floor Whitewater Suite with a separate bedroom and sitting room is larger.

> **Instead of having breakfast in the inn, guests walk next door whenever it suits them, settle into a booth or table in the ice cream parlor, and order hotcakes, eggs and bacon, or pastry and muffins, served with fruit, juice, coffee, or tea by cheerful college students who work there.**

The rooms tend to be small, but guests who need space find plenty in the living room. Tastefully decorated in peach and pastel green, it has hardwood floors set off by Oriental rugs, a clutch of wicker furniture, two sofas, a decorative fireplace, and a television. Photos of the house being moved hang on one wall, while the front windows open to views of the river. There is more white wicker on the riverfront porch outside, making it a favorite place to gather in warm weather. A nearby footbridge arches over the river to the University of Montana campus.

What's missing from Goldsmith's, however, is any sense of warmth or ambience or personal attention. Few guests ever meet the absentee owners, and the students who check guests in and out at the ice cream parlor, while amiable, are no substitute for an on-site innkeeper. They may know where to find the best burgers in town but not necessarily the best cuisine, for example, and their dual responsibilities mean they can't give inn guests their undivided attention.

NOXON

Bighorn Lodge

710 Bull River Road
Noxon, MT 59853
406-847-5597
Fax: 406-847-5022

*An elegant
four-room inn
at the edge of
the wilderness*

Innkeeper: Inez Wates. **Accommodations:** 4 rooms, all with private bath. **Rates:** Single $65, double $105. **Included:** Full breakfast. **Minimum stay:** None. **Added:** 4% tax. **Payment:** MasterCard, Visa (4% surcharge); cash or checks preferred. **Children:** Discouraged. **Pets:** Prohibited. **Smoking:** Prohibited in rooms. **Open:** Year-round; reserved for hunters in May, early September to early October, late October–November.

Nestled in northwest Montana's scenic Bull River Valley, the Bighorn Lodge combines the warmth of an elegant bed-and-breakfast home with the look and feel of a hunting lodge and the recreation of a guest ranch. This sophisticated hybrid came about when Rus Willis, a hunting and fishing guide, convinced his mother, Inez Wates, to give up her landscape and interior design businesses in Virginia and move west.

Though constructed of cedar, pine, Douglas fir, and larch and set in a forest of evergreens, the two-story log lodge nonetheless hints at southern plantation architecture, especially in its broad front porch. Lawns, shrubs, and beds of flowers adorn the circular drive in front. Off to one side stands a satellite dish.

Inside, the entrance foyer opens into a vast room two stories tall that runs the entire width of the lodge. At its center a half circle of elegant contemporary couches and chairs faces a towering stone fireplace. The dining area lies to the left, another sitting area with a television and VCR to the right. A stuffed mountain lion and many deer, bear, and elk trophy heads hang on the walls, and sliding doors open onto a back deck.

A stairway at one end leads to a mezzanine and the entrances to the four wood-paneled rooms, each furnished in a different motif but all having views of the Cabinet Wilderness. One has a queen-size four-poster bed and a palette of forest green. Another is filled with traditional Americana. A third has a mural of a forest scene and mountain lion whimsically decorated with appliqued cartoon drawings of ants on vacation. All have modern, private baths.

> **Inez Wates built Bighorn Lodge "for those who like a little luxury with their wilderness." She presides over the lodge with a southern accent and a flare for entertaining.**

Inez, a congenial and charming hostess, encourages guests to help themselves to coffee and beverages in the kitchen and to make themselves at home. There's no fixed menu at breakfast, so guests order whatever they want — eggs, pancakes, French toast — and it comes with fruit, juice, and huckleberry muffins. On nice days, many choose to eat outside on the deck.

Bighorn Lodge's location between the Cabinet and Scotchman's Peak wilderness areas means recreation options abound. Guests can horseback ride, fish, canoe, or explore lost canyons on four-wheel-drive safaris, either on an à la carte basis or by booking packages that also include lunch and dinner. During certain months in the fall and spring, Inez turns the lodge over to her son for his hunting trips.

SEELEY LAKE

The Emily A. Bed & Breakfast

Rt. 83, Mile Marker 20
P.O. Box 350
Seeley Lake, MT 59868
406-677-3474

> *A lakefront log home in its own 160-acre wilderness*

Innkeepers: Marilyn and Keith Peterson. **Accommodations:** 5 rooms and 1 suite, 3 with private bath. **Rates:** Rooms $85, suite $150. **Included:** Full breakfast. **Minimum stay:** 2 nights preferred on weekends. **Added:** 4% tax. **Payment:** Cash, checks, or traveler's checks. **Children:** Welcome. **Pets:** Allowed. **Smoking:** Prohibited, even outdoors. **Open:** Year-round.

Marilyn Peterson's roots in this sunny valley between Kalispell and Missoula date to 1917, when her family began spending summers here. Though she and her husband Keith left the state after graduating from the University of Montana, they always intended to find a way back. So in 1992, they built this bed-and-breakfast on a 158-acre wilderness ranch not far from where Marilyn used to spend her summers. They named it for her pioneering grandmother, Emily Alvis Stinson Shope.

Constructed of larch logs, the two-story house stands in an open meadow at the edge of a lake formed by the Clearwater River. Its picture windows frame views of the valley and the Swan and Mission Mountains. The exceptionally peaceful setting lures not only guests eager to get away but also an abundance of ospreys, eagles, loons, deer, moose, snow geese, and herons.

Inside, a two-story stone fireplace impregnated with geological specimens dominates a large, atriumlike living room with oak floors, antique furnishings, and the Petersons' collection of western art. Stairs lead to the second floor, where quilts drape over the railings of the balconies that wrap around three sides. On that level, there is a U-shaped common area with a television, children's play area, and another fireplace. It has doors that open onto a broad deck at the front of the house with views toward the Swan Mountains. There are also four bedrooms on the second floor, each named for one of their children and decorated with feather duvets and, in season, fresh flowers.

> This is a place to get lost, wandering off down the roads and hiking trails that lace the ranch, canoeing, or fishing in the river.

The largest of the four is Julie, all lace and an antique cherrywood bed. It has a private deck overlooking the river and a private bath. The three sons' rooms share a tiled bath with a shower but have individual personalities: John has a pencil-post bed and oak antiques, Eric features walls of sports posters, and Chris has a vaulted ceiling and an in-room sink and vanity.

There are two other rooms: the Grandparents' Room on the main level, which has twin beds and a private but detached bath; and the Family Suite, downstairs off a private patio facing the river. It has two bedrooms with hand-crafted log beds and furnishings, a foldout couch, and a complete kitchen, making it ideal for families.

Every afternoon, Marilyn serves afternoon tea, and each morning, classical music plays as guests sit down to huge breakfasts of homemade granola, huckleberry muffins or pancakes, fresh fruit, potatoes and vegetables, and homemade breads. No one leaves hungry.

SOMERS

Osprey Inn Bed & Breakfast

5557 Highway 93 South
Somers, MT 59932
406-857-2042
800-258-2042
Fax: 406-857-2019

*A modern B&B
on Flathead Lake*

Innkeepers: Sharon and Wayne Finney. **Accommodations:** 2 rooms, 1 suite, 1 cabin, all with private bath. **Rates:** Room and cabin $85, suite $160. **Included:** Full breakfast. **Minimum stay:** 2 nights in July and August. **Added:** 4% tax. **Payment:** Major credit cards. **Children:** Over age 9. **Pets:** Prohibited (they have a cat). **Smoking:** Prohibited. **Open:** Year-round.

When a guest complained of being chilly at breakfast, Sharon Finney offered to fetch her a sweatshirt. Rather than simply fetching it, however, Sharon popped it in the dryer for a few minutes so it was warm. More than anything else, that kind of creative personal attention is what makes the Osprey Inn such an appealing bed-and-breakfast.

The inn itself is a three-story modern home at the northern end of Flathead Lake. Decks at the back look across the lake at the Mission Mountains, and a well-tended lawn with beds of roses and iris gently slopes down to the shore and a pebbly beach and boat dock, where they keep a canoe and rowing shell for guests to use.

Their warm personalities also find expression in the accommodations. They've taken the typically nondescript bedrooms of a modern home and transformed them with rustic country beds that Wayne himself built and colorful quilt-print down comforters. Antique dressers and nightstands hold potpourri, a bedside basket of fresh fruit, and for new arrivals, a complimentary bottle of wine.

Two rooms have views of the lake: Squirrel Run and Island View, both on the second floor and both with private baths. Downstairs, there are two rooms on either side of a guest parlor, which has a woodburning stove, telephone, and racks of local information (Sharon is a former president of the local Chamber of Commerce). Since these rooms share a bath, however, they are either rented as a suite (one has a queen-size bed, the other twins) or the second room is left empty.

The most unusual of the accommodations is a cozy one-room log cabin, slightly separated from the house near some cherry trees in the backyard. Though without plumbing, it has a private bath inside the house.

> Each evening in good weather, the Finneys gather their guests in Adirondack chairs around a campfire on the beach to find out what everyone has planned for the following day. Native Montanans and members of the Audubon Society, they are invaluable sources of information, especially about Glacier National Park, an hour to the north, and about birding.

When weather permits, breakfast is served outside on the second-floor deck. It typically consists of the inn's own fresh cherries or raspberries in season, along with muffins, cinnamon rolls, and perhaps huckleberry pancakes with homemade syrup and country sausage or French toast with bacon. Guests call them "no-lunch breakfasts." Coffee is available early and throughout the day. In late afternoon, guests come back to fresh-baked brownies and an outdoor hot tub, where they can watch the sun set or the osprey, loons, grebes, and other shore birds. Next to the hot tub stands a small refrigerator for guests to use. Inside, there is a TV/VCR lounge, a library, and a living room with a fireplace and player piano.

TROUT CREEK

Blue Spruce Lodge & Guest Ranch

451 Marten Creek Road
Trout Creek, MT 59874
406-827-4762
800-831-4797

> *A completely barrier-free guest ranch*

Proprietors: Russ, Karen, and Deonne Milleson. **Accommodations:** 8 rooms, 1 with private bath. **Rates:** June–August, single $800/

week, double $1,500/week; lower rest of year. **Included:** All meals and, in summer, airport transfers and three outings. **Minimum stay:** None. **Added:** 4% tax on lodging portion only. **Payment:** MasterCard, Visa. **Children:** Welcome. **Pets:** Allowed with prior approval (stables available for horses). **Smoking:** Allowed. **Open:** Year-round.

Poised high on a razorback ridge in the foothills of the Bitterroot Mountains, the Blue Spruce Lodge could easily be just another rustic backcountry hideaway. What sets it apart is its dedication to providing recreation to those in wheelchairs or otherwise physically challenged, and to their families.

Russ Milleson himself uses a wheelchair. Injured in an industrial accident in 1974, he abruptly discovered that few facilities provided opportunities for him to continue to hunt, fish, and enjoy the outdoors as he had before his injury. After more than a decade of frustration, he built the Blue Spruce Lodge. He designed it to be totally wheelchair accessible, providing a ramp leading to the front door, barrier-free public spaces, and an elevator for access to rooms on the upper floors.

> Milleson has a full program of whitewater raft trips and fishing, hunting, and sightseeing excursions, all accessible to those in wheelchairs. He has his own pontoon boat on Noxon Reservoir and vans to transport guests back and forth. Even the sauna and hot tub accommodate wheelchairs.

Otherwise, Blue Spruce functions much like a typical guest ranch. The lodge has nine rooms, one with private bath, while the remainder share three large baths. Some have bunk beds, one has a canopy bed, others have doubles or queens in brass or wood. All have pine armoires. The four corner rooms have private decks with views of the Cabinet Wilderness and the Bitterroot foothills. Every landing has a sitting area with sherry and bowls of fruit. The third floor has a small workout area with a Universal-type weight machine.

Dinner in the main-floor dining room (its cedar floors free of obstructive rugs) could be quiche, lasagna, or steak. There's a big-screen television (with a satellite dish) and a pool table. Milleson, who lives next door, takes an active part in everything that goes on, from the cooking to the outings.

When summer ends, the lodge shifts its orientation first to hunting and then to winter sports like snowmobiling, sight-seeing in amphibious all-terrain vehicles, sledding, horse-drawn sleigh rides, and ice fishing.

WEST GLACIER

Mountain Timbers Lodge

5385 Rabe Road
P.O. Box 94
West Glacier, MT 59936
406-387-5830
800-841-3835
Fax: 406-387-5835

*A huge, secluded
log home
near Glacier
National Park*

Innkeeper: Don Hansen. **Accommodations:** 6 rooms, 1 suite, 1 3-bedroom cabin. **Rates:** Rooms $55–$125, cabin $175–$250. **Included:** Full breakfast. **Minimum stay:** None. **Added:** 4% tax. **Payment:** MasterCard, Visa. **Children:** Welcome. **Pets:** With prior approval (he has an outside dog). **Smoking:** Prohibited. **Open:** Year-round.

Don Hansen's tastefully furnished 5,000-square-foot log home stands in an open meadow, with the peaks of Glacier National Park behind. Built from 450-year-old larch logs, the secluded two-story lodge and its broad outdoor decks anchor a 220-acre tract of fields and forest on a little-used country road. The west entrance to the park is only seven miles away, but the wilderness seems even nearer at hand. Deer and elk wander through the meadow in summer, while in winter the lodge's own 15-kilometer system of groomed cross-country ski trails laces the meadow and surrounding hills. Everything conspires to create a feeling of total escape.

The focal point is the log-and-timber living room, which soars 24 feet to a vaulted ceiling. A massive flagstone fireplace dominates one wall. A baby grand piano stands in one corner, not far from six-foot-high picture windows that frame vistas of the meadow and the park's Cannon Peak and Great Wall. Oil paintings of famous Indians decorate the walls. Ficus trees and fresh flowers add to the sense of warmth.

Comfortable sofas and chairs make this a favorite place to gather, maybe after picking out a book from the lodge's 1,500-volume library.

Hansen has seen to guests' comfort in other ways, too. They're encouraged to use the picnic tables and barbecue grills on the outside decks (and, for that matter, the kitchen inside), to work out in a small fitness center, find relief in the outdoor hot tub overlooking the meadow, hang out in the game room playing pool or Ping Pong, or lounge in a room with a big-screen television (connected to a satellite dish), VCR, and audio system.

> **The room with the best views is the Master Suite on the main floor. An oversize chamber with log walls, a four-poster country bed, leather sofa, and antique armoire, its windows overlook the meadow and park.**

After the Master Suite (see sidebar), the most appealing chambers are those on the second floor. They share the warmth of log walls and sloping log-and-timber ceilings, but each has its own allure. Number 1 has views across the meadow, number 2 opens onto a private deck, and number 3 is a cozy chamber with views of the forest. There are three smaller but functional rooms off the parlor in the basement. All have private baths.

In July and August, Hansen also rents the three-bedroom, two-bath cabin where he normally lives. Set in another meadow of wildflowers, this one even deeper within the 220-acre property, it has a two-story river rock fireplace, an expansive front deck with the same view of Glacier as the lodge but from a higher elevation, its own workout room, a satellite TV, and a fully equipped kitchen, right down to an icemaker.

Cabin guests who'd rather not cook can join everyone else in the lodge for a full breakfast at the long table in the dining room. Hansen's usually there to help guests sort out their plans for the day, helped by his mother, Alice.

WHITEFISH

Duck Inn

1305 Columbia Avenue
Whitefish, MT 59937
406-862-3825
800-344-2377

*A peaceful, quiet
inn near
Big Mountain's
ski slopes*

Innkeepers: Phyllis and Ken Adler. **Accommodations:** 10 rooms, all with private bath. **Rates:** June–September, $79–$89; rest of year, $59–$69. **Included:** Continental breakfast, airport or train transfers. **Minimum stay:** None. **Added:** 4% tax. **Payment:** Major credit cards. **Children:** Welcome. **Pets:** Prohibited. **Smoking:** Prohibited. **Open:** Year-round.

Phyllis and Ken Adler built the brown clapboard Duck Inn in 1984, choosing a quiet spot just above a deep part of the Flathead River, a few blocks from the heart of Whitefish. Ducks do in fact gather here, along with geese, otter, and beaver. A deck with umbrella tables provides a breezy viewing area in summer; a glass-enclosed Jacuzzi in back is a warm retreat in any season.

The side of the lobby nearest the river soars almost two stories; it's a wonderful sunlight-flooded space. Green and gold sofas with duck motif pillows hunker in front of the flagstone fireplace, and books line the shelves. Every morning, the Adlers set out baked goods, juice, coffee, and tea at the tables on one side; guests can eat here or take breakfast back to their rooms.

Bedding down at the inn means settling into a handsomely countrified room with a gas-log fireplace, a brass or white iron queen-size bed, pine armoire, white wicker chairs, and a large bath with a soaking tub. An old-fashioned phone is on the nightstand; there are also cable TV and air conditioning. Each room has a deck; those on the river side are more desirable. The two in front also have bay windows.

> **The lure is the peace and quiet the Adlers insist on — they prefer children only in the off season — and the inn's proximity to the slopes of Big Mountain, nine miles to the north.**

In winter, the inn runs its own ski shuttle back and forth to Big Mountain. Though never obtrusive, the Adlers are constantly on hand to provide information about local attractions or restaurants.

The Garden Wall

504 Spokane Avenue
Whitefish, MT 59937
406-862-3440

> *A clapboard inn with Art Deco style*

Proprietors: Rhonda and Mike Fitzgerald, Terri and Andy Feury. **Innkeeper:** Chris Schustrom. **Accommodations:** 3 rooms, all with private bath, 1 suite. **Rates:** Rooms $85–$95 single, $95–$105 double; suite $175 (for 4); $10 less April 15–May 30 and September 15–December 15. **Included:** Full breakfast. **Minimum stay:** 7 days over Christmas holidays. **Added:** 4% tax. **Payment:** MasterCard, Visa. **Children:** Well-behaved children over age 10. **Pets:** Prohibited. **Smoking:** Prohibited. **Open:** Year-round.

With a broad front porch anchored by columns, the Garden Wall looks at once homey and full of character. The gray clapboard two-story inn with white trim stands on the corner of a tree-lined street a few blocks from downtown. It was built in 1923, which makes it one of the oldest houses in Whitefish, and its age shows mainly in the details of its construction, like the unusual barnlike roof line and the beveled glass windows. It had been for sale for a few years in 1985 when Rhonda Fitzgerald, who lives a block away, saw it and thought that buying it and turning it into a bed-and-breakfast would provide an excuse to buy, she says, "lots of wonderful furniture."

> **Terri Feury serves breakfast at an oak table on Glacier National Park's original blue willow china, as soft jazz plays. The often extravagant meal consists of fresh orange juice, baked goods, and such specialties as huckleberry waffles, eggs in puff pastry, or chicken and green chili omelettes.**

Though it was in good condition, right down to its inlaid fir moldings, it took two years of work for Rhonda and her partners to get it ready. After renovating the baths and bedrooms, they filled the rooms with period furnishings from northwest Montana. Peach and avocado Art Deco chairs now stand in front of the brick fireplace in the parlor, lace curtains hang in the windows, and Audubon bird prints decorate the walls.

They wallpapered and furnished each of the bedrooms differently, putting an Art Deco bird's-eye maple bedroom set in one, graceful iron beds in another. The suite, whose two bedrooms share a connecting bath, has a four-poster in the larger room, twin beds in the smaller. All have comforters, fresh flowers, and lace curtains.

Innkeeper Chris Schustrom lives here, and one of the four owners is almost always on hand. Since all of them ski, hike, swim, canoe, and ride mountain bikes, they can provide the inside scoop on what to see and do.

Grouse Mountain Lodge

1205 Highway 93 West
Whitefish, MT 59937
406-862-3000
800-321-8822
Fax: 406-862-0326

> *A modern*
> *hunting lodge with*
> *resort facilities*

Director of operations: Art Dull-inger. **Accommodations:** 133 rooms, 12 suites. **Rates:** Rooms, high season (June–September, Christmas holidays, winter weekends) $99–$149; rest of year, $60–$89; suites, $145–$175. **Included:** Airport and rail transfers. **Minimum stay:** None. **Added:** 4% tax. **Payment:** Major credit cards. **Children:** Free under age 12. **Pets:** Prohibited. **Smoking:** Nonsmoking rooms available. **Open:** Year-round.

The name suggests a rustic retreat for bird hunters, and that may very well have been the inspiration behind Grouse Mountain Lodge's architecture. Built from cedar and field-stone, the gabled three-story inn could almost be a modern hunting lodge, except that it trails along a golf course a few blocks from downtown Whitefish. Stuffed ringneck pheasants do decorate Logan's Grill, one of the dressier restaurants in town, but the talk there and in the adjacent Logan's Bar is not about wildfowl but about birdies and eagles.

Though the game played outside is Scottish, the lodge is quintessentially Montanan. Built in 1984, it combines contemporary with rustic. The mauve, green, and blue color scheme mirrors the hues of Big Sky's rocks, forests, and lakes. The lobby floors are slate; the towering fireplaces river rock. Thick panels of pale green glass etched with scenes of Glacier National Park line one wall of Logan's Grill, and more original art is on display.

The accommodations soar beyond the ordinary. Comfortably spacious, they weave stylish fabrics and rich colors like salmon, royal blue, mauve, and claret. Sheer drapes let in the light. The cable television comes with free HBO and Disney channel. Of the suites, several are two-level, condominium-like units with fully equipped kitchens and a second level connected to the first by a spiral staircase.

> **The public areas showcase spectacular examples of taxidermy. A mountain goat stares down from its precarious perch on a rock outcrop immediately above the check-in desk. Bighorn sheep, a Canadian lynx, and an elk warily survey diners in Logan's Grill, while the bar holds two stuffed black bears and a moose.**

The adjacent 27-hole Whitefish Lake Golf Course does not belong to the hotel, nor do the three tennis courts in front, but guests can use both. In addition, the lodge has an indoor pool, indoor and outdoor spas, a sauna, rooms for waxing skis, and a guest laundry. In winter, the golf course becomes a lighted cross-country ski center. Big Mountain Ski Area is eight miles away, Glacier National Park 25 miles. And with nightly entertainment in Logan's Bar and such entrées as buffalo steak, trout amandine, and sautéed duck breast in Logan's Grill, Grouse Mountain makes a good all-around base for exploring northwestern Montana.

Kandahar Lodge

P.O. Box 1659
Whitefish, MT 59937
406-862-6098
Fax: 406-862-6095

> *A cozy ski lodge*
> *right at the base*
> *of the slopes*

Innkeepers: Buck and Mary Pat Love. **Accommodations:** 34 rooms, 16 studios and lofts. **Rates:** (Higher over Christmas holidays) Rooms $90–$110 summer (mid-May–late November), $120–$160 winter (late November–mid-April); studios and lofts $100–$130 summer, $132–$184 winter. **Minimum stay:** None. **Added:** 4% tax. **Payment:** Major credit cards. **Children:** Free under 13. **Pets:** Prohibited. **Smoking:** Nonsmoking rooms available. **Open:** Year-round.

Though often overshadowed by Big Sky, its more famous rival in southern Montana, Big Mountain Ski Area is actually much larger. In fact, its 4,000 acres of skiable terrain dwarf anything else in the state. Situated high on the slopes of Big Mountain, eight miles from Whitefish, the ski area looks south across the expanse of the Flathead Valley and east to the snow-capped peaks of Glacier National Park.

When Buck and Mary Pat Love built their slopeside Kandahar Lodge in Big Mountain's ski village, they included accommodations for themselves and their daughters. Having the Loves there, personally seeing to the comfort of guests, imbues this ski-in/ski-out lodge of 50 cozy pine-paneled rooms with the warmth and appeal of a family-run inn. No one gets lost in the shuffle.

The layout helps assure it. An inviting sunken lobby, paneled in golden knotty cedar, is the centerpiece of the lodge. Skiers returning from the slopes eventually end up here — after a detour to one of the two Jacuzzis or saunas — for après-ski, sinking into one of the sumptuous sofas or chairs in front of a floor-to-ceiling river rock fireplace.

All of the rooms have been refurbished within the last few years. Comfortably spacious, they feature reproductions of country antiques — among them pine beds with high headboards and armoires with remote control cable televisions — brass lamps, and eye-soothing wildflower-print fabrics. Framed photos of Glacier National Park provide a sense of place. In addition to the rooms, the Kandahar has 16 studio apartments with kitchenettes and, in a few cases, lofts.

> **Kandahar's back doors open directly onto the slopes, which allows skiers to finish their day right at the lodge and drop their equipment in a heated ski and boot room.**

There are several places to eat in the ski village, but none comes close to the savory bistro fare — pecan-stuffed game hen, chicken Sonoran, linguini olio santo, Lindser schnitzel — in the 10-table Café Kandahar, which ranks among the top restaurants in the valley.

Southern Montana

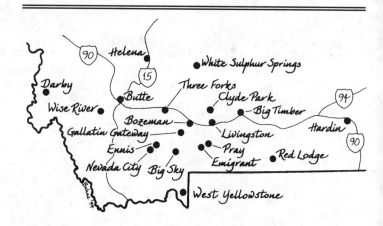

Best Bed-and-Breakfast Homes

Bozeman
  The Silver Forest Inn
  Torch & Toes
Hardin
  Kendrick House Inn
Helena
  The Barrister
West Yellowstone
  Sportsman's High

Best Bed-and-Breakfast Inns

Bozeman
  The Voss Inn
Butte
  Copper King Mansion
Helena
  The Sanders
Livingston
  Greystone Inn Bed & Breakfast
Three Forks
  Sacajawea Inn

Best Condominiums, Apartments, and Cabins

Big Sky
  Big Sky Ski & Summer Resort
  Shoshone Condominium Hotel
Red Lodge
  Rock Creek Resort
West Yellowstone
  Sportsman's High

Best Fishing Lodges

Ennis
  T Lazy B Ranch

Hardin
  Eagle Nest Lodge
West Yellowstone
  Firehole Ranch
Wise River
  The Complete Fly Fisher

Best Guest Ranches

Big Sky
  Lone Mountain Ranch
Big Timber
  Lazy K Bar Ranch
  Sweet Grass Ranch
Clyde Park
  G Bar M Ranch
Darby
  Triple Creek Ranch
Emigrant
  Mountain Sky Guest Ranch
Livingston
  Sixty-Three Ranch
White Sulphur Springs
  Elk Canyon Ranch

Best Historic Hotels, Inns, and Lodges

Big Timber
  The Grand
Gallatin Gateway
  Gallatin Gateway Inn
Livingston
  The Murray Hotel
Nevada City
  The Nevada City Hotel
Pray
  Chico Hot Springs Lodge
Red Lodge
  The Pollard

Best Resorts and Spas

Big Sky
  Big Sky Ski & Summer Resort
Red Lodge
  Rock Creek Resort

Best Ski Area Hotels & Lodges

Big Sky
  Lone Mountain Ranch
  Shoshone Condominium Hotel

Montana's southern tier braids strands of the Old West with the new. Though it has the state's largest city in Billings, a spiffy and thoroughly modern destination resort in Big Sky, and a knack for luring movie production companies, southern Montana gets its identity from its frontier past. Many of the guest ranches still run cattle, the rivers teem with trophy trout, and a roadless wilderness lies only a few miles off an interstate highway.

Two national monuments memorialize conflicts with the Indians: the Big Hole Battlefield west of Wisdom, and Little Bighorn Battlefield south of **Hardin.** The broad Big Hole is a hauntingly beautiful valley hard by the Continental Divide. It was there, in 1877, that U.S. troops attacked five so-called "nontreaty" bands of Nez Perce Indians. The visitors' center has exhibits recounting the battle, and there are several self-guided trails through the siege area. A year earlier, in 1876, Sioux and Cheyenne warriors had overwhelmed General Custer's U.S. Army troops at Little Bighorn. Guided tours of the battlefield leave from the visitors' center there, and every June, Custer's last stand is reenacted, accompanied by Native American dances, rodeos, and games.

A different kind of reenactment takes place at **Nevada City** and Virginia City. These two restored mining camps border what was called Alder Gulch when gold was discovered there in 1863. Melodramas take place during the summer in Virginia City's Old Opera House, while Nevada City recreates the look and feel of a mining camp with actual buildings from the period, including stores, homes, a school, music hall, and hotel.

It was out of just such a camp that **Helena,** the state capital, evolved. Founded in 1864, when gold was discovered in

Last Chance Gulch, it has become the state's fourth largest
city and a center for agriculture, industry, and government.
The old gulch has been reborn as a fetching main street of
new and restored shops. The Montana Historical Society Museum maintains a Montana Homeland exhibit of the state's
history as well as a collection of Charles M. Russell's art and
a gallery of Montana photography. Also worth seeing is the
original Governor's Mansion, a restored 22-room brick house
built in 1888, and the stained glass windows of the Gothic
Cathedral of St. Helena.

Those attractions notwithstanding, southern Montana's
most powerful lure is its abundant recreation. Three of the
five entrances to Yellowstone National Park are in Montana
at **West Yellowstone,** Gardiner, and Cooke City. That last entrance lies at the end of the Beartooth Highway, a National
Forest Scenic Byway that begins in **Red Lodge,** dips into
Wyoming, and returns. The 69-mile drive reaches dizzying
heights as it winds through a landscape of snow-capped
peaks, glaciers, and alpine lakes. Charles Kuralt called it "the
most beautiful drive in America."

Red Lodge is also one gateway to the Absaroka-Beartooth
Wilderness, a one-million-acre tract of primitive backcountry
along the border with Yellowstone. It encompasses 12,799-
foot Granite Park, Montana's highest, as well as more than a
thousand alpine lakes and 700 miles of hiking trails.

Though there is good fishing in that wilderness, dedicated
anglers head for southern Montana's Yellowstone, Madison,
Gallatin, Beaverhead, Clark's Fork, and Big Hole rivers, to
name only the most prominent. Every valley, it seems, has its
blue ribbonwaters, bordered on either side by picturesque
mountains. Robert Redford's evocative film about fly fishing,
A River Runs Through It, was filmed near Livingston.

The same corridor contains some of Montana's oldest and
newest guest ranches. They range from no-frills to drop-dead
luxury while maintaining a boots-and-jeans informality. And
it also has hot springs at **Pray,** two notable downhill ski areas
at **Big Sky** and Bridger Bowl. And once the snows melt, Big
Sky shifts gears to become a major summer resort, where hiking and mountain biking share a roster with golf and tennis.

BIG SKY

For other lodging in the area, see the town of Gallatin Gateway.

Big Sky Ski & Summer Resort

P.O. Box 1
Big Sky, MT 59716
406-995-4211
800-548-4486 in U.S.
Fax: 406-995-4860

> *A year-round resort near Yellowstone National Park*

General manager: John Kircher. **Accommodations:** 204 rooms, 845 condos. **Rates:** Summer (May–October), rooms $100–$140, condos $90–$450; winter, rooms $91–$170, condos, $105–$600; higher over Christmas holidays. **Minimum stay:** 7 days over Christmas holidays; up to 7 days other times depending on the property. **Added:** 7% tax. **Payment:** Major credit cards. **Children:** Free under age 11. **Pets:** Prohibited in most properties. **Smoking:** Nonsmoking rooms and condos available. **Open:** Year-round

Originally developed by newscaster Chet Huntley in the early 1970s, Big Sky has blossomed into a year-round resort community. It comprises two villages: one in an alpine meadow along the Gallatin River, 43 miles south of Bozeman; the other almost 1,000 feet higher, on the slopes of 11,166-foot Lone Mountain. Together they offer a wealth of summer and winter recreation.

It was 3,000 vertical feet of crowd-free skiing that first put Big Sky on the map. Today, the tentacles of its ski lifts extend across Andesite Peak in one direction and high into the bowls of craggy Lone Mountain in the other. Every year, an average of 400 inches of powdery fluff sift down onto 55 runs spread over 2,400 acres that mount above timberline. Big Sky supplements this alpine terrain with 45 miles of groomed cross-country trails at Lone Mountain Ranch (see below).

Apart from the Huntley Lodge, a slightly dated hotel partly redeemed by its slopeside views and its outdoor pool and two hot tubs, all of the lodging in the Mountain Village consists of condominiums. None is richer in features than the Shoshone

Condominium Hotel (see listing), though anyone looking for luxury space and a ski-in/ski-out location should check out the Beaverhead and Arrowhead complexes as well.

In summer, golfers arrive at Meadow Village to test its 6,748-yard Arnold Palmer golf course, which winds around the middle fork of the Gallatin River. There is tennis in both locations, but the Big Sky Tennis Club has more organized activities. Condos in the meadow can be booked through the Golden Eagle (800-548-4488) or Triple Creek (800-548-4632) management companies.

> **Hikers and mountain bikers will find trailheads scattered through the resort. The gondola operates in summer as well as winter, providing a top-of-the-world panorama of the glacier-carved Spanish Peaks and the Gallatin and Madison ranges.**

Blue ribbon trout fishing is as near as the Gallatin River across from the entrance, and there are four other rivers within easy driving distance. Finally, Yellowstone National Park lies 47 miles to the south, close enough to reach on day trips.

Lone Mountain Ranch

Lone Mountain Ranch Road
P.O. Box 160069
Big Sky, MT 59716
406-995-4644
Fax: 406-995-4670

> *A guest ranch
> also known for
> hiking and cross-
> country skiing*

Proprietors: Bob and Vivian Schaap.
Accommodations: 23 cabins, all with private bath. **Rates:** Summer (Memorial Day to mid-October), single $1,275/week, double $1,975–$2,520/week; winter (December–early April), single $1,250–$1,465/week, double $2,460–$2,890/week. **Included:** All meals, airport transfers, entertainment; summer: horseback riding, all ranch activities, tours of Yellowstone; winter: cross-country skiing, sleigh rides. **Minimum stay:** 7 nights preferred. **Added:** 4% tax and 14% service charge. **Payment:** MasterCard, Visa. **Children:** Free under age 2; reduced rates under age 12 in winter, under 5 in summer. **Pets:** Prohibited. **Smoking:** Prohibited in public areas. **Open:** Memorial Day to mid-October, December to mid-April.

Bob and Vivian Schaap took over Lone Mountain Ranch in 1977, and it hasn't been the same since. Their first act was to introduce cross-country ski trails so the ranch could remain open in the winter. That alone distinguishes Lone Mountain from dozens of other Rocky Mountain guest ranches. But what draws guests back year after years is the Schaaps' inability to rest on their laurels. Not a season goes by without their finding some new way of redefining what a traditional guest

ranch can be. So along with a superb horseback riding program and exceptional western hospitality, the Schaaps have
introduced naturalist-guided hikes, children's programs that
teach about nature and the backcountry even as they entertain, and an Orvis-endorsed fishing program.

> **Over the years the Schaaps have used a blend of hands-on attention and limitless quantities of congeniality to create a first-rate family haven. "We believe very strongly in change," says Bob Schaap. "There's nothing we aren't willing to try to improve."**

Another aspect that sets Lone Mountain apart from most other ranches is its location. Though set below the rugged Spanish Peaks on the threshold of the Lee Metcalf Wilderness Area, the ranch itself lies within the Big Sky Ski & Summer Resort (see above). That endows it with rare assets. Hiking and horseback riding trails plunge directly into the scenic Montana high country, even as the ranch road connects the 140-acre spread with a host of resort facilities, including downhill skiing, a golf course, tennis courts, shops, and restaurants, none more than a few miles distant.

Horseback riding remains a staple of the Lone Mountain summer. The secret to its appeal lies in the ranch's Horse Sense program, whose intent, says Bob Schaap, is "to teach people to think like horses." The attentive, gentle instruction continues on the trail. As many as seven rides of varying degrees of difficulty leave from the corrals each morning. To ensure personal attention, none has more than seven riders. Children as young as six can mount up, often going out on the trails with adults, while those younger join a wrangler-led pony ride around the corral.

As good as the riding program is, it has been rivaled in recent years by the growing popularity of Lone Mountain's wilderness walks. Led by resident naturalists, these treks into the backcountry wind through Manet landscapes of wildflowers, with backdrops of the rugged Spanish Peaks. Along the way, guides may point out the difference between moose and elk prints, encourage hikers to taste wild strawberries, and talk about local Indian lore. Once each week, Lone Mountain turns its attention to Yellowstone National Park, 50 miles to the south, for a guided hike to explore the wildlife, birds, flora, and geology of the park's unique ecosystem.

That ecosystem and the nearby watersheds also happen to contain several blue ribbon trout streams, among them the Gallatin River just across the highway from the entrance to Big Sky. Lone Mountain not only has a fully-stocked Orvis tackle shop on the property but has also become a base for fly-fishing instruction and guided tours (both at added cost).

In winter, Lone Mountain looks and feels like a different place. Once the snows fall, the emphasis shifts to cross-country skiing. Its 75 kilometers of immaculately laid track, supplemented by Nordic instruction and backcountry tours, have made it one of the nation's great Nordic ski touring centers. A free shuttle runs to Big Sky for the downhill slopes and other winter diversions, like sleigh rides and on-the-snow luncheons.

Summer or winter, guests bed down in one of 23 log cabins. These range in size from a single room to two-bedroom, two-bath suites capable of sleeping up to nine people. Many date from the 1920s but a few are brand new. Exceptionally well maintained, all have modern private baths, handmade furnishings, covered porches with log chairs or swings, and amenities like coffeemakers. Almost all have either a fireplace or woodstove. Housekeepers arrive each night to turn down the queen-size beds.

It's a short walk from the cabins to the main lodge and a hot tub and massage rooms. The lodge also contains the Horsefly Saloon, a favorite place to gather before the fresh, healthy dinners (at large tables for those who relish company or small ones for those who don't) of chicken breast stuffed with Boursin, buffalo steak with lingonberries, pheasant with pistachio crust, or a vegetarian dish that changes nightly. There are steaks on the menu, too, but this is otherwise a far cry from typical ranch fare.

The Schaaps are almost always present at dinner. Their personal involvement is one key to the ranch's success. Another is their staff, who opted to live in Montana after finishing college because of their love for the Big Sky state. It's evidently infectious: more than 70 percent of Lone Mountain guests come back, many year after year.

Shoshone Condominium Hotel

Big Sky, MT 59716
406-995-4211
800-548-4486
Fax: 406-995-4860

> *A ski apartment's
> amenities plus
> hotel services*

General manager: John Kircher.
Accommodations: 94 condos.
Rates: Summer (May–October) $160–$260, winter $215–$375;
higher over Christmas holidays. **Minimum stay:** 7 nights over
Christmas holidays. **Added:** 4% tax. **Payment:** Major credit
cards. **Children:** Welcome. **Pets:** Prohibited. **Smoking:** Nonsmoking rooms available. **Open:** Year-round.

Like all ski resorts, the Big Sky's Mountain Village on the
slopes of Lone Mountain contains an abundance of condominiums. Only one property, however, the ski-in/ski-out
Shoshone Condominium Hotel, combines the space and convenience of an apartment with the assets of a full-service
hotel. That includes daily maid service, bellman assisted
check-in, and room service.

The distinctive seven-story wing of 94 one-bedroom units
opened in 1990 as one part of a complex that includes the
Huntley Lodge (now somewhat past its prime; see Big Sky Ski
& Summer Resort, above), a conference center where ski
movies or recent releases are screened in winter, a health
club, and two heated swimming pools.

The Shoshone condos feature gas fireplaces, doors that
open onto a balcony with views of the mountains or the val-

ley, and living rooms with both a Murphy bed and a foldout sofa. A three-quarter bath off the living area supplements the full bath attached to the large separate bedroom. Kitchens come with every essential, from full-size refrigerators and dishwashers to microwaves, coffeemakers, dishes, and pots and pans. Fifteen larger units on the seventh floor are identical to these except for the addition of a loft with a queen-size bed and extra bath.

> **What the Shoshone dubs a standard condo contains 790 to 900 square feet, all of it outfitted in an easy-to-live-with contemporary decor.**

Choices for après-ski are the subdued Chet's Bar in the Huntley Lodge or the livelier Whiskey Jack's in the mall next door. The mall also harbors restaurants, a grocery/sundries/liquor store, several clothing and souvenir shops, and an ATM. Perhaps the only people who can't spend a winter vacation entirely at the Mountain Village are cross-country skiers, who must travel a few miles down the road to the Nordic center at Lone Mountain Ranch (see above).

BIG TIMBER

The Grand

McLeod Street
Big Timber, MT 59011
406-932-4459

> *An 1890 hotel with a notable restaurant and wine list*

General manager: Lawrence Edwards. **Accommodations:** 7 rooms, 2 with private bath. **Rates:** $55–$85. **Included:** Full breakfast. **Minimum stay:** None. **Added:** 4% tax. **Payment:** Discover, MasterCard, Visa. **Children:** Welcome. **Pets:** Allowed if quiet. **Smoking:** Prohibited in rooms and dining room. **Open:** Year-round.

Built to serve railroaders and land speculators, cattlemen and sheepherders, the two-story red brick Grand became a major business and social gathering place for the community of Big Timber. That earned it a listing on the National Register of Historic Places but couldn't prevent its slide into near dereliction. The Grand was battered and rundown when owner Suzanne Wilson undertook its salvation in 1986. By the time she finished, it had seven cheerfully decorated rooms and a restaurant with inventive American cuisine and a Wine Spectator award for having one of the best wine lists in Montana.

> The exposed brick, wainscoting, comforters, ceiling fans, and sophisticated color schemes suggest an attention to comfort and style almost certainly missing in the original hotel, most of whose rooms were tiny, utilitarian cubicles.

The front door opens onto a sunny corner lobby with windows on two sides and new oak trim, oak wainscoting, and a floral carpet. Part of the original pressed tin ceiling survives. An old safe now doubles as a plant stand. Black and white photos of Big Timber at the turn of the century decorate the walls, along with western paintings of forest fires. A door to one side leads into the saloon with its original mahogany back bar.

All of the accommodations are on the second floor off a long hall anchored at the near end by a sitting area with parquet floors, reupholstered antique chairs and sofas, and a small TV. The rooms themselves suggest the past in their antique beds and dressers, most purchased at estate auctions. Many of these rooms are still on the small side, but there are exceptions, among them number 4, which has a brass bed and air conditioning, and number 6, which has a private half bath. Largest of all is number 7, which has ample space for a king-size brass bed, a sitting area with wicker furnishings, and a private bath with modern fixtures. Beds in the other rooms vary, from white iron or brass to burled maple or rustic log. Five of the rooms share four detached baths, with robes provided for getting back and forth.

It isn't so much those refurbished rooms that put the Grand on the maps, however, as its restaurant, which is now under the care of Lawrence Edwards, formerly of Chico Hot Springs fame (see Pray, Montana). Though there are steaks and rack of lamb on the menu — this is still grazing country, after all — Edwards also serves dishes not usually found on menus of restaurants in small western towns, including a tasty Key lime chicken, champagne shrimp, and daily fresh fish specials. People drive for miles just to dine.

Lazy K Bar Ranch

P.O. Box 550
Big Timber, MT 59011
406-537-4404
Fax: 406-537-4404

An old, family-run ranch with 100-mile vistas

Proprietors: The Van Cleve family.
Accommodations: 22 cabins, 20 with private bath. **Rates:** Single $695–$955, double $1,150–$1,660. **Included:** All meals and activities. **Minimum stay:** 7 nights. **Added:** $35/person/night tax. **Payment:** Cash, personal checks, or traveler's checks. **Children:** Nurse or nanny required under age 6. **Pets:** Prohibited. **Smoking:** Allowed. **Open:** June 23 through Labor Day

Founded by the Van Cleve family in 1880, this 22,000-acre paradise of high plains, glacier-chiseled peaks, and 100-mile vistas is one of the oldest and most celebrated family operations in the Rockies.

The lodge and cabins huddle among the Douglas fir above Big Timber Creek, 25 miles northwest of the town of Big Timber, at the end of an unmarked gravel road. Barbara Van Cleve, wife of the founder's son, and her three children run it with an uncharacteristic minimum of structure and virtually no organized activities except the Saturday night square dance and Sunday breakfast walk. Guests must stay at least a week but may arrive on any day. With people constantly coming and going, the following day's schedule is typically made up at dinner the night before, after polling guests about their preferences.

Most want to ride. With so much terrain open to the ranch, the choice of trails verges on endless. Guests may opt to take a short jaunt to the reservoir for a swim or an all-day ride to a meadow at the timberline (coupled with a hike to the top of Big Timber Peak for a spectacular panorama of the Big Sky country). In between are trails to an outlaw's hideout or to pools inhabited by prehistoric fairy shrimp. Children six to twelve have their own wrangler, who often sets up all-day rides that culminate in a cookout or keeps them busy hunting fossils or playing softball or volleyball. Parents can spend as much or as little time with their children as they want.

> **Still a working ranch, the Lazy K first accepted guests in 1922, letting them help move cattle or simply ride through country the Crow Indians called "the perfect place."**

The command center is the old log lodge itself, with its big stone fireplace, western antiques, an 1882 grand piano, and an 1885 Brunswick billiards table. Guests gather in the lodge for family-style meals of ranch-raised beef and pork, vegetables fresh from the garden, Guernsey milk, and homemade breads. Nearly all the food is grown on the property. Barbara's bouquets of wildflowers decorate the tables.

The log and timber cabins, like the lodge, radiate rustic warmth. Ranging from one to four bedrooms, they feature log beds, vegetable-dyed Navajo rugs, and in most cases private baths and a Franklin stove or a fireplace. Most have porches, the perfect place to read a book from the lodge library.

Strenuous activity is not required, of course. In addition to riding there are lakes and streams to fish, hiking trails, and a swimming pool, but no one cares if guests prefer to gather wildflowers — something Barbara loves to do — or relish the mountain air and views of the Crazy Mountains. The ranch fills quickly, though, so for the best choice of dates, book right after Christmas.

Sweet Grass Ranch

Melville Route, Box 167
Big Timber, MT 59011
406-537-4477
Fax: 406-537-4497

> *A picturesque cattle ranch, steeped in western hospitality*

Proprietors: Shelly and Bill Carroccia. **Accommodations:** 4 rooms with shared bath; 8 cabins, 6 with private bath. **Rates:** Rooms $625/person/week, cabins $590–$685/person/week. **Included:** All meals, horseback riding, and activities. **Minimum stay:** 7 nights. **Added:** 4% tax on lodging portion only. **Payment:** Cash, personal checks, or traveler's checks. **Children:** No charge under age 3; reduced rates under age 6. **Pets:** With prior approval. **Smoking:** Prohibited in main lodge and on trails. **Open:** Mid-June through Labor Day; a cabin is also available the rest of the year at the Carroccias' winter home at Otter Creek Ranch.

All heart and minimal frills, Sweet Grass Ranch captivates everyone who endures the 17 miles of sometimes bad road to find it. Its peculiar power begins with the picturesque setting: the red-roofed lodge and cabins edge along the pines and cottonwoods on the banks of the Sweet Grass River in a narrow canyon 40 miles from Big Timber. Corrals and a fenced meadow fill the space in front of the lodge, while the granite wedge of Big Timber peak pierces the sky behind it. Yet even beyond that dazzling scenery, the Sweet Grass Ranch traces its magic to the Carroccia family's friendliness and accommodating spirit.

Still a working ranch with 200 head of cattle, Sweet Grass begins at 6,100 feet in the foothills

> There is no structure to the day unless cattle have to be moved, in which case guests are encouraged to come along. Otherwise, the Carroccias find out what people want to do and then accommodate them, whether they prefer to spend an hour or all day in the saddle, or just hang around and maybe fish.

and literally goes on for miles, alternating its 20,000 acres with sections of the Gallatin National Forest as it spreads west into the Crazy Mountains. The riding is spectacular. Some trails lead up above the timberline to alpine lakes and 300-mile views. Pronghorns, eagles, and hawks are common.

All the ranch's riding instruction is informal. Guests may saddle their own horses or ride bareback, take moonlight rides, help milk cows, check fences, or clear trails. "We want people to get a sense of what living on a ranch is all about," says Shelly. "We run it very much like a large family; guests can take part in anything." Kids are welcome, and although there are no special programs, children can take part in much of the activity, riding their own horse or doubling up with an adult. Babysitting can be arranged for the very young.

Listed on the National Register of Historic Places, the Sweet Grass is a classic example of what homesteaders could accomplish using little more than materials found on the land. The rustic, two-story log lodge radiates character. In the dining room guests sit down at long tables for tasty fare (served family-style) such as ranch-raised beef, milk and cream from Sweet Grass's dairy cattle, greens from the garden, homemade breads, and desserts. Afterward, they gather around the massive stone fireplace in the adjoining living room for conversation, a game of pool, or sing-alongs. No one stays up very late. Some go back to cabins with woodstoves and private baths, others to rooms in the lodge with shared baths, and a few to tiny cabins without heat or running water.

"It's basically a no-frills working ranch," says Bill. "We emphasize riding, that's all." Maybe, but the people who come back year after year, captivated by the Carroccias' infectious joy, think it's much more.

BOZEMAN

For other lodging in the area, see the towns of Big Sky, Emigrant, Gallatin Gateway, and Three Forks.

Silver Forest Inn

15325 Bridger Canyon Road
Bozeman, MT 59715
406-586-1882

*A turreted B&B
near Bridger Bowl*

Hosts: Kathryn and Richard Jensen. **Accommodations:** 5 rooms, 3 with private bath. **Rates:** $60–$90. **Included:** Full breakfast.

Minimum stay: None. **Added:** 4% tax. **Payment:** MasterCard, Visa. **Children:** Welcome. **Pets:** Small pets considered. **Smoking:** Prohibited, except in a few restricted areas. **Open:** Year-round.

This log house with turret clings to a hillside in Bridger Canyon, 15 miles north of Bozeman and a half mile from the Bridger Bowl Ski Resort. Built in 1934 as the residence for the founder of a summer artists' colony, it merges the charm of a cabin with the spaciousness of a lodge.

After a day of skiing, the outdoor hot tub is the most popular gathering place at the inn, followed by the living room, where Richard Jensen's artwork adorns one wall and the mountain landscape, seen through two huge windows, adorns the other.

> Deer and moose sometimes wander by, oblivious to the guests relaxing in the outdoor hot tub or the spectacular panorama of the Bridger Range across the valley.

Richard and Kathryn, a massage therapist, are affable hosts, eager to please and quick to treat guests like friends. So is their school-age son.

All three Jensens love it when guests bring children. Those who do often book one room for themselves and another for their kids, though the Forest Room with its wood-paneled walls, two queen-size beds, handwoven rugs, and private bath can handle a family of four. Two of the most enchanting rooms beg for romantic couples. Everyone's favorite — even if it does share a bath down the hall — is the Turret Room. Though tiny, it has log walls on eight sides, a queen-size bed, floral quilts and drapes, and panoramic views of the Bridger Mountains. Two floors below it, in a secluded corner of the house, is Bridger View, a sun-drenched hideaway with low ceilings, a queen-size bed, and detached but private bath. The dusky rose McKinney Room, by contrast, trades spectacular views for a sitting area and private attached bath, making it the most comfortable room for long stays.

Sandwiched between the two rooms in the turret is a tiny breakfast nook with room for six. Guests gather here or beneath the chandelier at the dining room table to devour generous helpings of quiche, crêpes, or Belgian waffles while gazing at the mountains and ski slopes.

Torch & Toes

309 South Third Avenue
Bozeman, MT 59715
406-586-7285
800-446-2138

A historic-district B&B, cheery and unpretentious

Hosts: Ronald and Judy Hess. **Accommodations:** 4 rooms, 2 with private bath. **Rates:** Single $55, double $65–$70. **Included:** Full breakfast. **Minimum stay:** None. **Added:** 4% tax. **Payment:** MasterCard, Visa. **Children:** Welcome. **Pets:** Prohibited. **Smoking:** Prohibited. **Open:** Year-round.

While trying to decide what to call their new bed-and-breakfast, Judy and Ron Hess chanced upon an old photo of the first pieces of the Statue of Liberty to arrive in the United States: the torch and a foot. Taken by the whimsy, they decided to dub their Colonial Revival house the Torch & Toes. The photo that inspired the offbeat name now hangs in the entryway, to amuse guests as much as to enlighten them. It is the first clue to the Hesses' approach to innkeeping.

Built in 1906 and part of Bozeman's Bon Ton Historic District, the Torch & Toes refuses to take itself too seriously, even though it exemplifies the kind of residential architecture popular during the early 20th century. The Hesses have tried here and there to suggest the feel of a turn-of-the-century guest house. The two high-ceilinged parlors contain period furnishings, as does the oak-wainscoted dining room. Moreover, they decorated the Alyssum Room with a Jenny Lind spool bed, an antique washstand and lavabo, and some family antiques. But they couldn't resist capricious touches, like the ice cream parlor chair in the Flower Room or the soft-sculpture doll in the Elaine Room, both of which have bay windows and a few antiques. The carriage house has a sunny room with Mission style furniture, a lodgepole pine queen-size bed, a private bath with a clawfoot tub, and a loft with a rug that Judy, a weaver, created out of 45 pairs of jeans.

> **A few period furnishings, leaded glass windows, and lace curtains suggest the past, but they must vie for attention with collections of gargoyles, mousetraps, old postcards, and a Victrola with vintage Frank Sinatra records. As historic B&Bs go, this one is very relaxed.**

The Hesses serve huge and varied breakfasts — eggs baked with leeks and tarragon, pan-fried trout, apple ricotta pie, buttermilk waffles with chokecherry syrup — in front of the dining room fireplace in winter or, weather permitting, on the redwood deck outside in summer. Downtown Bozeman is a short three blocks away.

The Voss Inn

319 South Willson
Bozeman, MT 59715
406-587-0982

> *An 1883 mansion turned romantic B&B*

Hosts: Bruce and Frankee Muller. **Accommodations:** 6 rooms, all with private bath. **Rates:** Single $65–$75, double $70–$80. **Included:** Full breakfast. **Minimum stay:** None. **Added:** 4% tax. **Payment:** MasterCard, Visa. **Children:** Welcome over age 5. **Pets:** Prohibited. **Smoking:** Prohibited except in the parlor. **Open:** Year-round.

Every afternoon, Frankee Muller sets out scrumptious homemade pastries and tea in the Victorian parlor of the Voss Inn, an 1883 two-story mansion converted into a comfortably elegant bed-and-breakfast. A scattering of Empire-style furniture stands before the parlor fireplace beneath a brass chandelier. Bold wallpapers set off oil paintings of Victorian ladies. Sunlight streams through bay windows, falling on the oriental rugs that accent the polished hardwood floors.

> The spacious guest rooms are rich in Victoriana. They feature brass or iron beds — including one with a dramatic nine-foot-high brass headboard — vivid wallpapers, a scattering of antiques, and vases of fresh flowers often picked from the inn's own gardens. Half of the rooms have clawfoot tubs.

The Mullers bought the inn in 1989, when they decided to start a family but didn't relish the idea of having babies in the wilderness of Botswana, where they had been leading photographic safaris. Adept at hospitality, they took over a B&B that had been renovated and decorated with exceptional style and taste.

Each room has a small table and chairs, so guests can have breakfast in the privacy of their own rooms. Every morning the Mullers set out a breakfast buffet at one end of the second-floor hall. In addition to coffee, fruit, and juice, it consists of something hot, like an egg and cheese dish in individual ramekins, plus fresh muffins or cinnamon rolls from an antique bun warmer built in to the 1880s radiator.

Since guests are not thrown together at breakfast, Frankee's afternoon teas become the excuse for them to get together with one another and the Mullers. In winter, everyone gathers in front of the parlor fireplace; in summer, they may drift out onto the front porch. The Voss is only a few blocks from Montana State University, and Yellowstone National Park, though not close by, can be reached on an independent day trip or on one of the Mullers' Jeep safaris.

BUTTE

Copper King Mansion

219 West Granite Street
Butte, MT 59701
406-782-7580

> *A copper baron's
> ostentatious
> mansion turned
> museum and inn*

Managers: Maria and Chris Wagner. **Accommodations:** 4 rooms, 2 with private bath. **Rates:** $55–$95. **Included:** Full breakfast; mansion tour. **Minimum stay:** None. **Added:** 4% tax. **Payment:** Major credit cards. **Children:** Free; $10 for roll-away. **Pets:** Allowed if well behaved. **Smoking:** Prohibited. **Open:** Year-round.

William Andrews Clark, who became a prominent Montana political figure, spent $300,000 in 1884 to construct this opulent 34-room mansion in historic uptown Butte. At that time, the Montana mining city had a reputation as "the richest hill on earth," and Clark, who owned not only mines but supply stores, transportation systems, real estate, and banks ranked among the nation's 100 richest men. In this mansion, now listed on the National Register of Historic Places, he seems to have set out to display his wealth in the most ostentatious way possible.

Like Donald Trump, Clark never opted for the simple and elegant if there was an opportunity to be ornate and showy. Stained glass windows and magnificent hand-carved woodwork vie for attention with frescoed ceilings and inlaid floors, much of the work having been done by European craftsmen brought over specifically to work on the mansion.

The wonderful opulence of these interiors gets a boost from the furnishings. Though only 20 or so are original to the mansion, the remainder all come from the same period — or, in the case of a 1917 addition to the house, from the 1920s. Yet the decor goes beyond highback burled walnut beds and clawfoot tubs with golden feet; it also includes an astonishing array of collectibles, from antique perfume bottles to turn-of-the-century combs and purses. The mansion has been not merely furnished but accessorized.

> **The Copper King Mansion is a monument to Victorian excess. Somewhat the worse for 100 years of weather, the three-story medley of porches, gables, and bow windows only hints at the fantastic interiors that lie within.**

Delightful to wander through — it's open for guided tours from May through October — the house that Clark built is even more special as a place to stay. Five of the rooms can accommodate overnight guests. For lavish surroundings, nothing surpasses the Master Suite. Its large sitting room with bird's-eye maple woodwork, fireplace, and frescoed ceiling adjoins Clark's own sycamore-paneled bedroom furnished with a burled walnut highback bed and matching dresser. It has a large private bath with a pedestal sink, huge tub (but no shower), and a collection of antique combs and purses. The vast Family Room, by contrast, was built as a place for the Clarks to gather. In it, hand-painted watercolor frescoes on the ceiling cap a huge space lined with cherry woodwork and furnished with a fireplace, lace curtains, and two African mahogany sleigh beds with matching dressers. It has a private half bath with five doors and a clawfoot tub. Of the others, the Hugette Room, added in 1917, stands out for its Art Deco furnishings, while the Andrea Room, which belonged to one of the Clark children, has a golden oak bed, lace and rose plush curtains, and an Oriental rug.

The Hugette and Andrea rooms share a bath containing both a huge tub and a bizarre "birdcage" shower, which sprays water not only from above but also from the sides. "It comes with 10 minutes of instructions," quips manager

Maria Wagner, the granddaughter of the woman who bought and refurbished the mansion in 1952.

The mansion's dual role for part of the year as tourist attraction and a bed-and-breakfast imposes some peculiar strictures. Guests are expected to have finished breakfast and checked out by 9 A.M. when the tours start. Guests on multinight stays may leave their things in their rooms but need to be aware that people will come traipsing through every hour from 9 A.M. to 5 P.M. Still, it seems worth it for the opportunity to bed down in what amounts to a museum of late 19th-century American opulence.

CLYDE PARK

G Bar M Ranch

Clyde Park, MT 59018
406-686-4687

A small, family-run ranch where guests feel like family

Proprietors: Mary, George, and Hank Leffingwell. **Accommodations:** 4 rooms, 2 cabins, all with private bath. **Rates:** Rooms $650/week single, $1,200/week double; cabins $600/person, 3-person minimum. **Included:** All meals, activities, and taxes. **Minimum stay:** 7 nights. **Added:** Nothing. **Payment:** Cash, personal checks, or traveler's checks. **Children:** Reduced rates under age 12. **Pets:** Prohibited. **Smoking:** Allowed. **Open:** May through September.

At the G Bar M, guests, ranch hands, wranglers, and the Leffingwell family all eat together at big tables. Mary Leffingwell, who's now in her 70s and gets around in an electric wheelchair, is supposed to join the gathering, but she often rolls off to the kitchen to fetch or fix something else. "They tell me to supervise," she says, "but I can't stay out of the kitchen. I have my sourdough pancakes that I won't let anyone else do, and all the breads."

Mary has been doing this since 1934, when her father first started accepting guests at the cattle ranch he'd established around the turn of the century. Now her sons, George and

Hank, are also involved, as are George's wife and sons and Hank's wife. All of them have the rare gift of easygoing warmth and genuine western hospitality. Guests no sooner come through the door than they are made to feel like family.

The G Bar M, one of a diminishing number of working ranches, still rides herd on 150 head of cattle on its 3,200 acres of sagebrush-covered foothills in Brackett Creek Valley, along the Bridger Mountains. Part of the property is a wildlife reserve where no hunting is allowed. Thus, eagles, elk, and deer frequent the ranch, as does a wide variety of birds.

> **The ranch can handle a maximum of 15 people (and usually has fewer), so guests receive an abundance of personal attention and are encouraged to take part in the ranch routine, right down to saddling, currying, and feeding the horses if they're so inclined. Mainly, however, they ride.**

At the beginning of the week, wranglers match each person to an appropriate horse and make sure they can handle it before leading them out on the trail. These rides, while often scenic, tend to be connected to some aspect of the ranch operation: checking fences, placing salt licks, or visiting the ranch's sawmill. At certain times of the year the cattle have to be moved, and guest participation is not only welcome but encouraged. "They're a big help," George Leffingwell says of the guests who help. "The cattle don't know they're inexperienced."

Accommodations at the G Bar M consist of four rooms with private baths in the main house and two cabins, one with two bedrooms and a clawfoot tub, the other with three bedrooms and a fireplace. Ranch-made quilts cover the brass or log beds in rooms that are as homey as they are immaculately clean.

Dinners of spaghetti, stews, casseroles, steaks, and roasts, accompanied by at least two salads and Mary's fabulous breads, are served family-style in the dining room of the main house. Afterward, guests sometimes gather in the pine-paneled living room, which has an upright piano, a television, and a VCR with a selection of videotapes. More often than not, they go to bed early, like the ranch hands.

Embraced by the Leffingwells' warmth and good humor, 80 percent of them come back. "It's like a family," says George. "They cry when they leave and so do we."

DARBY

Triple Creek Ranch

5551 West Fork Stage Route
Darby, MT 59829
406-821-4664
800-654-2943
Fax: 406-821-4666

A ranch secluded from everything but luxury

General managers: Wayne and Judy Kilpatrick. **Accommodations:** 17 cabins. **Rates:** Single $425–$715/day, double $475–$765/day. **Included:** All meals, activities, wine with dinner, and drinks. **Minimum stay:** None. **Added:** $4.50–$5.70/cabin/day lodging tax. **Payment:** Major credit cards. **Children:** Under age 16 not allowed unless entire facility is reserved. **Pets:** Prohibited. **Smoking:** Prohibited in dining room. **Open:** Mid-May to mid-October and late December through February.

West of Darby, the last of Montana's paved roads turns to gravel before dissolving into the rugged Bitterroot Range along the Idaho border. More than a million acres of wilderness takes over, dominated by the rocky crest of 10,157-foot Trapper Peak. It's an unlikely place to find one of the West's most exclusive and seductive hideaways, which is only part of what makes the Triple Creek Ranch so enchanting.

Poised at the edge of that pristine backcountry, Triple

Creek seems a million miles from civilization and its discontents. Wildflowers bloom in the meadows. Whitetail deer wander through the firs. Nothing disturbs the silence but the sound of rushing creeks and tumbling waterfalls.

The staff — more than one per guest — exists to help. No one seems to mind unusual or last-minute requests, and many of the activities — including horseback rides and guided fly-fishing outings — tend to be organized on an individual basis. Guests are even encouraged to drop in to the kitchen to talk to the chef about special dietary requirements.

> **The attentiveness of the staff and their consistent attempts to provide the warmhearted, personal service typical of a first-class hotel helps underpin this ranch's appeal.**

The lavish accommodations show the same thoughtful attention to detail. The 14 cabins have from one to three rooms. Country elegant rather than rustic, even the smallest have outside decks, queen-size log-post beds, stone fireplaces, plump furnishings, refrigerators (fully stocked with beverages, beer, wine, and the guest's favorite liquor and mixers), coffeemakers, remote-control satellite TVs and VCRs, phones, bowls of fruit, fresh-baked cookies, an eclectic selection of paperbacks and magazines, and a rechargeable flashlight. The larger units add separate living areas and in some cases huge baths with double steam showers and private hot tubs.

The heart of the ranch is a cedar lodge containing an elegant oak-furnished dining room, a scenic upstairs bar with a fireplace and outside deck, and a library/conference room with comfortable sofas. Each night, casually attired guests sit down to hearty table d'hôte dinners as sumptuous as the rest of the ranch. On Friday and Saturday evenings, the public can dine (reservations required).

Those who opt to stay around the ranch during the day can bask in the heated pool or hot tub, play tennis, or fish for trout in a stocked pond.

EMIGRANT

Mountain Sky Guest Ranch

Big Creek Road
Emigrant, Montana
406-333-4911 (summer only, at
    ranch)
Mailing Address:
P.O. Box 1128
Bozeman, MT 59715
406-587-1244
800-548-3392
Fax: 406-587-3977

> *A guest ranch with
> resort amenities,
> near Yellowstone*

Proprietors: Alan and Mary Brutger. **Accommodations:** 25 cabins, all with private bath. **Rates:** $1,645–$1,890/person/week. **Included:** All meals, horseback riding, other ranch activities, and gratuities. **Minimum stay:** 7 nights in high season; otherwise 3 nights. **Added:** 1% tax. **Payment:** MasterCard, Visa. **Children:** Reduced rates under age 13. **Pets:** Prohibited. **Smoking:** Prohibited in dining room. **Open:** Late May to early October.

Guests lounging around the pool at Mountain Sky banter about "power hikes" and try to work out how many hours they must spend in the mirrored aerobics dance studio to work off the calories of the previous night's tortellini-garnished rack of lamb and scrumptious desserts. This is strange talk for one of Montana's oldest guest ranches, whose tradition of welcoming guests dates from the 1930s and whose history as a working ranch dates from 50 years before that. But ever since the Brutger family took over in the late 1970s, the 4,000-acre gem has been pushing the envelope of the traditional ranch by expanding the available amenities while preserving the essential western hospitality.

Draped across the slopes of the Gallatin Mountains, 60 miles southeast of Bozeman, the Mountain Sky spread backs up against the Gallatin National Forest. From its perch 5,300 feet above sea level, it looks east at the Absaroka Mountains on the opposite side of Paradise Valley. That location puts it within an easy 30-mile drive of Yellowstone National Park and a mere 4½ miles from the blue ribbon trout fishing on the Yellowstone River on the valley floor below.

Like all guest ranches, Mountain Sky takes pride in its horseback riding. Wranglers lead small groups into the scenic backcountry twice a day, choosing trails to match the skills of the riders. Those who prefer to travel under their own power can use the half dozen hiking trails that lace the surrounding forest, some over gently rolling hills covered with wildflowers, others rising to higher elevations and views east across Paradise Valley. Guests who stay behind can look forward to a stocked fishing pond and several trout-rich creeks, a heated swimming pool, a hot tub and sauna, two tennis courts, stretch-and-relax exercise classes, and those early-morning power hikes.

> **As good as the riding program is, the ranch stands out for its determination to offer much more than a day in the saddle. Escaping to the mountains does not, in this case, mean having to do without amenities typical of a resort hotel.**

That's true of the cabins as well. Though a handful were carpentered together in the 1930s and remain popular for their streamside locations and lodgepole pine furnishings, most were built after the Brutgers took over in the 1980s. Whether old or new, the one- to three-bedroom pine-paneled hideaways feature woodstoves, down comforters, country prints, small refrigerators, and full modern baths. Baskets of fresh fruit are refilled whenever they run low; so is the coffee for the in-room coffeemakers.

Cabins comfortably accommodate families, who come in force, lured by the ranch's exceptional children's programs. Teens get their own set of organized diversions, including a special table in the dining room. While adults feast at the twice-a-week gourmet dinners, kids go off for pizza or burgers and maybe a trip into Bozeman for the rodeo. The Brutgers have turned this old Montana ranch into a very special kind of family getaway.

ENNIS

T Lazy B Ranch

532 Jack Creek Road
Ennis, MT 59726
406-682-7288

> *A haven for
> avid fishermen
> near the Madison*

Proprietors: Bob and Theo Walker.
Accommodations: 3 cabins, share
separate bathhouse. **Rates:** $120/
person. **Included:** All meals and taxes. **Minimum stay:** None.
Added: Nothing. **Payment:** Cash, personal checks, or traveler's checks. **Children:** Welcome, but caters to fishermen and
has no special activities. **Pets:** Allowed. **Smoking:** Allowed.
Open: Mid-June through September.

The T Lazy B Ranch straddles Jack Creek as it flows out of the
Madison Range nine miles east of Ennis. Apart from the private fishing it offers on the creek, the ranch specializes in
guided float trips on the legendary Madison River ($235 for
two), where fly-rodders have a shot at catching trophy-size
rainbow and brown trout ranging up to 22 inches. The ranch
also provides easy access to more than half a dozen other blue
ribbon streams and rivers.

Bob Walker has been a fishing guide in this area since 1977,
when he and his wife, Theo, bought the 33-acre ranch. They
have deliberately kept the operation small in order to give
more personal attention and get to know their guests. Everyone is encouraged to drop in to the kitchen and help himself
to coffee or fruit. Homestyle meals of spaghetti, loin of pork,

steaks, chicken, or whatever guests want revolve around fishermen's schedules. Many of the vegetables come from the garden in front of the lodge, a single-story log structure built in 1935 that contains the dining room and a parlor with a small fireplace where guests gather in the evening.

> **In addition to float trips on the Madison River, the T Lazy B also arranges (at extra cost) guided wading trips on any of the nearby rivers, or courses of instruction for everyone from beginners to advanced fly rodders.**

An apron of lawn extends from the lodge to Jack Creek, where a wooden footbridge provides access to three no-frills cabins. Hand-crafted in the 1930s, they have been simply furnished, though one does have an antique walnut sleigh bed that once belonged to Theo's grandfather. None has running water. Instead, they share a sparkling clean, modern bathhouse containing showers, toilets, sinks, and even a washer and dryer.

The ranch has none of the traditional dude ranch activities or children's programs. In the fall, emphasis shifts from angling to upland bird hunting, but throughout the summer its only passion is fishing.

GALLATIN GATEWAY

Gallatin Gateway Inn

U.S. 191
P.O. Box 376
Gallatin Gateway, MT 59730
406-763-4672
800-676-3522
Fax: 406-763-4672

> *An exotic gem
> in primitive
> surroundings*

General manager: Colin Kurth Davis. **Accommodations:** 32 rooms, 3 suites. **Rates:** Rooms $75–$85, suites $95–$100. **Included:** Continental breakfast. **Minimum stay:** None. **Added:** 4% tax. **Payment:** Major credit cards. **Children:** Welcome. **Pets:** Prohibited. **Smoking:** Nonsmoking rooms available. **Open:** Year-round.

The Chicago, Milwaukee and St. Paul Railroad built the elegant Gallatin Gateway Inn in 1927, hoping to lure easterners to attractions like Yellowstone National Park and, of course, to the rail service it provided to take them there. Some 10,000 people attended the grand opening of the buff-colored stucco and red tile inn, marveling at the stenciled Philippine mahogany beams, the carved stone mantel, and the graceful arched windows of its expansive lounge.

Unfortunately, the decline of rail travel after World War II set the fashionable two-story Spanish Colonial hotel on a downward course through a succession of owners who used or abused it variously as a showroom for antique cars, a live music club, and, at its nadir, an arena for women's mud wrestling.

A $1.5 million renovation restored its former glory. It's worth stopping by just to have a drink in that magnificent lounge, gazing up at the 23-foot beamed ceiling from one of the beautifully upholstered chairs or sofas, or to dine beneath Spanish chandeliers on dishes like Thai scampi, braised rabbit, or grilled pheasant.

> It took landmark status, $1.5 million, and the blood, sweat, and tears of current owners Catherine Wrather and her son Bill Keshishian to restore it to its former glory. For their efforts, they won the 1986 Montana Historic Preservation Award.

Guests have a choice of bedding down in the inn itself or in a 1993 annex. The rooms in the main building, though on the small side, have been appointed with pastel Indian print comforters and brass lamps. Most — but not all — have full private baths. The accommodations in the two annex buildings, by contrast, trade history for roominess. Although their decor includes wall sconces saved from the original hotel, and the walls have a similar rough plaster finish, the rooms themselves are more spacious. Each has two queen-size beds with handmade pine headboards, a full bath, and air conditioning. All the rooms, whether in the inn or annex, have phones and cable televisions. Rates in either place include a breakfast of fresh fruit, muffins, and juice, which the young, pleasant staff sets out each morning in the colonnade.

Yellowstone National Park is roughly an hour's drive to the south, while the hotel itself diverts guests with an outdoor heated pool and hot tub, a tennis court, a fly-casting pond, and an array of rental mountain bikes.

HARDIN

Eagle Nest Lodge

P.O. Box 470
Hardin, MT 59034
406-665-3799

An ultra-exclusive fishing lodge on the Big Horn

General managers: Nick and Francine Forrester. **Accommodations:** 5 rooms, all with private bath; 1 cabin. **Rates:** $1,600/person for 5 days on standard package; custom packages available. **Included:** All meals, taxes, guides, boats, and flies. **Minimum stay:** None. **Added:** Nothing. **Payment:** Cash, personal checks, or traveler's checks. **Children:** Welcome, but no special activities or babysitters. **Pets:** Prohibited indoors; must have own kennel. **Smoking:** Allowed. **Open:** Late April to Thanksgiving.

By some estimates, the Big Horn River contains more than 7,000 trout per mile, many of them between 18 and 22 inches long, a distinction that ranks it among America's richest trout streams. The only Orvis-endorsed facility on the river is the Eagle Nest Lodge.

Built in 1985 of honey-colored pine, the ultra-exclusive lodge sits among a stand of cottonwood trees within the Crow Indian Reservation a few miles outside of Hardin. Its five air-conditioned rooms and two-bedroom cabin accommodate a maximum of 15 guests in spiffy comfort. There's also a small Orvis shop on the premises.

With the help of the amiable guides, one for every two fly fishermen — or fisherwomen, who constitute roughly a third of guests — even intermediates boast of catching 10 or more big rainbows or browns a day, while experts have been known to reel in as many as 50. Although there is some float fishing, boats tend to be used only to move from place to place, letting fishermen out to wade the river's edge (easy to do, because the bottom is not slippery).

Everything revolves around fishing, including dinner, which is served as late as 10 P.M. if anglers dally. Francine Forrester, who studied classical French cuisine in New York City, prepares what she calls "country gourmet with a French accent": tasty five-course affairs featuring roast Cornish game hen, red snapper with cilantro and black beans, or stuffed tenderloin. Many of the vegetables come from her garden, and everything is homemade, including the white chocolate mousse, ice creams, and profiteroles.

> **This is the quintessential fly-fishing camp, where the talk around the fireplace every evening inevitably runs to the relative merits of blue wing olives or pale morning duns and the fish that did, or did not, get away.**

Because the Big Horn is a tailwater fishery unaffected by spring runoff, the lodge enjoys a long season, with the best fishing from May to September. Packages include everything except a fishing license and alcohol (none is sold at the lodge, but guests are welcome to bring their own). In the fall, fishermen share the lodge with upland bird hunters, who have access to 50,000 private acres of rolling grasslands and wheat fields that are home to pheasants, Hungarian partridge, and sharptail grouse.

Kendrick House Inn

206 North Custer Avenue
Hardin, MT 59034
406-665-3035
Fax: 406-665-3035

> *A renovated 1915 home near Custer's last stand*

Hosts: Marcie and Steve Smith. **Accommodations:** 7 rooms with shared baths. **Rates:** Single $45, double $55. **Included:** Full breakfast. **Minimum stay:** None. **Added:** 4% tax. **Payment:**

MasterCard, Visa. **Children:** Welcome. **Pets:** Prohibited (they have a cat). **Smoking:** Prohibited. **Open:** Year-round.

As the town closest to Little Bighorn Battlefield National Monument and the Bighorn River's blue ribbon trout fishing, Hardin snags carloads of tourists who might otherwise stay in Billings, 60 miles to the west and 20 times larger. That's especially true during Little Bighorn Days, the third week in June, when the reenactment of Custer's last stand takes place.

> **Steve and Marcie Smith's renovated home provides an alternative to the campsites, RV parks, and motels that are standard fare near Little Bighorn Battlefield National Monument.**

Now listed on the National Register of Historic Places, this brick two-story dwelling was the most elegant boarding house Hardin had ever seen when it was built in 1915. Later gutted by fire, it stood empty for years until the Smiths bought it in 1988 and set about restoring it to its former grandeur.

Despite an unhappy location next to a car dealership, the B&B is successful because of Steve Smith's almost obsessive attention to detail and Marcie's skill at interior design. They furnished the rooms with pieces they found in antiques shops, thrift stores, and auction houses, added a television and guest phone to the library, hung a swing in the enclosed first-floor porch, and placed white wicker furniture on the deck.

The decor varies from bedroom to bedroom, with brass beds in some, oak or iron in others. Antique dressers, lace curtains, and period prints enhance the turn-of-the-century look. Each room has its own pedestal sink to take the pressure off seven rooms sharing two baths.

Born in Billings, Steve has a native's intimate knowledge of the area's attractions and a western warmth that Marcie, who's from Oregon, shares. Their handiwork shows in everything from her collection of plates to the polished fir flooring and hand-painted hot air registers. Guests linger over hearty Montana breakfasts of homemade coffee cake, fruit, French toast, eggs, bacon, and sausage; after all, Custer's battlefield isn't going anywhere.

HELENA

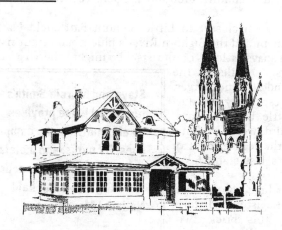

The Barrister

416 North Ewing Street
Helena, MT 59601
406-443-7330

*A Queen Anne
B&B facing
Helena's gothic
cathedral*

Hosts: Connie and Nick Jacques. **Accommodations:** 5 rooms, all with private bath. **Rates:** $75–$90. **Included:** Full breakfast. **Minimum stay:** None. **Added:** 4% tax. **Payment:** MasterCard, Visa. **Children:** Over age 9. **Pets:** With prior approval (they have a dog). **Smoking:** Prohibited. **Open:** Year-round.

In a city rich in Victorian homes, the Barrister seems to merit no more than a passing glance. Built in 1874, the Queen Anne three-story inn stands on a shady corner in a quiet residential neighborhood just across from one of Helena's most impressive architectural monuments: the Gothic Cathedral of St. Helena, a twin-spired beauty renowned for its stained glass windows. But its location aside, it looks neither more nor less spectacular than numerous other historic houses lining the streets on either side of Last Chance Gulch, the site of the 1864 gold strike that turned Helena into a boomtown. What makes the Barrister special, however, lies inside. Connie and Nick Jacques have transformed the century-old mansion —

and former rectory for the cathedral — into an elegant bed-and-breakfast, as warmly hospitable as it is tastefully decorated.

That extends to the five guest rooms, all on the second floor. The most romantic of these is the Norway Room, a junior suite with a four-poster canopy bed, sitting area with a bow window, a decorative fireplace, and attached bath. Each of the others is decorated individually, from the cheerful yellows of the Garden Room to the oak woodwork and nautical theme of the Captain's Room (which used to be the bishop's changing room when this was a rectory). All have been furnished with queen-size beds, antiques or reproductions and hidden cable televisions. Like the Norway, two others have decorative fireplaces. All have private baths, though three are detached (in which case the room comes with robes).

> Ornate fireplaces, bold Victorian wallpapers, and lace and plush curtains decorate rooms furnished with superb antiques and oil paintings. The bow-windowed parlor, part of 2,000 square feet of common area, is particularly impressive for its high ceilings, walnut fireplace surround, and gas lamp–style chandelier in etched glass and brass.

Besides providing a full breakfast, served either in the formal dining room or on the enclosed sun porch, the Jacques serve complimentary hors d'oeuvres and beverages each afternoon. "We love to be around people when they're having a good time," says Nick, an attorney who grew up four blocks away.

They live there on the third floor, giving guests free run of not only the parlor, dining room, and sun porch but also the library and den/television room. Outside, guests can sit on white wicker furnishings on a covered porch fragrant with lilacs and look across at the cathedral. It couldn't be more pleasant.

The Sanders

328 North Ewing
Helena, MT 59601
406-442-3309

An opulent 1875 senator's mansion, romantically refurbished

Innkeepers: Bobbi Uecker and Rock Ringling. **Accommodations:** 7 rooms, all with private bath. **Rates:** Single $65–$70, double $75–$95. **Included:** Full breakfast. **Minimum stay:** None. **Added:** 4% tax. **Payment:** Discover, MasterCard, Visa. **Children:** Welcome (but no roll-aways or cribs available). **Pets:** Prohibited. **Smoking:** Prohibited. **Open:** Year-round.

When gold was discovered in 1864 in the area now called Helena, cabins sprouted like mushrooms along Last Chance Gulch. The gulch has since been transformed into an inviting main street lined with shops and restaurants, many of them in renovated turn-of-the-century buildings, and the town has become the state capitol. A vestige of that opulent era survives in the Wilbur F. Sanders mansion.

Built in 1875 for one of Montana's first senators, the bay-windowed, three-story Victorian stands on a residential street in the heart of Helena, a block from the original Governor's Mansion. Some renovations were undertaken during the ensuing 120 years, but much of the original interior survives.

Beautifully hand-crafted woodwork panels the walls and frames the doorways and windows, and crystal chandeliers hang from the high ceilings above oak floors. The living room stands out for its coffered walls and ceiling, carved fireplace surround, and painted and stenciled canvas wall covering, while the most impressive feature of the parlor sitting room is a built-in china cabinet of oak and beveled glass. Ornately framed pictures accent the walls, while Sanders's collection of rocks found in the area's mines injects a touch of the original owner's personality.

> **To step through the front doors, their glass windows etched with the monogram WFS, for Senator Wilbur F. Sanders, is to enter another century.**

The same turn-of-the-century grandeur suffuses the seven guest rooms. At once richly old-fashioned and comfortably modern, they combine brass, iron, and hand-carved antiques, thick quilts, colorful Ralph Lauren fabrics, and floral wallpaper — some of it original — with renovated private baths, phones, and color televisions (the latter two hidden from view). Most have queen-size beds, and all have air conditioning.

The couple responsible for this live upstairs. Young and affable, they could not be more pleasant hosts. They are also caterers, which explains the sumptuous Montana-size breakfasts that feature Grand Marnier French toast, orange soufflé, sourdough pancakes, and yogurt smoothies, all served with coffee and accompanied by a newspaper. The shops and restaurants of Last Chance Gulch are only blocks away.

LIVINGSTON

Greystone Inn Bed & Breakfast

122 South Yellowstone Street
Livingston, MT 59047
406-222-8319

> *A stone house
> turned inn,
> an hour
> from Yellowstone*

Innkeepers: Lin and Gary Lee. **Accommodations:** 4 rooms, 1 with private bath. **Rates:** Summer (May–September) $50–$65, Winter $40–$55. **Included:** Full breakfast. **Minimum stay:** None. **Added:** 4% tax. **Payment:** Cash, checks, or traveler's checks. **Children:** Welcome if supervised (crib available). **Pets:** Prohibited. **Smoking:** Prohibited. **Open:** Year-round.

Lin and Gary Lee renovated this turn-of-the-century house intending to move in themselves. But when the time came, Lin couldn't bear to leave the home they owned, two doors away, which was even older. At the same time, she had come to love their second home so much that selling it was equally out of the question. So early in 1992, they opened it as the Greystone Inn.

Along the front of the house runs an unusual fence of wrought iron and sandstone, fashioned to mimic the Georgian window just below the eaves. The architectural detail continues inside in Corinthian columns, oak woodwork, pocket doors, and windows of leaded beveled glass. There are also homey touches, as if the Lees had actually moved in: Lin made a stained glass window for the dining room and collected antiques wherever she could, including four vintage radio/phonographs, and she draped the dining room table with a crocheted table-cloth. Every day she sets out sherry, Amish cinnamon bread, and the fixings for coffee and tea on a sideboard.

> **The handsome two-story inn, constructed of hand-quarried sandstone, reposes beneath some trees on a quiet street two blocks from the heart of Livingston.**

Though Lin lives two doors away, she spends most mornings at the inn. She is always there for breakfast, making buttermilk pancakes called *abelskiver*, pastries, and waffles on the 1920s Paramount Match stove in the kitchen. A resident of Livingston for 25 years, she knows everything there is to do, whether it's skiing in Bridger Bowl (25 minutes away) or hiking in Yellowstone National Park (50 miles south).

Of the four guest rooms, only one is on the main level: Muriel's Room, which still has its original 90-year-old wallpaper and a private bath with a 1930s tub and pedestal sink. The three rooms on the second level share a large pink bath. The largest of these is the Sunrise Room, a junior suite with a highback oak bed, a fireplace, and a white iron day bed. Both the others have charm, however, born of their brass beds, ceiling fans, and colorful wallpapers.

Because the Lees live elsewhere, guests have full run of the house, including the living room, which has a television. But it's always warmest when Lin's around. "We have a lot of fun with this house," she says. "Talk about finding your niche in life. I couldn't be happier." Neither can her guests.

The Murray Hotel

201 West Park
Livingston, MT 59047
406-222-1350
Fax: 406-222-6745

> *A recovering railroad hotel with a Hollywood clientele*

General managers: Dan and Kathleen Kaul. **Accommodations:** 41 rooms (29 with private baths), 5 suites. **Rates:** Rooms $34–$54; suites $65–$150. **Included:**

Continental breakfast in rooms with shared baths and in suites. **Minimum stay:** None. **Added:** 4% tax. **Payment:** Major credit cards. **Children:** Welcome. **Pets:** Allowed. **Smoking:** Allowed. **Open:** Year-round.

Like much of downtown Livingston, the Murray Hotel is listed on the National Register of Historic Places, and like parts of downtown Livingston, it is not immediately obvious why. Built in 1897 and originally dubbed the Elite, the Murray owes its existence to the coming of the railroad and was once considered one of the grandest hostelries of the northwest. The Queen of Denmark spent the night here during her travels in the West. So did the humorist Will Rogers and railroad tycoon Walter Hill. That pair tried to bring their favorite saddle horse up to their third-floor suite in an old hand-cranked 1905 Otis elevator — the town's first.

> The Murray has an aura and mystique hard for the uninitiated to fathom.
> The four-story brick box looks unassuming, perhaps even a little seedy, though its marble lobby, antique furnishings, and hand-painted murals do hint at grander times.

Though it would later see its moment of greatness flicker, it continued to lure celebrities. Film director Sam Peckinpah lived there on and off, listing the Murray as one of his residences but keeping a low profile except for occasionally firing a shot through the roof. More recent guests have included Jimmy Buffett, Jack Palance, and Richard Brautigan, not to mention a host of celebrated bar patrons like Robert Redford, Peter Fonda, and Whoopi Goldberg. On any given summer night an assorted crowd of locals, tourists bound for Yellowstone, fishermen, and the merely curious wander in and out of its lobby and bar, hoping to spot someone famous or at least find out what all the fuss is about.

Since 1991, some of that fuss has been about the concerted effort being made to upgrade the facilities by the latest owners, Dan and Kathleen Kaul. By their own admission, the Murray is a work in progress, but that doesn't diminish the enormous strides they've made. Gone are the partitions that used to divide the lobby, leaving a sunny open space with marble wainscoting, Mission oak furnishings, an old pump organ, and the requisite elk and buffalo trophy heads. The Winchester Cafe under celebrated Montana chef Mark Glass has become one of *the* places to dine in southern Montana, with entrées ranging from superb steaks to pasta and Montana trout.

The guest quarters on the floors above are in different states of renovation and redecoration. Of those that have been redone, no two are alike. One may be decorated in cowboy prints, another in lace and chenille, a third in country prints and ruffles, with whatever antique or reproduction furnishings seem appropriate. The renovated baths retain an old-fashioned look in their clawfoot tubs, but most have showers as well. A dozen rooms still have shared baths, though as compensation guests there get a complimentary Continental breakfast.

Sixty-Three Ranch

Mission Creek Canyon
P.O. Box 979
Livingston, MT 59047
406-222-0570

*A historic
guest ranch
long on horses
and hospitality*

Proprietors: Virginia Christensen and Sandra, Bud, and Jeff Cahill. **Accommodations:** 9 cabins, all with private bath. **Rates:** Single $830/week, double $1,620/week. **Included:** All meals, horseback riding, ranch activities. **Minimum stay:** 7 nights. **Added:** 4% tax on lodging portion. **Payment:** Cash, personal checks, or traveler's checks. **Children:** Reduced rates under age 12. **Pets:** Prohibited. **Smoking:** Discouraged in main lodge and dining room. **Open:** June to mid-September.

The first guest ranch in Montana to be declared a National Historic Site, the Sixty-Three Ranch was founded in 1930 on a ranch that dates to 1863 (hence the name). To this day the 2,000-acre spread remains in the hands of the family that founded it. They run it like the traditional ranch it is, with an emphasis on horseback riding, and it's as comfortable as old jeans. Horses outnumber people two to one.

Virginia Christensen started the guest ranch and continues to operate it with the help of her daughter Sandra, Sandra's husband, Bud, and their son Jeff. Determined to offer lots of personal attention, they take no more than 30 guests a week. That way, they can match each of them to a great horse, teach those who need lessons how to ride, and head off at full gallop up mountain passes, into wooded canyons, or across hills that stretch down toward the Yellowstone River. Since this is a working ranch, guests are encouraged to help with any of the ranch chores, whether moving cattle, haying, or fencing.

> Set at 5,600 feet at the mouth of Mission Creek, on the north slope of the mountains the Indians called "big black bird," the collection of rustic log cabins, wildflower meadows, creeks, and granite peaks is what the whole world would look like if God were a Montana cowboy.

Accommodations consist of nine log or timber cabins with from one to four bedrooms. The most appealing are original to the ranch's beginnings in the 1930s, but all have distinctive handmade log furniture, wood floors with braided rugs, and private baths. A few have big decks with knockout views.

As at most traditional guest ranches, dinner brings guests and staff together at big tables in the main lodge. Though there is plenty of ranch-raised beef on the menu, the Sixty-Three also serves fish and their own poultry and pork, and willingly adapts to low-cholesterol, vegetarian, or other diets. After dinner, the evening diversions run to square dancing, staff vs. guest volleyball games, billiards on a 100-year-old pool table, or just sitting around the fireplace in comfortable old sofas.

The Sixty-Three does not have a children's program; it does, however, teach those as young as four to ride, and there are cats and dogs for them to play with and a pond stocked with trout. Fly-rodders have 3½ miles of Mission Creek all to themselves and the Yellowstone River within easy reach. Twice a year the ranch hosts photo workshops. It may be well run and traditional, but it isn't lost in another century.

NEVADA CITY

The Nevada City Hotel

Highway 287
Nevada City, MT 59755
Reservations: P.O. Box 338
Virginia City, MT 59755
406-843-5377
800-648-7588
Fax: 406-843-5377

> *A western hotel
> and cabins
> in a recreated
> mining town*

General manager: Kirk Hansen. **Accommodations:** 13 rooms, 2 suites, and 14 cabins, all with private bath. **Rates:** Rooms and cabins $45; suites $60. **Included:** Coffee. **Minimum stay:** None. **Added:** 4% tax. **Payment:** Major credit cards. **Children:** Free under age 12. **Pets:** Allowed in cabins. **Smoking:** Prohibited. **Open:** Late May to mid-September.

Nevada City and nearby Virginia City sprang to life in 1863, with the discovery of the richest placer deposit in history in Alder Gulch. Within months, 10,000 fortune seekers arrived. They washed $300 million in gold out of the gulch and attracted so many desperadoes that there were 191 murders in little more than half a year. When the deposits played out, Nevada City became a ghost town. A restoration project begun in 1946, however, has brought back the mining era.

Five streets lined with wooden sidewalks and historic buildings make up the core of Nevada City. There are early mining-camp stores, homes, a school, and offices. The Music Hall displays a large collection of mechanical bands. Staged gunfights and medicine shows take place in the streets.

The Nevada City Hotel faces the highway, but its back

door opens to the town. The rough-timbered two-story hotel originally stood in the town of Bollinger (now Twin Bridges); it was moved here in 1958 along with 14 mining-era cabins.

> **Kids especially love staying in a place that seems straight out of the Wild West. The Nevada City Hotel was not meant to be a museum of the mining era; it was meant to be fun, and it succeeds.**

Now renovated, it's a playful place to stay. Best are the two one-room Victorian suites at the front of the hotel and the two Victorian cabins (numbers 5 and 6) at the back. These have two antique double beds made of burled wood, matching dressers, and armoires, set against white wood walls. Handwoven rag rugs cover the floors. The cabins — three of which have two rooms — can easily handle a family of four and are a little quieter than the hotel, where sound carries through the walls.

PRAY

Chico Hot Springs Lodge

Chico Road
P.O. Drawer D
Pray, MT 59065
406-333-4933
Fax: 406-333-4694

> *A quirky hotel and a highly regarded restaurant*

General managers: Mike and Eve Art. **Accommodations:** 52 rooms in main lodge (14 with private bath), 24 motel units, 4 cabins, 4 cottages. **Rates:** Lodge rooms $36–$69, motel rooms $59–$84, cabins $59–$74, cottages $99–$295. **Included:** Coffee. **Minimum stay:** None. **Added:** 4% tax. **Payment:** Discover, MasterCard, Visa. **Children:** Free under age 6. **Pets:** Allowed ($2 housekeeping fee). **Smoking:** No smoking in the dining room. **Open:** Year-round.

To the uninitiated, Chico Hot Springs Lodge appears to be just another white clapboard Victorian relic, one that in this case abuts 11,000-foot Emigrant Peak in south-central Montana's Paradise Valley. There are, however, unmistakable clues to its offbeat charm. For one thing, the county road leading to it doubles as an airstrip, with signs that warn "Caution: Aircraft Operations." For another, someone attached a bar countertop — complete with drinks, scattered peanuts, and an ashtray with cigarettes — upside down on Chico's saloon ceiling, apparently to give anyone lying drunk on the floor the illusion of lying drunk on the ceiling.

> **The Chico's off-beat attitude, plus two pools fed by hot springs and the best restaurant for miles around, account for its popularity.**

Chico has become a popular watering hole for everyone from cowboys to the local colony of Hollywood expatriates, among them Jeff Bridges and Dennis Quaid, and the tourists who come to rub elbows with both.

It didn't start out that way. Following the discovery of gold in nearby Emigrant Gulch in the 1860s, miners began using the hot springs as a place to bathe. Its full-fledged transition to a health resort took place in 1900, when the current clapboard and shingle structure was erected. Noted cowboy artist Charlie Russell often stayed here, trading paintings for drinks, and President Theodore Roosevelt stopped over on his way to Yellowstone Park, 30 miles to the south.

Mike and Eve Art adopt an essentially lighthearted attitude to this history. Old milk cans, a baby grand piano, and a scattering of old — as opposed to antique — couches and chairs decorate the lobby, whose walls bear the requisite deer and elk trophy heads. Though there are more private baths than when Roosevelt visited, the rooms in the historic main lodge remain tiny and tend to be filled with an eclectic collection of brass beds and oak dressers, some of them the worse for wear. None has a television or phone. Floors creak; sound carries.

But Chico's stock in trade is conviviality and activity, not luxury. Guests get free access to the mineral pools, the larger one kept at 100 degrees, the smaller one at 108. There is great fishing three miles away in the Yellowstone River, horseback riding in Paradise Valley, and scenic flights along the Absaroka and Gallatin Mountain Ranges, with planes taking off and landing from the county road. Weekend nights sometimes find live bands in the barn-size saloon.

To fuel these diversions, Chico has a pasta bar, whose tables spill out onto a deck overlooking the front yard, and a casual, family-oriented poolside grill. But its culinary fame rests with its main dining room, dubbed the Chico Inn. Every night a packed house of eager diners, clad in anything from jeans to fancy duds, pores over menus trying to decide among choices like buffalo steaks, basil roasted Cornish hen, and salmon Marie au poivre. Reservations are essential, and it's best to make them at the same time you book your room.

RED LODGE

The Pollard

2 North Broadway Avenue
Red Lodge, MT 59068
Reservations:
406-446-0001
800-POLLARD
Fax: 406-446-3733

A resurrected grand hotel on a scenic byway

General manager: Ken Bate. **Accommodations:** 33 rooms and 11 suites, all with private bath. **Rates:** Rooms $65–$95, suites $110–$125. **Included:** Use of fitness center. **Minimum stay:** None. **Added:** 4% tax. **Payment:** Major credit cards. **Children:** Welcome. **Pets:** Prohibited. **Smoking:** Prohibited. **Open:** Year-round.

The first brick building in Red Lodge opened with great fanfare in 1893. Called the Spofford Hotel, it had cost $20,000 to construct, served elegant meals, and became the preferred place for galas and balls. Unhappily, the first landlord bilked creditors and absconded for parts unknown.

Thomas Pollard and his wife took possession in 1902 and renamed it the Pollard. They added 25 more rooms — bringing the total to 60 — space for a store, a stately dining room and ornate mahogany bar, display areas for traveling salesmen, and a bowling alley. It blossomed only to fade, and by the 1970s the Pollard had become another derelict hotel, scarred by an attempt to build a swimming pool beneath it.

Resurrected in the early 1990s, it reopened long enough to be the site for a fashion shoot in *Vogue* and then closed again, this time for even more extensive renovations. While those were going on, the architect discovered an unsound wall, which had to be replaced. Somehow it survived to reopen in 1994, after making the National Trust for Historic Preservation's list of Historic Hotels of America.

> In its heyday, the Pollard was a gathering place for celebrities of every stripe, including orator William Jennings Bryan, copper king William Andrews Clark, and Buffalo Bill Cody, Calamity Jane, and Jeremiah "Liver-eatin'" Johnson.

Today, its most remarkable feature is a three-story interior gallery with decorative stained glass panels at the east end. Some of the rooms open onto this interior space, rather than outside, and have windows or wrought-iron balconies with views of the sitting area and wood-burning fireplace below. Fine oak woodwork runs through the lobby, restaurant, and a history room, the latter with a bar and library of books and memorabilia.

The rooms themselves shun heavy Victoriana in favor of reproduction antiques in oak or cherry, lace curtains, and modern tile baths with pedestal sinks. All have cable TVs and phones. Two are wheelchair accessible.

The swimming pool had to be given up; however, the basement does hold a small fitness center and two racquetball courts. There is also a hot tub and ski lockers (the shuttle for the Red Lodge ski area leaves from the corner outside).

The owners want the hotel to once again become a place for elegant, talked-about dining. Frank Grovenstein, lately of Chico Hot Springs Lodge's restaurant, calls his cuisine "eclectic," as it draws on influences as different as the Southwest, the Mediterranean, and the Pacific Rim. On any given night you may find pheasant with cranberry marmalade, smoked duck lasagna, or brie and pear quesadillas on the menu.

Rock Creek Resort

Rt. 2, Box 3500
Red Lodge, MT 59068
406-446-1111
Fax: 406-446-3688

An intimate resort near wilderness and a scenic highway

General manager: John Siebring. **Accommodations:** 33 rooms in lodge, 38 1- to 3-bedroom condos and 2 studios (with total of another 53 rooms). **Rates:** Rooms $80–$200, condos $60–$260. **Minimum stay:** 4 nights at Christmas, 3 nights over major holidays. **Added:** 4% tax. **Payment:** Major credit cards. **Children:** Under 11 free. **Pets:** Prohibited. **Smoking:** Nonsmoking rooms available. **Open:** Year-round.

With fewer than 100 rooms, Rock Creek nonetheless has a full panoply of amenities, including access to an 18-hole golf course, tennis courts, a heated indoor swimming pool, fitness center, restaurants, conference facilities, and even a soccer field and children's playground. It sits just off the highway, five miles southwest of the town of Red Lodge, astride the stream that inspired the name.

Built by the world-renowned Austrian ski racer Pepi Gramshammer and opened in late 1990, Rock Creek is a relatively new addition to the Rocky Mountain resort landscape. Its heart is the Beartooth Lodge, a cedar-and-stone three-story inn on the banks of the creek. Arched windows in the lobby soar nearly to the ceiling framing views of the mountains. A huge river rock fireplace anchors one wall facing a cluster of whitewashed lodgepole pine furniture covered in southwestern prints in teal, burgundy, and sandstone. Deer-antler chandeliers and Crow Indian art pieces accent this western theme. Off to one side, doors open into the Kiva Restaurant and Lounge, which overlooks the creek through a wall of greenhouselike windows. On warm days, tables dot the deck outdoors.

Accommodations in the lodge range from standard rooms (one of them wheelchair accessible) to studios, the latter with kitchenettes, Murphy beds, and a foldout couch. All have been decorated in a style that hints at the Indian Southwest. Some of these rooms have decks (the most appealing overlook the creek), and some have Jacuzzi tubs.

Families needing something larger can opt for the Grizzly Condominiums just next door. The condos have up to three bedrooms and have full kitchens and woodburning stoves. A few connect via hidden spiral staircases. Unlike the lodge rooms, however, few of the condos have outside decks (though those with even numbers do have views of the creek).

> Its location puts it within easy reach of the hiking and fishing in the half-million-acre Beartooth-Absaroka Wilderness Area, and Yellowstone lies two hours to the west over 11,000-foot Beartooth Pass, on a scenic byway that Charles Kuralt called "the most beautiful roadway in America." In winter, the major lure is skiing at Red Lodge Mountain, nine miles away.

From either the lodge or condominiums it's a few steps to the Old Piney Dell, the second of the resort's restaurants, this one housed in a 1920s homesteader's cabin. Though there have been later additions, the original log structure survives, complete with its river rock fireplace and collection of Montana wildlife trophies. The menu in the 100-seat restaurant runs not to pemmican and hardtack, however, but to verdure pasta, medallions of pork Jezebel, and chicken with artichokes.

THREE FORKS

Sacajawea Inn

5 North Main Street
Box 648
Three Forks, MT 59752
406-285-6515
800-821-7326
Fax: 406-285-6515

> *A railroad hotel reborn as a country inn*

Innkeepers: Smith and C. Jane Roedel. **Accommodations:** 33 rooms, all with private bath. **Rates:** Single $49, double $59–$99. **Included:** Coffee and pastry. **Minimum stay:** None. **Added:** 4% tax. **Payment:** Major credit cards. **Children:** Free under 12. **Pets:** Limited. **Smoking:** Prohibited. **Open:** Year-round.

The Jefferson, Madison, and Gallatin rivers converge not far from Three Forks to form the headwaters of the Missouri River. Lewis and Clark passed this way in 1805 in their search for the Northwest Passage; a century later, when John Quincy Adams (a descendent of the sixth president) built a hotel to serve the passengers of the Milwaukee Railroad, he named it for the Shoshone Indian woman who guided the great explorers.

Now on the National Register of Historic Places, the three-story hotel stands at the top of Main Street, half a mile off I-90. The white clapboard structure trimmed in green looks rather like a displaced New England inn. Dormer windows accent the pitched roof, and a covered porch, its roof supported by paired columns, extends across the front of the building. From rocking chairs on the porch, guests can look out on the comings and goings of small-town America.

Although it looks fabulous now, the 1910 inn had languished in disrepair until Smith and C. Jane Roedel refurbished it in 1992. They opted for an arts and crafts simplicity. The lobby has hardwood floors, dark wood molding, and tapestry-print furnishings but otherwise little adornment, not even a fireplace, beyond lace curtains.

The rooms are similarly simple and under-

> **Accommodations on the first floor soar to 14-foot ceilings, while those on the third floor — once a dorm for railroad workers — have lower ceilings but are otherwise just as large or even larger. Most are very sunny, and all have phones and televisions.**

stated. Furnished with antiques and reproductions, these generally small to average-size quarters have queen-size beds with quilted comforters, brass lamps, and oversize baths with modern fixtures. There are lace curtains and a decorative wallpaper border, but otherwse little ornament. One room on the first floor is fully wheelchair accessible.

Part of the inn's appeal can be attributed to the Roedels themselves. He was in the hotel business, she a nurse, in Key West, Florida, when they set out looking for an inn to purchase and found the Sacajawea. Hands-on owners, they live on the premises, the better to see to guests' needs, something the whole staff does extremely well.

Dining, meanwhile, is as close as the inn's restaurant, whose menu includes not only the usual steaks but also blackened seafood, lemon basil chicken, and several pastas. Lewis and Clark never had it so good.

WEST YELLOWSTONE

Firehole Ranch

11500 Hebgen Lake Road
P.O. Box 686
West Yellowstone, MT 59758
406-646-7294, summer only
Reservations:
P.O. Box 360
Jackson, Wyoming 83001
307-733-7669
Fax: 307-733-7669

> *A lakefront fishing retreat and stylish guest ranch*

General manager: Stan Klassen. **Accommodations:** 8 cabins, all with private baths. **Rates:** Single $250, double $390; 7-day fly-fishing packages $2,710 single, $3,690 double. **Included:** All meals, liquor, airport transfers, and activities except fishing guides (unless on fly-fishing package). **Minimum stay:** 4 nights. **Added:** 4% tax on lodging portion, 15% gratuity. **Payment:** Cash, personal checks, or traveler's checks. **Children:** Welcome over age 11. **Pets:** Prohibited. **Smoking:** Prohibited in lodge. **Open:** June through September.

Firehole Ranch sprawls across 500 sagebrush-covered acres between Hebgen Lake and snow-covered Coffin Peak in the heart of America's blue ribbon trout fishing country. Though the majority of Firehole's guests come to fish, the ranch does have other diversions. In fact, prior to extensive renovations in 1981, Firehole was a guest ranch. The corrals are still here, and so are a dozen horses. Wranglers schedule half-day or all-day trail rides to such spectacular alpine aeries as Coffin Lakes, two liquid mirrors in the granite cirque between Coffin Peak and Mt. Baldy. Fishermen often go along for the joy of catching lots of little rainbows. Firehole also has mountain bikes, canoes, miles of hiking trails (supplemented by those in Yellowstone National Park), and occasional sunset cocktail cruises. Four or five times a summer, the ranch brings in live entertainment. This diversity makes it popular with couples and families with older children.

The staging area for all of this activity is a 1947 log house with a massive stone fireplace, overstuffed couches, Indian print rugs and drapes, an elegant mahogany bar, and a spacious dining room that looks out on the lake and its mountain backdrop. The lodge is only a short walk from the eight duplex log cabins, all of which have fireplaces, pine-paneled walls, carpeted floors, cozy sitting areas (three actually have a separate living room), and spiffy modern baths with showers. Fresh towels arrive every evening with turndown service.

Many of the Firehole's friendly staff — 19 members for the 20 guests — come back every summer, including its inventive French chef, who consistently wins raves for meals like soft-shell crab on capillini, veal chops with wild mushrooms, grilled fresh Alaskan halibut with cilantro, lime, and jalapeño butter, and other selections not usually dished out at a guest ranch. With them the ranch offers a selection of 20 complimentary wines. Air service into West Yellowstone itself makes access to the ranch unusually easy.

> **Half a dozen legendary rivers — the Madison, Gallatin, and Yellowstone among them — lie within an hour's drive. These high-mountain waters contain an abundance of rainbow and brown trout, some as large as 22 to 24 inches. The ranch's eight full-time guides know all of these fisheries intimately.**

Sportsman's High

750 Deer Street
West Yellowstone, MT 59758
406-646-7865
800-272-4227
Fax: 406-646-9434

> *A playful B&B
> eight miles from
> Yellowstone*

Hosts: Diana and Gary Baxter. **Accommodations:** 5 rooms, all with private bath, plus carriage house and 2 homes, all with full kitchen. **Rates:** Rooms, single $55–$75, double $65–$85; houses, $135–$175. **Included:** Full breakfast with the rooms. **Minimum stay:** 3 nights in carriage house and homes. **Added:** 4% tax. **Payment:** Master-Card, Visa. **Children:** Over age 9 in rooms, no restrictions elsewhere. **Pets:** Prohibited (they have 2 dogs). **Smoking:** Prohibited. **Open:** Year-round.

This winsome bed-and-breakfast appears to be the result of a collision between a two-story ranch house and a Dutch barn. Painted sky blue and trimmed in white, it sits on three acres of aspens and pines in a development called Lazy Acres, eight miles west of the entrance to Yellowstone National Park. A covered porch with white wicker chairs wraps around three sides, ending at a back deck with a hot tub, umbrella tables, and bird feeders.

Diana and Gary Baxter built a tiny log cabin here in 1984 as a vacation retreat, then added the unusually designed house and opened it as a bed-and-breakfast in 1989. Like the architecture of Sportsman's High, the playful interiors reflect the

Baxters' personalities. The front door opens onto an entryway with a hand-decorated floor, the first of many clues that Diana is an accomplished tole and decorative painter. Immediately to the left is a colonial-style kitchen and dining room with a deal table and wood-burning stove. It's here that guests meet for huge homemade breakfasts of Diana's own variation on eggs Benedict (with hard-boiled eggs and cheese sauce), burritos, stuffed croissants, or quiches served with her muffins and breads.

Four of the guest rooms are upstairs off a sitting area paneled in knotty pine and furnished with a television and a guest phone. Each of these quarters has been individually decorated in floral prints, with curtains, dust ruffles, and decorative wreaths that Diana makes herself. Each has a few antiques and a private bath.

The largest room, Deer Haven, opens onto a deck with views of a small pond that attracts wildlife. It has an antique dresser and desk. Another room is a little log cabin, built in the same ogee arch shape as one wing of the house and decorated with a log headboard, pine armoire, and plaid fabrics. It has a swing on its tiny front porch.

For those who need more space, the Baxters also have a 950-square-foot carriage house, which sleeps six, and two even larger homes, which sleep as many as 12. Each of these has a full kitchen, washer-dryer, private hot tub, and TV/VCR. Breakfast is not, however, included with their rental.

WHITE SULPHUR SPRINGS

Elk Canyon Ranch

Rural Route One
White Sulphur Springs, MT 59645
406-547-3373
Fax: 406-547-3719

*A secluded
guest ranch for
those inclined to
luxury*

General managers: John and Kay Eckhardt. **Accommodations:** 8 cabins, all with private bath. **Rates:** $250/person/day. **Included:** All meals, horseback riding, and most other ranch activities. **Minimum stay:** 7 nights. **Added:** 4% tax to lodging portion only. **Payment:** Cash or checks. **Children:** Reduced rates under age 12; supervised programs for ages 4–14. **Pets:** Prohibited. **Smoking:** Discouraged. **Open:** Late May through mid-October.

Elk Canyon's posh log cabins and two-story log lodge perch atop a ridge in a picturesque setting above the Smith River. The ranch's own 3,000 acres blend seamlessly with the surrounding Lewis and Clark and Helena national forests to create a panoramic tapestry of wildflower meadows and ridges timbered with ponderosa pine. Wildlife abounds, from skittish pronghorns and mule deer to eagles and osprey. The nearest town, White Sulphur Springs (population 1,302), is 28 miles away. Bozeman airport is 2½ hours to the south.

The time it takes to reach Elk Canyon is the only sacrifice guests have to make, for creature comforts abound. The reward for a day spent riding the range, trout fishing on four miles of private beats along the Smith River, or hiking with a guide to an eagle's nest or Indian cave is cocktails at the lodge (also John and Kay Eckhardt's home) followed by a four-course dinner of sirloin of lamb, roast pork, or pan-seared scallops, served with a selection of wines. Afterward, guests retire to the "cabins": beautifully appointed log cottages with spacious living rooms, hand-carved cedar furnishings, rock fireplaces, and from one to four bedrooms, each with a private bath. The units also feature wet bars, ice makers, coffeemakers, and washer/dryers.

The lodge has a fireplace, a telescope, and a jar that's always full of homemade cookies. The Eckhardts, who have a long history of operating guest ranches, are caring and personable hosts.

Horseback riding is an important activity, with daily trips along the valleys or up into the mountains. Other diversions include guided nature hikes, fishing, trap and skeet shooting, tennis on two courts, lounging around the pool, or sitting on the front porch of a cabin and taking in the views.

> **Elk Canyon has a fabulous children's program with enthusiastic guides to make sure kids have fun and at the same time learn something about riding and the outdoors. Kids may have dinner in the dining room, but most of them opt out of the four-course feasts in favor of their own cookouts and marshmallow roasts.**

WISE RIVER

The Complete Fly Fisher

Highway 43
P.O. Box 105
Wise River, MT 59762
406-832-3175

> *A riverside fishing camp in relentless pursuit of perfection*

Proprietors: Dave and Christine Decker. **Accommodations:** 5 cabins. **Rates:** $2,000/person for 6-night packages. **Included:** All meals, liquor, guides, instruction, fishing equipment, boats, and airport transfers. **Minimum stay:** 6 nights. **Added:** 1% tax; 10% for gratuities. **Payment:** Cash, personal checks, or traveler's checks. **Children:** Welcome. **Pets:** With prior approval. **Smoking:** Allowed. **Open:** March through October.

Since he took over the Complete Fly Fisher in 1983, Dave Decker has had one simple philosophy: "If you're going to take care of people, take good care of them." This tenet shows in everything from his guides, all of whom have put in at least 1,500 days on the river here, to the immaculate cedar-paneled cabins in a pasture that borders the Big Hole River. He can accommodate only 10 guests at a time, but 85 percent return, convinced that there is no finer fishing lodge on the planet.

One reason, of course, is that the river teems with brown, rainbow, brook, and cutthroat trout. Much of the fishing is done from Avon rafts outfitted with comfortable chairs. With no more than two fishermen per guide, everyone gets personal attention. Even rank novices spend most of the week on the river, learning the art of fly-fishing by casting flies under the watchful eye of a skilled instructor/guide. CFF loans equipment at no charge and has a complete retail tackle shop. The fishing season on the Big Hole River runs from June through September, but in the months before and after Decker uses the camp as a base to fish other rivers in the region, including the Bitterroot, Clark Fork, and Beaverhead.

> "Fishing is all we do," says Decker adamantly. Hardcore fishermen can fish from before dawn till after dark, knowing that they'll get breakfast before they leave and dinner after they return. At the same time, Decker gears his marketing to couples, so roughly half the guests in camp are women.

The focal point of CFF is Decker's former home (he now lives across the road), a modern house that perches on the banks of the river. Guests gather in its living room for cocktails (Decker takes the trouble to find out what they like before they arrive) and in its glass-enclosed porch for sumptuous dinners of leg of lamb, standing rib roast, paella, or Argentine asado, all served with lots of fresh vegetables and wine. Classical music or jazz plays softly in the background.

The cabins have pine furnishings, striped Hudson Bay blankets, walk-in closets, spiffy bathrooms with thick towels, vases of fresh flowers, and a complimentary bottle of wine. One cabin can even accommodate fishermen in wheelchairs, and the house, too, is barrier free. In every detail, the Complete Fly Fisher is a thoroughly professional operation.

Utah

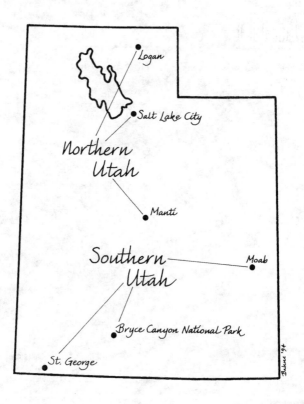

Logan

Salt Lake City

Northern Utah

Manti

Southern Utah

Moab

Bryce Canyon National Park

St. George

Bahma '94

Utah's Wasatch Mountains slice through the western third of the state, roughly dividing the gray desert of the Great Basin to the west from the spectacular red rock country of the Colorado Plateau to the east. Geologic phenomena punctuate much of the state's 85,000 square miles, creating landscapes of rare and magnificent beauty. Within Utah lie five national parks, six national monuments, two national recreation areas, and a national historic site, as well as 45 state parks and 3,000 lakes, the hypersaline Great Salt Lake among them.

Though the state's name derives from the Ute Indians who still live there, its modern history dates from 1847, when wagonloads of Mormon pioneers led by Brigham Young arrived in the valley of the Great Salt Lake. Thousands more followed, setting up agricultural communities along the

Wasatch Front, which extends north-south from Ogden through Salt Lake City and on to Provo and points farther south. Each of these communities, large or small, follows a prescribed layout, with the Mormon chapel or tabernacle at the center of a grid of broad streets, all numbered in precisely the same way to indicate how far any given point lies from the center. Almost 70 percent of Utah's population belongs to the Mormon Church — more formally, the Church of Jesus Christ of Latter-Day Saints — whose world headquarters is in Salt Lake City, the state capital. But beyond its urban sprawl lie the most compelling reasons to visit Utah: the great national parks.

Any one of them — Arches, Bryce Canyon, Canyonlands, Capitol Reef, or Zion — would be excuse enough to put the Beehive State on a Rocky Mountain itinerary. Collectively, they almost demand it. Eons of erosion have sculpted the Colorado Plateau into wondrous galleries of multicolored sandstone and limestone cliffs, pinnacles, spires, arches, fins, balanced rocks, needles, grabens, hoodoos, and domes. In Zion, one of the oldest national parks, vermilion and ivory cliffs with evocative names like the Great White Throne, the Watchman, Angels Landing, and Weeping Rock tower above the unprepossessing Virgin River, which carved out the deep canyon that gave the park its name. A scenic highway parallels the river for six miles, dead-ending at the Temple of Sinawava and the Gateway to the Narrows and the start of the park's most popular off-trail hikes.

Each of the other parks has its own theme and variations on geologic sculpture. In Bryce Canyon, thousands of delicately carved spires, banded with color, line a vast amphitheater. The world's largest concentration of natural stone arches can be found in Arches National Park. Capitol Reef is a wilderness of sandstone formations and cliffs set off by fruit orchards. And Canyonlands is renowned for its jeeping, hiking, and whitewater rafting through a labyrinth of canyons. Dinosaur National Monument contains the largest quarry of dinosaur bones, and the terraced bowl of Cedar Breaks contains stone pinnacles, columns, and intricate canyons in shades of red, yellow, and purple.

Bass fishermen, houseboaters, and photographers head for Lake Powell, the second largest reservoir in North America, attracted by its hundreds of scenic side canyons, inlets, and coves, some of which hold Indian dwellings. Whitewater rafters thrill to the rapids on the Colorado and Green rivers.

And skiers converge on Utah's 16 ski resorts — Park City, the soignée Deer Valley, Snowbird, and Alta among them — attracted by their easy accessibility to Salt Lake City.

For information about what to see and do, contact the Utah Travel Council, Council Hall/Capitol Hill, Salt Lake City, Utah 84114 (801-538-1030).

Northern Utah

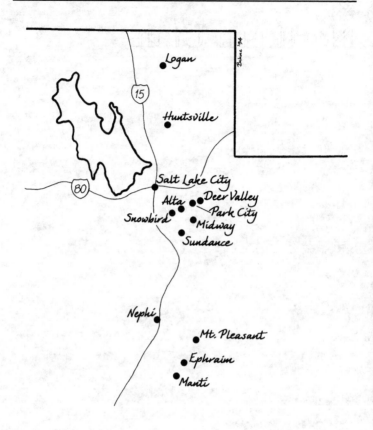

Best Bed-and-Breakfast Homes

Ephraim
  Ephraim Homestead
Manti
  Brigham House Inn
  The Yardley Inn
Nephi
  The Whitmore Mansion Bed & Breakfast Inn
Park City
  Old Town Guest House
Salt Lake City
  Anton Boxrud B&B
  Saltair Bed & Breakfast

Best Bed-and-Breakfast Inns

Logan
  Center Street Bed & Breakfast Inn
Manti
  Manti House Inn
Midway
  Inn on the Creek
Mt. Pleasant
  The Mansion House
Park City
  The Old Miners' Lodge
  Washington School Inn
Salt Lake City
  Brigham Street Inn
  The Inn at Temple Square
  The Pinecrest Bed & Breakfast Inn

Best Condominiums, Apartments, and Cabins

Park City
  Blue Church Lodge
Sundance
  Sundance Resort

Best Country Inns

Huntsville
  Jackson Fork Inn
Park City
  The Snowed Inn

Best Historic Hotels, Inns, and Lodges

Park City
  The Imperial Hotel
Salt Lake City
  The Peery Hotel

Best Resorts and Spas

Midway
  The Homestead

Best Ski Area Hotels and Lodges

Alta
  Alta Lodge
  Rustler Lodge
Deer Valley
  Goldener Hirsch Inn
  Stein Eriksen Lodge
Snowbird
  Cliff Lodge
Sundance
  Sundance Resort

Utah's northern tier encompasses the state's greatest cities and most forbidding wilderness, its most fashionable ski areas and hottest springs, its biggest caves and saltiest lake, its highest point and flattest flats. The Wasatch Mountains, one of the nation's most rugged ranges, slice through the center from north to south. They separate the Great Basin on the west from the glacier-capped Uinta Range, the only major U.S. mountain range to run east-west. They also provide a grand backdrop for the capital of **Salt Lake City.**

This thoughtfully planned city of 160,000 sprawls along the base of the mountains in what was once a desert wilderness. It dates to 1847, when Brigham Young led a band of his Mormon followers into the basin and declared, "This is the place." With remarkable foresight, he laid out a wonderfully open city of 10-acre blocks and 132-foot boulevards, with a soaring Mormon Temple at the center of the grid and views of the mountains to the east and west.

Temple Square, at the heart of the city, welcomes the public with free guided tours conducted by Mormon volunteers. The oldest structure is the temple itself, a triple-spired cathedral begun in 1853 and finished four decades later. However, since the temple is closed to non-Mormons, the 1867 tabernacle attracts the most attention. It houses the 11,623-pipe organ used to accompany the Mormon Tabernacle Choir. Anyone may attend their Thursday evening rehearsals or Sunday morning concerts. Also on the site are a monument to the sea gulls that saved crops from locusts in 1848 and the world's largest geneaology library.

Salt Lake City carries the cultural and entertainment banner for the state. It has a symphony orchestra and opera company, an arts center, and a sports arena for its Golden Eagles NHL hockey team and NBA Jazz basketball team.

It takes less than an hour to drive from Temple Square to any of 10 ski areas that drape the Wasatch Mountains immediately to the east. That includes the fabled slopes of **Alta, Snowbird, Park City,** and **Deer Valley.** It also includes **Sundance,** which not only has skiing but hosts an annual January film festival.

These nearby mountains also harbor hot springs, at **Midway,** and Timpanogos Cave National Monument, east of American Fork. The caves are three small limestone chambers spiked with imaginatively named formations of stalactites and stalagmites and large numbers of gravity-defying helictites that grow directly out from the walls. Note, however, that reaching the cave entrance requires a strenuous 1½-mile hike, and that once inside you'll need a sweater or jacket to ward off the 43-degree chill.

In the other direction sprawls the Great Salt Lake, a shallow inland sea twice as salty as the ocean. Beyond the lake lie the Bonneville Salt Flats, a hundred square miles of perfectly flat salt as hard as concrete. Race-car drivers often take their machines there in an attempt to set land speed records.

Transportation of another sort is commemorated at Golden Spike National Historic Site, 32 miles west of Brigham City.

There, on May 10, 1869, a golden spike was driven to complete the transcontinental railroad. The visitors' center shows interpretive movies year-round, and working replicas of 1869 steam locomotives operate from May through October.

South of Salt Lake, an unforgettable scenic byway winds for 20 miles around the eastern flank of 11,877-foot Mt. Nebo, the highest point in the Wasatch Range. Beginning in the canyons outside of Payson, it reaches an elevation of 9,000 feet, where it skirts a wilderness area and commands panoramic views across the colored canyons of Devils Kitchen before dropping down into **Nephi.**

South of Nephi, the town of **Manti** stages Utah's largest pageant every July on the grounds of the Manti Temple. As many as 20,000 spectators arrive to see musical dramatizations of American and Mormon history.

ALTA

Alta Lodge

Utah 210
Little Cottonwood Canyon
Alta, UT 84092
801-742-3500
800-747-2582
Fax: 801-742-3504

> *A family-run
> ski lodge, with
> children's après-ski*

General manager: Julie Faure. **Accommodations:** 55 rooms, 2 dormitories. **Rates:** Rooms, winter (mid-November to late April) single $136–$225, double $197–$287; summer (early

June–mid-October) single $56–$85, double $63–$95. Dorms, winter $86/person. **Included:** Breakfast and dinner in winter; Sunday brunch in summer. **Minimum stay:** None. **Added:** Winter, 10.625% tax on lodging, 8.125% tax on food, and 15% service charge; summer, 10.625% tax. **Payment:** Cash or checks in winter; MasterCard, Visa in summer. **Children:** Welcome. **Pets:** Prohibited. **Smoking:** Prohibited in public areas. **Open:** Year-round except for 6 weeks in spring and from Columbus Day to mid-November (or the reopening of the lifts).

The Alta Lodge inspires affection and fierce loyalty in some people (William F. Buckley among them), and incomprehension in others. Built in 1939 by the Denver & Rio Grande Railroad, it is the oldest ski lodge at Alta. Its rooms, even those in the newer wing (added in the 1960s), tend to be small by today's standards and for the most part spartan.

> No one has ever described the Alta Lodge as posh or trendy. Nevertheless, it is so warm, relaxed, and comfortable that guests come back time after time — 80 percent, in fact, have been there before.

Part of the lodge's attraction can be traced to the family who runs it. Alta's mayor, Bill Levitt, and his wife, Mimi, bought the lodge 25 years ago and continue to be involved with the help of their children and their children's spouses. Their caring attitude extends to the staff, who are friendly and attentive.

Its location further contributes to its appeal. A side door opens onto a short, gentle slope that ends in one of Alta's two base areas (a rope tow hauls skiers back up to the lodge). Skiers who return before the lifts close can sit in either of the lodge's two Jacuzzis and watch the hardcore tackle High Rustler, the most famous of Alta's expert slopes. To make it easy on parents, the lodge runs a special children's après-ski program, entertaining them with arts and crafts or sled races from 4 P.M. on. There's even an optional children's dinner hour, with menus of foods they like.

In the end, Alta Lodge is about much more than the extraordinary skiing available just outside. Three days a week the lodge serves afternoon tea and tea breads in the lobby, and every afternoon a private club called the Sitzmark (which can serve liquor) draws a crowd for après-ski. The conviviality extends to dinner, where guests sit down at large tables to dine on such entrées as roast New York strip, broiled yellowtail snapper, or spinach fettuccine. The food is excellent; the conversation and friendships are what people remember.

Nightlife is virtually nonexistent in Alta, and that, frankly, is part of its attraction. By 9:30 P.M. almost everyone, having put in a long day on the slopes, has gone to bed, grateful to rest without feeling that they're missing anything.

Rustler Lodge

Utah 210
Little Cottonwood Canyon
Alta, UT 84092
801-742-2200
800-451-5223
Fax: 801-742-3832

*A spacious
ski lodge, with
views of the slopes*

General manager: Tom Pollard. **Accommodations:** 52 rooms, 3 suites, 1 dorm. **Rates:** Rooms $85–$165/person, suites $165–$215/person, dorm $75–$85. **Included:** Breakfast and dinner. **Minimum stay:** 7 nights over Christmas holidays, February, and March. **Added:** 10.625% lodging tax, 8.125% meal tax, 15% service charge. **Payment:** Cash, personal checks, or traveler's checks. **Children:** Welcome. **Pets:** Prohibited. **Smoking:** Prohibited except in lobby. **Open:** Before Thanksgiving to late April

Alta attracts skiers with copious amounts of ultralight powder, the most reasonably priced lift tickets of any major ski area, and a chronically low-key, unpretentious style. Those who love Alta willingly put up with long traverses to reach some of the most fabled terrain, like High Rustler, which plunges down the front face. They endure long lift lines, because that reduces congestion on the slopes. And they live for those days when avalanches close the highway through Little Cottonwood Canyon, because then the only people cutting tracks through fresh powder are those who had the good sense to stay at the mountain rather than in Salt Lake City, 45 minutes to the west.

In Alta, there are only two places to stay with any kind of

panache: the Alta Lodge and the Rustler. Though they have approximately the same number of rooms, the Rustler is more spacious. It has an open, expansive lobby with window

> **Those posh digs, with amenities like phones and a wet bar, break with an unwritten Alta tradition that says accommodations don't matter very much.**

views up and down the valley, and wrought iron chandeliers hanging from the heavy ceiling beams. Clusters of leather chairs are a comfortable spot to read the morning paper or a novel. There is a bar with a fish tank and a dining room with wide views of the ski slopes on the far end. It's an easy place to drink in the beauty of the canyon.

So are the deluxe rooms, whose country decor features handsomely upholstered chairs and sofas, beds with dust ruffles, dark wood paneling set off by white cinder block walls, and a full-width balcony and wall of windows facing the slopes.

People stay in Alta's lodges in order to meet other skiers, if not at big tables in the dining room then certainly in the Jacuzzi, pool, or bar, all of which the Rustler has. Under those circumstances, rooms are places of last resort, where you go only to clean up or sleep. The Rustler's old rooms tack closer to that tradition, though even the standard versions, with their dormitory-style furnishings, have views up or down the mountain.

The Rustler is also a cut above the others in that it pays more attention to cuisine. The four-course nightly menu always includes a choice of two entrées, among them grilled mahi-mahi with roasted red pepper coulis, rack of lamb, and stuffed chicken breast. The restaurant even has a maître d', a title seldom uttered in Alta. At the same time it is a little less social, a little less inclined to cram people together at big tables or in tiny bars just so they can meet, a little more aloof. And for the many who love the Rustler, that's just fine.

DEER VALLEY

Goldener Hirsch Inn

7570 Royal Street
P.O. Box 859
Deer Valley, UT 84060
801-649-7770
800-252-3373
Fax: 801-649-7901

> *An Austrian-
> inspired ski inn,
> elegant and informal*

Innkeeper: Jeanne Lehan. **Accommodations:** 3 rooms, 17 suites. **Rates:** (higher over Christmas holidays and Presidents' week) Rooms, summer (Memorial Day–mid-November) $100, winter (January 4–end of ski season) $280; suites, summer $140–$200, winter $350–$550. **Included:** Full breakfast. **Minimum stay:** 4 days in winter. **Added:** 10.25% tax. **Payment:** Major credit cards. **Children:** Welcome. **Pets:** Prohibited. **Smoking:** Prohibited except in lounge. **Open:** Year-round except early April–mid-June.

Stenciled filigrees on the white stucco above the windows and wooden balconies with cutout designs give the Goldener Hirsch a playful Austrian appearance. Named for the venerable Goldener Hirsch in Salzburg, Austria — and built and furnished with the advice of its former doyenne, the Countess Harriet Walderdorff — this magnificent 1990 addition to Deer Valley lodgings has much of its ancestor's European style but none of its Old World stodginess.

Most of the accommodations are suites, except for three oversize hotel

> **Poised in the center of Deer Valley's midmountain village, the inn succeeds in being at once comfortably elegant and informal. Everything is infallibly tasteful.**

rooms on the first floor that are wheelchair accessible, and are reached by hallways wide enough to accommodate sitting areas. In every room, sunlight streams in through abundant windows and reflects off the white plaster walls, making the rooms exceptionally bright. They are furnished in Austrian tradition with painted antique reproduction furniture (an armoire hides a television with remote), carved pine doors, and wrought-iron hardware. The pine beds have down comforters in duvet covers. Double doors open onto decks with views of the mountain. All the suites have fireplaces and huge bathrooms with separate tub and shower. Color schemes vary from blues to pinks to greens.

Like all good ski lodges, it has indoor and outdoor hot tubs and saunas. The inn is rare, however, in also having an excellent restaurant, which serves traditional Austrian fare like wiener schnitzel and fondues, supplemented by hearty soups and stews, with game in winter and lighter cuisine like house smoked trout with grapefruit vinaigrette or salmon with caviar buerre blanc in summer. Meanwhile, all of the staff, who dress in loden jackets and dirndls, are as warm and unpretentious as the inn is full of character.

Stein Eriksen Lodge

7700 Stein Way
P.O. Box 3177
Park City, UT 84060
801-649-3700
800-453-1302
Fax: 801-649-5825

A Valhalla for skiers, down to its superb restaurant

General manager: Richard L. Erb. **Accommodations:** 74 rooms, 44 suites. **Rates:** (higher over Christmas holidays and Presidents' week) Rooms, summer $130–$225, winter $275–$500; suites, summer $205–$500, winter $500–$1,200. **Minimum stay:** 4–7 nights during some winter and holiday periods. **Added:** 10.25% tax. **Payment:** Major credit cards. **Chil-

dren: Welcome. **Pets:** Prohibited. **Smoking:** Nonsmoking rooms available. **Open:** Year-round

A Scandinavian vision in stone and timber, this rustically elegant, ski-in/ski-out hostelry hugs the slopes just above Deer Valley's 8,200-foot midmountain village, where it enjoys 360-degree views of the valley. Arriving guests following signs for the Stein Eriksen Lodge are directed into a heated underground parking structure. The lobby entrance is there, with bellmen by the door and a welcoming blaze in the fireplace just inside.

The Stein Eriksen is often held up as the epitome of stellar ski-country lodging. Even a standard room has elegant pine furnishings, Scandinavian down comforters, heavy exposed beams, a bay window with a window seat, a large bath with a Jacuzzi tub, and in some cases a fireplace. Moving up to a deluxe room guarantees the fireplace and adds a sitting area with two sofas, vaulted ceilings, a private balcony, and a second sink in the bath. Three of these are wheelchair accessible.

> **The main lobby has towering stone fireplaces and a thick-beamed ceiling. This could be a modern Valhalla, especially when Stein Eriksen himself, the legendary Olympic gold medalist, shows up in the lounge, as he often does in the late afternoon. Eriksen is part of the mystique that clings to the lodge.**

It is, however, the baronial splendor of the one- to four-bedroom condominium suites next to the lodge that lures Johnny Carson, Sylvester Stallone, and other celebrities. Spacious and amenity-rich, each of these features a gracious living room, dining area, fully equipped European kitchen, and a master bedroom with a king-size bed and its own fireplace and deck. A pine armoire in the living room conceals a fold-down queen-size bed. There are heavy brushed pine chairs from Spain, hand-painted chandeliers from Italy, hand-painted kitchen tiles from Portugal. No detail has been overlooked.

A true ski-in/ski-out hotel, the lodge provides ski lockers immediately inside the door skiers use to go to and from the slopes. Any tuning or repair can be handled overnight. Lift tickets can be purchased at the front desk. Naturally, there is a heated pool, Jacuzzi, and workout room. Massages are available, as is a beauty salon. A sundries shop also carries wine and liquor. Tea and fresh pastries are served every afternoon in front of a roaring fire as a pianist plays in the background. There's an outstanding restaurant in Glitrelind, just off the lobby. The service is unstintingly personal.

If anyone complains, it's about how far some of the suites and condos are from the main lobby. That quibble aside, the elegant, secluded lodge is one of the world's great mountain retreats.

EPHRAIM

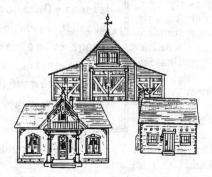

Ephraim Homestead

135 West 100 North
Ephraim, UT 84627
801-283-6367

A fairy-tale cottage and cabin as B&B

Hosts: Sherron and McKay Andreasen. **Accommodations:** 2 rooms with shared bath; 1 cabin and 1 cottage with private bath. **Rates:** Rooms $35–$45, cabin or cottage $75. **Included:** Full breakfast. **Minimum stay:** None. **Added:** 9% tax. **Payment:** Cash, personal checks, or traveler's checks. **Children:** Welcome. **Pets:** Prohibited (they have a dog and a cat). **Smoking:** Prohibited, as is drinking. **Open:** Year-round except the cottage (June–August).

In a way, Ephraim Homestead recreates an aspect of Mormon history: the classic family plot that consisted of a house, a granary, and a barn. What makes it special, however, has far less to do with 19th-century pioneering history than with the talent of McKay and Sherron Andreasen.

For most of the year the Andreasens live in the main house, but in summer they retreat to the basement, turning the parlor, bath, and two tiny upstairs bedrooms of this fairy-tale cottage over to guests. Heavy drapes, tasteful floral wallpaper, a potbelly stove, a German chandelier with candles,

> **Using more imagination than money, and McKay's extraordinary woodworking skills, the Andreasens have turned an 1880s adobe house, an 1860s Norwegian cabin (once a granary), and a barn into a bed-and-breakfast that is a sheer delight.**

and a scattering of antiques — among them a Chicago organ — give the tiny parlor a Victorian feel. Its red, gold, and green color scheme is Scandinavian, like the Andreasens.

Even the bathroom is fun. Apart from its clawfoot tub, it has a marble corner sink with antique brass fixtures and a capricious collection of old apothecary and liniment bottles. An old crank phone hangs on the wall just outside, concealing a real phone.

Steep, narrow stairs off the kitchen climb to the two bedrooms cozied in beneath the eaves. The master bedroom contains Sherron's great-grandparents' brass bed, lace curtains and heavy drapes, another potbelly stove, and a half bath. The second, smaller bedroom holds an oak bed with a hand-appliquéd quilt.

The quaint two-story cabin shows the same engaging attention to detail. The main floor, which has very low ceilings and a fireplace, looks like a museum reconstruction of a pioneer dwelling. Authentic handmade pioneer furniture — including a mahogany rocker — competes for attention with a spinning wheel, electrified hurricane lamps, and an antique cast-iron cookstove. The single upstairs room contains a 200-year-old four-poster bed, a twin four-poster, a Danish child's bed, and a crib, all of them with quilts. The bathroom has a clawfoot tub and an 1890s corner sink.

The barn loft contains two rustic rooms, a large one at the

front and a small one at the back, with heavy beamed ceilings, plank floors, and antique iron beds covered with quilts. Though they share a three-quarter bath, each has its own antique washstand.

Sherron cooks wonderful breakfasts of apple muffins and pancakes, eggs, waffles, or French toast on the woodstove in the main kitchen. Guests staying in the main house or the barn eat at an oak table in the dining room, but Sherron delivers breakfast to those in the cabin, which makes it a favorite with honeymooners.

The Ephraim Homestead is especially irresistible because every dab of paint, every piece of woodwork, and every homemade apple muffin seems to express the care and enthusiasm of the Andreasens.

HUNTSVILLE

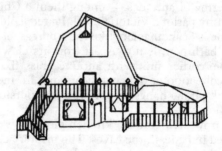

Jackson Fork Inn

Utah Highway 39
7345 East 900 South
Huntsville, UT 84317
801-745-0051
800-255-0672
Fax: 801-745-0052

> *A country inn
> in a former
> dairy barn*

Innkeeper: Vicki Petersen. **Accommodations:** 8 rooms. **Rates:** $50 without Jacuzzi, $90 with. **Included:** Continental breakfast. **Minimum stay:** None. **Added:** 9.25% tax. **Payment:** Major credit cards. **Children:** Free under age 11. **Pets:** Prohibited. **Smoking:** Discouraged. **Open:** Year-round.

The huge white clapboard structure that houses the Jackson Fork Inn was originally a rustic dairy barn. When it was slated for demolition, Vicki Petersen's father, who had milked cows in it, bought the barn and moved it to its current location across the highway from Pineview Reservoir in the scenic Ogden Valley Recreation Area. It was converted first into a private club and later a restaurant. Further renovations in the early 1980s added rooms upstairs. In 1987, Vicki, who had been managing properties in southern California, came home to take over as innkeeper.

> Since Vicki took over, the once-dreary lodgings have taken on country charm. The decor is as warm and unpretentious as she is.

The inn consists of a restaurant on the main floor — paneled in gleaming knotty pine — and the guest rooms upstairs. All but one has a sitting area furnished with a trundle bed or fold-out couch and a spiral staircase leading to a loft with one or two queen-size beds. In addition, five of the rooms (including the small one without a loft) feature Jacuzzis. All have televisions but no phones.

Vicki stenciled designs around the doors, added colorful fabrics, painted, and is halfway through replacing the nondescript furnishings with antiques her father has collected and the brown carpet with pastels. The same country look pervades the lobby, which has a potbelly stove and a collection of porcelain animals.

Rates include a limited buffet breakfast of muffins and coffee. The restaurant serves reasonably priced lunch and dinner Monday through Saturday, and Sunday brunch. There are three ski areas within a 15-mile radius; summers bring a boating and fishing crowd to Pineview Reservoir (which has a yacht club) and Causey Reservoir as well as a collection of hikers and picnickers.

LOGAN

Center Street Bed & Breakfast Inn

169 East Center Street
Logan, UT 84321
801-752-3443

> *An artist's imagination runs riot through a dozen rooms*

Innkeepers: Ann and Clyne Long. **Accommodations:** 13 rooms, all with private bath. **Rates:** Weekdays $48–$108, weekends $48–$158. **Included:** Continental breakfast. **Minimum stay:** None. **Added:** 9.25% tax. **Payment:** Major credit cards. **Children:** Infants welcome; otherwise, over age 10 only. **Pets:** Prohibited. **Smoking:** Prohibited. **Open:** Year-round.

From the outside, this stately 1879 red brick mansion in Logan's historic district looks like an elegant 19th-century home, complete with carriage house. The front door opens onto a turn-of-the-century parlor with plush Victorian couches, oak floors, Oriental carpets, and a fireplace. At first glance it seems little different from other Victorian houses on the National Register of Historic Places, yet there are hints that another sensibility is at work here. The oil paintings on the wall include copies of the *Mona Lisa* and *Blueboy,* and the muraled ceiling suggests Michelangelo except in the boldness of its colors.

The innkeeper, Ann Long, is also an artist (those are her oil paintings hanging in the parlor) with an eclectic style who approached each room as a fresh canvas. Only one relatively small antique-filled chamber, called the Victorian Suite, is traditional; the others flit off into fantasy. Thus, the Arabian Nights Suite has a king-size round bed covered with a sultan's tent, sand-colored carpet, walls painted with palm trees, and a red heart-shaped spa tub separated from the main room by stained glass windows shaped like onion domes. Jungle Bungalow features a king-size bed with a leopard skin cover and mirrored canopy, muraled walls depicting a rain forest, a plashing waterfall, a green and white marble Jacuzzi, and environmental sounds.

Next door, in a turn-of-the-century two-story home dubbed the White House, Long has created half a dozen more fantasy rooms, ranging from an Egyptian Suite, with a mural of the pyramids and sphinx at sunset, to Space Odyssey, with black-light illuminated stars, planets, and nebulae. All of the rooms have big-screen televisions and VCRs (the inn has a free library of 85 movies). Some have gas-log fireplaces and a second television visible from the Jacuzzi. For added privacy, Long's staff delivers a breakfast of fruit cups, pastries, yogurt, hash browns, juice, coffee, and tea to the room each morning.

Long's playful imagination often sails dangerously close to Las Vegas glitz, to the horror of those enamored of traditional bed-and-breakfasts. That hardly diminishes Center Street's popularity, however, especially with honeymooners.

> **The room called Aphrodite's Court has Greek statues, an antique brass four-poster bed beneath a peach and white canopy, faux marble walls, and a rectangular Jacuzzi spa framed by pillars and flowering plants.**

MANTI

Brigham House Inn

123 East Union
Manti, UT 84642
801-835-8381

> *A house of warmth
> built long ago by a
> Mormon bishop*

Innkeepers: Helen and Lee Thurston. **Accommodations:** 4 rooms. **Rates:** $40–$65. **Included:** Full breakfast. **Minimum stay:** None. **Added:** 10% tax. **Payment:** Cash, personal checks, or traveler's checks. **Children:** Welcome. **Pets:** Prohibited. **Smoking:** Prohibited. **Open:** Year-round.

The Brigham House Inn has two-foot-thick walls in places, a construction feature typical of Mormon handiwork during the last century. Bishop Moffatt had it built for himself in 1865, a few years before construction began on the Manti Temple. Brigham Young stayed there on his visits to town.

It never hurts for a bed-and-breakfast to have that kind of resonant history, though something much more immediate underpins the Brigham House's beguiling charm. Every nook and cranny of this house seems to radiate not only the enthusiasm of the Thurstons but also their past.

No two guest rooms are alike. The most impressive one, off the parlor on the main floor, has a 250-year-old French Empire bed, a burled armoire, and a six-foot clawfoot tub with brass feet and brass and porcelain fixtures. Photos of the Thurston ancestors hang on the walls. The three other rooms also have character, featuring handmade quilts, a four-poster bed, or reproductions of antique French dressers.

The parlor itself has a player piano and a carved wood mantel that came from Lion House in Salt Lake City. But since the fireplace is only decorative, guests often gather in the dining room, which has a wood-stove, or the sun porch, which has views of Manti Temple. Or they can be found upstairs relaxing on leather couches in the large Indian Room, which contains Navajo rugs, an American Flyer train set, and a television and VCR.

> **Lee Thurston's mother bought the house, and the eclectic furnishings have evolved through two generations, as one added to the legacy of the other. It is warm because it is unmistakably someone's home.**

The sun porch is part of an addition built to accommodate the Thurstons. So is the dining room, where Helen, whose Australian birth is betrayed by her gentle accent, serves an all-you-can-eat American breakfast of banana bread, apple rolls, and dishes like cheese soufflé, pancakes with raspberry jam, omelettes, or sausage rolls. Guests adore her.

Manti House Inn

401 North Main Street
Manti, UT 84642
801-835-0161

> *A romantic inn in the shadow of Manti's Mormon Temple*

Innkeepers: Beverly and Charles Futrell. **Accommodations:** 4 rooms, 3 suites, all with private baths. **Rates:** Rooms $45–$70, suites $65–$100. **Included:** Full breakfast. **Minimum stay:** None. **Added:** 10% tax. **Payment:** MasterCard, Visa. **Children:** Over 17. **Pets:** Prohibited. **Smoking:** Prohibited. **Open:** Year-round.

Around 1880, the workers commissioned to erect the Manti Mormon Temple honed their skills by building this two-story house. Then they moved in, living there until the temple was completed.

Today the Utah landmark has become an endearing inn full of craftsmanship and detail. The rooms, decked out in eye-catching wallpapers, all have bold color schemes. All have private baths with either oversize Roman tubs or clawfoot tubs. Each has a brass, white iron, or hand-made four-poster bed covered with a handmade quilt. Some have capricious decorations, like a tin child's bathtub from England. One, the former innkeepers' quarters, has been converted into a two-bedroom suite with a private entrance, oak floors, sitting room, and television.

> The workers who built Manti House faced the adobe brick exterior with the same cream-colored limestone, called oolite, that they used in the temple a block away. They also gave it a staircase identical to the one later installed in the temple.

The current owners, Beverly and Charles Futrell, live across the street. Though they'd been living in California, they had honeymooned at the inn, which gives them more than the usual affection for the place. They've set about a general beautification, from new carpet to beds of flowers around the inn and its gazebo.

In summer, wicker furniture and rockers adorn the front porch, and an ice cream parlor opens in back. Winter provides an excuse to sink into one of the sofas in front of the lobby's gas-log fireplace or take advantage of the inn's glass-enclosed Jacuzzi. At any time of the year guests are treated to hearty breakfasts of sausage-cheese casserole, peach French toast, or sour cream buttermilk pancakes, depending on what they want and what Beverly feels like preparing.

The Yardley Inn

190 West 200 South
Manti, UT 84642
801-835-1861
800-858-6634

> *A turn-of-the-century B&B with surprises*

Hosts: Gill and Marlene Yardley.
Accommodations: 5 rooms, 1 suite, all with private bath. **Rates:** Rooms $40–$60, suite $95. **Included:** Full breakfast. **Minimum stay:** None. **Added:** 10% tax. **Payment:** MasterCard, Visa. **Children:** Welcome if supervised. **Pets:** Prohibited. **Smoking:** Prohibited. **Open:** Year-round.

Gill Yardley is an enthusiastic cowboy poet, and his wife, Marlene, used to conduct the church choir, so guests who stay in their turn-of-the-century bed-and-breakfast sometimes return from dinner to find the Yardleys and their friends engaged in impromptu entertainment in the music room. But then this is a house that seems to invite theatricality. The structure itself dates to 1898, and in subsequent expansions and renovations it acquired, among other things, the arched windows from Salt Lake City's old Hotel Newhouse, a slate and bronze fireplace, and a collection of artifacts gleaned from flea markets and salvage outlets. Crystal chandeliers hang throughout. Nothing is quite what you'd expect.

The old-fashioned kitchen, for example, showcases an ornate woodstove and gives onto an expansive dining room open to the second-floor ceiling. From there, stairs lead to the rooms on the floor above and a guest parlor outfitted with a big-screen television, lots of couches, and an old organ. Those guest quarters, like the rest of the house, bear the stamp of the Yardleys' style, Marlene's in particular. Most have been extensively redone in recent years, many to the point of requiring a change of names to reflect their new decors. Each is a little different. The Show Business Room, for example, has two brass beds — one of them very large — old theater posters on the walls, and a detached bath down the hall. In the Rose Room, a white iron and brass bed and antique dresser stand in front of a fireplace. All the rooms have cable television.

> **Largest and most dramatic of all is the Honeymoon Suite. Plush ivory carpet runs from the bedroom with its king-size bed and antique armoire into the sitting room with a gas-log fireplace, a Victorian heart-shaped leaded glass window, and two-person Jacuzzi beneath a mural of painted lilacs.**

Breakfast at the Yardleys reflects Marlene's holistic health background. Guests gather at a long table in the country kitchen for nine-grain waffles, cornbread pancakes with black beans and salsa, turkey sausage, farm fresh fertile eggs, and herbal teas, supplemented occasionally by Gill's specialty chile relleno. There's also an afternoon tea with scones and crumpets. Both Gill and Marlene clearly enjoy dishing out hospitality. "This is very close to our hearts," says Marlene.

MIDWAY

The Homestead

700 North Homestead Drive
P.O. Box 99
Midway, UT 84049
801-654-1102
800-327-7220
Fax: 801-654-5087

> *A hot springs gives rise to Utah's only complete resort*

General manager: Britt Mathwich. **Accommodations:** 97 rooms, 12 suites. **Rates:** Rooms $75–$129, suites $145–$295. **Included:** Continental breakfast for guests of Virginia House only. **Minimum stay:** 3 nights over Christmas holidays. **Added:** 9% tax. **Payment:** Major credit cards. **Children:** Welcome except in Milk House and Virginia House. **Pets:** Prohibited. **Smoking:** Nonsmoking rooms available. **Open:** Year-round.

Looking like a Currier & Ives painting, the Homestead nestles in the foothills above Heber Valley, 60 miles southeast of Salt Lake City. Its guest houses and cottages — some more than 100 years old — cluster to one side of the pillared main building along winding paths landscaped with flowers and shrubbery. Horses and cattle graze in the fields below, which are separated from the inn by a corridor of golf fairways. Yet there are peculiar features in this otherwise bucolic landscape, among them a 30-foot-high mound that emits clouds of steam.

What has become a classic country resort started out as a farm. The Swiss-born Simon Schneitter attempted to grow alfalfa, but the water seeping from the warm springs that dot his property turned crops soggy. He did notice, however, that neighbors liked to bathe in the springs, so he built an enclosed pool, filled it with hot mineral water piped in from the mother of all springs in that huge mound, and opened S. J. Schneitter's Famous Hot Pot Resort.

> Among the newest accommodations are the cottage suites, chock-a-block with luxury amenities like fireplaces, stocked refrigerators, coffeemakers, jetted tubs, and enough room to sleep as many as six in comfort. In all, 109 rooms are scattered through 15 buildings.

It remained popular for decades before lapsing into genteel decline, only to be rescued in 1986, its centennial year, by Great Inns of the Rockies, who invested $3.8 million in its rehabilitation and expansion while preserving its down-home hospitality. The resort has never looked better. Antiques accent the main building, which dates from the 1950s and has walls built of pot rock, the incredibly hard mineral residue of the warm springs. The original guest house built in 1886 was reborn as an adults-only bed-and-breakfast called Virginia House, with tiny rooms that are models of Victorian country elegance, and a solarium with a Jacuzzi. Others, like the remodeled Bunkhouse, have two rooms with a queen and bunk beds and make ideal family lodging.

For recreation, the Homestead features not only those historic hot springs pools — now open only to resort guests — but also a golf course, tennis courts, riding stables, and a summer Kid's Kamp. In winter, there are sleigh rides, cross-country skiing, and easy access (and very economically priced packages) to eight downhill ski areas. If its main dining room has a penchant for showy entrées like chateau-briand flamed at the table, it can also turn out delicious fresh fish, and there's an informal grill room as well. Think of it as a country inn magically transformed into Utah's most complete resort.

Inn on the Creek

375 Rainbow Lane
Midway, UT 84049
801-654-0892
Fax: 801-654-5871

*A Swiss inn
on a golf course*

Innkeepers: Becky and Joel Van Leeuwen. **Accommodations:** 8 rooms and 5 cottages. **Rates:** Rooms $95, cottages $250–$295. **Included:** Full breakfast in rooms. **Minimum stay:** None. **Added:** 9% tax. **Payment:** Major credit cards. **Children:** Over age 8 in inn. **Pets:** Prohibited. **Smoking:** Prohibited. **Open:** Year-round.

First settled by the Swiss, the town of Midway has an emotional commitment to preserving its Swiss heritage, so when Becky and Joel Van Leeuwen built the Inn on the Creek in 1991, they looked to Alpine lodges for inspiration. Their three-story inn thus has a cedar shake roof, stucco walls, an octagonal turret and forest green shutters with Christmas tree cutouts. Midway is not Gstaad, however, so rather than having views of towering peaks, the Inn on the Creek overlooks the golf course at the Homestead.

Amenities abound: all guest rooms have gas-log

> However geographically displaced, the inn stands out for its wonderfully spacious rooms, large enough to qualify as junior suites. There are eight in all, each individually decorated in styles that range from country elegant to antique Victorian.

fireplaces, televisions, patios or balconies with golf course or mountain views, and huge tiled baths with Jacuzzi tubs and a separate shower. Those on the third floor have vaulted ceilings and a skylight over the tub.

The common areas are similarly expansive. The front door opens into a lobby paved with ivory and green stone tiles. The turret holds a parlor with another fireplace, a few couches, and window banquettes. There's also a dining room, where guests meet for breakfast, and beyond that a broad deck, whose balusters have the same Christmas tree cutouts as the shutters. Beyond lie the cottages. While somewhat more casually decorated than the inn, each has a living area with fireplace, three bedrooms, Jacuzzi tubs, and a full kitchen.

If there's any fault to be found with this little inn, it's not with the staff, who are very accommodating, but with a curious absence of coziness or intimacy. That probably does not matter for the executive retreats the Van Leeuwens encourage but may put off some vacationers. On the other hand, guests get reduced greens fees at the Homestead, and there are plans to serve dinner on Friday and Saturday evenings.

MT. PLEASANT

The Mansion House

298 South State Street
P.O. Box 13
Mt. Pleasant, UT 84647
801-462-3031

> *A B&B inn with respect for privacy*

Innkeepers: Denis and Terri Andelin. **Accommodations:** 3 rooms, all with private baths.

Rates: Single $40–$46, double $50–$62. **Included:** Full, Continental, or no breakfast, depending on rate. **Minimum stay:** None. **Added:** Nothing. **Payment:** MasterCard, Visa. **Children:** Over age 11 welcome. **Pets:** Prohibited. **Smoking:** Prohibited. **Open:** Year-round.

When Denis and Terri Andelin saw this two-story red brick Victorian in 1976, it had deteriorated, says Denis, to the point of looking "like a haunted house." Porches drooped, balconies threatened to collapse, and the cover to the ornate parlor fireplace lay in the gutter. Miraculously, however, the hand-painted mural on the ceiling, the ornate plaster rosettes, as well as the stained glass windows remained intact.

> Built in 1897 by James Larsen, a prominent sheep rancher, the house had been a showplace where Larsen and his wife entertained presidents and apostles of the Mormon church, government officials, and other dignitaries. The Andelins set out not so much to remodel as to restore it to its former glory.

Originally the Andelins had planned to live in the house, using the grand parlor as Denis's photography studio, but so many people stopped to photograph the house that the Andelins decided to open the rooms to guests.

A private entrance leads up a scrolled-oak staircase, past a stained glass window, to three cheerful bedrooms tastefully decorated with quilted bedspreads and colorful fabrics. All have modern private baths and color televisions.

For some, the inn's chief shortcoming is its failure to provide a place for guests to congregate. All of the first floor, excluding the foyer and check-in desk, is given over to the Andelins' living space and photography studio. Even breakfast is a private affair, delivered to the room rather than savored with other guests. There is a warmth missing here, peculiar in so small an inn. On the other hand, anyone looking for privacy will find it in abundance.

NEPHI

The Whitmore Mansion
Bed & Breakfast Inn

110 South Main Street
Nephi, UT 84648
801-623-2047

> *An uncommonly
> genial classic
> Victorian*

Hosts: Dorothy and Bob Gliske. **Accommodations:** 5 rooms, all with private bath. **Rates:** $50–$70. **Included:** Full breakfast. **Minimum stay:** None. **Added:** 9% tax. **Payment:** MasterCard, Visa. **Children:** Welcome if well behaved. **Pets:** Prohibited. **Smoking:** Prohibited. **Open:** Year-round.

The Whitmore Mansion appears in some architectural textbooks as a classic example of Queen Anne Eastlake Victorian design. Built in 1898 of red brick and sandstone, it has a turret at one corner, the original leaded and etched-glass windows, and a huge front porch. Inside, massive pocket doors, European oak woodwork — including a magnificent staircase — and carved fireplace mantels add to the grand atmosphere, but there is whimsy, too, like the hand-carved ticket booth from a French theater now used as a check-in desk.

When the Gliskes bought the mansion in 1987, it had already been converted to a B&B by Californians who decorated the rooms according to their rather eccentric tastes (the three-room Tower Suite, with a sitting room at the top of the turret, still has shingles on an inside wall, for example). But Dorothy, whose father was an artist, wanted wallpapers and fabrics that set off the antiques. She decorated the Attic Room in blues and whites, covering the high-back oak bed with a ruffled comforter and pillows and a teddy bear. The Sewing Room has a floral canopy over the white-iron bed, louvered windows, and a pink plaid wallpaper. An old Underwood typewriter sits capriciously on a table in the turret, not far from a daybed with a crocheted coverlet. Loveliest of all is the master bedroom/ honeymoon suite, which has a clawfoot tub in its oversize bath, a French desk set facing the rounded windows in the turret, and silvery white wallpaper with tiny blue cornflowers. Each of the other rooms has a private bath and its own charms, including handcrafted rugs, crocheted afghans, and lace curtains. A particular favorite, especially for families, is that three-room suite at the top of the tower.

> **Dorothy Gliske is not the sort to take living among antiques in a house listed on the National Register of Historic Places all that seriously. Warm, talkative, and willing to please, she dons different outfits depending on whether she's being cook or waitress. In all guises, she tends to favor long skirts that let her go barefoot without anyone's noticing.**

Dorothy is also a fine cook, serving not only hearty breakfasts of German pancakes with hot applesauce or various kinds of eggs (with her own homemade muffins) but also five-course dinners of chicken, beef stroganoff, and lasagna, followed by fabulous desserts (reservations required two days ahead; guests may bring their own wine). In warm weather, she'll sometimes serve homemade ice cream on the outside porch, or in winter, hot cider around the fireplace.

Her husband, Bob, helps out on weekends when he's not working, but it's Dorothy's presence you'll feel most. She attributes her success as an innkeeper to the skills she learned raising children. She treats her guests with the same loving care.

PARK CITY

The Blue Church Lodge

424 Park Avenue
P.O. Box 1720
Park City, UT 84060
801-649-8009
800-626-5467

> *A ski area inn
> with apartments
> rather than rooms*

General manager: Nancy Schmidt.
Accommodations: 12 apartments. **Rates:** $120–$375. **Included:** Continental breakfast. **Minimum stay:** 6–7 nights preferred. **Added:** 10.25% tax. **Payment:** MasterCard, Visa. **Children:** Welcome. **Pets:** Small pets allowed with prior approval. **Smoking:** Allowed. **Open:** Thanksgiving to Easter

The Blue Church Lodge clings to a hillside in Park City's historic district. The blue and white wood frame structure dates from the turn of the century, when it was built as the first Mormon Church in town. It continued to be their meeting hall until 1962. Though converted now to an inn, the Victorian exterior survives, and the building is listed on the National Register of Historic Places.

The Blue Church's history and its accommodations make it an unusual bed-and-breakfast inn. Instead of typical rooms, the Blue Church consists of apartments (five in the modern annex across the street). They range from studios to four bedrooms and feature fireplaces and fully equipped kitchens. The contemporary decor combines oak and pine furnishings, brass beds, custom-made comforters with matching dust ruffles and pillow shams, fold-out sofas, track lighting, and the occasional skylight. The annex condos have all been recently redone in a southwestern lodge motif and tend to be larger; staying there does, however, mean having to cross the street to get to breakfast and the Jacuzzi.

The town ski lift is three blocks away — a long way in ski boots — but the restaurants and shops of Park City's historic Main Street are a mere block below. Also at the inn, you'll find a library with a fireplace, a game room with table tennis, covered parking, and a coin-operated laundry. The resident manager even supplies cribs.

> **The fact that guests gather for breakfast makes the atmosphere unusually convivial for a condominium. It's not unusual to hear them making plans at breakfast or in the Jacuzzi to meet again the next year.**

The Imperial Hotel

221 Main Street
P.O. Box 1628
Park City, UT 84060
801-649-1904
800-669-8824
Fax: 801-645-7421

> *A landmark hotel on Park City's historic Main Street*

Manager: Todd and Ann Hoover. **Accommodations:** 8 rooms, 2 suites. **Rates:** (higher during Christmas holidays) Rooms, summer (mid-April–mid-November) $60–$75, winter $90–$140; suites, summer $85, winter $145–$175. **Included:** Full breakfast. **Minimum stay:** 3 nights in ski season. **Added:** 10.25% tax. **Payment:** Major credit cards. **Children:** Welcome (no cribs or roll-aways). **Pets:** Prohibited. **Smoking:** Prohibited. **Open:** Year-round.

The miners who streamed into Park City at the turn of the century hoping to make a fortune on silver spawned a forest of boardinghouses. A scant four remain, among them the landmark 1904 Imperial Hotel, which is now listed on the National Register of Historic Places.

> **Miners probably enjoyed the parlor, but it's certain they didn't bed down in such cheerful rooms.**
> **A festival of Victorian wallpapers, often in bold colors, gives the hotel rooms a country house atmosphere, as do the antique iron, wicker, or brass beds, down comforters, and lace curtains.**

The white clapboard Victorian rises 2½ stories at one end of Main Street. A steep set of stone stairs leads up to the entrance and a high-ceilinged hallway lined with wainscoting and Victorian wall sconces. Oak antiques, wing chairs, and painted murals decorate the parlor, an inviting room where fires blaze in stone fireplaces in winter.

Each room is differently appointed, though all have phones and televisions. Seven have deep Roman tubs (all have private baths). The suites both have two bedrooms (or a bedroom and sleeping loft) and so can easily accommodate a family. One of the suites also has a kitchen.

Guests get together in the breakfast room off the parlor for pancakes, waffles, French toast, hot and cold cereal, fruit, and several kinds of muffins. They can also gather in the Jacuzzi, which has been rather drearily closeted in a windowless downstairs room. For dinner, guests need go no farther than Park City's Main Street at the bottom of the steps.

The Old Miners' Lodge

615 Woodside Avenue
P.O. Box 2639
Park City, UT 84060
801-645-8068
800-648-8068
Fax: 801-645-7420

> *An inn that cele-brates Park City's colorful past*

Innkeepers: Hugh Daniels, Susan Wynne, and Liza Simpson.
Accommodations: 7 rooms, 3 suites. **Rates:** Rooms, summer (mid-April–mid-November) $50–$70, winter $85–$95; suites, summer $70–$90, winter $145–$165. **Included:** Full breakfast. **Minimum stay:** None. **Added:** 10.25% tax. **Payment:** Major credit cards. **Children:** Welcome. **Pets:** Prohibited. **Smoking:** Prohibited. **Open:** Year-round.

This two-story frame house in Park City's National Historic District has a Victorian pedigree dating from 1893, when it first opened as a boarding house for miners. Despite its history, Hugh Daniels and Susan Wynne opted for less elegance and more whimsy when restoring the inn, packing the rooms with an eclectic mix of antiques, reproductions, and collectibles.

Each of the guest rooms celebrates a colorful character linked to Park City's past. Thus, Susanna Emery-Holmes, a flamboyant woman who married so often and so well that she became known as Utah's "Silver Queen," is memorialized with a room that has a four-poster bed, antique white furnishings, and peach walls. Mother Urban, a 200-pound madam with a wooden leg, inspired the use of a queen-size brass bed and black soaking tub. Most of the others adopt loosely Victorian themes played out with brass or iron beds, clawfoot tubs (in baths that are otherwise modern), and turn-of-the-century accessories. A notable exception, however, is Fort Bridger, named for the frontiersman Jim Bridger, which contains a log bed, hopsack curtains, and rough-hewn cedar walls decorated with a buckskin shirt and old animal traps.

> It's often possible to ski up to the back of the lodge from the slopes of the adjacent Park City Ski Area, whose town lift, like the shops and restaurants of Park City's historic Main Street, is a block away. It could not be more conveniently situated.

Though the trio of owners — which now includes Liza Simpson — have a sense of humor, it does not come at the expense of guests' comfort. Every room has down comforters, terry robes, and fluffy towels, and at night guests find their beds turned down, chocolate kisses on the pillows, and in winter the electric blanket set to low. Hot cider is served by the living room fire in winter, lemonade on the porch in summer; there's an outdoor hot tub year-round.

Breakfast, which is served at a long table in the dining room, could be anything from French toast with their own homemade syrup to cheese eggs, quiche, or the miner's special (potatoes with bell peppers and cheese). It always comes with fresh fruit and some kind of meat. Hugh generously offers seconds.

Old Town Guest House

1011 Empire Avenue
P.O. Box 162
Park City, UT 84060
801-649-2642

> *A hillside haven for adventurous travelers*

Innkeepers: John Hughes and Debbie Lovci. **Accommodations:** 4 rooms, 2 with private bath. **Rates:** Summer, $45–$75; winter, $100–$175. **Included:** Full breakfast in winter; Continental-plus in summer. **Minimum stay:** 3 nights in winter. **Added:** 10.25% tax. **Payment:** Cash, checks, or traveler's checks. **Children:** Welcome. **Pets:** Prohibited (they have a dog). **Smoking:** Prohibited. **Open:** Year-round.

John Hughes and Debbie Lovci, the personable young couple whose house this is, love the mountains and the outdoors. John guides skiers into the backcountry in winter; Debbie spends the summer leading mountain bike tours.

Built in 1925, the large house stands on a hillside a few blocks above the shops and restaurants of Park City's historic district and about the same distance from the town ski lift. It has four guest

> **One clue to the atmosphere at the Old Town Guest House is that each of its rooms has been named for a ski run at Park City.**

rooms, each furnished with lodgepole pine beds. The one called Treasure Hollow lies just off the parlor but also has a private entrance. Its decor runs to southwestern mountain man, with a rough log bed, a convertible loveseat, an Indian print rug, log rocker with a rawhide seat and back, and a mix of old wainscoting, new wood veneer, and a southwestern print wallpaper. Accents take the form of an Indian print rug and some old snowshoes. It has a three-quarter bath.

Upstairs, Hughes and Lovci opted for a cowboy theme for a two-bedroom suite with a queen-size log bed in one room, two twins in the other, and a bath with a jetted tub. In a new addition off the back, they installed two small bedrooms with ruffled curtains and log beds. The two rooms share a shower, but each has its own half bath.

The focal point of the house is its cozy parlor, where there's a flagstone fireplace, and the adjacent dining room, which has a rustic pine table and pine benches. It's there that guests gather for an après-ski (or après-bike) of cookies and brownies and for huge breakfasts in winter and health-conscious fare in summer. There's also a hot tub to soothe aching muscles year-round.

The Snowed Inn

3770 North Highway 224
Park City, UT 84060
801-649-5713
800-545-7669
Fax: 801-645-7672

> *A ski-country
> inn modeled on
> a farmhouse*

General Manager: Robin Sletten.
Accommodations: 8 rooms, 2 suites. **Rates:** (higher during
Christmas holidays) Rooms, summer $100–$140, winter
$175–$195; suites, summer $160, winter $225. **Included:** Full
breakfast. **Minimum stay:** None. **Added:** 9% tax. **Payment:**
Major credit cards. **Children:** Welcome. **Pets:** Prohibited.
Smoking: Prohibited. **Open:** Year-round.

The Snowed Inn is impossible to miss. Standing beside the
highway, about three miles from the ski slopes at Park City,
the blue and white two-story inn looks like a Victorian farmhouse, with a gazebo on
one side and a carriage
house and horse corral on
the other. A porch wraps
most of the way around.

> **Antiques, high ceilings,
> colorful wallpapers, and
> lace curtains give the
> rooms a turn-of-the-century
> feel, though the down
> comforters, televisions,
> carpeted floors, terrycloth
> robes, and private baths
> with oversize soaking tubs
> guarantee modern comfort.**

Yet the inn is hardly
old or rustic. Modeled on
the Iowa farmhouse that
belonged to the owner's
grandmother, it was built
in 1987. Guests come in
to a two-story lobby with
marble floors and dark
paneling. On the right, a
staircase leads past an
oval stained glass window
to an L-shaped balcony overlooking the lobby. To the left,
pocket doors, guarded by a grandfather clock, open into a convivial parlor turned restaurant, where in winter a fire blazes
in a fireplace framed by a massive mahogany mantel supported by Doric columns. Alex Duffer, noted for his restaurant, Alex's, on Main Street, has opened at the Snowed Inn,
serving French-Continental fare like pike dumplings in lobster sauce, duck flambé, and pepper steak.

The rooms, individually decorated, lie off narrow hallways.

A couple of the rooms (erroneously billed as suites on the rate card) are quite small; the Family Suite, on the other hand, has a master bedroom with a sitting area and a fireplace, two twin beds (separated from the main room by a screen), and a huge mirrored armoire. A full breakfast is served in the library.

The Snowed Inn's only disadvantage is its location, neither in town (and thus close to restaurants) nor at the ski area. On the other hand, it does have a hot tub on the back deck, plenty of parking, a petting zoo with fallow deer, and a sleigh-ride company.

Washington School Inn

543 Park Avenue
P.O. Box 536
Park City, UT 84060
801-649-3800
800-824-1672
Fax: 801-649-3802

An 1889 school magically changed into a romantic inn

Innkeeper: Nancy Beaufait. **Accommodations:** 12 rooms, 3 suites. **Rates:** (higher during Christmas holidays) Rooms, ski season $190, rest of year $75–$100; suites, ski season $230–$250, rest of year $110–$150. **Included:** Full breakfast. **Minimum stay:** Over Christmas holidays, 3 nights in rooms, 7 nights in suites; rest of year, none in rooms, 3 nights in suites. **Added:** 10.25% tax. **Payment:** Major credit cards. **Children:** No children under 12. **Pets:** Prohibited. **Smoking:** Prohibited except in mezzanine library. **Open:** Year-round except for 2 weeks late April–early May.

Of all the structures in Park City's hillside historic district, none is more distinctive than the Washington School Inn. Built in 1889 of limestone from a nearby quarry, the old schoolhouse is one of the few buildings in town to survive the great fire of 1898. Now listed on the National Register of Historic Places, it stands out for its bell tower, pediment-shaped dormers, and oversize 3-by-9-foot windows.

> **Downstairs, there's a hot tub, sauna, steam showers, and ski lockers. Out front are historic Main Street's restaurants, shops, and galleries, and Park City's town ski lift lies at the end of Park Avenue, a two-minute walk away.**

Light from those windows illuminates a 16-foot-high lobby and marble-topped check-in desk. An oxblood leather parlor set faces a huge fireplace with a massive rough-hewn mantel. An antique oak sideboard anchors the cheerful dining room; the mezzanine above — the one place indoors where guests may smoke — holds a book-lined reading and television room with a VCR.

The rooms, though small, have the feel of a turn-of-the-century country inn, with brass or wooden beds covered with quilts and private baths with old-fashioned pewter and porcelain fixtures. Each is named for a schoolteacher. Better still are the spacious suites, two of which have fireplaces. The one called Miss Uriel runs the width of the building beneath a sloping attic ceiling. A festival in yellow and plum, it has a four-poster pine bed, an etched-glass chandelier, and windows with sitting areas.

It's the friendly, attentive staff and lots of extras that set the Washington School Inn apart. Besides a hearty full breakfast (set out buffet-style in winter), guests get afternoon snacks like hot appetizers or chicken wings with hot cider or wine in winter, and lemonade in summer. There is brandy in the living room each evening.

SALT LAKE CITY

The Anton Boxrud Bed & Breakfast

57 South 600 East
Salt Lake City, UT 84102
801-363-8035
800-524-5511

> *A B&B with
> history and
> sociable hosts*

Hosts: Mark Brown and Keith Lewis. **Accommodations:** 5 rooms, 2 with private bath, 1 suite. **Rates:** Single $55–$89, double $49–$109. **Included:** Full breakfast. **Minimum stay:** None. **Added:** 10.85% tax. **Payment:** Major credit cards. **Children:** Welcome (cribs available). **Pets:** Prohibited. **Smoking:** Prohibited. **Open:** Year-round.

Anton Boxrud is a rarity among turn-of-the-century homes: its original plans survived, making it possible to restore this 1901 two-story home to something approximating the house Anton and Minnie Boxrud moved into. The front door opens to another era. Beveled glass, burled woodwork, pocket doors, oak wainscoting, and maple flooring enrich the interiors. Remarkably, even some of the furnishings are original, having been stored in the attic when the Boxruds passed away.

Mark Brown and Keith Lewis bought the B&B in 1993 after renovating a couple of other houses in Salt Lake City. Moving in antiques of their own and others they acquired, they set about enhancing the look of the place with new carpet and wallpaper, floral print comforters, and new linens and towels. All of that and their love of socializing with their guests has brought a new element of conviviality to this historic home.

And a new level of comfort. The sparely furnished front parlor and den now have the kinds of sofas and chairs that encourage guests to gather. The front porch, too, has been made more appealing by painting its columns to look like marble and its floor to look like stone. The gardens have more flowers and a well-tended look.

> The largest room is the original master bedroom, done in dark forest green. Its queen-size mahogany bed faces a gorgeous stained glass window. It also has a private bath.

Five of the rooms occupy the second floor. Each of them has a scattering of antiques, some of them original to the house, and down comforters in duvet covers. Room 1, though smaller and without a private bath, stands out for its sunny location on the front of the house and old antique brass bed. Mark and Keith added a honeymoon suite to the attic space on the third floor. Accessible by the back stairs, it has a polished steel headboard, wicker furnishings, marbleized walls with a stenciled border, a small sitting area, and a tiny private bath. Televisions are available on request, and there's a phone for guests to use in the entrance foyer.

Breakfast has become a sumptuous repast of stuffed French toast, pancakes with raspberry syrup, quiches, or soufflés complemented by fresh fruit and yogurt. There's coffee and tea out all day, and a small refrigerator stocked with complimentary sodas and juice. Mark and Keith, who live downstairs, serve munchies every evening — one more chance to get together with their guests.

Brigham Street Inn

1135 East South Temple
Salt Lake City, UT 84102-1605
801-364-4461
Fax: 801-521-3201

A showcase of interior design in a 19th-century mansion

Owner: Nancy Pace. **Accommodations:** 8 rooms, 1 suite, all with private bath. **Rates:** Rooms, single $75, double $105–$115; suite $150. **Included:** Continental breakfast. **Added:** 10.85% tax. **Payment:** Major credit cards. **Children:** Under 3 free. **Pets:** Prohibited. **Smoking:** Allowed. **Open:** Year-round.

Most late-19th-century mansions make the transition to bed-and-breakfasts by becoming living museums of Victoriana, chock full of antiques and turn-of-the-century memorabilia. Not the delightful Brigham Street Inn. The 2½-story red brick inn with deep green pillars hints at the belle époque, with its high ceilings, rounded bay windows with leaded glass, pocket doors, and staircase of quartersawn oak. But only one bedroom — and a single at that — contains Victorian antiques. The rest are cheerful, contemporary, and unique.

In 1981, Nancy Pace, now vice president of tourism for the Convention & Visitors Bureau, decided to buy the dilapidated 1898 mansion she'd fallen in love with and turn it into an inn. While undertaking the renovations she lent the house, which is on the National Register of Historic Homes, to the Utah Heritage Foundation for use in its annual fund-raiser, a designers' showcase. When it ended, Pace opened the richly decorated rooms to guests.

She hired young, personable managers to staff the desk 24

hours a day and serve Continental breakfast at a long oak table in the dining room. Their attentive professionalism, coupled with features such as phones with data ports in

> The Utah Heritage Foundation brought in 12 interior designers to create a model bed-and-breakfast inn, assigning each a room to decorate, and then opened the house to public tours. When it was all over, Pace bought the contents from the decorators and began her new career as an innkeeper.

the rooms and the inn's proximity to the University of Utah, attracts not only tourists but business travelers as well. Guests often gather on the comfortable sofas in the parlor (with an original bird's-eye maple mantel) to compare notes on their rooms, from the bay-windowed elegance of Room 1 with southern exposure to the contemporary style of the basement suite, with its private entrance, brass bed, double Jacuzzi tub, and kitchen with microwave. Evening turndown includes mints and fresh towels.

The Inn at Temple Square

71 West South Temple
Salt Lake City, UT 84101
801-531-1000
800-843-4668
Fax: 801-537-7272

> *A European-style hotel across from Temple Square*

General manager: Marge Taylor.
Accommodations: 75 rooms, 15 suites. **Rates:** Rooms, weekdays $95–$102, weekends $73–$93; suites $140. **Included:** Full breakfast. **Minimum stay:** None. **Added:** 10.85% tax.

Payment: Major credit cards. **Children:** Free under age 18. **Pets:** Prohibited. **Smoking:** Prohibited and subject to fine. **Open:** Year-round.

When the venerable Hotel Utah closed, Salt Lake City plunged into an accommodations Dark Age, no longer able to offer travelers a truly distinctive hotel in the heart of downtown. That changed in 1990 with the reopening of the Inn at Temple Square.

Though originally constructed in 1930 as a transient hotel, the seven-story red brick inn bears no resemblance to its Depression-era ancestor except in its distinguished architecture. The new inn is a European-style hostelry whose staff greets guests like friends.

The rooms continue the European style, with custom-made dark wood furniture and heavy Edwardian drapes.

> The intimate lobby rises two stories from its green marble floors to a coffered ceiling. Sunlight illuminates a hand-painted frieze of bluebells and reflects off brass chandeliers. Many afternoons, live piano music drifts down from the mezzanine library.

The smallish standard rooms, which face the back courtyard, have queen-size beds, feather pillows, thick comforters, fine linens, armoires with remote-control televisions, small refrigerators with complimentary soft drinks, and two-line phones with data ports. The spacious deluxe rooms, with their king-size beds, have the same amenities but look out on Temple Square — site of the Mormon Temple and Tabernacle — directly across the street. Businesspeople like the Parlor Suites, which include a completely separate sitting room with a table, chairs, and half bath; honeymooners love the Bridal Suites for their four-poster beds and Jacuzzi tubs. Five of the rooms are fully wheelchair accessible, and the hotel has been ramped throughout.

The price of the room includes a buffet breakfast of fresh fruit, pastry, eggs, pancakes, bacon, and more amid the Tiffany lamps and upholstered banquettes of the hotel's Carriage Court Restaurant. The restaurant also serves lunch and good, moderately priced dinners of seafood fettuccine, breast of chicken Oscar, and tournedos of beef. The hotel does not have a liquor license and is so adamant about its nonsmoking policy that guests risk eviction and a fine for lighting up.

The Peery Hotel

110 West 300 South
Salt Lake City, UT 84101
801-521-4300
800-331-0073
Fax: 801-575-5014

> *A restored hotel
> dating to the era
> of train travel*

General managers: Michael Fletcher and Darrel Newman. **Accommodations:** 71 rooms, 6 suites. **Rates:** Rooms $59–$89, suites $99–$109. **Included:** Continental breakfast. **Minimum stay:** None. **Added:** 10.85% tax. **Payment:** Major credit cards. **Children:** Free under age 16. **Pets:** Prohibited. **Smoking:** Permitted on third floor. **Open:** Year-round.

Listed on the National Register of Historic Places, the Peery Hotel is a three-story brick structure faced with gray sandstone that stands halfway between the Rio Grande Railway Station and Temple Square. Constructed in 1910, its unprepossessing architecture suggests a history of transient guests, people who needed rooms for a night or two and cared more about cost than comfort. But the Peery is much more.

A half moon of stained glass caps double birch doors that open onto an elegant lobby dominated by a grand staircase. Thick, dusky plum carpet covers the floor and stairs. Many of the lobby's furnishings are antiques, among them a monumental carved wood breakfront. More antiques create mini-parlors on each of the upper floor landings.

Rooms feature high ceilings, decorative wood moldings, and tile baths. The layouts and decor vary. The standard rooms, although small and without desks and tubs, occupy corners and thus have two windows. The deluxe rooms are roughly the size of most other standard hotel rooms, while suites are really large rooms with sitting areas and perhaps a partial divider. The only disappointment is the bland furnishings, which seem more appropriate to a motel than a historic hotel.

But the Peery's amenities and services help balance those shortcomings. All the rooms have televisions, and rates include a Continental breakfast and newspaper, free parking, free airport shuttle, and access to a tiny workout

> **The fine turn-of-the-century workmanship shows everywhere, from the dentil moldings on the lobby's high wooden ceiling to twin square pillars that anchor the staircase.**

room, a hot tub, and a sauna. There are two restaurants off the lobby (one of them the very affordable Peery Pub & Café), both of which offer room service. There's also a sundries shop.

The Pinecrest Bed & Breakfast Inn

6211 Emigration Canyon Road
Salt Lake City, UT 84108
801-583-6663
800-359-6663

> *A quiet canyon inn on a historic Mormon route*

Innkeepers: Phil and Donnetta Davis. **Accommodations:** 3 rooms, 1 suite, 1 guest house, 1 cabin, all with private bath. **Rates:** Rooms $70–$175, guest house $135, cabin $120. **Included:**

Full breakfast. **Minimum stay:** None. **Added:** 9.75% tax. **Payment:** Major credit cards. **Children:** Welcome in suite, guest house, or cabin. **Pets:** Prohibited. **Smoking:** Prohibited. **Open:** Year-round.

Pinecrest dates from 1915, when quarry owner W. S. Henderson had it built as his home, using red and white stone from a quarry nearby. He chose a location six miles up Emigration Canyon, the historic Mormon route into the Salt Lake Valley, setting the house alongside a gurgling trout stream on six acres wooded with pines, cottonwoods, and river birch. His son, David, inherited the estate and added wrought iron gates (which originally graced Paramount Studios in Hollywood) and formal gardens. The setting is so peaceful it takes effort to remember that Salt Lake City is a mere 20-minute drive away.

> The original master bedroom, which takes up the entire upper floor, has become an opulent Oriental Suite furnished with Ming silk couches, a king-size bed, and a Chinese screen. It has views of the gardens, its own rose-colored Jacuzzi tub, and a separate room with two twin beds, making it ideal for families.

Phil and Donnetta Davis purchased the house in 1986 and, except for modernizing a couple of the baths, kept it much as they found it. A huge living room runs across the main floor, with windows looking onto the gardens. Paneling covers the walls and ceiling, Belgian carpet covers the floors, and a fireplace adorns a wall of flat fieldstone.

There are three rooms and a suite in the inn proper, each with a different decor and private bath. The smallest is done in Holland blue with white wicker, the largest (after the master bedroom) in a Jamaican decor complete with its own Mexican tile Jacuzzi and a sauna. Also special is the two-story Stetson Guest House, which has hardwood floors, a fireplace, kitchen, and Western memorabilia. It holds a queen-size bed on the main level and four bunk beds and a bath downstairs (Robert Redford stayed here in the years before the Davises bought it). Tucked into the pines near the Davises' own home a mile and a half away is a 1940s log cabin with its own fireplace, full kitchen, and two double beds in a loft.

Phil Davis prides himself on the sour cream banana pancakes he serves for breakfast, dishing them out at an antique dining table in the living room in winter, on a deck overlooking the gardens in summer. Beyond that, he is intermittently on hand to give advice and answer questions, leaving guests full run of the property. Guests can follow hiking trails that lead into the woods, or the Davises can arrange horseback riding and dinner.

Saltair Bed & Breakfast

164 South 900 East
Salt Lake City, UT 84102
801-533-8184
800-733-8184

A sunny Victorian B&B, a mile from downtown

Hosts: Jan Bartlett and Nancy Saxton. **Accommodations:** 5 rooms, 2 with private bath. **Rates:** Single $38, double $55–$95. **Included:** Full breakfast. **Minimum stay:** None. **Added:** 10.85% tax. **Payment:** Major credit cards (subject to 4% surcharge); checks or cash preferred. **Children:** Welcome if well behaved. **Pets:** Prohibited. **Smoking:** Prohibited. **Open:** Year-round.

When Nancy Saxton and her husband, Jan Bartlett, wanted to open a bed-and-breakfast, they visited Saltair and immediately fell under its spell. "We believe in the spirit of homes," says Nancy, "and this one feels very comfortable."

This homey Victorian with a long covered porch is situated on a residential street a mile from downtown. Though outwardly little different from its neighbors, it is listed on the National Register of Historic Places. Built in 1903, it was sold in 1920 to Italian vice consul Fortunato Anselmo. Among his overnight guests were the cardinal who later became Pope Pius XII, Mussolini's secretary (who was also Anselmo's mistress), and members of the Italian Olympic team. During Prohibition, Anselmo made wine in the cellar, but authorities couldn't touch him since the house was regarded as occupying foreign soil.

Though the still in the basement didn't survive, much of the house's fine interior detail did. Snowflakes etched in beveled-glass panes to resemble winter frost frame the oak front door. Inside, sunlight floods through large leaded glass windows into a living room and dining room rich with original oak millwork. Antiques and plants abound.

> **Healthy breakfasts, served family style on a long oak table in the dining room, consist of fresh fruit, home-made muffins and granola, fruit smoothies (blended fruits and yogurt), and French toast, pancakes, or waffles. Guests can have as much as they want.**

A polished oak staircase leads to the five main bedrooms, each furnished with antiques, family heirlooms, and fresh flowers. What they lack in size they make up for in cheerful comfort. Quilts or crocheted bedspreads cover the brass beds, adding to the feeling of warmth and freshness. The most inviting of all are the Blue Crystal room, which has a sunny southern exposure, bay window, and queen-size brass bed (its private bathroom is down the hall), and the Sweet Sage room, which has a queen-size brass bed and potbelly stove.

On winter afternoons, Nancy puts out hot cider and veggies, cookies, or popcorn. In summer, there is sometimes homemade ice cream (an old-fashioned crank machine that guests help with) and fresh lemonade. The atmosphere could not be warmer.

SNOWBIRD

Cliff Lodge

State Highway 210
Little Cottonwood Canyon
Snowbird, UT 84092
801-742-2222
800-453-3000
Fax: 801-742-3300

> *A slopeside hotel and spa in concrete and glass*

General manager: John Warner. **Accommodations:** 532 rooms, suites, and dorms. **Rates:** Rooms, winter (late December–late March) $178–$285, summer $92–$143; suites, winter $480–$756, summer $235–$378; dorms, winter $50, summer $26. **Minimum stay:** 3–4 nights in winter. **Added:** 9.75% tax. **Payment:** Major credit cards. **Children:** Welcome. **Pets:** Prohibited. **Smoking:** Nonsmoking rooms available. **Open:** Year-round.

The flagship hotel for owner/developer Dick Bass's 2,000-acre Snowbird ski resort is the 13-story Cliff Lodge. A modern Stonehenge in concrete and glass, this angular monolith anchors one end of the village about 150 yards from Snowbird Plaza's shops, restaurants, and ski-tram maze. It looks stark from outside, as if it could withstand an avalanche of Little Cottonwood Canyon's fabled ultralight powder snow, but inside an 11-story atrium with a wall of windows on the slopes helps temper the cold grayness, as does an abundance of blond wood and a permanent art collection.

Basic lodging consists of comfortably large standard-issue hotel rooms, some with balconies. They are redeemed by wall-to-wall windows with views of the slopes or the canyon.

Guests who need their space (or who abhor boring rectangular quarters) should book a deluxe room, some of which have king-size Murphy beds.

> Every afternoon, guests who haven't booked herbal wraps or massages head for the rooftop whirlpool and lap pool, whose glass walls provide unobstructed views of the slopes.

There are three restaurants in the lodge, ranging from the aptly named (and pricey) Aerie and its sushi bar to casual Keyhole and its Mexican food. Valet parking, efficient ski lockers, and state-licensed child care and nursery (for children six weeks and up) complete the assets.

SUNDANCE

Sundance Resort

R.R.#3
Box A-1
Sundance, UT 84604
801-225-4107
800-892-1600
Fax: 801-226-1937

> *A resort for all seasons and a retreat for filmmakers*

General manager: Bill Shoaf. **Accommodations:** 57 studios and 2- to 3-bedroom cottages; 15 3- to 5-bedroom homes. **Rates:** (higher over Christmas holidays) Rooms, winter (early December–late April) $150–$240, rest of year $110–$155; studios and cottages, winter $295–$590, rest of year $175–$455; homes $575–$675. **Included:** Full breakfast. **Minimum stay:** 3 nights over Christmas holidays. **Added:** 9% tax. **Payment:** Major credit cards. **Children:** Welcome. **Pets:** Prohibited. **Smoking:** Prohibited. **Open:** Year-round.

Long before there was a Sundance Institute or a Sundance Resort, a not-yet-famous Robert Redford camped in the wilderness below 11,750-foot Mt. Timpanogos and later built a house there. He found solace in this part of Utah's Wasatch Mountains, a solace he eventually sought to introduce to a wider audience by building an arts community. In the ensuing quarter century, Sundance has evolved into a year-round resort, known not only as a retreat for independent filmmakers and playwrights, but also as the most unpretentious of a corona of ski resorts situated within an hour's drive of Salt Lake City.

Yet Sundance remains less a place than a mood. To the degree possible, structures disappear: constructed of stone and unpainted wood, they intrude as little as possible on the natural beauty of the woods and mountains that surround them.

> **Whether Robert Redford happens to be visiting or not, his love of this wilderness invests everything from the limited scope of the development — fewer than 100 houses and cottages on its 5,000 acres — to the restaurants' emphasis on fresh, local ingredients.**

Redford designed the Sundance Cottages, scattering them along a creek that winds through the aspens, yellow oak, and scrub maple behind the main lodge. Most have three bedrooms, typically consisting of a one-bedroom suite, a studio, and a bedroom, each with a private entrance off a shared foyer so they can be rented together or separately. Inspired by cabins in the woods, the cottages adopt a rustic tone in their rough pine interiors and stone fireplaces. Most have a kitchen or kitchenette. Indian rugs and old photographs provide color and a sense of place. Sliding glass doors open onto a deck with views of the trees and either Mt. Timpanogos or a limestone cliff on the opposite side of the canyon about half a mile away. The cottages' rustic appearance blends perfectly with the beauty of the canyon, which Redford fans will recognize as the setting for much of *Jeremiah Johnson*. Even more impressive are the privately owned mountain homes. Like the cottages, many of them make liberal use of stone and woods, while ranging in size up to five bedrooms. They cling to the hillside and have sweeping views of the surrounding peaks.

As a ski area, Sundance lacks the notoriety of nearby Alta, Snowbird, Deer Valley, and Park City. Its vertical drop at 2,150 feet is respectable, but its relatively modest 450 acres pales in comparison to its sister ski areas, all of which have three to five times as much skiable terrain. Nevertheless, skiers who ignore statistics discover an appealing intermediate-expert bowl and enough variety to be glad they came. Those who decide to stay overnight discover a sybaritic sanctuary with some of the most sensually satisfying lodgings anywhere.

There are two restaurants: the more casual Grill Room, decorated with photos from the Sundance Institute summer workshops; and the Tree Room, which shows native art and antiques from Redford's own collection (among them a huge Indian rug given to Redford by an admirer of his environmental work). With differing degrees of sophistication, both restaurants showcase native American cuisine, which translates into simple preparations of Utah trout, range-fed lamb, prairie chicken with cider cranberry sauce, and salmon, accompanied whenever possible by organic vegetables from the Sundance garden.

Sundance's other amenities include a Nordic center with trails through the Elk Meadows Preserve five minutes away, all-day supervision in ski school for kids six to twelve, a ski shop, a general store, and a boutique selling the same items available through the Sundance catalog. In summer, the canyon is, if possible, even more beautiful, and the activities shift to hiking, mountain biking, horseback riding, and fishing, and evening performances of the Sundance Summer and Children's theaters. Its rustic style and intimate scale make it an exceptional place to get away.

Southern Utah

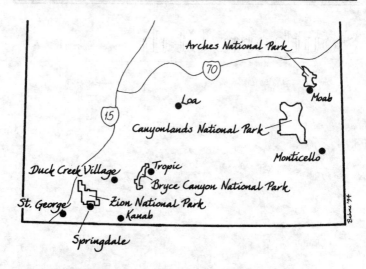

Best Bed-and-Breakfast Homes

Kanab
   Nine Gables Inn
Springdale
   Harvest House Bed & Breakfast
   O'Tooles' Under the Eaves
Tropic
   Bryce Point Bed & Breakfast

Best Bed-and-Breakfast Inns

Duck Creek Village
   Meadeau View Lodge
Moab
   Castle Valley Inn Bed-and-Breakfast
   Sunflower Hill Bed-and-Breakfast Inn
Monticello
   The Grist Mill Inn Bed & Breakfast
St. George
   Greene Gate Village
   Seven Wives Inn

Best Condominiums, Apartments, and Cabins

Moab
   Pack Creek Ranch

Best Country Inns

Loa
   Road Creek Inn
Moab
   Pack Creek Ranch

Best National Park Lodges

Bryce Canyon National Park
   Bryce Canyon Lodge

Zion National Park
Zion Lodge

Best Resorts and Spas

St. George
Green Valley Spa & Tennis Resort

Though the larger cities of Utah's southern tier stake their own claims on travelers' affections — Cedar City with its annual summer Shakespeare Festival and **St. George** with its salubrious climate and 19th-century red sandstone tabernacle — this region's extraordinary power to enchant radiates from five wondrous national parks in a playground of recreation. To drive through the region inspires awe; to hike, raft, Jeep, ride horseback, or bike through is to cross an invisible threshold into a sculpture garden of cliffs, pinnacles, spires, arches, fins, balanced rocks, needles, grabens, hoodoos, and domes. Much of the southern Utah landscape seems to belong to another world.

The oldest of these parks is **Zion,** in the southwestern corner near St. George. The Mormons first gave this wilderness of cliffs and canyons a name that means "heavenly city of God." Few roads penetrate its 230 square miles. One that does follows the course of the Virgin River through a narrow canyon bordered by 2,000- to 3,000-foot sandstone cliffs. Smaller canyons branch off to either side. Turnouts provide a chance to gaze up at formations, while hiking trails, including a few that have been paved and ramped for wheelchairs, take off at various points for higher perspectives. One of the wettest and most popular hikes, called Gateway to the Narrows, follows the course of the Virgin River through a canyon so narrow that at times it's necessary to wade up the river itself.

The road into Zion Canyon can be reached from the south at **Springdale** or from the east via Mt. Carmel Junction.

Whereas the great features of Zion are massive cliffs and deep canyons, **Bryce Canyon National Park** resembles a surreal petrified forest. Thousands of spires delicately carved from limestone cliffs stand in odd formations around a dozen amphitheaters within the 56-square-mile park. The stratified rock varies in color, layer by layer. Shades of red, orange, brown, ivory, and soft yellow change intensity and hue with the changing light, making the view at sunrise different from the view at sunset. The Rim Drive through the park follows the edge of a plateau, with overlooks on the amphitheaters below.

From the west, the park entrance can be reached along the Red Canyon Scenic Byway. That road (Route 12) continues east, rambling along the Kaiparowits Plateau, then north over a mountain pass, in what is consistently one of the most riveting drives in a region laced with scenic byways. At Torrey, it intersects with another scenic byway into Capitol Reef National Park. There red sandstone domes wear grayish white caps in a 75-mile-long wilderness occasionally interrupted by fruit orchards, the legacy of early settlers. Several fairly easy hiking trails lace the interior, and there is a 25-mile scenic drive, some of it unpaved, beginning at the visitors' center.

The two great parks of eastern Utah are Arches and Canyonlands. More than 1,500 natural stone arches cover the 114-square-mile park named for its most prominent feature. A 41-mile paved road through it laces together many of the major formations, including Balanced Rock, Skyline Arch, Double Arch, and the Fiery Furnace. But the best way to explore this museum of sandstone sculpture is on foot. That not only lets you see sites inaccessible by car, like Delicate Arch, but takes you past Indian petroglyphs. The entrance is five miles northwest of **Moab.**

Canyonlands, south of Arches, is the largest of all these parks. It provides two perspectives on the artistic power of rivers: one from below, gazing up, the other from above, gazing down into the canyon at the rushing whitewater below. The Colorado and Green rivers carved Canyonlands into three districts, each named for its distinctive landscape: Island in the Sky, Needles, and the Maze. The first two are accessible by passenger car: Island in the Sky lies 30 miles from Moab, Needles 50 miles from **Monticello.** But the Maze reveals its secrets only to hikers, mountain bikers, and four-wheel-drive enthusiasts. Whitewater rafting trips through the park can be arranged in Moab.

When the Colorado River leaves Canyonlands, it enters Glen Canyon, where it backs up behind a dam to form the 190-mile-long Lake Powell. Hundreds of side canyons, inlets, and coves, some sheltering Indian ruins, make this a wonderland for houseboating and photography. There are three marinas in Utah, at Hite, Bullfrog, and Hall's Crossing.

BRYCE CANYON NATIONAL PARK

For other lodging in the area, see the towns of Duck Creek
Village, Kanab, and Tropic.

Bryce Canyon Lodge

Bryce Canyon National Park
Bryce, UT 84764
801-834-5361
Reservations:
TW Recreational Services, Inc.
P.O. Box 400
Cedar City, UT 84721
801-586-7686
Fax: 801-586-3157

> *A vintage lodge
> and cabins
> near a multihued
> wonderland*

General manager of TW Services: John Shafer. **Accommodations:** 70 rooms, 4 suites, 40 cabins. **Rates:** Rooms $69, suites
$105, cabins $79. **Minimum stay:** None. **Added:** 9% tax. **Payment:** Major credit cards. **Children:** Free under age 13. **Pets:**
Prohibited. **Smoking:** Nonsmoking rooms available. **Open:**
Mid-April through October.

From any of the rooms or cabins at Bryce Canyon Lodge, it is
only a few hundred yards to the rim of Bryce Amphitheater
and a multicolored geologic masterpiece of intricately eroded
limestone. For that reason alone, the lodge could be a hovel
and still be the first choice of places to stay in the park.
Fortunately, it is something far grander. Built in the 1920s by
the Union Pacific Railroad, Bryce Canyon Lodge and its
entourage of cabins are fresh from a $1.5 million restoration.
Using historic photos, architects and designers stripped away
modern accretions and recreated lost fixtures to turn the
clock back 60 years. Log candelabra once again hang above the
copper-hooded stone fireplace in the lobby. Park benches and
hickory furniture invite guests to sit around the courtyard
entrance. The false ceiling has been stripped from the auditorium to reveal the vaulted beams, and the original post office
has been restored and reopened. In the dining room, thick
steel girders still run wall to wall, a legacy of the railroad
bridge engineers who built the lodge.

Some things are new. The old dormitories upstairs in the
lodge have been converted to four suites and have white

wicker furnishings. The western-style log cabins, built in 1928 of unpeeled ponderosa pine, still have vaulted ceilings, windows on both sides, porches, and what are now gas-log fireplaces, but the furnishings and carpets are brand new, and the private baths were completely redone. Even the motel units, which lack the character of the cabins and lodge, have spiffy new appointments to go with their log exteriors and decks.

> **It's desirable to stay near the canyon because the hues and tones of its pinnacles and walls shift with the quality and angle of light. Sunrise is a completely different experience from sunset.**

So Bryce Canyon Lodge is once again the place to stay in the park, so much so that reservations for the busy summer months can book out a year ahead (for last-minute cancellations, call no more than 24 to 48 hours ahead). But it's worth it to have that spectacular natural amphitheater just a few steps from your room.

DUCK CREEK VILLAGE

Meadeau View Lodge

P.O. Box 1039
Duck Creek Village, UT 84762
801-682-2495

> *A homey inn high in the Dixie Forest*

Innkeepers: Harris and Val Torbenson. **Accommodations:** 6 rooms, 2 suites, 1 2-bedroom family loft, 2 cabins, all with private bath. **Rates:** Rooms, single $33, double $50; suites, single $43, double $60; family loft $50 double plus $10 for each child over age 5; cabins $125-$150. **Included:** Full breakfast in lodge. **Minimum stay:** None. **Added:** 9% tax. **Payment:** MasterCard, Visa. **Children:** Free under age 6. **Pets:** Small pets allowed. **Smoking:** Prohibited in rooms. **Open:** Year-round.

Built of peeled pine logs and capped by a shingle roof, the two-story Meadeau View Lodge sprawls beneath the aspens and pines 8,400 feet above sea level in the heart of the Dixie National Forest, 29 miles east of Cedar City. Though missing on some maps, this roadside cluster of cabins, cafés, and a gas station and grocery store makes up Duck Creek Village.

> The movie *My Friend Flicka* was shot in this wildflower-strewn meadow. More recently, the village has become known for the trout fishing in nearby lakes and for its proximity to the painted cliffs of Cedar Breaks National Monument.

That and a homey atmosphere at budget prices are at the heart of Meadeau View's appeal. The six simple rooms have knotty pine walls, wildflower-print spreads, and spotless baths with showers but no tubs. Families gravitate to the suites, whose sitting areas have a pull-out sofa, or to the family loft, with a queen and twin bed in one room, four twins in the other. Adjacent to the lodge there are also two-bedroom, $1\frac{3}{4}$-bath contemporary cabins with lofts, fully equipped kitchens, and washer-dryers.

Like any good lodge, Meadeau View encourages guests to mingle, gathering around the polished rock fireplace in the middle of the two-story lobby or on the outside patio watching the squirrels, marmots, and birds.

Harris and Val Torbenson, who manage the lodge, have a gift for making people feel at home. Warm and welcoming, they seem to understand which couples prefer to have their own table at breakfast and which would love to have company. And because the mountain air inspires big appetites, they serve a huge breakfast of homemade goods and Val's stuffed French toast or oven omelettes. With advance notice, they'll also fix dinners like roast beef or rolled chicken breast.

KANAB

Nine Gables Inn

106 West 100 North
Kanab, UT 84741
801-644-5079

An inviting B&B convenient to Bryce, Zion, and Grand Canyon

Hosts: Frank and Jeanne Bantlin. **Accommodations:** 4 rooms. **Rates:** Single $60, double $70. **Included:** Continental breakfast. **Minimum stay:** None. **Added:** 10% tax. **Payment:** Discover, MasterCard, Visa. **Children:** Not suitable for small children (no cribs or roll-aways available). **Pets:** Prohibited. **Smoking:** Prohibited. **Open:** Mid-May through mid-October.

Frank Bantlin is one of those rare people to whom hospitality comes naturally. "I love to talk," he says, "and to cook and entertain." So when he retired from the phone company in 1986, it was not long before he took up another project: redoing the historic house he and his wife, Jeanne, had purchased in Kanab in order to turn it into a bed and breakfast.

A Mormon pioneer started building the house one room at a time, so that even the interior walls are fabricated from adobe-like Kanab brick. Among its later owners was Mary Woolley Chamberlain, the first woman mayor to have an all-female council.

Yet despite its age, the

> **Zane Grey once stayed in what is now Nine Gables Inn, as did Buffalo Bill Cody and Brigham Young — but then, Young stayed in as many different places as George Washington. The best guess dates the house from 1872, making it the oldest extant dwelling in town.**

house is anything but a fusty Victorian. Sunlight streams in through the many lace-curtained windows to fall on hardwood floors and family heirlooms. Nine Gables looks cheery and lived-in and altogether inviting.

All but one of the guest rooms are upstairs off a guest parlor furnished with a television, wet bar, refrigerator, wood stove, phone, and an old Victrola. The bedrooms themselves come with wonderful antique beds in oak or cherry with matching chests or dressers. Watercolors and Frank's mother's hand-made doilies decorate the walls. All have spiffy private baths with pedestal sinks.

In summer, the garden out back produces so many vegetables that guests are encouraged to pick some to take with them. Breakfast — "served when you want it," says Frank — consists of juice, fresh seasonal fruit, muffins, bagels, toast with mesquite honey, hot or cold cereal, coffee, and tea, with the option of a full breakfast on request. All in all, the Bantlins couldn't be nicer, saying, "We want to be known for our homeyness."

LOA

Road Creek Inn

98 South Main
P.O. Box 310
Loa, UT 84747
801-836-2485
800-388-7688
Fax: 801-836-2489

> *A country inn renowned for its trout dinners*

Owner: Mark Leavitt. **Innkeepers:** Evan and Ramola Harding. **Accommodations:** 10 rooms, 3 suites. **Rates:** Rooms $50–$65, suites $65–$85. **Included:** Full breakfast. **Minimum stay:** None. **Added:** 9% tax. **Payment:** Major credit cards. **Children:**

Welcome. **Pets:** Prohibited. **Smoking:** Prohibited. **Open:** Year-round.

Even if the Road Creek Inn did not harbor a dozen charming rooms behind its buff stucco facade, it would be worth a trip to Loa just for the inn's mouth-watering rainbow trout. Every night at dinner, this 10-table restaurant (hung with local artwork) delights diners with the freshest, most succulent fillets of that classic Rocky Mountain fish. Only those caught wild with a rod and reel are tastier.

The Road Creek Inn's rainbow trout is so superb because its owner, Mark Leavitt (son of state senator Dixie Leavitt) raises them on his Road Creek Ranch. The dinner menu features eight different preparations — Oriental, amandine, and *en papillote* among them — but it's hard to beat the simplest: charbroiled with parsley and lemon.

> A few of the ranch ponds have been stocked with two- to ten-pound trout and are open for fishing (for a daily or hourly fee) on a catch-and-release basis. But to dine on these succulent fish, you need to drop by the restaurant.

The inn is exceptional in other ways, too. Built in 1912 as a mercantile store, it became a co-op for farm supplies before Leavitt converted it to a bed-and-breakfast inn in 1990. In the plans he included such unexpected features as a sauna, hot tub, small workout room, game room, and conference center. Except for two small, windowless rooms in the basement, the accommodations are oversize. Color schemes vary — blue and mauve predominate — though the basic look is country cheerful. A few rooms have walnut headboards or reproduction antiques; all have down comforters. The two front corners contain huge family suites — one with a loft — furnished with brass beds, sofas, televisions, and phones. The loft holds a second bed and fold-out sofa.

Stay overnight if you can, but whatever you do, don't miss the trout.

MOAB

Castle Valley Inn Bed-and-Breakfast

CVSR Box 2602
Moab, UT 84532
801-259-6012

*A secluded B&B
amid red rocks
and fruit trees*

Hosts: Eric and Lynn Forbes Thomson. **Accommodations:** 8 rooms, 3 bungalows, all with private bath. **Rates:** Rooms $75–$105, bungalows $125. **Included:** Full breakfast. **Minimum stay:** 2 nights. **Added:** 9% tax. **Payment:** MasterCard, Visa. **Children:** Over age 7. **Pets:** Prohibited. **Smoking:** Prohibited. **Open:** February–November.

The Castle Valley east of Moab gets its name from the towering red sandstone formations and parapetlike walls that loom above its irrigated fields. Castle Creek meanders through on its way to the Colorado River, providing the water to make the lower end of the desert valley green. The Castle Valley Inn sits on 11 acres at that verdant end of the valley. Its driveway edges along rows of fruit trees and a broad lawn dotted with willows, Russian olive trees, evergreens, and flower beds. The property slopes down to Castle Creek and a stand of cottonwoods. Deer and pheasant occasionally pass through.

The inn is a contemporary ranch-style house and three bungalows constructed of red stone and unpainted lumber. Eric and Lynn Forbes Thomson opened it in 1989, decorating the interiors with Eric's handmade furniture and with art and artifacts collected on their world travels. Tinwork mirrors from Mexico share space with African masks, 1,000-year-old ceramics from China, rugs from Central America, and basketry from Southeast Asia. Photos of Vietnam and Thailand decorate the walls. "Everything has a story," says Lynn. Yet despite this exotic tinge, a glance out any of the picture windows reveals a landscape that could only belong to the desert Southwest.

Except for having private baths with Spanish tiles, the guest quarters are much like the bedrooms of any late-vintage western home, comfortable to be sure but hardly remarkable. They have a scattering of antiques, ceiling fans, and walk-in closets. There are eight such rooms in the main house, supplemented by three more spacious one-room bungalows, each with a kitchenette, VCR, and patio or balcony.

> **Because of the inn's out-of-the-way location, the Thomsons prepare "Desert Survival Kit" lunches and optional dinners for guests who want them. And they're invaluable sources of information about the area, having seen and done much that there is to see and do themselves.**

But although there are more interesting bed-and-breakfast lodgings in the Rockies, there are few more interesting hosts. Eric spent time with the Peace Corps in Africa, Lynn is an archeologist, and they have lived in the Philippines and traveled extensively in the Americas and Asia. People drawn to this part of Utah by Arches National Park (35 minutes to the west) and the mountain biking, hiking, camping, and river rafting return to an inn whose owners share their passion for travel and outdoor activity.

The Thomsons themselves think of the inn as a retreat. "We give people plenty of attention," Lynn notes, adding, "but not too much attention." They've scattered benches at the margins of the property so guests can escape. They put in an outdoor hot tub but opt not to run the jets, since sound echoes off the red-rock cliffs.

"We really have a good handle on this part of the country because we travel one day every week," says Lynn. The inn is closed for two months in the winter while the Thomsons head for another remote corner of the planet, collecting more art and stories along the way.

Pack Creek Ranch

Off LaSal Mountain Loop Road
P.O. Box 1270
Moab, UT 84532
801-259-5505
Fax: 801-259-8879

*A country inn
and cabins
near Arches and
Canyonlands*

Proprietors: Ken and Jane Sleight. **Accommodations:** 9 cabins. **Rates:** Summer (April–October) $125/person, rest of year $57/person, $85/couple. **Included:** Breakfast, lunch, dinner, and taxes in summer; taxes in winter. **Minimum stay:** None. **Added:** Nothing. **Payment:** Major credit cards. **Children:** Reduced rates under age 12. **Pets:** Allowed. **Smoking:** Prohibited in lodge or restaurant. **Open:** Year-round; restaurant open Saturdays only in winter.

Pack Creek Ranch is a 300-acre oasis of lawns, hayfields, and an apple orchard in the adobe-colored foothills of the La Sal Mountains, 14 miles southeast of Moab. The original Indian inhabitants of this area were followed by cattle and sheep ranchers. But since the mid-1980s, when Ken and Jane Sleight transformed the ranch cabins and lodge into a country inn, Pack Creek has been a gathering place for the motel-averse: people who, after a day wandering through the sandstone arches, pinnacles, spires, and labyrinthine canyons of nearby Arches or Canyonlands National Parks, prefer a comfortable log cabin — even if it lacks a phone and television and lies a bit out of the way — to a characterless room in the heart of town.

In some ways, the inn's location is an asset. Set at 6,000 feet in the transition zone between the desert and mountains, it never suffers from the 115-degree temperatures that sometimes suffocate Moab in July and August. Trails — for hikers, horses, and mountain bikers — lead even higher, toward the dark green forests above the piñon pine, juniper, and yellow rabbitbrush that surround the ranch.

> Ute Indians used to camp in the shade of the cottonwoods that line the creek and marvel at the beauty of the 12,004-foot mountain they called Tukuhnikivatz, or "the place where the sun lingers longest."

During the summer, Pack Creek runs horseback rides lasting anywhere from an hour to days, the swimming pool is at its most inviting, and a live band often entertains on weekends. In winter, there is cross-country skiing right outside the cabin doors and the outdoor hot tub becomes an even more popular gathering place than it is in summer. Those who can, however, come in spring and fall, when the parks are less crowded and wildlife more abundant.

The cabins range in size from one to four bedrooms. All have pine-paneled walls, comfortable couches and chairs, and lots of books, and many have a stone fireplace. Some also have kitchens, a convenience during most of the year but crucial during the winter months when the restaurant is closed.

For most of the year everyone meets in the dining room of the central lodge, which also has an old upright piano and a huge fireplace. The patio out back is a favorite place for beer before and after dinner. The limited menu always features a selection of meats, seafood, poultry, and vegetarian entrées, accompanied by homemade breads. No one goes hungry.

Sunflower Hill Bed-and-Breakfast Inn

185 North 300 East
Moab, UT 84532
801-259-2974

*A home turned
family-run inn*

Innkeepers: Richard and Marge Stucki and family. **Accommodations:** 5 rooms, 1 cottage, all with private bath. **Rates:** Rooms $78–$86, cottage $86. **Included:** Continental-plus breakfast. **Minimum stay:** None. **Added:** 11% tax. **Payment:** MasterCard, Visa. **Children:** Welcome over age 7. **Pets:** Prohibited. **Smoking:** Prohibited. **Open:** Year-round.

Sunflower Hill is a Stucki family trademark: it was the name of the bakery and antiques shop they used to own, and it's the name of their fruit farm in Castle Valley. So when they opened this B&B in 1989, they knew what to call it.

The name fits. The turn-of-the-century adobe house with a cedar shake roof has an almost storybook appearance. Painted pale yellow, it stands behind a split-rail fence amid well-tended gardens on a cul-de-sac three blocks from Moab's Main Street. Fruit and nut trees stipple the broad lawn to one side, separating the inn from its cottage next door and providing room for an outdoor hot tub amid some pines and poplars.

The guest quarters in the inn adopt an essentially country decor. The Rose Room contains a four-poster bed and a scattering of antiques. Stenciled roses accent the walls. The Sun Porch stands out for its floor-to-ceiling windows on the garden, wicker chairs, and private entrance. The newest room, Morning Glory, also has a private entrance and views of the garden, and has morning glories stenciled on the walls. All these rooms have private baths and televisions.

The artist responsible for all of the decoration is Richard and Marge's daughter, Robin Officer, who illustrates children's books when she isn't brightening the rooms or tending the gardens. Their son Jeff and his wife, Pam, also help out, making this very much a family operation. Says Richard, "We try very hard to give strangers somebody they can rely on as a friend" for information about the area.

The Stuckis live in separate quarters at the back of the inn, leaving the main house to guests. Apart from a tiny library with a phone and collection of guidebooks, there is no place for guests to gather inside, but there is that yard and a patio. The Stuckis have provided an honor bar filled with soda, robes to use when going to and from the hot tub, gas grills, and bike storage.

> **The Garden Cottage has two bedrooms, a living room with a sleep sofa, and more examples of hand-painted flowers and stenciling. One bedroom wall has, in fact, been covered with flowers.**

Breakfast consists of the farm's fruit, baked goods (which could include any of nine different types of muffins or wholewheat raisin bread), yogurt, and their own honey-almond granola, served in a breakfast room decorated with gingham tablecloths and warmed by a woodstove.

MONTICELLO

The Grist Mill Inn Bed & Breakfast

64 South 300 East
P.O. Box 156
Monticello, UT 84535
801-587-2597
800-645-3762

> *A derelict mill, imaginatively converted*

Owners: Dianne and Rye Nielson.
Innkeepers: Mike and Maggie Heronema. **Accommodations:**

6 suites, 1 caboose. **Rates:** Single $50, double $66. **Included:** Full breakfast. **Minimum stay:** None. **Added:** 9.53% tax. **Payment:** Major credit cards. **Children:** Welcome if well behaved. **Pets:** Prohibited. **Smoking:** Prohibited. **Open:** Year-round.

Most people in town looked at what had been the Monticello Flour Mill and saw a derelict three-story building that hadn't been used for more than two decades. And for years, so did Dianne Nielson. But after searching in vain for a historic building that she could convert to a bed-and-breakfast, she bought the atrocious and dilapidated 1933 structure, gutted it, installed six guest suites and quarters for her family, and created a remarkable bed-and-breakfast.

> **The newest addition is an old caboose, set on some railroad tracks and converted to a Victorian suite in the dark greens and rusts that would have suited a railroad baron. It has a sitting area, bedroom, private bath, and a small refrigerator and microwave.**

The Old Grist Mill Inn charms guests with its playful and imaginative decor. Some of the original grain-grinding machinery stands in the lobby and on a second-floor sitting area. One suite has a collection of antique phones and an old telephone switchboard. Another features an antique Corona typewriter sitting on the floor and bedside tables made from old school desks. In yet another, the bathroom sink sits in a vanity made from a sewing machine table. Dianne's sense of humor and flare show everywhere.

Each suite is different. All are really junior suites, since no wall separates the sitting area from the bedroom, but that seems like quibbling given their size (two even have a second bedroom with a daybed). Guests sleep on antique beds of brass, wood, or painted iron covered with floral- or country-print comforters. No suite is simply rectangular or square, and one actually has four levels: one for the raised entryway, one for the master bedroom, and one each for a second bedroom and a bath with clawfoot tub. Whether staying in the mill or the caboose, guests also have access to a library–sitting room with a television and a hot tub.

Mike and Maggie Heronema, who run the inn for the Nielsens, serve a huge country breakfast in a high-ceilinged dining room with an old-fashioned stove that they use to keep coffee and homemade breads and muffins hot. The menu varies, based mainly on the Heronemas' sense of what guests want, though quiche and egg dishes are favorites.

ST. GEORGE

Greene Gate Village

62-78 West Tabernacle
St. George, UT 84770
801-628-6999
800-350-6999
Fax: 801-628-5068

An inn created from restored Mormon pioneer houses

Innkeepers: Barbara, Mark, and John Greene. **Accommodations:** 13 rooms, 5 suites, 2 houses. **Rates:** Rooms $45–$95, suites $60–$80, houses $95–$175. **Included:** Full breakfast. **Minimum stay:** None. **Added:** 9% tax. **Payment:** Major credit cards. **Children:** Welcome. **Pets:** Prohibited. **Smoking:** Prohibited. **Open:** Year-round.

Greene Gate Village's wrought iron and red rock fence encloses a collection of lovingly restored, 19th-century, Mormon pioneer houses. The tiny, picturesque village clusters around a brick courtyard containing a swimming pool, gazebo, and cast iron street lamps topped with eagles. Given its meticulous reconstruction, it could be a museum; instead it is a bed-and-breakfast inn, rich with a feeling of history.

Barbara Greene, a petite, savvy dynamo, and her surgeon husband, Mark, spent 12 years getting the project started, occasionally buying historic houses sometimes so dilapidated, she says, that "others considered them hopeless." The worst one crumbled into a pile of adobe rubble as it was being moved into place and had to be rebuilt. All needed plumbing and electrical work. Somehow the Greenes stuck to it and were finally able to open in 1986. Work on the eighth, and probably last, house ended late in 1991.

> Accommodations within the village vary from spacious, high-ceilinged rooms with fireplaces and porches to two-bedroom suites and houses suitable for families. All have been tastefully furnished with antiques, lace curtains, quilts or comforters, phones, and televisions.

Honeymooners adore the Lysann room in the Bentley House for its dark Victorian woods, queen-size bed, sitting room, and private balcony. The Morris House has two bedrooms, a living room with a hideaway bed and fireplace, and a kitchenette. Family reunions or small groups book the four-bedroom Greenehouse and its bunkhouse-style carriage house. That complex, though several blocks outside the village, has a private swimming pool, tennis court, and hot tub and can comfortably sleep 20.

The focal point of the village is the 1878 Bentley House, which has hand-painted faux-grain woodwork throughout. Guests register in a hall lined with exposed adobe brick and gather in a sunny breakfast room for pecan waffles, biscuits with sausage gravy, cheese blintzes with strawberries, homemade granola, and fresh seasonal fruit. From Thursday through Saturday nights, its ornate parlor and Victorian dining room become the setting for popular homemade suppers from a limited menu that features filet mignon, stuffed chicken breast, trout, and halibut. Early reservations are essential — something the amiable staff occasionally forgets to tell guests until it's too late.

Green Valley Spa & Tennis Resort

1515 West Canyon View Drive
St. George, UT 84770
801-628-8060
800-237-1068
Fax: 801-673-4084

> *A spa-cum-tennis school near Zion*

General manager: Alan Coombs. **Accommodations:** 60 condominiums (1–3 bedrooms). **Rates:** Summer (March–November) $1,798/person/week, winter (December–February) $1,598/person/week. **Included:** Use of workout room, outdoor tennis courts, swimming pools; choice of spa or tennis program or combination; all meals. **Minimum stay:** 7 nights with some programs. **Added:** 9% tax, 10% service charge. **Payment:** Discover, MasterCard, Visa. **Children:** Welcome. **Pets:** Prohibited. **Smoking:** Prohibited. **Open:** Year-round.

The first Mormon pioneers to visit what is now St. George dubbed this southwestern corner of Utah "Dixie" because of its mild winters. More than a century later, it is still the weather that lures visitors, many of them snowbirds from northern Utah. They arrive with their golf clubs, tennis racquets, hiking gear, and mountain bikes, lured by ample recreation facilities, clear air, and easy access to Zion National Park, 42 miles to the east.

> **Green Valley Resort contributes to the region's sports mystique with two outstanding facilities: a highly regarded spa and one of the West's foremost tennis schools.**

Green Valley's spa rose to national prominence for its unusual exercise program. Committed to pampering clients while helping them lose weight and become fit, Green Valley starts each day of its week-long program with a three-hour hike along trails in Bryce, Zion, or Grand Canyon National Parks led by cheery counselors. Fat-burning aerobics, aquacize, and weight-training classes follow. In the afternoons, however, the hard work is rewarded with a round of spa treatments — massages, facials, herbal wraps, and pedicures. Interspersed through the regimen are three daily meals in the spa dining room, whose fiber-rich fare is low in salt, fat, and cholesterol and devoid of sugar, artificial sweeteners, caffeine, and preservatives.

Tennis players who opt for the Vic Braden Tennis College curriculum, by contrast, spend five or more hours of their day on Green Valley's 19 courts — the largest resort complex in the Rockies — or on its 13 hitting lanes. Renowned tennis guru Vic Braden does not personally run the clinics but appears daily in instructional videos, joking about "fuzz sandwiches" and trotting out the scientific research that underpins his teaching methods.

Since Green Valley is a condominium community, spa guests, tennis college campers, and residents — many of them families — bed down in spacious one-to-three-bedroom units with simple, contemporary decors and oversize terraces. Nearby are two large swimming pools — one outdoor, the other covered — Jacuzzis, a baby pool, basketball courts, and a children's play area. And while there are no supervised children's programs, parents who need a break can find reasonably priced babysitters willing to take kids to the pool, rent videotapes, and generally amuse them.

Seven Wives Inn

217 North 100 West
St. George, UT 84770
801-628-3737
800-600-3737

A grand house where polygamists hid out

Hosts: Jay and Donna Curtis, Jon and Alison Bowcutt. **Accommodations:** 11 rooms, 1 suite, all with private bath. **Rates:** Rooms $50–$75, suite $100. **Included:** Full breakfast. **Mini-**

mum stay: None except Easter and marathon weekends. **Added:** 9% tax. **Payment:** Major credit cards. **Children:** Welcome. **Pets:** Prohibited. **Smoking:** Prohibited. **Open:** Year-round.

In 1873, Edwin G. Woolley built a grand house in St. George, with foot-thick walls of native gray adobe, long covered porches, and second-floor balconies. He had the pine trim inside painstakingly painted to resemble oak and bird's-eye maple. But the house's fame and its ticket to a place on the National Register of Historic Places originate with the passage in 1882 of a federal law banning polygamy. Woolley, not a polygamist himself, sympathized with those who were and hid many from persecution, giving them access to the attic via a secret door. Among those he sheltered was Donna Curtis's great-grandfather, a man who had seven wives.

> **In Jane, the converted attic where the polygamists hid, queen and single beds with oak headboards stand on wood floors adorned with rag rugs.**

So when the Curtises bought the house and turned it into a B&B, they named seven of the bedrooms for her ancestor's wives. The huge master bedroom, called Melissa, contains a wood-burning fireplace, a high-back oak bed beneath a crystal chandelier, a pegged oak armoire, lace curtains, and a door opening onto the front deck. It also has a sitting room on one side of its entrance foyer and a two-person Jacuzzi tub on the other, while its bath, though tiny, has room enough for a clawfoot tub. Sarah adjoins Susan, together making a good family suite, with high beamed ceilings, a fireplace, and a sun porch. Sunlight filters into Lucinda through a stained glass window, falling on a brass bed with a pink and white quilt. All have antiques, lace curtains, handmade quilts, cable televisions, and private baths, some with clawfoot tubs. A brief account of each wife hangs in the bedroom that bears her name.

The Curtises also own the 1883 Whitehead House next door, a dignified adobe with an ornate Victorian parlor and four bedrooms decorated with white wicker and chintz. A small swimming pool, usable in summer, helps separate the two houses.

The Curtises run the inn with the help of their daughter

and son-in-law, Alison and Jon Bowcutt. After more than a decade, they have an easy way with guests, treating them so much like family that no one wants to leave. They serve excellent breakfasts of homemade granola, blueberry or German apple pancakes, sausage or bacon. The spacious breakfast room also doubles as a gallery for Jon Bowcutt's abstract oil paintings and sketches, creating a modest sort of time warp as evidence of the late 20th century crops up in this 19th-century haven.

SPRINGDALE

Harvest House Bed & Breakfast

29 Canyon View Drive
P.O. Box 125
Springdale, UT 84767
801-772-3880

*A contemporary
B&B in the
shadow of Zion*

Hosts: Barbara and Steven Cooper. **Accommodations:** 4 rooms, all with private bath. **Rates:** Single $60–$80, double $70–$90. **Included:** Full breakfast. **Minimum stay:** 2 nights on holiday weekends. **Added:** 10% tax. **Payment:** MasterCard, Visa. **Children:** Welcome with prior arrangement. **Pets:** Prohibited. **Smoking:** Prohibited. **Open:** Year-round.

The crimson rock wall known as the Watchman stands sentinel at the entrance to Zion National Park as a kind of preview of the sculpted rock formations, narrow chasms, and hanging gardens that lie beyond. For guests of the Harvest House, the Watchman is also a reminder of what brought them to this southwestern corner of Utah. That great cliff looms just outside, making it the first thing they see each morning when they come down to breakfast.

Barbara Cooper's flare for interior design and great eye for color accounts for the inviting decor. All the rooms have comforters, plants, thick towels, and unusual additions like suitcase stands and extra pillows. The largest bedroom, in a corner on the second floor, stands out for its vaulted ceiling, sitting area, and private sundeck. Others have capricious accessories like a glove mannequin.

> **Erected in 1989, Harvest House is that rare modern bed-and-breakfast unafraid to be contemporary. It isn't neo-Victorian or country cottage or western ranch; it's an up-to-date clapboard two-story building with lots of windows and well-chosen furnishings from Conran's.**

Barbara's training as a professional caterer accounts for the wonderful breakfasts of brewed coffee, black and herbal teas, freshly baked muffins, scones, pastries, and breads, homemade preserves, and a delectable assortment of superb entrées including cheese blintzes with fresh fruit, almond French toast with caramelized bananas, poached eggs with tomato-basil hollandaise sauce, and corn-banana pancakes.

The Coopers take exceptional care of guests in other ways, too. Hot and cold beverages are available anytime from the wet bar in the dining room. The living room has not only a fireplace but also a library of art books and cookbooks, a television, VCR, and library of classic movies. Steve's cactus garden ornaments the backyard, which contains a hot tub. A competitive bicycle racer, Steve is a fountain of information about outdoor activities in the area, including that most spectacular of Utah's national parks, Zion.

O'Tooles' Under the Eaves

980 Zion Park Boulevard
P.O. Box 29
Springdale, UT 84767
801-772-3457

*An English
cottage in
red rock country*

Hosts: Michelle and Rick O'Toole.
Accommodations: 4 rooms, 2 with
private baths; 1 suite. **Rates:** Rooms $55–$85, suite $125. **Included:** Full breakfast. **Minimum stay:** None. **Added:** 10%
tax. **Payment:** MasterCard, Visa. **Children:** Over age 9. **Pets:**
Prohibited. **Smoking:** Prohibited. **Open:** Year-round.

Springdale, a town with a population of roughly 350, huddles
beneath the multihued cliffs at the southern entrance to Zion
National Park. Ersatz Indian pueblos crop up frequently along
its main drag, so it is an arresting sight to approach the center
of town and come upon an English cottage. The seemingly
misplaced little two-story house has a postage stamp yard and
a porch furnished in white wicker in front and a terraced garden and little cabin in back.

Michelle and Rick O'Toole bought Under the Eaves in
1993, giving up professional careers in Salt Lake City in order
to be closer to the hiking, bicycling, and golf they love. By
then the storybook cottage had variously housed the town library, the post office, an antiques store, and a kindergarten,
before the previous owners converted it into a winsome bed-and-breakfast. Taking over at the height of the season, the
O'Tooles added their own family heirlooms to the antiques
that came with the house and began a gradual refurbishing,
intent on restoring the cottage to its period warmth.

Accommodations in the main house consist of two small

guest rooms and a suite. The guest rooms lie at the back of the house just off the dining area. One has a black iron bed with a white eyelet lace coverlet, the other a white iron bed beneath a blue and white comforter. Though they share a bath, each has an in-room sink. The suite occupies the entire second floor. Ogee windows from a church frame spectacular views of Zion, and sloping rafters form a canopy above an antique English oak bed and two single beds. There is still room left over for two roll-aways. The suite also has a small kitchen with a table, a tiled bath with a clawfoot tub and hand-held European shower, and a private entrance.

> **This dollhouse, built in 1935 as a wedding present, was designed by the architect responsible for many of the national park lodges. Massive red sandstone blocks quarried in nearby canyons make up the foundation. From there up it is all white stucco beneath a steeply pitched shingle roof.**

There are two additional rooms in a 1920s park cabin that now stands behind the house. If their windows are disappointingly small given the surroundings, the bedrooms are homey, having ash or twig beds, pastel floral comforters, private tiled baths with showers, and private entrances onto the terraced gardens. That puts them only steps away from an outdoor Jacuzzi.

Breakfasts, served family style in the dining room, feature fresh-baked breads and biscuits, homemade granola, fresh fruit, and perhaps a frittata, soufflé, or Belgian waffles. Best of all, the main entrance to Zion National Park is less than a mile away.

TROPIC

Bryce Point Bed & Breakfast

61 North 400 West
P.O. Box 96
Tropic, UT 84776-0096
801-679-8629

> *A room with a view of Bryce's fairyland spires*

Hosts: LaMar and Ethel LeFevre.
Accommodations: 5 rooms. **Rates:**
Single $55, double $65. **Included:** Full breakfast. **Minimum stay:** None. **Added:** 10% tax. **Payment:** MasterCard, Visa; cash or checks preferred. **Children:** Welcome with advance notice. **Pets:** Prohibited. **Smoking:** Prohibited. **Open:** Year-round.

The picture windows in Bryce Point's guest rooms overlook the spires and crimson cliffs of Bryce Canyon National Park, a 20-minute drive to the west. That alone makes it the best alternative to staying inside the park itself, but the contemporary bed-and-breakfast also has other appealing features, not the least of them owners who grew up in Tropic and know the surrounding countryside intimately.

Always busy with outside interests even when he had a full-time job as a teacher and school administrator, LaMar LeFevre retired with a long list of postponed projects. One of them was to convert their 1930s house into a bed-and-breakfast, which meant adding a new two-story wing on the back for the oversize guest rooms. He gave them modern ranch decor, western art, private baths with showers, and lace-curtained picture windows.

Next, he added flagstone and rose beds to the front yard and a redwood sun deck along the side near the fruit and vegetable garden. He refurbished the living room, installing a pellet stove set on alabaster slabs. By early 1991, the LeFevres were ready to entertain their first guests, giving them the run of the house and feeding them huge breakfasts of juice, fresh fruit, homemade muffins and bread, homemade preserves, and whatever hot dishes they favored, from eggs to pancakes to French toast.

And of course he hasn't come close to finishing his list of projects. He bought an old Bryce Canyon cabin with the idea of converting it into a honeymoon hideaway with a king bed, whirlpool tub, sunroom, and porch. He points to a space near the garden where a hot tub

> **While Ethel goes about feeding everyone, LaMar tells stories about life in this valley, going back 60 years or more. He will gladly recommend a place to eat or suggest the best hiking trails in the park.**

will go someday. He might arrange for local artists to display their work in the living room and common areas or put televisions in each of the rooms. Making Bryce Point better for guests promises to be a never-ending project.

ZION NATIONAL PARK

For other lodging in the area, see the towns of Kanab, St. George, and Springdale.

Zion Lodge

Zion National Park
Springdale, UT 84767
801-772-3213
Reservations:
TW Recreational Services, Inc.
P.O. Box 400
Cedar City, UT 84721
801-586-7686
Fax: 801-586-3157

> *A midpark lodge and cabins below 3,000-foot cliffs*

General manager of TW Services: John Shafer. **Accommodations:** 75 rooms, 6 suites, 40 cabins. **Rates:** Rooms $68, suites $104, cabins $76. **Minimum stay:** None. **Added:** 9% tax. **Payment:** Major credit cards. **Children:** Free under age 13. **Pets:**

Prohibited. **Smoking:** Nonsmoking rooms available. **Open:** Year-round.

Sandstone cliffs in shades of vermilion and ivory tower 2,000 to 3,000 feet above the floor of Zion Canyon, the narrow chasm that is the centerpiece of Utah's oldest national park. Few roads penetrate this wilderness of sculpted rock, deep canyons, and high plateaus, but one exceptionally scenic highway begins at the southern entrance near Springdale and runs for nine miles to the formation called the Temple of Sinawava. The only lodging in the park, apart from campgrounds, is Zion Lodge, nestled beneath the cliffs halfway along that route.

> **Several hiking trails begin near the lodge, including the short, relatively undemanding path to Emerald Pools. The Virgin River flows nearby, and deer frequent the lawn in front of the lodge. Only hikers camped out along Zion's trails awaken to a more beautiful setting.**

The original lodge, built in the 1920s, burned down in 1966. It was replaced with a two-story timber and concrete structure, more functional than attractive, containing a pine-paneled restaurant (serving reasonably priced broiled Utah trout, mesquite-grilled steaks, and pasta), a gift shop, snack bar, and some meeting rooms. Its lobby, though paneled in pine and furnished with log couches and chairs, lacks a fireplace and is little more than a place to check in and check out. Zion Lodge is redeemed, however, by a friendly, exceptionally attentive staff and by refurbished rooms that are both comfortable and cheery.

Two-thirds of the rooms occupy separate two-story, motel-like wings painted national park brown and accented with red stone. These accommodations have spacious decks facing the canyon walls, two double beds, tasteful wallpapers and bedspreads, and modern private baths. Two rooms are wheelchair accessible. They are supplemented by a cluster of cabins, built in the 1920s and renovated in the late 1980s. Each of them contains from one to four rooms, all with gas-log fireplaces of red stone, porches, two double beds, and a full bath with his and hers sinks. Most are oriented to have views of the towering red canyon walls.

Wyoming

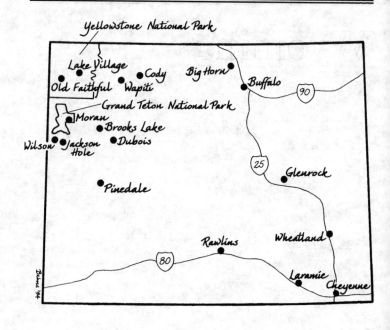

Best Bed-and-Breakfast Homes

Big Horn
Spahn's Big Horn Mountain Bed & Breakfast
Cheyenne
Rainsford Inn Bed & Breakfast
Cody
Parson's Pillow Bed & Breakfast
Jackson Hole
Wildflower Inn
Laramie
Annie Moore's Guest House
Rawlins
Ferris Mansion
Wheatland
The Blackbird Inn
Wilson
A Teton Tree House Bed & Breakfast

Best Bed-and-Breakfast Inns

Jackson Hole
Nowlin Creek Inn
Rusty Parrot Lodge

Best Condominiums, Apartments, and Cabins

Jackson Hole
Dornan's Spur Ranch Log Cabins

Best Fishing Lodges

Wilson
Crescent H Ranch

Best Guest Ranches

Buffalo
Paradise Guest Ranch

Dubois
Absaroka Ranch
Bitterroot Ranch
Jackson Hole
Gros Ventre River Ranch
Lost Creek Ranch
R Lazy S Ranch
Pinedale
Flying A Ranch
Wapiti
Cody's Ranch Resort
Rimrock Dude Ranch

Best Historic Hotels, Inns, and Lodges

Brooks Lake
Brooks Lake Lodge
Cody
The Irma Hotel
Glenrock
Hotel Higgins
Jackson Hole
The Wort Hotel

Best National Park Lodges

Grand Teton National Park
Jackson Lake Lodge
Jenny Lake Lodge
Yellowstone National Park
Lake Yellowstone Hotel
Old Faithful Inn

Best Resorts and Spas

Jackson Hole
Teton Pines
Spring Creek

The name Wyoming is a corruption of an Indian word meaning "large plateau between the mountains." That description does not fit the eastern quarter of the state, which lies mainly in the Great Plains, but it accurately depicts a recurring feature of the landscape farther west. There, more than a dozen mountain ranges, oriented for the most part north-south, are separated by basins that resemble valleys or plains. The best known and most scenic example is Jackson Hole, in the state's northwest corner, where mountains surround a 600-square-mile valley.

For decades, Wyoming was one of the places settlers had to cross to reach points farther west on the Oregon, Overland, and Mormon trails. Cities like **Cheyenne,** the capital, and **Laramie** sprang up after the transcontinental railroad was completed. Cattlemen and sheepherders fought over its open ranges, and though they've settled their differences, cattle and sheep still outnumber people four to one — but then, this most sparsely populated of the lower 48 states doesn't have all that many people to begin with.

Although French fur trappers visited the area as early as 1743, the most pivotal of the early explorers was John Colter. A member of the Lewis and Clark Expedition, Colter broke away and wandered for months before returning with tales of "steaming geysers and bubbling mud pots and a river that ran so fast over the rocks it boiled." His friends dubbed his find "Colter's Hell," though when it became the world's first national park in 1872 it took the name of its principal river: Yellowstone.

Today, **Yellowstone National Park** sprawls over 3,472 square miles, covering more area than Rhode Island and Delaware combined. Its best known attraction is Old Faithful, which has been erupting on average every 70 minutes since before the park was established. There are, however, 200 other geysers in the basin and so much to see that no vacation seems long enough. Among the park's other marvels are the highest large lake in the world (Lake Yellowstone, at 7,733 feet), a waterfall almost as tall as Niagara, and a 1,200-foot-deep canyon. Bison roam through the park, bringing traffic to a standstill whenever they near a highway. So do deer and elk.

Although the park spills over into Montana, which has three entrances, and Idaho, within Wyoming there are two gateways: one on the south from Jackson and **Grand Teton National Park,** the other on the east, 52 miles from Cody. What they all have in common during the busiest months of July and August is heavy traffic, the worst of it arriving from the south through Jackson and from the west through West

Yellowstone, Montana. After Labor Day the flood abates, and although snows can close portions of the park as early as mid-September, the greatly diminished crowds on trails and roads make the risk worth taking. Once the roads close, the park becomes a winter wonderland beloved by snowmobilers and cross-country skiers.

Wyoming's other national park, Grand Teton, lies just south of Yellowstone, thus doubling the pleasure of visitors to the state's northwest corner. But whereas Yellowstone expresses the raw, primal forces deep within the planet, Grand Teton embodies the pure pleasure of dramatic scenery. Its 310,000 acres encompass the young, athletic peaks of the Grand Tetons themselves. Wind, water, snow, and glaciers stripped the peaks of their sediment, exposing the jagged granite beneath. They are not inordinately high as the Rocky Mountains go, but they do constitute one of the most dramatic ranges because they rise straight from the valley floor without foothills to diminish their impact. The lakes at the base reflect the peaks and the blue sky above. More than 200 miles of hiking trails penetrate the park, and even some relatively easy hikes lead to panoramic vistas of Jackson Hole and its flanking mountains.

In winter, **Jackson Hole** is renowned for its skiing. Its aerial tram drops skiers off 4,200 feet above the valley floor, with miles of trails spread out through the 2,000 snow-covered acres below. Winter also brings elk down from their summer pastures to the National Elk Refuge. Thousands of the huge animals gather in the plain north of Jackson, and visitors can take horse-drawn sleighs out into the herds for a closer look. **Jackson** itself has two must-see, if completely different, attractions, both right on Jackson Square. The first and most significant is the superb Wildlife of the American West museum, with a large collection of North American wildlife paintings and sculpture, among them a comprehensive collection of the works of Carl Rungius. The second is everybody's favorite hangout, the Million Dollar Cowboy Bar, where the stools are saddles and live bands play nightly for those who want to dance the Texas two-step or country swing.

Wyoming's other attractions revolve around its Wild West and cattle-ranching past. Guest ranches speckle the landscape, ranging from luxury retreats within easy reach of Jackson to remote working spreads far from everything except wide-open vistas and western hospitality. From Moran Junction in Jackson Hole, the road east has been designated a scenic byway. It crests the Continental Divide over Togwotee Pass before dropping into **Dubois.** At the heart of ranch country, it has a small museum depicting early life in the area and the National Bighorn Sheep Interpretive Center, a winter refuge that is home to the largest Rocky Mountain bighorn sheep herd in North America.

The town of **Cody,** east of Yellowstone National Park, has the stellar Buffalo Bill Historical Center, a magnificent four-museum complex that displays not only the historical memorabilia of the famous showman and scout but also a comprehensive collection of western art, firearms, and artifacts of the Plains Indian.

For rodeos, nothing compares with Cheyenne's Frontier Days, which have been held every July since 1897.

For more information about the Cowboy State, contact the Wyoming Division of Tourism, I-25 and College Drive, Cheyenne, WY 82002 (307-777-7777 or 800-225-5996).

BIG HORN

Spahn's Big Horn Mountain Bed & Breakfast

P.O. Box 579
Big Horn, WY 82833
307-674-8150

> *A log home with see-forever views and attentive hosts*

Hosts: Ron and Bobbie Spahn. **Accommodations:** 2 rooms and 2 cabins, all with private bath. **Rates:** Summer (late June–mid-September), rooms $80–$95, cabins $85–$105; rest of year, rooms $65–$85, cabins $65–$80. **Included:** Full breakfast. **Minimum stay:** None. **Added:** 6% tax. **Payment:** MasterCard, Visa; cash or checks preferred. **Children:** Welcome. **Pets:** Prohibited (they have a dog, outside cats, rabbits, sheep). **Smoking:** Prohibited. **Open:** Year-round.

When the sun rises on Spahn's Big Horn Mountain Bed & Breakfast, the rays actually slant upwards. The log home and cabins perch among the ponderosa pines on a steep hillside, 6,000 feet above sea level and nearly 2,000 feet above the town of Sheridan, 15 miles to the northeast. Little Goose Valley — where Queen Elizabeth II and former vice president Dan Quayle have vacationed — stretches out below it, and the vistas extend to the mountains on the horizon and as far north as Montana. And Hemingway wrote *A Farewell to Arms* in a cabin on the slopes behind.

Ron Spahn built this home himself in 1986 out of lodgepole pine while he and his family lived in one of the two cabins. He gave it a broad deck to make the most of those views and an open design inspired by the lobby of the Old Faithful Inn (see Yellowstone National Park), with its balconies above balconies. A sunken living room with a wood-burning stove, television, and stereo soars past log-banistered landings to the rafters three stories above. It connects with the outside deck in one direction and the many-windowed hexagonal dining room in the other. Solar panels provide some of the electricity, propane generators the rest.

> **Deer, moose, eagles, hawks, and owls frequent the area, and the Spahns have a menagerie of dogs, cats, rabbits, and sheep.**

There are two guest quarters in the main house. The Red Room, which opens onto a balcony, has both a queen-size and a twin hand-peeled log bed, handmade patchwork quilts, and ruffled curtains, while the Green Room, whose dormer windows frame views through the treetops of the valley below, contains antique oak furnishings and a loft overlooking the living room. Both have private baths.

The cabins provide yet another experience. The Homestead, where the Spahns lived while building the house, has one room with a queen-size bed, a loft with two doubles, a fully equipped kitchen, and a sitting porch with 100-mile views. Eagle's Nest, though tiny, basks in wonderful seclusion a five-minute walk from the house along a shady trail. Its single room contains a queen-size bed beneath a country quilt, but its most outstanding feature is an east-facing porch with mountain vistas framed by massive cliffs.

Ron, a lawyer and geologist by training and a former Yellowstone National Park ranger, presides over the bed-and-breakfast full time with the help of Bobbie, who is a nurse, and their two teenage children. Their attention to guests is unstinting. "We're here to give them guidance, provide a social situation, and advise them about what to do," says Ron. That includes serving full breakfasts that one guest characterized as "remorselessly large," and optional dinners or even adventure tours into the high country. There's also a hot tub.

Mostly, though, there are those stunning views and the Spahns' warm hospitality. Or as Ron describes it: "I think of it as putting on a party every night when you don't know who the guests are going to be."

BROOKS LAKE

Brooks Lake Lodge

Brooks Lake Road
P.O. Box 594
Dubois, WY 82513
307-455-2121

> *A sanctuary in a wilderness of peaks and forests*

General managers: Rebecca and Will Rigsby. **Accommodations:** 6 rooms, 6 cabins, all with private bath. **Rates:** Rooms, summer (July–September 15) $150/person double, winter (December 15–April 15) $115/person double; cabins, summer $170/person double, winter $140/person double. **Included:** All meals and activities in summer; breakfast, dinner, cross-country ski equipment in winter. **Minimum stay:** 3 nights in summer. **Added:** 6% tax on lodging portion. **Payment:** Major credit cards. **Children:** Free under age 4, half price under 7. **Pets:** Prohibited. **Smoking:** Allowed only in bar and lobby. **Open:** Late June to mid-September and late December to mid-April.

A classic example of what American craftsmen can do with logs and stone, the dazzling Brooks Lake Lodge hides out in a lake-dotted alpine valley 9,200 feet above sea level. The Continental Divide rises just to the west, but it's the eye-popping views of the Pinnacle Mountains, jutting above the mirrored surface of Brooks Lake, that lure guests to pull up a chair on the lodge's front porch. Even though the cowboy town of Dubois is a mere 23 miles to the east, the setting recalls what the west must have looked like to early mountain men and explorers.

> In any season, guests rave about the food, which could be rack of lamb with rosemary one night, grilled ahi with lemon-dill butter another, and turkey breast stuffed with ricotta and spinach on a third, followed by dessert and coffee in front of the fire in the lobby as the sun sets behind the Continental Divide.

Built in 1922 and now on the National Register of Historic Places, the lodge found new life in the late 1980s when Richard Carlsberg, a California developer and big-game hunter, and his wife, Barbara, restored the deteriorated structure. They installed modern baths, lodgepole pine furnishings, and country-chic wallpapers in the six lodge rooms, and built or refurbished six one- and two-room cabins, giving them nouveau-rustic interiors of pine paneling, antiques, woodstoves, and lace and fabric curtains.

The most impressive room in the lodge is the Great Hall, a cavernous space two stories high at the peak of its log rafters. A massive stone fireplace stands at one end; dozens of Carlsberg's hunting trophies decorate the walls and floors. Clusters of green wicker furniture with floral-print cushions evoke the country interiors favored by designer Ralph Lauren, while an elk mounted on a movable platform seems to eavesdrop on conversations.

In summer, those conversations are likely to be about the scenic horseback rides to places like upper and lower Jade Lake, or about the canoeing, hiking, and lake and stream fishing (there's a tackle shop out back). In winter the subject turns to cross-country skiing across the frozen flats of the lake or through the magnificent Shoshone National Forest or snowmobiling up to 12,000-foot Austin Peak, which has a herd of bighorn sheep and vistas of the Teton Mountains.

Rebecca and Will Rigsby, the Carlsbergs' daughter and son-in-law, head up the friendly, helpful staff. In summer, the lodge functions much like a dude ranch, with daily rides and all meals included in the fee. In winter, 600 to 900 inches of snow falls, burying the road. The staff thus meets guests at the highway, ferrying them into the lodge by snowmobile for days of backcountry skiing (the lodge supplies equipment) or snowmobile tours (available at extra cost). Afterward, the indoor hot tub looks even more inviting than in summer, as does the fire in the hearth. But in any season, Brooks Lake is one of the Rockies' most appealing retreats.

BUFFALO

Paradise Guest Ranch

Hunter Creek Road
P.O. Box 790
Buffalo, WY 82834
307-684-7876
Fax: 307-684-9054

A storybook ranch, steeped in amenities and kids' programs

Proprietors: Jim and Leah Anderson. **Accommodations:** 18 cabins. **Rates:** Single (May and September only) $1,290, double $2,180. **Included:** All meals, horseback riding, ranch activities, airport transfers. **Minimum stay:** 7 nights. **Added:** 5% tax. **Payment:** Cash, personal checks, or traveler's checks.

Children: Reduced rates under age 12. **Pets:** Prohibited. **Smoking:** Prohibited in dining room. **Open:** Mid-May to late September.

Paradise Ranch trails along the edge of a rolling meadow in a secluded mountain valley 17 miles west of Buffalo. The snow-capped peaks of the Big Horn Mountains rise majestically to the west. A million acres of forest lands surround it.

> Kids not only learn to ride but even have their own rodeo. For those too young to handle a horse alone there are pony rides, nature hikes, a talent show, a swimming pool, baby animals to meet, and an overnight campout. They won't even miss television.

Lured by its soul-soothing beauty and myriad activities, guests have been coming to the ranch since 1907. Its reputation as one of the country's foremost family destinations, however, dates only from the 1980s. It was then that the hundred-year-old ranch underwent a $1 million facelift that infused its old log cabins with modern creature comforts and added several new cabins with as many as four bedrooms. Guests can look forward to exceptionally spacious lodgings and outstanding children's programs.

Riding remains the ranch's mainstay. Every one of the 60 or so guests gets his or her own horse for the week, including kids six and over. Twice a day they head out on trails through meadows painted with lupine and balsamroot, spending as little as an hour or as much as a day in the saddle. Fishermen can put the horses to use, too, riding up to reach mountain lakes full of large trout. There is more good fishing as close as the streams that flow through the meadow.

Although the cabins lack phones and televisions, though most guests regard that as an asset, especially since the amenity-rich accommodations lack nothing else. The smallest is a suite with a large bedroom and separate living room/dining room with a stone fireplace, overstuffed furniture, kitchenette, coffeemaker, full modern bath, and in many cases a washer-dryer. All of them open onto spacious decks with views of the meadows.

It's a short walk from any of the cabins to the pool and hot tub and to the French Creek Saloon in one of the oldest buildings on the ranch. On the night of the kids' campout, adults are treated to a gourmet dinner in the dining room, where the fare otherwise runs to ranch traditional. Everyone looks forward to the twice-weekly cookouts and to the Saturday night square dance. The conveniences may be modern, but Paradise remains true to dude ranch tradition.

CHEYENNE

Rainsford Inn Bed & Breakfast

219 East 18th Street
Cheyenne, WY 82001
307-638-BEDS
800-638-BEDS
Fax: 307-634-4506

*A historic house
with a new heart*

Hosts: John and Nancy Drege. **Accommodations:** 5 rooms, all with private bath. **Rates:** $75–$95 (higher during Frontier Days). **Included:** Full breakfast. **Minimum stay:** None. **Added:** 7% tax. **Payment:** Major credit cards. **Children:** Not suitable for children under 10. **Pets:** Prohibited. **Smoking:** Prohibited. **Open:** Year-round.

Built in 1900 and listed on the National Register of Historic Places, the Rainsford Inn evokes an era when Cheyenne was part frontier town, part burgeoning rail center, and already Wyoming's largest city and its state capitol. The first man to own it was Willis VanDeVanter, the only Wyoming judge to serve on the U.S. Supreme Court. Decades later, that was not enough to protect the once proud two-story house from a slow devolution, first into a boarding house and then a warren of tiny offices. Somewhere along the way it acquired an encrustation of chartreuse metal siding.

When John and Nancy Drege rescued it in the early 1990s, not much of the original interior remained to restore. They set about a conversion instead, reintroducing oak floors and antiques as they carved out five rooms with private baths from the gutted shell. They stripped off the awful siding, and the house again took its place among its elegant neighbors. In 1992 they opened to guests, banishing themselves to back quarters off the kitchen.

> This is not a house for those who want to step back to the beginning of the century but for those who like spiffy, modern lodgings with hints of the past.

Each room is different. Moonlight and Roses has a bow window, a Victorian bed from the Stanley Hotel in Estes Park, and a sitting area with a gas-log fireplace. The masculine Cattle Baron Corner has been decorated with a cow pelt and a stained glass horse head framed in a horse collar. The sunny corner School Room features old-fashioned school desks — both the Dreges work for the school district. Those three open off a second-floor sun room. On the third floor, Grandma's Attic takes up the entire width of the house with dormer windows on each end and windows into a raftered area capriciously decorated with old photos, knick-knacks, and antique clothes. Finally, the bay-windowed Garden Room, on the main floor, adopts a floral motif. It is the only room without a whirlpool tub; however, it is also fully handicapped accessible, a rarity in bed-and-breakfasts. Phones and televisions are available on request. And breakfast is pretty much whatever you want, provided they have it in the kitchen, from granola and fruit to eggs or waffles.

CODY

For other lodging in the area, see the town of Wapiti.

The Irma Hotel

1192 Sheridan Avenue
Cody, WY 82414
307-587-4221

> *The hotel that
> Buffalo Bill built*

General manager: Doug Greenway.
Accommodations: 25 rooms and 15 suites. **Rates:** Rooms $58–$71, suites $87–$98. **Included:** Airport transfers. **Minimum stay:** None. **Added:** 5% tax. **Payment:** Major credit cards. **Children:** Free under age 9. **Pets:** Prohibited. **Smoking:** Allowed. **Open:** Year-round.

The great frontiersman and showman William F. "Buffalo Bill" Cody had the Irma Hotel built in 1902, naming it for his youngest daughter. The early ads promised "Celebrated Ostermoor matresses [sic] and springs used exclusively. Telephone in every room. Everything modern and first-class."

Buffalo Bill often stayed at the Irma between tours with his Wild West Show, and that contributed to its notoriety. So did Queen Victoria's gift of a magnificent cherrywood bar that is now the focal point of the Irma Restaurant,

> **The sandstone and timber two-story hotel quickly became the town's social hub and remains so, a place where tourists rub elbows with cowboys in the Silver Saddle Lounge.**

where the food, locals report, ranges from okay to awful. Nevertheless, it wasn't cuisine but the Irma's long, rich history that earned it a listing in the National Register of Historic Places.

The rooms that most merit attention are the suites, which were created by combining rooms in the original hotel (an annex was added in 1937). Each one bears the name of a notable town resident and has been decorated with Victorian antiques, many of them original to the Irma. Though each is different, they share an affinity for high ceilings, Victorian floral-striped wallpapers, heavy drapes with tasseled valances, carpeted floors, and modern baths. Some have pocket doors between the bedroom and parlor. Others, like the skylighted Colonel Cody Suite, are L-shaped and open onto the second-floor deck. All have telephones, television, and air conditioning. The one caveat is that those at the front, along Cody's main street, can be noisy. The remainder of the rooms in the hotel have contemporary furnishings and completely lack the turn-of-the-century character that makes the suites so appealing.

The Irma is in the heart of town, convenient to shops and restaurants. It's only five blocks from the stellar Buffalo Bill Historical Center, which contains Bill Cody's personal and historical memorabilia as well as collections of firearms, Plains Indian artifacts, and a comprehensive gallery of western art. The center alone is sufficient reason to include Cody on a travel itinerary. That and Yellowstone Park, whose east entrance is 52 miles away.

Parson's Pillow Bed & Breakfast

1202 14th Street
Cody, WY 82414
307-587-2382
800-377-2348

A cheerful B&B near the Buffalo Bill Historical Center

Hosts: Lee and Elly Larabee. **Accommodations:** 4 rooms, 2 with private bath. **Rates:** Summer (May–September) $65–$75; $10 less rest of year. **Included:** Full breakfast. **Minimum stay:** None. **Added:** 6% tax. **Payment:** MasterCard, Visa (with 4% surcharge). **Children:** Not suitable for children under 13. **Pets:** Prohibited. **Smoking:** Prohibited. **Open:** Year-round.

Lee and Elly Larabee came to Cody to visit friends and fell under the spell of this western town of 8,000. Before long, they sold their health food store in California and moved there themselves, buying a wood-frame two-story building that had once been the town's first church and converting it into a bed-and-breakfast. With a nod to its early history, they dubbed it Parson's Pillow.

The building dates to 1902, and while the exterior —

minus the steeple — looks much as it does in old photos of Cody, little of the interior of the church survived. To compensate, the Larabees engaged a local woodworker to craft beaded woodwork for the parlor, dining room, and the staircase leading to the rooms on the second floor.

Walls of books line the slightly old-fashioned parlor. The parlor also has the inn's only television and a VCR. A huge breakfast is served in the adjacent dining room on a table laid with china and crystal.

In contrast to the somewhat traditional quality of those public areas, the rooms upstairs are all very lighthearted. The Garden Room has latticework over mint green walls, white wicker furnishings, a comforter patterned with hydrangeas and chrysanthemums, and a bath with a pedestal sink and antique tub. The Rose Room could be a setting for a Barbara Cartland romance (a selection of her novels stands on the bedside table), all roses, plants, gilt-framed mirrors, and even a painting of a voluptuous nude. It, too, has a private bath. Memories has an antique bed with feather pillows and shares a bath and antique clawfoot tub with Western, whose bed is log.

> Guests like to gather in the parlor, something the Larabees encourage by serving snacks in the afternoon, keeping a supply of menus for local restaurants, and generally making themselves available for advice. In the evening Elly sometimes plays the piano and Lee the fiddle, encouraging guests to join in.

Among the nice touches are early morning coffee and newspapers and a small refrigerator (whimsically painted to look like an old safe) on the second floor filled with complimentary sodas, juices, and fruit. There's also a microwave for guests to use. Cody's Main Street is only a block away, but the pale yellow inn itself stands in a quiet residential neighborhood beneath a shady tree. A porch extends across the front, providing guests a place to sit outdoors. Window boxes of petunias provide color. All in all, it's an engaging little bed-and-breakfast run by a very pleasant couple.

DUBOIS

Absaroka Ranch

Star Route
Dubois, WY 82513
307-455-2275

A secluded working ranch with limitless vistas

Proprietors: Budd and Emi Betts. **Accommodations:** 4 cabins. **Rates:** $900/person/week. **Included:** All meals, horseback riding, other activities. **Minimum stay:** 7 nights. **Added:** 2.2% tax, 10% service charge. **Payment:** Cash or checks. **Children:** Reduced rates under age 13. **Pets:** Prohibited. **Smoking:** Prohibited in dining room. **Open:** Mid-June to mid-September.

Intimate and family-oriented, Absaroka Ranch sits high on the slopes of a rugged and picturesque plateau that overlooks the immense Dunoir Valley, 16 miles northwest of Dubois. It is a world of sage-cloaked hills, alpine forests, snow-capped peaks, and limitless vistas. Wildlife abounds in this unspoiled landscape, and so does a sense of complete escape.

Most guests come to ride. Ranch owners Budd and Emi Betts have virtually unlimited access to the surrounding Shoshone National Forest, where miles and miles of trails etch the backcountry. Matched with horses appropriate to their riding experience, guests take off across the plains headed for wildflower meadows and exhilarating high-country vistas of the encircling peaks. There are hidden streams along the way, and chance encounters with wildlife.

Children, too, can ride and that and the out-of-harm's-way location make it a favorite with families. Three of the cabins have two bedrooms with a connecting bath — ideal for four people. All four cabins have propane heat, firm pine beds, and a front porch with views of the mountains.

None is more than a few steps from the quaint log ranchhouse, where guests gather for cocktails and hors d'oeuvres followed by delicious family-style meals of lasagna, paella, chicken in phyllo, and beef tenderloin, always served with home-made breads, lots of fresh fruits and vegetables, desserts, and wine. One night a week there's a steak cookout. After dinner guests might find themselves playing in an impromptu whiffleball game, singing songs around the campfire, or listening to a cowboy poet. There's also a game room with bumper pool and a jukebox. On weekends the Bettses sometimes round up a crew and head into the cowboy bars in Dubois.

> After some initial riding instruction, the patient, amiable wranglers feel guests out about how much more they want and teach accordingly. Kids as young as five can have their own horse; for the younger ones, there is a wrangler to give them pony rides and a babysitter to care for them while their parents are on the trail.

There's more to the ranch than riding, though. Hikers and photographers can take off with a pack lunch on many of the riding trails and reach stunning vistas without the aid of a horse. The ranch also arranges guided fishing trips for experienced fly-rodders to nearby lakes and trout streams. With a maximum of 15 guests to tend to, Budd and Emi Betts can see to everyone's needs personally. It's as guest-oriented as they come.

Bitterroot Ranch

East Fork Road
P.O. Box 807
Dubois, WY 82513
307-455-2778
800-545-0019
Fax: 307-455-2354

A horse ranch for equestrians, deep in a scenic valley

Proprietors: Bayard and Meloena Fox. **Accommodations:** 11 cabins. **Rates:** $1,150/person/week. **Included:** All meals, taxes, and horseback riding. **Minimum stay:** 7 nights. **Added:** Nothing. **Payment:** Cash, personal checks, or traveler's checks. **Children:** Reduced rates for children under 16. **Pets:** Prohibited. **Smoking:** Allowed. **Open:** Late May–late September.

Remote and secluded, the Bitterroot Ranch trails along both sides of a river in the East Fork Valley, 26 miles northeast of Dubois and four miles from its nearest neighbor. Its setting out in the open provides expansive vistas in every direction. Set on 1,300 acres, it borders a 50,000-acre winter elk reserve on one flank and the Shoshone National Forest on another. There are stunning vistas in every direction, none more dramatic than the sight of the snow-capped Wind River Mountains.

A working ranch that raises purebred Arabian horses, the Bitterroot differs from many guest ranches in its emphasis on equestrian training and serious riding. "We like to ride fast and hard and we like people to hold their weight properly so they don't interfere with the horses," says Bayard Fox, who owns the ranch with his wife Meloena. Many of the wranglers perfected their riding technique in England. The Foxes have a winter business (called Equitour) of conducting riding tours all over the world. They cater to those interested in riding as a sport rather than merely as a means to explore Wyoming's vast scenery.

The ranch is nonetheless surrounded by limitless opportunities for exceptional rides. The terrain varies from sagebrush flats and open meadows to timbered hills and 10,000-foot peaks. Elk, deer, and bighorn sheep abound, as do wildflowers. To ensure that everyone makes the most of his or her time at the ranch, riders are divided into small groups by ability, provided with a fresh horse in the morning and another in the afternoon, and given the opportunity to ride as far and as fast and as long as their abilities allow. And the Foxes ride with them: one or both goes out every day.

To ensure plenty of personal attention, they accept a maximum of 30 people. Children have their own riding program but no other supervised activities. Everyone eats together in the lodge on such fare as roast turkey, roast beef, or pork chops accompanied by fresh-baked breads and salads made from the ranch's own lettuce. Afterward, if they're not watching videotapes of their lessons, guests can search the library for books, gather around the piano in the lodge, or catch whatever video movie the ranch decides to show.

> **The weekly calendar includes two days of formal riding lessons, videotaped for after-dinner evaluation, on everything from the basics to show jumping. The ranch even has a cross-country course with 60 jumps.**

The log cabins lie along both sides of the river. Some date to the turn of the century, but whether old or new, all have a western decor of pine paneling, wood-burning stoves, private baths, and a rustic air. Their simplicity mirrors the ranch itself, which has no such amenities as a swimming pool or hot tub. "We shun that kind of thing like the plague," notes Bayard. "We cater to riders."

GLENROCK

Hotel Higgins

416 West Birch Street
P.O. Box 741
Glenrock, WY 82637
307-436-9212
800-458-0144
Fax: 307-436-9213

> *A hotel with flare
> and great food*

Innkeepers: Jack and Margaret Doll. **Accommodations:** 4 rooms and 2 suites, all with private bath. **Rates:** Single $44, double $58; suites $54–$68. **Included:** Full breakfast. **Minimum stay:** None. **Added:** 7% tax. **Payment:** MasterCard, Visa. **Children:** Welcome. **Pets:** Prohibited. **Smoking:** Allowed. **Open:** Year-round.

The discovery of oil on John Higgins's ranch near Casper propelled him to wealth and to Wyoming's legislature. When he built this three-story hotel in 1916, he and his wife sought to invest it with a touch of class still evident in the oak and mahogany woodwork, beveled glass doors, terrazzo tile, and alabaster chandeliers. Elegant appointments, cut crystal, and sterling silver lured turn-of-the-century luminaries like William Jennings Bryan and Wyoming's first governor, Robert Carey.

But it fared less well in the decades that followed. A later owner covered its original cedar shake exterior with its current bland vinyl siding and turned it into a workingman's hotel. But when Jack and Margaret Doll bought it in 1974, they had other ideas. They set about restoring the rooms to their former richness, filling them with furnishings from the 1920s, 1930s, and 1940s.

Now on the National Register of Historic Places, the hotel

has a flare impossible to find elsewhere in eastern Wyoming. The lobby looks much as it did when the Higginses opened it, right down to the softly ticking Seth Thomas wall clock and a Toledo scale, both dating from around 1900. The ballroom has become the Paisley Shawl restaurant (open for lunch and dinner, Tuesday–Saturday), whose warm and tasteful decor makes it an excep-

> **There is not a better restaurant than the Hotel Higgins's Paisley Shawl within a radius of 150 miles.**

tionally comfortable venue for the fixed-price, five-course dinners ($24) featuring choices like rack of lamb marinated in rosemary and Alaskan snow crab crêpes.

The guest rooms, though individually decorated and furnished, share a homey feel, with brass, iron, or wooden beds, chenille spreads and lace curtains. All have private baths with old-fashioned tubs or stall showers. None has a phone, and only one of the suites has a television.

The hotel also offers an exquisite breakfast of champagne, fruit compote, juice, muffins, and baked French toast (a favorite), omelettes, or quiche with ham or Canadian bacon. A few times each week, the man in charge is Rusty Paquette, a former resort chef, who charms guests with lines like, "Have some more bubbly. It'll be eight or ten more minutes before I get up the nerve to look in the oven."

GRAND TETON NATIONAL PARK

For other lodging in the area, see Jackson Hole and Wilson.

Jackson Lake Lodge

Grand Teton National Park
P.O. Box 250
Moran, WY 83013
307-543-2811
Reservations: 307-543-2855
800-628-9988
Fax: 307-543-2869

> *A midpark lodge facing the Tetons*

General manager of Grand Teton Lodge Co.: Clay James. **Accommodations:** 381 rooms, 4 suites. **Rates:** Rooms $89–$159, suites $300–$450. **Minimum stay:** None. **Added:** 8% tax. **Payment:** Major credit cards. **Children:** Free under age 12. **Pets:** Subject to stringent park restrictions. **Smoking:** Prohibited in dining room; nonsmoking rooms available. **Open:** Late May to mid-October.

From its perch on a bluff in the heart of Grand Teton National Park, the Jackson Lake Lodge looks across a broad expanse of willow flats to the lake and its awesome backdrop of the Grand Tetons. The three-story lodge, built in 1954, was designed by a prison architect with an apparent fondness for concrete. To his credit, he tried to soften its institutional lines by giving the exterior walls and interior beams the texture of wood, etching the concrete floors to make them look like blocks of stone, and installing twin fireplaces. But his greatest contribution was a three-story wall of windows in the main lounge that frames awesome views of the Grand Tetons.

> The most desirable — and expensive — rooms look across Willow Flats at the Tetons, a fabulous sight to awaken to.

Renovations completed in 1993 softened the lobby interiors by facing the concrete pillars with flagstone and adding oak paneling to parts of the walls. At the same time, the lodge introduced new furnishings upholstered in stripes, subdued plaids, and Indian prints. Warmer and more appealing, it has also become a showcase for some of the Rockefeller collection of southwestern art.

The rooms upstairs also underwent a desperately needed refurbishment. They now sport Indian print bedspreads, wooden headboards with carved relief mooseheads, and new blue and white tile baths with modern fixtures. The most desirable rooms face west, where they have vistas across Willow Flats at Mt. Moran and the Grand Tetons. They also have the added amenities of down comforters, a wet bar, and small refrigerator.

The remaining accommodations consist of motellike rooms on the short streets to either side of the main lodge. Though constructed in the 1950s, they've all been redone since 1990 with flagstone entryways, much new furniture — including the same carved moosehead headboards — colorful pastel print bedspreads, soft green carpets, and bright new baths in green and white. Most have two double beds. All have patios in front, and some have a second patio in back, though not necessarily with views.

All of these units are within walking distance of the lodge, which has several restaurants, a bar, and shops. Its Mural Room, a large, tiered space decorated with Carl Roters's western murals, has views of the Tetons. Reservations are required for what are nonetheless only average dinners of prime rib and Rocky Mountain trout. Those who forget to make reservations gladly drop in on the Pioneer Grill, a 1950s-style soda fountain with U-shaped Formica counters, green vinyl chairs, and very inexpensive dinners, sandwiches, and ice cream treats. Several nights a week the lodge books live entertainment into its cocktail lounge, which has its own views of the Tetons.

The lodge's amenities include an outdoor swimming pool, several shops, and a beauty parlor. But its greatest asset is its central location, which makes it a good base for exploring both Grand Teton and Yellowstone National Parks.

Jenny Lake Lodge

Grand Teton National Park
P.O. Box 250
Moran, WY 83013
307-733-4647
Reservations: 307-543-2855
800-628-9988
Fax: 307-543-2869

> *A Rockefeller legacy in elegant cabins and superb food*

General manager of Grand Teton Lodge Co.: Clay James. **Accommodations:** 31 cabins, 6 suites. **Rates:** Rooms, single $255, double $320; suites $460. **Included:** Breakfast and dinner, horseback riding, bicycles. **Minimum stay:** None. **Added:**

8% tax. **Payment:** Major credit cards. **Children:** Under age 7 discouraged. **Pets:** Prohibited. **Smoking:** Prohibited in public areas; nonsmoking rooms available. **Open:** Late May to mid-October.

John D. Rockefeller, Jr., built this compound in the 1920s, setting the stage for what has become one of America's most engaging national park lodges. Part guest ranch, part sybaritic retreat, the cottage colony nestles beneath a canopy of fir trees alongside two alpine meadows at the very heart of Grand Teton National Park. Noteworthy cuisine is as close as the rustic log and timber lodge.

> The awesome granite spectacle of 13,770-foot Grand Teton itself looms immediately to the west. Hiking and horseback riding trails begin virtually on the cabin doorsteps.

The main lodge has been expanded and refurbished since Rockefeller sowed those first seeds, but guests still bed down beneath handmade quilts and electric blankets in three dozen log cabins, some of them original to the ranch and seven that are brand-new. New or old, they have log walls, wood floors with braided rugs, one king- or two queen-size beds, pine dressers, modern baths, and porches with rocking chairs. A few are two-room suites with fireplaces or wood-burning stoves. Among the added amenities are terrycloth robes, hair dryers, walking sticks, and umbrellas.

Those who stay at Jenny Lake ride horseback, hike, and fish amid the park's breathtaking surroundings. Most of the time they dine on such succulent fare as poached fresh Snake River trout, hickory-smoked buffalo sirloin, or pheasant breast with pheasant sausage (the restaurant is also open to the public; jackets for men are requested). But one night a week, they ride off to the steak fry, which differs from the usual barbecue because the picnic tables are set with linen, china, and crystal. On Sundays there is a legendary buffet whose centerpiece is always an elaborate ice sculpture.

Couples adore all of this and the informal warmth and enthusiastic, capable young staff. Families, disenchanted by the hefty prices and the absence of much for children to do, opt instead for Jackson Lake Lodge or accommodations in town.

JACKSON HOLE

For other lodging in the area, see Grand Teton National Park and Wilson.

Dornan's Spur Ranch Log Cabins

P.O. Box 39
Moose, WY 83012
307-733-2522
Fax: 307-733-3544

A cluster of spiffy cabins right outside the park

Manager: Sherida McKie. **Accommodations:** 12 cabins. **Rates:** Summer (mid May–mid-October) and winter (mid-December–March) $100–$175, rest of year $75–$125. **Minimum stay:** 2 nights. **Added:** 8% tax. **Payment:** MasterCard, Visa. **Children:** Welcome. **Pets:** Prohibited. **Smoking:** Prohibited. **Open:** Year-round.

This cluster of new log cabins sits in the open just outside the southern entrance to Grand Teton National Park, 12 miles north of Jackson's town square. Forget rustic. Though built of honey-colored logs and paneled in pine, these are thoroughly modern one- and two-bedroom units with locally made lodgepole pine furnishings, fully equipped kitchens, Scandia down comforters and pillows and Ralph Lauren linens on queen-size beds, modern baths, and phones (but no televisions or fireplaces). Braided rag rugs accent the wood floors, the living room couches convert to beds, and all have porches with chairs and a barbecue grill.

The cabins are arranged in a rough circle around a field of wildflowers and grasses. Most have views of the Teton Mountains either from their kitchen or a bedroom window.

The Dornan family, who homesteaded this spot in 1919, built the cabins in 1992, adding yet another element to the large Dornan's Spur complex, which includes a small deli/grocery, an exceptional wine shop, a restaurant and lounge, a clothing and sporting equipment store, and a whitewater outfitter. The cabins occupy their own 10-acre plot alongside the Snake River, just below the rest of the Dornan enterprises.

Each cabin bears the name of a local flower. Larkspur, a two-bedroom unit, stands out for having views of the river as well as the mountains. The town of Jackson lies 12 miles to the south, Yellowstone National Park 35 miles to the north.

The cabins remain open year-round, easily accessible on well-maintained roads.

Gros Ventre River Ranch

Gros Ventre Road
P.O. Box 151
Moose, WY 83012
307-733-4138
Fax: 307-733-4272

> *A guest ranch with modern comforts, close to Jackson*

Proprietors: Karl and Tina Weber.
General managers: Brad and Carrie Robicheaux. **Accommodations:** 10 cabins. **Rates:** Summer (May–October), single $1,740–$1,950/week, double $2,080–$2,776; winter, $90–$150/person with meals or $150/cabin (up to 4 people) without meals. **Included:** All meals, activities, airport transfers. **Minimum stay:** 7 nights from mid-June through mid-September, otherwise 3 nights. **Added:** 3% tax and 15% service charge. **Payment:** Cash or checks. **Children:** Free under age 2; reduced rates under 7. **Pets:** Prohibited. **Smoking:** Prohibited in dining room. **Open:** May–October and December–March (lodge open January–March)

The decks of the L-shaped lodge at the Gros Ventre River Ranch look across the river at the sagebrush plains of the National Elk Refuge, deserted in summer, and the majestic panorama of the Tetons, which spread out along the horizon to the west. The soft rushing of the Gros Ventre River flowing to join the Snake River in the valley below is often the only sound to break the silence.

This is a mid-sized operation, with room for no more than 40 guests, but one that weaves together the best traditions of dude ranches with modern comfort. The ranch started taking guests in the 1950s, and many of its older log cabins date from that era. However, when Karl and Tina Weber bought it in 1987, they set out to upgrade the creature comforts while still preserving the western flavor. Their success shows in everything from the new lodge, built to take advantage of those Teton views, to the friendly staff and multidimensional programs.

Like all good ranches, Gros Ventre assigns each guest a horse and makes sure he or she gets plenty of good instruction, including children as young as six. Half-day and full-day rides are scheduled throughout the week.

Fishermen appreciate the ranch for its easy accessibility to fine trout streams. They have an entire mile of the Gros Ventre River all to themselves as it flows through the property, making for great cutthroat and rainbow fishing — on a catch-and-release basis — just a few steps from the cabins. Guides are available if guests want them, and the legendary Snake River is a short trip away. The ranch also has a stocked fishing pond, not only for kids but also for adults (the chef will cook anything you catch).

> The ride that has guests buzzing around the fireplace in the main lodge in the evening is a spectacular nine-hour excursion up into the snow above the timberline near 11,000 feet on Sheep Mountain. From that point it's possible to see the entire Jackson Hole valley, flanked by the Tetons and the Gros Ventres.

The cabins come in two basic models, old and new. The older log cabins, which date from the 1950s, lie closer to the lodge at the edge of the forest. All have front porches that face a lawn with swings and hammocks. Inside, log beds and peeled pine walls square off with contemporary pull-out sofas and modern baths. Of theseolder cabins, only the one called the Homestead has that magnificent view. None of the others lets you sit on the porch and watch the sun set behind the Tetons.

To rectify that, the Webers had an additional set of cabins built farther from the lodge but positioned so that their decks and windows to that sweeping panorama. These hideaways also have large living rooms with vaulted ceilings and woodstoves, a huge master bedroom and smaller second bedroom each with its own deck, full kitchens, modern baths, wall-to-wall carpeting, and contemporary ranch furnishings set off by Audubon prints. These cabins are also available in winter, with or without meals, though the ranch suspends organized activities when the snow falls.

The cuisine shows a similar bent for blending the traditional with the contemporary as guests chow down at a steak fry one night and dine on swordfish or Cornish game hen the next. Wine is available for those who want it, otherwise the ranch is BYOB.

The ranch's seclusion and its small number of guests engender an easy camaraderie, yet there are times when people turn up missing from the dinner table. The reason is that while the ranch may be secluded, it is not isolated. Teton and Yellowstone National Parks lie close enough to visit on day trips, and the town of Jackson is only 18 miles away, luring guests with a craving for movies, shopping, or a restaurant dinner. Far from discouraging such off-site ventures, the staff willingly packs picnic lunches for anyone who wants to make a day of it. It is an exceptionally well-run operation.

Lost Creek Ranch

P.O. Box 95
Moose, WY 83012-0095
307-733-3435
Fax: 307-733-1954

A sybaritic ranch with panoramic Teton vistas

General manager: Wanda Smith.
Accommodations: 10 cabins. **Rates:**
$3,595/couple/week. **Included:** All meals, horseback riding,

ranch activities, float trip, Yellowstone park tour, airport transfers, laundry service, and gratuities. **Minimum stay:** 7 nights. **Added:** 2.5% tax. **Payment:** Cash, personal checks, or traveler's checks. **Children:** Best suited for ages 6 and up. **Pets:** Prohibited. **Smoking:** No smoking in dining room. **Open:** June through September.

Exclusive and sybaritic, Lost Creek Ranch captivates its guests with big-as-all-outdoors views of Jackson Hole and the 13,000-foot Grand Tetons. Its lodge and cabins trail along a bench 600 feet above the sagebrush-tufted valley. The broad decks lure many of the 45 or so guests out in the evening to watch the sun set behind the peaks. Nothing obstructs the panoramic vista except perhaps the tip of a spruce tree.

Surrounded by Grand Teton National Park and the Bridger-Teton National Forest, the ranch is an oasis of creature comforts. Original art and custom-made furniture decorate its elegant main lodge. The rambling structure shelters a huge living room with a vaulted ceiling, terra cotta tile floors, and a soaring fireplace. Chairs with hand-carved and hand-painted wildflowers flank dining room tables set with silver, crystal, and linen. Even the fireplace screen, made from old barbed wire, is a work of art.

> With almost as many staff members as guests, Lost Creek provides a level of service unknown at most guest ranches. The nightly turndown brings fresh towels; laundry service is part of the package, and so are babysitting during the dinner hour and an overnight campout for kids.

There are more custom furnishings and original art in the handsome cabins. All of them have both queen and single beds, sitting areas, full modern baths, refrigerators, and porches. The larger two-bedroom family units add a living room with full kitchen, fireplace, and sleep sofa.

Each guest has his or her own horse, as much riding instruction as wanted, and the chance to venture out twice a day on two- to three-hour rides. But whereas horseback riding is the mainstay of most ranches, at Lost Creek it constitutes one diversion in a lengthy agenda of daily activities that includes (at no extra charge) float trips on the Snake River, hiking in Grand Teton, and a tour of Yellowstone. For those who stay behind, the ranch has a heated pool and a tennis court.

With rare exceptions, kids are integrated into the adult program. Younger children eat early several nights during the week, happy to have pizza or fried chicken instead of grilled tuna with roasted red bell pepper sauce or rack of lamb with fresh rosemary. The ranch also has a special license allowing it to sell beer and wine with dinner only, and the eclectic wine list has about two dozen choices, mostly California vintages. Otherwise guests need to bring their own liquor. Entertainment follows dinner, perhaps Indian dances, western swing lessons, or a wilderness photography presentation. Once a week in summer, everybody piles into vans and heads for the rodeo in Jackson, 20 miles to the south.

Nowlin Creek Inn

660 East Broadway
P.O. Box 2766
Jackson Hole, WY 83001
307-733-0882
800-542-2632
Fax: 307-733-0106

A smart inn,
near the National
Elk Refuge

Innkeepers: Mark and Susan Nowlin. **Accommodations:** 5 rooms. **Rates:** $125–$155. **Included:** Full breakfast. **Minimum stay:** 2 nights on weekends. **Added:** 8% tax. **Payment:** Major credit cards. **Children:** Welcome. **Pets:** Prohibited. **Smoking:** Prohibited. **Open:** Year-round.

The Nowlin Creek Inn can be found in a quiet part of Jackson, directly across from the headquarters of the National Elk

Refuge. The unprepossessing two-story inn faced with unpainted wood and edged by aspen trees, gives few clues to the engaging interiors that lie within. But its door opens onto a vaulted, sunny living space furnished with overstuffed couches and chairs and decorated with historical prints of American Indians and original art — some of it done by Susan Nowlin.

Nowlin Creek was built in 1993, and although there are suggestions of the rustic West in its rough pine floors and of the Victorian era in its scattering of antiques, it

> **The inn was designed with the comfort of guests in mind, down to the hand-crafted furnishings, sun deck, and outdoor hot tub.**

is in every way a modern inn. Radiant heat, for example, runs beneath those floors, which bear hand-done stenciling of leaves and wildflowers.

The five rooms stand out for their spaciousness. Named for lakes, they meld western contemporary furnishings with Victorian antiques and family heirlooms. All have modern private baths and views of either the Elk Refuge or Snow King Mountain. Largest and most viewful of the lot is Solitude, a junior suite on the second floor containing a king-size bed with a lodgepole pine headboard, an antique dresser and nightstand, and a large bath with a whirlpool tub. Its windows frame vistas of Snow King Mountain on one side and of the Elk Refuge and Tetons on the other.

Oddly missing from all these rooms, however, despite the well-chosen furnishings and colorful Ralph Lauren linens, is a feeling of warmth. Empty expanses of white wall endow them with a hotel-like quality — but without amenities like phones or televisions. And some will miss not having a fireplace in the living room. At the same time, since the Nowlins live next door, guests have full run of the common areas, which are exceptionally appealing. And the Nowlins themselves help by providing hot beverages every evening and a full breakfast of decadent French toast, egg strata, or pancakes and sausage every morning. Mark Nowlin's grandparents homesteaded the valley, and he has long had a picture-framing business in a shop a few yards from the inn. He and Susan thus have a local's intimate knowledge of the area.

Jackson's town square is three-quarters of a mile to the west, and in winter the bus to the ski area stops a block away.

R Lazy S Ranch

P.O. Box 308
Teton Village, WY 83025
Summer: 307-733-2655
Winter: 801-628-6546

An old-fashioned ranch with old-fashioned hospitality

Proprietors: Howard and Cara Stirn. **General manager:** Claire Mc-Conaughy. **Accommodations:** 12 cabins, 2 dorms for teens. **Rates:** Cabins $840–$1,155/person/week, dorms $770/week. **Included:** All meals, horseback riding, activities, Jackson Lake boating. **Minimum stay:** 7 nights. **Added:** 6% tax on food and lodging portion. **Payment:** Cash, personal checks, or traveler's checks. **Children:** Age 6 and older; adults only in September. **Pets:** Prohibited. **Smoking:** Prohibited in dining room. **Open:** Mid-June through September.

The R Lazy S Ranch abuts the southern boundary of Grand Teton National Park and spreads east until it encounters the serpentine course of the Snake River. To the west lie the sky-piercing palisades of the Teton Mountains. Yet the setting is not nearly as remote as it seems: the town of Jackson is only 20 minutes away, and it's less than five minutes to Teton Village and the aerial tramway to the top of 10,400-foot Rendezvous Mountain. This doesn't prevent the ranch itself from being a 285-acre oasis of tranquility where old-fashioned western hospitality flourishes.

The McConaughy family, who started the ranch in 1947, still manage it, acting as co-hosts with Howard and Cara Stirn, who bought it in 1975. So an abundance of personal attention is lavished on guests, whether they come to ride, fish, hike, or do nothing at all.

For those who come to ride, the ranch offers thorough and patient instruction and 17 different all-day outings. Some leave directly from the ranch for scenic backcountry like Taggart Lakes or the showy views above the timberline in Death Canyon. Others bring riders to trailheads elsewhere in the valley, so guests can ride in the more difficult to reach summer range of Wyoming's elk, moose, antelope, bison, and deer. Fly-rodders, meanwhile, don't have to go any farther than a few steps from their cabins to find several miles of private fishing along the Snake River, one of the world's great trout streams.

For children, the ranch runs a special program for six- to twelve-year-olds. The wranglers teach horsemanship, lead rides to nearby lakes and a hot-springs pool, and teach the kids how to saddle and groom their own mounts. There's a swimming hole on the ranch, and kids can go inner-tubing on the river. Children and teens also have their own dining room.

> **Traditional to the core, the ranch remains free of any kind of resort amenity: no pools, no hot tubs, no television; just casual atmosphere, good horses, and friendly people.**

The one- to three-bedroom log cabins nestle among the aspens not far from the river. Built in the 1920s but thoroughly modernized, they feature porches, private baths, stylish country appointments, and amenities like coffeemakers, electric blankets, and in some cases woodstoves. Some have riveting views of the Tetons.

Overall, the atmosphere is very informal. After dinners of seafood, pasta, prime rib, or chicken, guests can look forward to square dances, slide shows, singalongs, or conversation around the fireplace in the main lodge. And whenever this soothing tranquility gets to be too much, there is always something going on in Jackson.

Rusty Parrot Lodge

175 North Jackson
P.O. Box 1657
Jackson, WY 83001
307-733-2000
800-458-2004
Fax: 307-733-5566

*A convivial lodge,
near everything
in town*

Innkeeper: Ron Harrison. **Accommodations:** 31 rooms, 1 suite. **Rates:** Rooms $98–$215, suite $245–$300. **Included:** Full breakfast. **Minimum stay:** 3 nights over summer and winter weekends; 5 nights over Christmas holidays. **Added:** 8% tax. **Payment:** Major credit cards. **Children:** Children under 12 discouraged. **Pets:** Prohibited. **Smoking:** Prohibited. **Open:** Year-round.

A classic log lodge with river rock fireplaces and pine furnishings, the Rusty Parrot would be completely at home deep in a remote Rocky Mountain valley. However, the timber and stone three-story lodge stands across from a city park, four blocks from galleries, restaurants, the Ralph Lauren Polo Factory Outlet, and the Million Dollar Cowboy Bar on Jackson's town square. Since it opened in 1990, the inn has introduced a convivial new dimension to Jackson Hole's hotel accommodations.

Furnished like an elegant country cottage, the lodge's spacious rooms have custom-made queen-size log or peeled-aspen beds, distressed pine armoires, and down comforters and wool blankets in reds and greens. Thick, forest green carpet runs wall to wall in rooms furnished with wicker chairs, pine tables, and brass lamps. Terra cotta and pine accent private baths, which feature large oval tubs and baskets of thick, colorful towels. Romantics can opt for a room with a fireplace and, if they want, a double Jacuzzi tub. Seven of the rooms have balconies; one on the first floor is wheelchair accessible. All have phones and remote-control televisions. The suite has fireplaces in both the living room and bedroom, a full kitchen, and a private bath with Jacuzzi tub. There's even a massage therapist.

> **Like any good lodge in ski country, the Rusty Parrot has a lobby fireplace with comfortable sofas; the requisite hot tub is on a second-floor deck with views of the heart-stoppingly steep slopes at Snow King, Jackson's lesser known ski area, right in town.**

Unlike many lodges, the Rusty Parrot's rates include a huge breakfast, offering guests a choice of three daily specials like banana bread French toast with blueberry sauce, eggs Benedict, or Rocky Mountain trout, served with pastries, muffins, and granola. Innkeeper Ron Harrison is often on hand, happy to help with anything from restaurant suggestions to finding the shuttle to the ski slopes (two blocks east). Skiers or sightseers returning in the afternoon find cookies, coffee, tea, and hot chocolate set out in the vaulted lobby, providing yet another excuse to bring guests together. It's the friendliest lodge in town.

Spring Creek

1800 Spirit Dance Road
P.O. Box 3154
Jackson, WY 83001
307-733-8833
800-443-6139
Fax: 307-733-1524

> *A blufftop sanctuary,*
> *between town*
> *and the ski area*

General manager: Steven F. Price. **Accommodations:** 36 rooms, 62 condominiums and homes. **Rates:** (Higher over Christmas holidays) Rooms, winter (January–March) $150, summer (June–September) $190, spring/fall $120; condos and homes, winter $180–$450, summer $205–$625, spring/fall $130–$300. **Included:** Full breakfast with rooms and studios during fall, winter, and spring. **Minimum stay:** None to 5 nights depending on season. **Added:** 8% tax. **Payment:** Major credit cards. **Children:** Free under age 12. **Pets:** Prohibited. **Smoking:** No pipes or cigars in dining room. **Open:** Year-round.

Its spectacular views of the Grand Tetons alone make Spring Creek one of the most desirable addresses in Jackson Hole. Poised on a sagebrush-covered ridge a few miles north of town, the combination hotel and condominium property has an elevated perspective on the 60-by-20-mile valley and its western palisade of saw-tooth granite peaks. On a clear morning, this is one of the most stunning vistas in the scenic Rockies.

> **Set on 1,000 acres and framed by cattle ranches and the National Elk Refuge, Spring Creek feels remote despite its proximity to town. It is itself a wildlife preserve, protecting the winter migration route of herds of mule deer.**

The serpentine road to Spring Creek ends amid a cluster of honey-colored, low-rise structures built of cedar, fir, pine, and spruce. Even the basic rooms have fireplaces, plaster walls, lodgepole pine furnishings, down comforters, remote-control cable TVs, and decks with at least a glimpse of the Tetons. The condos and deluxe houses range in size up to three bedrooms — some with lofts — and come with fully equipped kitchens. Some of their furnishings, too, are made of lodgepole pine, which, along with the quilted comforters and stone fireplaces, give the rooms uncommon warmth and character.

Staying at Spring Creek obviously means having all of Jackson Hole's abundant recreation at your doorstep. At the same time, this blufftop sanctuary holds out diversions of its own. In summer, guests can choose from horseback riding, hiking, tennis, and swimming, while in winter the resort has an ice skating pond, an outdoor hot tub, 20 kilometers of groomed cross-country track, and a free shuttle to the ski area. Its Granary restaurant, with a fireplace and cathedral ceiling, stands out for wall-to-wall views of the Tetons and some of the most scenic dining in the valley. Spring Creek is Jackson Hole's great sanctuary, promising splendid isolation, exceptional comfort, and some of the Rockies' most spectacular scenery.

Teton Pines

3450 North Clubhouse Drive
Jackson, WY 83001
307-733-1005
800-238-2223
Fax: 307-733-2860

A country club resort at the foot of the Tetons

General manager: Bob Marshall.
Accommodations: 16 suites. **Rates:** Summer (mid-June–late September) and Christmas holidays, rooms $250–$275, 1-bedroom suite $325–$360; winter (December–early April), rooms $125–$160, 1-bedroom suite $160–$195. **Included:** Continental breakfast, use of tennis courts, airport transfers, transportation to ski slopes. **Minimum stay:** None. **Added:** 8% tax. **Payment:** Major credit cards. **Children:** Free under age 3. **Pets:** Prohibited. **Smoking:** Allowed. **Open:** May–mid-October, December–early April.

A refined, country club atmosphere pervades Teton Pines, a mostly private resort development seven miles west of Jackson on the access road to the Jackson Hole Ski Area. Custom-built homes and luxury townhouses dot its 360 picturesque acres of golf fairways, small lakes, streams, meadows, and aspen groves laid out along the base of the Teton Mountains.

The epicenter of the resort is an elegant 27,000-square-foot clubhouse with vaulted ceilings and soaring windows. Clerestory windows in its cathedral ceiling flood the interior with sunshine, illuminating honey-colored beams and a restaurant with windows of the Tetons and the golf fairways.

On the manicured grounds adjacent to the clubhouse rise four two-story buildings, each containing four junior suites.

Contemporary in style and stylishly decorated in soft greens, blues, and mauves, each contains a king-size bed with a down comforter, a generous sitting-dining area, and two full baths — one with a whirlpool tub and well-lit makeup mirror, the other with a shower. There are also thoughtful touches like spacious mirrored closets, wet bars, refrigerator/ice makers, remote-control cable televisions, plenty of thick towels, a full complement of toiletries, and bowls of fresh fruit. The back door opens onto a deck or patio with views of the golf course or mountains. Those who need even more space can add the adjoining living room, which encompasses a travertine fireplace, half bath, and another refrigerator and wet bar. Either way, the room is stocked daily with everything essential for a Continental breakfast, including a coffeemaker, fruit, and breads or muffins.

> **Arnold Palmer and Ed Seay designed the 18-hole course, riddling it with 40 acres of water hazards and three acres of sand traps. It plays from 6,333 to 7,412 yards, every yard of it with stunning views of the craggy Teton peaks. When the snow falls in winter, it becomes a cross-country ski touring center with 13 kilometers of groomed trails.**

The resort complements an 18-hole golf course designed by Arnold Palmer and Ed Seay with an attractive tennis center, conveniently situated next to the heated swimming pool and outdoor Jacuzzi and anchored by its own two-story clubhouse staffed with pros. In winter, bubbles cover three courts, thus allowing play year-round. And the recreation does not end there. Guests can use the fitness center next door at the Aspens Athletic Club or attend a Jack Dennis Fly Fishing School, which uses a stocked pond by the golf course to teach the basics of fly fishing.

The two-tiered clubhouse restaurant is one of the best places to dine in town. Tables set with oil lamps have views of the golf course. The menu includes pastas, steaks, free-range chicken, and lamb but specializes in fresh fish — yellowfin tuna, Arctic char, and halibut among them — prepared in several ways: grilled, poached, baked, or blackened.

The Wildflower Inn

Shooting Star Lane
P.O. Box 3724
Jackson, WY 83001
307-733-4710

*A log B&B
on the road
to the ski area*

Hosts: Sherrie and Ken Jern. **Accommodations:** 5 rooms, all with private bath. **Rates:** $120–$130. **Included:** Full breakfast. **Minimum stay:** 3 nights preferred. **Added:** 8% tax. **Payment:** MasterCard, Visa. **Children:** Welcome. **Pets:** Prohibited (they have a cat). **Smoking:** Prohibited. **Open:** Year-round.

Ken and Sherrie Jern built the engaging Wildflower Inn themselves in 1988, designing it to be both their home and a bed-and-breakfast. Set back from the access road leading to the Jackson Hole Ski Area, eight miles west of town, the handsome two-story log house sits on three wildflower-covered acres amid a stand of aspen. Jackson's fabled ski slopes are only four miles away, and Grand Teton National Park lies seven miles beyond that.

> **The Jerns are ski instructors with a love of the outdoors. Ken spends part of his summers as a rock-climbing guide. Both offer invaluable advice about how to make the most of a northwestern Wyoming vacation.**

The rooms are as warm and inviting as the house. Color schemes vary according to which wildflower the room represents, but all have high lodgepole pine beds, down comforters, remote-control cable televisions, and thoughtful touches like luggage racks and alarm clocks. Each has a private bath with shower (Glac-

ier Lily's bath is detached), a pedestal sink, and thirsty Ralph
Lauren towels. Most rooms open onto decks. All have views
of the glacier-carved cirques and crags of the spectacular
Teton Mountains. Big country breakfasts, served on the back
deck overlooking a pond when weather permits, a towering
river rock fireplace, and a solarium with a hot tub and lots of
plants add to the inn's already considerable assets.

The Jerns can recommend local outfitters for whitewater
raft trips or snowmobile outings, and they know which hiking trails in Grand Teton are scenic without being overly
strenuous or time-consuming. Naturally hospitable, they relish spending time with guests, showing photos of how their
log house was built or suggesting restaurants, shops, and art
galleries. They make their terrific house seem even homier.

The Wort Hotel

50 North Glenwood
P.O. Box 69
Jackson, WY 83001
307-733-2190
800-322-2727
Fax: 307-733-2067

> *A modern version*
> *of a classic lodge,*
> *in the heart*
> *of town*

General manager: Lee Riley. **Accommodations:** 55 rooms, 5 suites. **Rates:** Rooms, summer
(June to late September) and winter (mid-December to mid-
April) $145, spring and fall $125–$130; suites, summer and
winter $190–$295, spring and fall $165–$295. **Included:** Airport transfers. **Minimum stay:** None. **Added:** 8% tax. **Payment:** Major credit cards. **Children:** Free under age 12. **Pets:**
Prohibited. **Smoking:** Nonsmoking rooms available. **Open:**
Year-round.

In 1915, local homesteader Charles J. Wort bought four lots in
Jackson and began talking about building a luxury hotel. He
died without realizing his dream, but his widow Luella and

son John carried on, opening the two-story Wort Hotel in 1941. It burned down in 1980 but was rebuilt and remains a Jackson Hole landmark, helped by its ideal location, a short half block from the Town Square.

Constructed of brick and local red stone, the two-story hotel has gabled roofs and a Tudor facade. Doors open onto a cozy pine-paneled lobby that is a modern take on a classic lodge. Local artwork decorates the walls, and a stone-block fireplace surmounted by the requisite moose head anchors the room. A grand staircase leads up to a mezzanine sitting area with another fireplace, this one with an elk head and still more art.

During a total renovation in 1989, the Wort's already spacious rooms exchanged their old Western look for an upscale

> **Off the lobby is the famous Silver Dollar Bar. With live entertainment and a serpentine bar inlaid with 2,032 uncirculated 1921 silver dollars, this is the second most popular place in town, after the Million Dollar Cowboy Bar on the square.**

country decor of reproduction antiques in pecan, brass fixtures, quilted floral bedspreads with matching curtains or an updated western look of lodgepole pine furnishings set off by leather chairs, paisley plum comforters, and walls decorated with an Indian saddle blanket and horseshoes. All have remote-control cable televisions, phones, and air conditioning. Modern tile baths come with toiletries and thick white towels. One is wheelchair accessible. Downstairs there are two Jacuzzis and a small workout room. A shuttle for the ski slopes leaves from right outside. Although all of this is new, the hotel has the same kind of friendly, capable staff as its ancestor.

LARAMIE

Annie Moore's Guest House

819 University Avenue
Laramie, WY 82070
307-721-4177
800-552-8992

> *An old boarding-house turned B&B, facing the university*

Hosts: Ann Acuff and Joe Bundy. **Accommodations:** 6 rooms, all with shared baths. **Rates:** Single $40–$50, double $50–$60. **Included:** Continental-plus breakfast. **Minimum stay:** None. **Added:** 8% tax. **Payment:** Major credit cards. **Children:** Discouraged under age 8. **Pets:** Prohibited (innkeepers have a cat). **Smoking:** Prohibited. **Open:** Year-round.

In 1981, a group of friends formed a co-op and took on a dilapidated three-story home with the intention of resurrecting it as a guest house. Eighteen months and a lot of blood, sweat, and tears later they succeeded, naming it for former owner Annie Moore.

Mrs. Moore, suddenly widowed at age 48, purchased the house in 1935 intent on supporting herself by using her cooking and housekeeping skills. She lived in the basement with her terrier, took in boarders on the upper floors, and prepared lunch and dinner for shifts of as many as 50 people, acquiring a reputation for hospitality along the way.

The three-story Queen Anne house itself dates from the turn of the century. Its hardwood floors and hand-crafted pine moldings give it warmth and character, as do the stained glass windows made by the co-op's president.

Of the six immaculate guest rooms, the most appealing are the three upstairs, all individually furnished with antiques or good reproductions. The corner Purple Room features a bay window and king-size brass bed, while the Blue Room has a white iron bed and a door that opens onto the sun deck. All have their own in-room sinks but share a full bath. The three cool downstairs rooms — sunnier than expected because they look out on a sunken garden — also share a bath (with shower only) and a second water closet. Only one room has a sink.

> **From the enclosed porch, called the Florida room, guests can sit in the sun and watch television or the parade of students coming and going from the University of Wyoming, directly across the street. Those who would rather relax outside can use the sun deck on the roof.**

Ann Acuff and her husband, Joe Bundy, joined the co-op when they came back from teaching English in Taiwan and eventually bought the house themselves. Like Annie Moore, Ann loves cooking and tending to guests. Breakfast consists of her homemade muffins, fresh fruit, cereal, and yogurt, and the kitchen is open during the day so guests can help themselves to juice, yogurt, coffee, and tea. The spirit of hospitality still reigns.

PINEDALE

Flying A Ranch

Route 1, Box 7
Pinedale, WY 82941
307-367-2385 in summer
800-678-6543 in winter
Fax: 607-336-8731 in winter

> *A ranch for romance,*
> *lost in a high valley*

Proprietors: Debbie Hansen and Keith Dagel. **Accommodations:** 6 cabins. **Rates:** Single $1,475–$1,575/week, double $2,000–$2,200/week. **Included:** All meals and activities. **Minimum stay:** 4 nights; 7 nights in July and August. **Added:** 4% tax, 15% service charge. **Payment:** Cash, personal checks, or traveler's checks. **Children:** No children under 16. **Pets:** Prohibited. **Smoking:** Prohibited. **Open:** Mid-June–early October.

Debbie Hansen and her husband, Keith Dagel, spent eight years restoring the 60-year-old log lodge and its hand-crafted cabins on the ranch her father bought during a 1965 hunting trip. Sequestered between the Gros Ventre and Wind River ranges, the 360-acre spread basks in timeless mountain vistas that have changed only imperceptibly since the ranch first accepted guests in the early 1930s. Moose occasionally take morning dips in the trout-filled lake, and deer and elk abound.

Hansen and Dagel have transformed the cabins into rustically elegant suites with hand-crafted furniture, oak floors, original art, porches with views of the Wind River Range, and in some cases fireplaces. And rather than make do with pemmican and hardtack, guests now sit down to charbroiled steaks, shrimp scampi, and Mexican fare.

The scenery invites guests to climb into the saddle, and those who want riding instruction get as much as they require. Set in a valley, the ranch has 360-degree views and access to more than 36,000 acres in the surrounding Bridger-Teton National Forest. Guests ride through meadows knee-deep in Indian paintbrush, visit waterfalls that plunge straight from the mouth of a cave, or climb onto the benches that divide the rocky pinnacles of the Gros Ventre from the pine and aspen forest below. Because groups are small and the setting remote, getting close to wildlife is easy. By bugling, Keith can sometimes lure elk to within 20 yards of the riders.

Magnificent though it is, riding is not the only diversion

open to guests. Fly-rodders can fish for trout weighing up to four pounds in the ranch's lakes, or arrange for a guide to take them to the nearby rivers and streams. There are also guided nature hikes and superb biking trails (the ranch has a couple of mountain bikes for guests). Deliberately missing from the ranch agenda are any programs for children. Hansen and Dagel have built a serene adult retreat, with a hot tub amid the pines, a cocktail lounge beside the lake, and deluxe hideaway accommodations. Lucky guests will catch a glimpse of the moose that sometimes swim in the lake, or hear the bugling of elk.

> **The scenery may be wild and primitive, but the ranch is not. Hansen and Dagel take only 12 guests at a time, which means that everyone gets an abundance of special attention.**

RAWLINS

Ferris Mansion

607 West Maple
Rawlins, WY 82301
307-324-3961

> *A century-old home, between Denver and Yellowstone*

Host: Janice Lubbers. **Accommodations:** 4 rooms, all with private bath. **Rates:** $55–$65. **Included:** Continental breakfast. **Minimum stay:** None.

Added: 7% tax. **Payment:** Discover, MasterCard, Visa. **Children:** Well-behaved older children welcome. **Pets:** Prohibited. **Smoking:** Prohibited. **Open:** Mid-March to mid-November.

When Janice Lubbers bought Ferris Mansion in 1979, the three-story turreted and gabled Queen Anne Victorian bore only a shadowy resemblance to the elegant home Julia Ferris had built in 1903. The grand oak staircase with its built-in banquette and carved newel post had been ripped out, and layers of paint covered the bird's-eye and curly maple fretwork and pocket doors. The once grand mansion had suffered an ignoble conversion to an apartment house. Few people would have attempted its resurrection.

> The turret room has a brass bed covered by a spread made from Janice's mother's hankies, a decorative fireplace, lavender carpet, and walls with a frieze of stenciled ribbon.

That Janice did shows how much she loved the house. Along the way she made a miraculous discovery: the original staircase minus the spindles had been put into storage in Encampment. She managed to get it back, enlisting a craftsman to make new spindles and adding a brass and etched-glass lamp above the carved leaf clusters on the newel post. The magnificent staircase winds up to the second floor, making it once again the centerpiece of Julia Ferris's former home.

Janice furnished the house with her own possessions and a miscellany of antiques, including her mother's oak dinette set and a 1925 Franklin baby grand player piano. She put rockers on the front porch and comfortable chairs and sofas in the sun room, which has rounded glass windows and a fireplace.

All four rooms are on the second floor. One holds a matching highback oak headboard and dresser, a loveseat, and lace curtains. The largest of all has another highback oak bed and matching dresser set before a tile and maple fireplace. All the rooms have private baths.

For breakfast Janice sets out a buffet of homemade granola, fresh caramel rolls, and several kinds of yeast breads next to a collection of antique toasters, which guests can use to make toast. Governor Sullivan had his own reasons for visiting Rawlins; most tourists stop en route to Grand Teton or Yellowstone national parks since this southern Wyoming town lies roughly midway between the parks and Denver.

WAPITI

Cody's Ranch Resort

Near Wapiti, Wyoming
Mailing address:
2604 Yellowstone Highway
Cody, WY 82414
307-587-6271

> *A country inn
> and guest ranch
> east of Yellow-
> stone*

Proprietor: Barbara Cody. **Accom-modations:** 14 rooms. **Rates:** Early June–August, $140/person/day; lower rest of year. **Included:** All meals and riding in summer. **Minimum stay:** 3 nights in summer. **Added:** 3.5% tax. **Payment:** Discover, MasterCard, Visa. **Children:** Welcome. **Pets:** Prohibited. **Smoking:** Non-smoking rooms available. **Open:** Year-round.

Bill Cody's Ranch Resort huddles beneath the lodgepole pines and aspens in a narrow draw along Nameit Creek, a quarter of a mile off Highway 14-16-20 and roughly 26 miles from the east entrance to Yellowstone National Park. It comes by its name legitimately: Bill Cody, the grandson of Colonel William F. "Buffalo" Bill Cody, owned and operated the ranch with his wife Barbara from 1971 until his death in 1992. Now Barbara runs it alone.

Part inn, part guest ranch, its rooms are all done in contemporary ranch style, with polished knotty pine walls, handmade four-poster beds, quilted comforters, original western artwork, and modern bathrooms. Half of them have two bedrooms. Only the exteriors are rustic.

Some guests stop for a single night; others spend days, dividing their time among the park, the riveting Buffalo Bill Historical Center (and other attractions in Cody), horseback riding at the resort, and the 2.8 million scenic acres of Shoshone National Forest. Just beyond the ranch lies the Absaroka Wilderness. Wildlife abounds. Barbara wants even rank beginners to have a chance to experience that backcountry on horseback, so she has patient wranglers and gentle horses. And although there is no separate children's program, kids as young as age five can take part.

If guests tend to go off in different directions during the day, they often meet up again either at the small hot tub, in the cozy bar, or in front of the woodstove in the rustic living room of the original 1925 lodge. There's also a convivial dining room, which serves homestyle chicken, fish, and beef at very reasonable prices. During the summer, when it stays light until very late, the ranch sometimes schedules rides after dinner.

> **The fence that marks the northern boundary of the ranch property is the last one, says Barbara, between there and Alaska.**

From early June until mid-September, Barbara requests that guests who want to stay longer than two days book a package that includes meals and horseback riding. In winter, the lure is cross-country skiing in the backcountry adjacent to the ranch or snowmobiling in and around Yellowstone National Park.

Rimrock Ranch

Near Wapiti, Wyoming
Mailing address:
2728 North Fork Road
Cody, WY 82414
307-587-3970
Fax: 307-527-4633

> *A homey ranch where western traditions run deep*

Proprietors: Glenn and Alice Fales, Colin and Connie Taylor. **Accommodations:** 9 cabins, all with private bath. **Rates:** Single $910/week, double $1,456/week. **Included:** All meals, horseback riding and activities, float trip, tour of Yellowstone, airport transfers. **Minimum stay:** 7 nights. **Added:** 6% tax and 10% service charge. **Payment:** Cash, personal checks, or traveler's checks. **Children:** Free under age 4 if not a rider. **Pets:** Prohibited. **Smoking:** Prohibited in lodge. **Open:** June to mid-September.

With three times as many horses as guests and more than 35 years experience running a guest ranch, native Wyomingites Glenn and Alice Fales make Rimrock one of the best-run and homiest ranches in the Rockies. She was born and raised on ranches; he has been a rodeo contestant, range cowboy, trapper, horse trader, timberjack, and guide-wrangler. Together they instill their 480-acre retreat with a deep sense of western tradition and hospitality.

Situated midway between Cody and the east entrance to Yellowstone National Park, the log house and cabins line both sides of a creek in a narrow canyon flanked by magnificent rock formations. Trails lead up the canyon sides and along the floor toward mountain passes as high as 10,000 feet in the Absaroka Range to the south. Several of the rides to higher ground last all day. The most spectacular winds up Table Mountain to a 360-degree vista. In the absence of a formal children's program, kids tend to ride with the adults.

> Those who want to can ride every day, although that would mean missing out on a float trip and a tour of Yellowstone.

There are times, though, when the wranglers do arrange special children's rides. With only 30 to 35 people to look after, the Fales can easily modify what is otherwise a fairly structured agenda to fit a particular week's crowd. Chances are they know most everyone already, since guests come back year after year, often staying two or three weeks.

The cabins aren't posh. Built in the 1930s, they range in size from one room to two bedrooms. They have western decor, old furnishings, private baths, and porches. Three have fireplaces. All are immaculately clean.

Rather than hang out in their cabins, guests tend to gather by the fireplace in the main house, in the dining room for hearty fare, or in the recreation room where saddles straddle the beam rafters above billiards and Ping-Pong tables, and trophy heads and pelts decorate the walls. At various times during the week there are talent shows starring guests and wranglers, square dances, and cookouts with campfire songs. Guests leave feeling like one of the family.

WHEATLAND

The Blackbird Inn

1101 11th Street
Wheatland, WY 82201
307-322-4540

> *A sociable B&B
> at budget prices*

Host: Dan Brecht. **Accommodations:** 4 rooms with shared baths, 1 suite. **Rates:** Single $30–$35, double $35–$40. **Included:** Continental-plus breakfast and tax. **Minimum stay:** None. **Added:** Nothing. **Payment:** Cash or checks. **Children:** Welcome. **Pets:** Prohibited (he has an outside dog). **Smoking:** Prohibited. **Open:** Year-round.

There are grander houses than the Blackbird Inn and certainly other bed-and-breakfasts with amenities like private baths, but few are warmer or more conducive to guests coming downstairs from their spacious rooms to chat. On summer afternoons, that typically happens on the wrap-around porch, in winter around the fireplace in the parlor or around the dining table, but gather they do.

Partly it's because Dan Brecht, who lives there with his son, Zachary, encourages people to treat this three-story Victorian home as theirs. Partly it's because he's a fund of information about what to see and do in the area — or where to hike and camp.

Brecht bought the historic house — which dates to 1910 — in 1988, and converted it to a bed-and-breakfast in 1988. It had been built by Thomas J. Carroll, a wealthy Wheatlander who was also responsible for putting in the town's sidewalks. It had survived with its oak doors, high ceilings, and trim intact. Brecht added antiques and white iron beds and then decorated each of

> **"Don't hang out in your room unless you want to," Brecht tells guests. "Join us downstairs."**

the four second-floor rooms according to a different theme with meaning for him. Wyoming, for example, contains a four-poster bed, ruffled lace curtains, original art by Brecht's friends, and a trunk full of books and magazines on Wyoming, while in the room called Whales he installed both a double and twin bed in white iron and decorated with pieces of baleen, soapstone carvings, and books and photos on the aquatic mammals, memories of his days teaching school in Alaska. All four rooms share a single bath on that floor and have access to a second bath downstairs. They also come with surprising touches, especially in rooms this inexpensively priced, such as potpourri and little tubes of toothpaste.

Breakfast at the Blackbird consists of juice, fresh fruit, yogurt, Brecht's own granola, and fresh homemade muffins, served at a table decorated with candles and napkin rings. He takes this trouble even during the school year, when he has to be out the door at 7:30.

Brecht teaches 5th grade, miraculously juggling single parenthood, a full-time job, and his B&B without stinting on attention to guests' needs. Since he was born here, Brecht has a local's intimate knowledge of the area, and he's eager to help and advise, whether it's with suggestions for day trips or hiking or places for dinner. Children are welcome; Zachary will share his favorite video movies with them.

WILSON

Crescent H Ranch

Wilson, Wyoming
Reservations: c/o Rivermeadows
P.O. Box 347
Wilson, WY 83014
307-733-3674 or 307-733-2841
Fax: 307-733-8475

> *A renowned
> fishing camp,
> fortified by
> ample amenities*

General manager: Scott Albrecht.
Accommodations: 12 cabins, all with private bath. **Rates:**
Summer, $1,925/person/week; winter, $140/person/day. **Included:** All meals and beverages, plus ranch activities, fishing
guides and instruction in summer, cross-country skiing and
equipment in winter. **Minimum stay:** 7 nights in July and August, otherwise 4 nights. **Added:** 6% tax plus 2% on lodging
portion, 15% service charge. **Payment:** Cash, personal checks,
or traveler's checks. **Children:** Children under age 12 discouraged in summer. **Pets:** Prohibited. **Smoking:** Discouraged at
dinner. **Open:** June through September and Christmas week
through March.

Tucked between the Bridger-Teton National Forest and the
Snake River, seven miles west of Jackson, the Crescent H has
a long-standing reputation as one of the West's foremost fly-fishing destinations. Seven miles of blue ribbon trout streams,
including three crystal-clear spring-fed creeks, flow through
its property. Not only do guests get private access to those
waters and their abundant cutthroat trout, they can also perfect their casting technique on the legendary Snake, Green,
and Yellowstone rivers, all of which run near enough to be
fished on day trips.

Built in 1927 as a fishing and hunting lodge, the Crescent H
spreads over 1,500 acres of unparalleled Wyoming scenery
within sight of the majestic Tetons. The land here has never
known hayfields or grazing cattle, so much of the native vegetation survives in wildflower-strewn meadows and fragrant
sagebrush. Moose, deer, elk, and songbirds abound.

In recent years the Crescent H has broadened its menu of
activities beyond guided fishing trips to include horseback

riding, hiking along game trails, tennis, and nature walks. A movie about trout and a fly-tying session now share evening billing with a cowboy poet or a trip to Jackson to see the rodeo. All of this has been done in an effort to lure more couples, thus there are no supervised children's programs.

Most of the cabins date to the 1920s. They fan out in a semicircle through a meadow ringed by aspens and lodgepole pines. Tiny and rustic, the shingle-

> **The Crescent H was the first ranch to garner an Orvis endorsement. It still hires only Orvis-certified guides and maintains a fully stocked tackle shop.**

roofed log cabins have modern baths and smart country appointments, including brass beds, firm mattresses, and lodgepole and antique furnishings. Two have fireplaces. Guests arrive to find baskets of fruit and cheese and bottles of chardonnay. Beds are turned down every night.

The heart of the ranch remains the old main lodge, large enough to need fireplaces at both ends. Wagon-wheel chandeliers hang from the rafters above giant couches and high-backed chairs upholstered in suede and leather. English antiques, western artifacts, American Indian weavings, and the obligatory moose head enhance the character.

When children do come, they have their dinner early, thus allowing adults to dine in peace at tables set with bone china, sterling silver, pewter, and crystal. An evening's menu typically lists four entrées, which could be grilled fillet of beef, fettuccini with roasted chicken pancetta, duck with dried cranberry and pear chutney, or the daily fish special, served with freshly made breads.

The amiable staff seems to have been chosen because of their innate western hospitality. One of the managers hosts dinner every night, taking an active role in organizing the next day's activities and personally seeing to the needs of the 35 to 40 guests.

In winter, the two largest cabins — lodges, really — remain open for cross-country skiing on 15 miles of groomed trails through the ranch's meadows and forests. Built in the 1980s, these cabins come with a chef and can accommodate six to twelve people.

A Teton Tree House Bed & Breakfast

6175 West Heck-of-a-Hill Road
P.O. Box 550
Wilson, WY 83014
307-733-3233
Fax: 307-733-3233

*A serendipitous
log house
in the trees
near Jackson*

Hosts: Denny and Chris Becker.
Accommodations: 5 rooms, all with private bath. **Rates:** $95–$145. **Included:** Continental-plus breakfast. **Minimum stay:** 4 nights July and August; otherwise 3 nights. **Added:** 8% tax. **Payment:** MasterCard, Visa. **Children:** Infants discouraged. **Pets:** Prohibited. **Smoking:** Prohibited. **Open:** Year-round.

It's a steep climb up 95 steps from the parking area to Denny and Chris Becker's secluded home near Wilson, seven miles west of Jackson. The multilevel structure clings to a hillside in a spruce and fir forest frequented by deer, moose, hummingbirds, and woodpeckers. It started out when Denny built a tiny cabin for himself and Chris. Then they had two daughters, which prompted the first set of additions, and in 1985 they decided to expand their home into a bed-and-breakfast, which prompted another. Now funny stairs and narrow hallways lead to a warren of host and guest quarters off both levels of the two-story great room. It seems not to have been planned so much as to have serendipitously evolved.

That has produced a mixed bag of rooms, in various sizes

and shapes. All of them have rough pine walls accented with wildlife photography, log beamed ceilings — some of which are very low — and a simple country decor of quilts, antique dressers, and dust-ruffled beds. Some have rockers, others cushioned window seats, and all have bookshelves — though some guests complain of the lack of comfortable reading chairs and adequate lighting. Each has a private bath with a shower (only one has a tub as well). And all but one opens onto a balcony with views of the trees or the Gros Ventre Mountains.

> **Before they had children, the Beckers were wilderness and whitewater guides. Attentive hosts, they can often be found huddled with guests around the woodstove in the great room's kiva fireplace plotting activities.**

"We spend a lot of time with guests, helping them find things to do," says Denny. "I go over maps for good hiking. What I haven't guided, I've done." At the end of the day, guests come back to a hot tub.

Breakfast, too, seems planned with active outdoor types in mind. Generally low cholesterol, it's heavy on fresh fruits, granola or homemade porridges, yogurt, whole-grain breads, and perhaps deep-dish French toast or pancakes.

YELLOWSTONE NATIONAL PARK

For other lodging near Yellowstone, see Jackson Hole and Wapiti in Wyoming and West Yellowstone in Montana.

Lake Yellowstone Hotel

Yellowstone National Park,
  Wyoming
307-344-7901
Reservations:
TW Recreational Services, Inc.
P.O. Box 165
Yellowstone National Park, WY
  82190-0165
307-344-7311
Fax: 307-344-7456

> *A regal lakefront hotel, deep inside the park*

General manager of TW/Yellowstone: Steve Tedder. **Accommodations:** 193 rooms, 1 suite, 102 cabins. **Rates:** Rooms $75–$110, suites $270–$290, cabins $55. **Minimum stay:** None. **Added:** 8% tax. **Payment:** Major credit cards. **Children:** Free under age 12. **Pets:** Prohibited in hotel; allowed in cabins. **Smoking:** Nonsmoking rooms available. **Open:** Mid-May to early October.

Yellowstone National Park's oldest and most elegant hotel started out in 1891 as a rather plain 80-room establishment. Built to replace a little-used tent camp, the Lake Yellowstone didn't need to offer guests much to be an enormous improvement on what had been available. Yet within a year of its opening, demand was such that steamboat service began to operate from West Thumb, bringing boatloads of passengers directly to the hotel's dock.

Its metamorphosis into a grand four-story Colonial dates

from 1903. Robert Reamer, the architect who also designed the Old Faithful Inn (see below) and other park buildings, masterminded its transformation, adding ionic columns, gables, balconies, and decorative moldings and almost tripling its size. Further additions occurred during the 1920s, among them the east wing, the lobby's tile-manteled fireplace, and the lakefront dining room, porte cochere, and sun room. More recent renovations, inside and out, for the hotel's centennial in 1991 have the rambling queen looking more regal than ever.

> The expansive, high-ceilinged lobby is richly decorated with painted wood moldings. It opens onto a lakeview sunroom with polished oak floors and cushioned wicker chairs and sofas.

Today's guests, who arrive by car rather than boat, get their first glimpse of the yellow clapboards and white trim from its less ornamented back, which faces the parking lot. It's only after they've checked in and begun to wander around that they realize it was built to be seen from the water.

Nothing surpasses the winsome accommodations in the old hotel. Though small by modern standards, these cheerful rooms feature brass and white iron beds, pine armoires, two comfortable armchairs, and large, modern baths. Everything is stylishly elegant, from peach-colored drapes to pottery lamps and pale gray and white wallpaper. Higher floors are better — even if that does mean climbing stairs — and nothing less than a lake view will suffice.

There are two other options, neither as appealing as the hotel itself: a detached annex, whose rooms suffer from a dated minimalist decor, and a cluster of clean, if characterless, wooden cabins a two-minute walk from the hotel.

Guests staying in the hotel have the further advantage of being a few steps closer to the chamber music concerts that take place in the lobby and to the charbroiled ahi, fettuccine with artichokes, teriyaki chicken, and prime rib in the moderately priced dining room. All that's missing is some way to arrive by boat.

Old Faithful Inn

Yellowstone National Park,
  Wyoming
307-344-7901
Reservations:
TW Recreational Services, Inc.
P.O. Box 165
Yellowstone National Park, WY
  82190-0165
307-344-7311
Fax: 307-344-7456

> *A log hotel
> beside the world-
> famous geyser*

General manager of TW/Yellowstone: Steve Tedder. **Accommodations:** 320 rooms, 141 with private bath. **Rates:** Rooms $40–$105, suites $175–$205. **Minimum stay:** None. **Added:** 8% tax. **Payment:** Major credit cards. **Children:** Free under age 12. **Pets:** Prohibited. **Smoking:** Nonsmoking rooms available. **Open:** Early May to mid-October.

When it was built in 1904, the Old Faithful Lodge was described as the largest log hotel in existence. Robert Reamer, who would later undertake the renovation of the Lake Yellowstone Hotel (see above), designed it to harmonize with its surroundings. He made extensive use of building materials at hand, including the logs and twisted wooden supports for the 85-foot lobby, and 500 tons of stone for its four-sided fireplace. Dormer windows light the four floors of overhanging balconies that cling to the lobby's interior walls. Reamer also designed the pendulum clock on the front of the fireplace and the copper light fixtures under the balconies, enlisting a local blacksmith to fashion them on site.

The imposing structure and its later east and west wings has become a National Historic Landmark. It does not face Old Faithful Geyser, as one would expect, but is instead perpendicular to it. For that reason it doesn't matter whether your room is at the front or back of the hotel, since few have views of the geyser anyway. What does matter is that those in the original lodge — now dubbed the "Old House" — have no private baths, while those in the wings have recently undergone a thorough renovation.

> **Some guests ask for rooms in the Old House for reasons of price — they are some of the least expensive accommodations in the park — and others because they adore the rooms' rustic charm.**

All of the rooms in the Old House have rough pine walls, brass beds, antique dressers, and original heavy cast-iron door latches (supplemented by a modern lock). All but the five on the front (the odd-numbered rooms from 221-229) share communal baths at the end (though they do have their own in-room sinks). Sound carries, so you'll hear the conversation of the people next door and the footfalls of the people upstairs.

Far more comfortable, though no longer nostalgically rustic, are the rooms in the wings. These have been completely redone so that all now have modern private tile baths, stylish wall-to-wall carpeting, wooden beds and tables, and wicker chairs. They also have phones. Some of those on the east side of the east wing have views of Old Faithful (the best views are from the third floor, but there are no elevators).

Whether or not your room has a view, staying in the old inn puts you within easy walking distance of Old Faithful. There's the soaring lobby to enjoy and a family restaurant serving acceptable trout, shrimp, chicken, and lasagna at reasonable prices. The inn also has a lounge called the Bear Pit, a deli, an ice cream parlor, a gift shop, an activities desk, and an ATM.

What's What

A cross-reference of accommodation types and special interests

Adults Only (no children under 12)

Colorado
  The Anniversary Inn, 39
  Castle Marne Bed & Breakfast, 29
  The Claim Jumper, 185
  C Lazy U Ranch (after Labor Day), 129
  Colorado Trails Ranch (after Labor Day), 194
  Forbes Trinchera Ranch, 68
  The Hardy House, 125
  Holden House 1902, 65
  Meadow Creek Bed & Breakfast Inn (weekends), 53
  Queen Anne Inn, 35
  Red Crags, 71
  RiverSong, 44
  Wilderness Trails Ranch (September), 180
  Williams House, 109
Montana
  Firehole Ranch, 344
  Triple Creek Ranch, 315
Utah
  Castle Valley Inn Bed-and-Breakfast, 420
  Center Street Bed & Breakfst Inn, 372
  Manti House Inn, 375
  Nine Gables Inn, 417
  Washington School Inn, 393
Wyoming
  Crescent H Ranch, 496
  Flying A Ranch, 488
  Parson's Pillow Bed & Breakfast, 456
  R Lazy S Ranch, Jackson Hole (September), 474

Backcountry Retreats

Bed-and-Breakfast Homes

Bed-and-Breakfast Inns

Budget (less than $60/couple)

Colorado

Condominiums, Apartments, and Cabins

Country Inns

Cross-Country Skiing

Family Affairs

Fishing Lodges

Golf

Guest Ranches

Health Spas

Colorado
The Broadmoor, 61
Lodge at Cordillera, 119
The Peaks at Telluride, 225
Sonnenalp Hotel and Country Club's Swiss Haus, 169
Utah
Cliff Lodge, 405
Green Valley Spa & Tennis Resort, 427

Historic Hotels, Inns, and Lodges

Colorado
Allenspark Lodge, 11
The Baldpate Inn, 40
The Broadmoor, 61
The Brown Palace Hotel, 26
Cleveholm Manor, 153
Elk Mountain Lodge, 189
General Palmer Hotel, 196
Glen-Isle Resort, 13
Grand Imperial Victorian Hotel, 223
Hotel Boulderado, 17
Hotel Jerome, 86
Imperial Hotel & Casino, 66
The Oxford Hotel, 33
The Peck House, 121
The Redstone Inn, 155
St. Elmo Hotel, 216
Strater Hotel, 199
Montana
Chico Hot Springs Lodge, 336
Copper King Mansion, 311
Gallatin Gateway Inn, 321
The Grand, 301
Historic Kalispell Hotel, 268
Izaak Walton Inn, 258
The Murray Hotel, 331
The Nevada City Hotel, 335
The Pollard, 338
Sacajawea Inn, 342

Horseback Riding (see also Guest Ranches)

Hot Springs Lodges

Wiesbaden Hot Springs Spa and Lodgings, 218
Montana
Chico Hot Springs Lodge, 336
Utah
The Homestead, 379

Kitchens Available

Colorado
Allenspark Lodge, 11
Alpine Lodge, 83
Avalanche Ranch, 151
Blue Lake Ranch, 206
Boulder Brook, 42
Brand Building, 85
Copper Mountain Resort, 118
Echo Manor Inn (one room), 220
Glen-Isle Resort, 13
The Inn at Rock 'n River, 51
The Kaiser House (one room), 127
Keystone Resort, 134
Park Plaza, 102
The Snowmass Lodge & Club, 157
Sonnenalp Hotel and Country Club, 169
Tamarron, 202
Trapper's Cabin, 105
Wiesbaden Hot Springs Spa and Lodgings, 218
Winfield Scott GuestQuarters, 22
Montana
Abbott Valley Accommodations, 269
Big Sky Ski & Summer Resort, 295
The Emily A. Bed & Breakfast (one room), 275
Grouse Mountain Lodge, 285
Kandahar Lodge, 287
Mountain Timbers Lodge's cabin, 280
Plum Creek House Bed & Breakfast, 254
Rock Creek Resort, 340
Shoshone Condominium Hotel, 300
Sportsman's High, 346
Turn in the River Inn, 256
Utah
The Blue Church Lodge, 386
Green Valley Spa & Tennis Resort, 427
The Imperial Hotel (one room), 387

Meadeau View Lodge, 415
O'Tooles' Under the Eaves (one room), 434
Pack Creek Ranch, 422
The Pinecrest Bed & Breakfast Inn, 401
Stein Eriksen Lodge, 366
Sundance Resort, 406
Wyoming
Dornan's Spur Ranch Log Cabins, 467
Gros Ventre River Ranch, 468
Spahn's Big Horn Mountain Bed & Breakfast (one room), 447
Spring Creek, 477

Near University

Colorado
Boulder Victoria, 14
Briar Rose, 16
Elizabeth Street Guest House, 46
General Palmer Hotel, 196
Hotel Boulderado, 17
The Magpie Inn on Mapleton Hill, 19
The Mary Lawrence Inn, 204
Pearl Street Inn and Restaurant, 21
Strater Hotel, 199
Montana
Goldsmith's Bed & Breakfast, 271
Torch & Toes, 308
The Voss Inn, 309
Utah
The Anton Boxrud Bed & Breakfast, 395
The Brigham House Inn, 374
Center Street Bed & Breakfast Inn, 372
Saltair Bed & Breakfast, 403
Wyoming
Annie Moore's Guest House, 484

Pets Allowed with Permission

Colorado
Alpine Lodge, 83
Avalanche Ranch, 151
Brand Building, 85

Resorts and Spas

Restaurant Open to Public

Romantic Hideaways

Ski Area Hotels & Lodges

Utah

Stellar Cuisine

Colorado
Montana
Utah
Wyoming

Swimming Pool

Colorado

The Homestead, 379
Inn on the Creek, 381
Pack Creek Ranch, 422
Rustler Lodge, 363
Seven Wives Inn, 430
Stein Eriksen Lodge, 366
Wyoming
Jackson Lake Lodge, 463
Lost Creek Ranch, 470
Paradise Guest Ranch, 451
Spring Creek, 477
Teton Pines (seasonal), 479

Tennis

Colorado
The Broadmoor, 61
C Lazy U Ranch, 129
Colorado Trails Ranch, 194
Copper Mountain Resort, 118
Great Sand Dunes Country Inn, 211
Keystone Resort, 134
Lodge at Cordillera, 119
Lost Valley Ranch, 24
The Peaks at Telluride, 225
The Redstone Inn, 155
Ski Tip Lodge, 136
The Snowmass Lodge & Club, 157
Sonnenalp Hotel and Country Club, 169
Tall Timber, 201
Tamarron, 202
Montana
Averill's Flathead Lake Lodge & Dude Ranch, 247
Big Sky Ski & Summer Resort, 295
Elk Canyon Ranch, 348
Gallatin Gateway Inn, 321
Grouse Mountain Lodge, 285
Mountain Sky Guest Ranch, 317
Rock Creek Resort, 340
Shoshone Condominium Hotel, 300
Triple Creek Ranch, 315

Utah
Wyoming

Water Sports

Colorado
Montana
Wyoming

Wheelchair Accessible

Colorado

Workout/Fitness Rooms

Recommended Guidebooks

The books noted below are excellent overviews of the Rockies and its attractions. One outstanding bookstore, said to be the largest independent bookstore in the U.S., deserves mention: the Tattered Cover Book Store in Denver (2955 E. First Ave., Denver, Colo. 80206; 303-322-7727 or 800-833-9327; fax: 303-399-2279). Its four floors of books include a large travel section, with special emphasis on Colorado and the Rockies.

The Rockies

APA Insight Guides: The Rockies. Houghton Mifflin Company, $19.95. Like other books in the Insight Guide series, this one combines breezily written text with wonderful color photography. It is best as an overview, providing background on the history, geography, people, and places in Colorado, Idaho, Montana, Utah, and Wyoming.

Fodor's The Rockies. Fodor's Travel Publications, $8.95. Fine for its practical information but lacking in critical authority, especially about restaurants and lodging.

A Historical Guide to the United States. Norton, $25. Another guide by state: each chapter has essays on the major historic sites as well as an annotated list of other places of historical interest, including the houses of prominent people.

Ranch Vacations. Gene Kilgore, John Muir Publications, 2nd ed. $18.95. This comprehensive survey covers a broad spectrum of guest ranches as well as those devoted to fly-fishing and cross-country skiing, not only in the continental U.S. but British Columbia and Alberta, Canada, as well. While not particularly critical, it does provide a wealth of useful information and cross referencing to help readers decide where they want to vacation.

Restored Towns and Historic Districts of America: A Tour Guide. Alice Cromie, Dutton (A Sunrise Book), $17.50. Concise and lucid, this is a state-by-state guide to the restored towns, villages, and preserved historic districts through the U.S. and Canada, with special emphasis on those less well known.

The Sierra Club Guide to the National Parks: Rocky Mountains and the Great Plains. Stewart, Tabori & Chang, $18.95. Filled with excellent color photographs, this intelligent guide covers the history and highlights of four of the great western national parks: Glacier, Grand Teton, Rocky Mountain, and Yellowstone. Also included are park maps and an appendix of plants and animals.

The Sierra Club Guide to the Natural Areas of Colorado and Utah and *The Sierra Club Guide to the Natural Areas of Idaho, Montana, and Wyoming.* John and Jane Greverus Perry, Sierra Club Books, $10 and $13 respectively These guides summarize the basic information about all the natural areas, including state and national parks, forests, wildlife preserves, and lands in the public domain.

The Smithsonian Guide to Historic America: Rocky Mountain States. Jerry Camarillo Dunn, Jr., Stewart, Tabori & Chang, $18.95. Background on towns, museums, forts, Indian sites, and buildings of historical importance for four western states. Illustrated with color photos.

Indian America

The Anasazi. J. J. Brody, Rizzoli Books, $75. The most recent, comprehensive, and expensive guide to the world of the Anasazi Indians.

Ancient Ruins of the Southwest. David Grant Noble, Northland Publishing, $14.95. General background on the prehistoric Southwest, including Colorado's Mesa Verde National Park and Utah's Hovenweep National Monument.

Book of the Hopi. Frank Waters, Penguin, $12; *The Fourth World of the Hopis.* Harold Courlander, University of New Mexico, $11.95. Both delve into the spiritual heritage of the Anasazi.

Indian America. Eagle/Walking Turtle (Gary McLain), John Muir Publications, $17.95. Eagle/Walking Turtle, who is also known as Gary McLain, is an Irish/Choctaw artist and writer. This award-winning guide to the world of Native Americans provides information on where to find more than 300 tribes, including those in Colorado, Montana, Utah, and Wyoming. A sourcebook illustrated with black and white archival photographs, it lists the tribal councils and Indian museums in the area and provides reasons for visiting all of them.

North American Indian Travel Guide. Ralph and Lisa Shanks, Costano Books, $14.95. Concise and thoughtful, this oversize paperback is one of the best at summarizing, state by state, the museums, national parks, historic sites, and tourist and cultural centers with Indian connections. The authors include tips about being a good guest in Indian country and advice on buying arts and crafts.

Snow Country

The Best Ski Resorts of America. Claire Walter, Randt & Co., $27.50 A veteran ski writer's look at 50 U.S. resorts. Ms. Walter combines local anecdotes, tidbits, and commentary to paint informative pictures of the resorts.

Colorado

The Colorado Guide. Bruce Caughey and Dean Winstanley, Fulcrum Publishing, $16.95. This tome (642 pages) covers the territory with intelligence and wit. It is the best of the books out, ranging over Colorado towns, attractions, outdoor activities, festivals, wilderness areas and forests, ghost towns, and hot springs. There are also chapters on the history of regions and towns and limited information on accommodations and campgrounds.

Fodor's Colorado. Fodor's Travel Publications, $10. Though bland, this is an otherwise useful compendium of what to see and do in the Centennial State. It is divided into four sections: Denver, Ski and Summer Resorts, Northwestern Colorado, and Southern Colorado. Each one has basic reviews of the major attractions followed by largely uncritical reviews of lodgings and restaurants in the major towns.

Montana

Montana. Norma Tirrel and Barry Parr, Compass American Guides, Inc., $14.95. Another in the Discover America series, and the best single source for a broad perspective on the Big Sky state, written by locals.

Utah

Utah. Tom and Gayen Wharton, Compass American Guides, Inc., $14.95. Part of the Discover America series, this volume takes up the geology, original inhabitants, early explorers, and Mormon pioneers before launching into a region by region overview of the cities, national and state parks, and ski areas. There is also practical information on climate, getting around, camping, outdoor activities, lodging, and restaurants.

Utah Handbook. Bill Weir, Moon Publications, $14.95. Compiled as much as written, this guide begins with plodding overviews of the geology, climate, flora and fauna, and people (with particular emphasis on Indians and Mormons) before taking on the state geographically. Missing from this book is the author's personality, which makes others in this series more fun to read. Still, its index and broad scope, coupled with useful charts summarizing accommodations and maps showing secondary byways, help redeem it.

Utah's National Parks: Hiking and Vacationing in Utah's Canyon Country. Ron Adkison, Wilderness Press, $18.95. This guide includes updated topographical maps and detailed descriptions of 125 hikes in Zion, Bryce, Arches, Canyonlands, and Capitol Reef national parks. The walks range from brief strolls to demanding treks.

Wyoming

Wyoming. Nathaniel Burt, Compass American Guides, $14.95. Another Discover America author sets out to put his state in perspective as he roams west with an engaging cowboy twang. It's illustrated with photos by National Geographic regulars Michael Freeman and Paul Chesley.

Index

Best Places Report

Authors of the Best Places to Stay series travel extensively in their research to find the best places for all budgets, styles, and interests. However, if we've missed an establishment that you find worthy, please write to us with your suggestion. Detailed information about the service, food, setting, and nearby activities or sights is most important. Finally, let us know how you heard about the place and how long you've been going there.

Send suggestions to:

The Harvard Common Press
Best Places to Stay Suggestions
535 Albany Street
Boston, Massachusetts 02118

NAME OF HOTEL _____

TELEPHONE _____

ADDRESS _____

_____ ZIP _____

DESCRIPTION _____

_____

_____

_____

_____

_____

_____

YOUR NAME _____

TELEPHONE _____

ADDRESS _____

_____ ZIP _____

Best Places Report

Authors of the Best Places to Stay series travel extensively in their research to find the best places for all budgets, styles, and interests. However, if we've missed an establishment that you find worthy, please write to us with your suggestion. Detailed information about the service, food, setting, and nearby activities or sights is most important. Finally, let us know how you heard about the place and how long you've been going there.

Send suggestions to:

> The Harvard Common Press
> Best Places to Stay Suggestions
> 535 Albany Street
> Boston, Massachusetts 02118

NAME OF HOTEL _____

TELEPHONE _____

ADDRESS _____

_____ ZIP _____

DESCRIPTION _____

_____

_____

_____

_____

_____

_____

YOUR NAME _____

TELEPHONE _____

ADDRESS _____

_____ ZIP _____

Best Places Report

Authors of the Best Places to Stay series travel extensively in their research to find the best places for all budgets, styles, and interests. However, if we've missed an establishment that you find worthy, please write to us with your suggestion. Detailed information about the service, food, setting, and nearby activities or sights is most important. Finally, let us know how you heard about the place and how long you've been going there.

Send suggestions to:

> The Harvard Common Press
> Best Places to Stay Suggestions
> 535 Albany Street
> Boston, Massachusetts 02118

NAME OF HOTEL _____

TELEPHONE _____

ADDRESS _____

_____ ZIP _____

DESCRIPTION _____

_____

_____

_____

_____

_____

_____

YOUR NAME _____

TELEPHONE _____

ADDRESS _____

_____ ZIP _____

Best Places Report

Authors of the Best Places to Stay series travel extensively in their research to find the best places for all budgets, styles, and interests. However, if we've missed an establishment that you find worthy, please write to us with your suggestion. Detailed information about the service, food, setting, and nearby activities or sights is most important. Finally, let us know how you heard about the place and how long you've been going there.

Send suggestions to:

The Harvard Common Press
Best Places to Stay Suggestions
535 Albany Street
Boston, Massachusetts 02118

NAME OF HOTEL _____

TELEPHONE _____

ADDRESS _____

_____ ZIP _____

DESCRIPTION _____

_____

_____

_____

_____

_____

_____

YOUR NAME _____

TELEPHONE _____

ADDRESS _____

_____ ZIP _____

Best Places Report

Authors of the Best Places to Stay series travel extensively in their research to find the best places for all budgets, styles, and interests. However, if we've missed an establishment that you find worthy, please write to us with your suggestion. Detailed information about the service, food, setting, and nearby activities or sights is most important. Finally, let us know how you heard about the place and how long you've been going there.

Send suggestions to:

> The Harvard Common Press
> Best Places to Stay Suggestions
> 535 Albany Street
> Boston, Massachusetts 02118

NAME OF HOTEL _____

TELEPHONE _____

ADDRESS _____

_____ ZIP _____

DESCRIPTION _____

_____

_____

_____

_____

_____

_____

YOUR NAME _____

TELEPHONE _____

ADDRESS _____

_____ ZIP _____

Best Places Report

Authors of the Best Places to Stay series travel extensively in their research to find the best places for all budgets, styles, and interests. However, if we've missed an establishment that you find worthy, please write to us with your suggestion. Detailed information about the service, food, setting, and nearby activities or sights is most important. Finally, let us know how you heard about the place and how long you've been going there.

Send suggestions to:

The Harvard Common Press
Best Places to Stay Suggestions
535 Albany Street
Boston, Massachusetts 02118

NAME OF HOTEL _____

TELEPHONE _____

ADDRESS _____

_____ ZIP _____

DESCRIPTION _____

_____

_____

_____

_____

_____

_____

YOUR NAME _____

TELEPHONE _____

ADDRESS _____

_____ ZIP _____

Best Places Report

Authors of the Best Places to Stay series travel extensively in their research to find the best places for all budgets, styles, and interests. However, if we've missed an establishment that you find worthy, please write to us with your suggestion. Detailed information about the service, food, setting, and nearby activities or sights is most important. Finally, let us know how you heard about the place and how long you've been going there.

Send suggestions to:

The Harvard Common Press
Best Places to Stay Suggestions
535 Albany Street
Boston, Massachusetts 02118

NAME OF HOTEL _____

TELEPHONE _____

ADDRESS _____

_____ **ZIP** _____

DESCRIPTION _____

_____

_____

_____

_____

_____

_____

YOUR NAME _____

TELEPHONE _____

ADDRESS _____

_____ **ZIP** _____

Best Places Report

Authors of the Best Places to Stay series travel extensively in their research to find the best places for all budgets, styles, and interests. However, if we've missed an establishment that you find worthy, please write to us with your suggestion. Detailed information about the service, food, setting, and nearby activities or sights is most important. Finally, let us know how you heard about the place and how long you've been going there.

Send suggestions to:

The Harvard Common Press
Best Places to Stay Suggestions
535 Albany Street
Boston, Massachusetts 02118

NAME OF HOTEL _____

TELEPHONE _____

ADDRESS _____

_____ ZIP _____

DESCRIPTION _____

_____

_____

_____

_____

_____

_____

_____

YOUR NAME _____

TELEPHONE _____

ADDRESS _____

_____ ZIP _____